Can We Afford to Grow Older?

A Perspective on the Economics of Aging

Richard Disney

The MIT Press
Cambridge, Massachusetts
London, England

Set in Palatino by Graphic Composition, Inc.
Printed and bound in the United States of America.

Library of Congress Cataloging-in-Publication Data

Disney, Richard.
    Can we afford to grow older? : a perspective on the economics of aging / Richard Disney.
        p.   cm.
    Includes bibliographical references and index.
    ISBN 0-262-04157-X
    1. Aging—Economic aspects. 2. Aged—Economic conditions 3. Age distribution (Demography) 4. Old age pensions. I. Title.
    HQ1061.D56   1996
    305.26—dc20   96-542
                                                            CIP

to Jamie, Larissa, and William—the next generation

Contents

Preface   ix

1 Overview   1

2 A Burden of Dependency? Social Security Programs and
   Intergenerational Redistribution   17

3 Overlapping-Generations Models, Feasible Pension Schemes,
   and Aging Populations   35

4 Social Security: Paying for Past Pension Promises   59

5 Private Pension Plans in the Demographic Transition   107

6 Productivity, Wages, and Educational Attainment: The Impact
   of Workforce Aging   153

7 Retirement: The Labor Supply of Older Workers in an Aging
   Society   193

8 Consumption and Saving: Life-Cycle Behavior and Population
   Aging   227

9 Financing Health Care   267

10 A Public-Choice Perspective   283

11 Some Salient Conclusions   307

Notes   311
Bibliography   323
Index   339

Preface

This book emerged at the suggestion of Terry Vaughn, of The MIT Press, who heard me present a paper with this title at the European Economic Association. Had we both realized the time that it would take to finish the book, in my case punctuated both by other research projects and by increments to the size of my family, we might have had second thoughts.

In writing the book, I came to realize that there was a good deal more literature in mainstream economics which addressed the topic of the book than I had at first realized. Even so, I am conscious that several topics are dealt with more cursorily than I would have wished and that other topics (notably those dealing with the "economics of population," such as endogenous fertility and family formation) are entirely ignored. The subject matter of this book therefore concerns the economic consequences of the dramatic present and prospective demographic shifts in Western industrialized (OECD) countries, not their causes.

My initial interest in the topic stems in large part from John Creedy; my intellectual debt to him is substantial as it is, more indirectly, to Peter Hart. Much of my recent research in the field has been with Edward Whitehouse; his contribution to this book is substantial. Other co-researchers, whose efforts appear directly or indirectly in this book, and to whom I am indebted, include James Banks, Richard Blundell, Agar Brugiavini, Andrew Dilnot, Tim Gallagher, Andrew Henley, Paul Johnson, Costas Meghir, Gary Stears, and Steven Webb. Other intellectual influences on the content will be apparent from the bibliography.

Past and present colleagues in the University of Kent's Department of Economics and at the Institute for Fiscal Studies have read drafts of parts of the book or endured my pronouncements on its contents; I single out Amanda Gosling, Andrew Henley, and John Van Reenen for particular awards. Emma Robinson is thanked for processing some of the figures. Three reviewers for The MIT Press made extremely helpful suggestions. I thank Paul Bethge for his splendid comprehensive editorial assistance, and The MIT Press for a fine all-round job.

My debt to my family is substantial: to my parents and to Marjorie and Gwen. Erika Szyszczak put up with the book intruding into our domestic life, and put me to shame by writing several books in the time it took to me to finish this one. In dedicating this book to our children, the standard disclaimer that it would have been finished a lot sooner in their absence is appropriate. But life would have been a lot less fun.

Can We Afford to Grow Older?

1   Overview

The economics of population aging is still seen as a subject in the back-waters of economics: as a topic for the specialists in demography and in pension economics. But changes in the age structure of the population impinge on most issues of interest in the economy, including labor-force participation, hours of work, accrual and disposal of wealth, the pattern of consumption, taxation and public expenditures, and the political economy of public policy. It is these issues, with particular emphasis on the developed industrialized countries, which form the focus of the present book.

The next decades will see major shifts in population structure in the developed industrialized countries. The numbers in the economically inactive age groups aged in their sixties or above will rise. People may well retire earlier as successive cohorts enter their sixties with greater wealth in the form of private pensions and assets such as housing. Governments may respond to the growing burden on social security programs by encouraging workers to remain active longer, but such policies may not outweigh the growing affluence of the elderly. The financial and political power of these elderly groups will grow.

Accompanying the growth in the numbers of the elderly will be a change in the age structure of the workforce. In the next decades, the process of aging will be reflected throughout the age structure of workers, but future trends will ultimately depend on the size of cohorts entering the labor force. An aging population is associated with increased longevity and decreasing fertility. The big leaps in longevity associated with improvements in public health and medical treatment are still affecting the age structure of populations, especially in developing countries, but it is increasingly the change in fertility rates that will determine the extent of population aging. In the postwar period, the trend in fertility rates in the developed world has generally been downward, although forecasters typically assume approximately replacement fertility rates into the future.

In the developing world, the relative youthfulness of the population conceals the significance of aging. Indeed, the maturation of the young into productive adults may prove a bonus rather than a hindrance. However, for those countries (notably the People's Republic of China) where stringent birth control has been practiced, the problems associated with a growing number of elderly are already apparent. With an underdeveloped pension scheme and a relatively limited asset base, the scope for supporting the economically inactive is much more limited.

Population Aging: A Boon or a Burden?

In the 1960s, concern about the "population time bomb" and the views of the new Malthusians led to an emphasis on controlling the population by reducing fertility rates. In the 1990s the twin issues of environmental damage and of the consequences of a growing world population's demand for fossil fuels for global temperature levels and atmospheric pollution have led to a similar advocacy of restraint in population growth.

Yet influential demographers have always been cautious in preaching the advantages of an aging population, which is the inevitable consequence of fertility reduction. Alfred Sauvy, who died in 1990, was the doyen of economic demographers. Although he was by no means an advocate of unbridled growth in population, advocating instead a balanced population structure, the tone of his arguments against "demographic aging" perhaps reflected a particularly Gallic obsession with the link between national prestige and a youthful and flourishing population.[1]

Sauvy's concerns as to an aging population were divided into the economic, the sociological, and the psychological. On the economic side, he was critical of those who perceived demographic issues in purely microeconomic terms, as questions of intertemporal consumption allocation and of income transfers. He emphasized that aging populations had effects on aggregate production. For example, a smaller population with a given capital stock would have higher productivity per capita but might not be able to benefit from economies of scale in production.

Labor economists would of course argue that changes in age structure will also affect overall productivity levels by changing the distribution of human capital in the population. Sauvy, too, felt that productivity would be associated with aging, but adversely. Furthermore, an aged population, he felt, would have detrimental effects on the productivity of the young through what we might call social externalities. "A population without children does not believe in the future and can hardly be expected to have the pioneering spirit . . . ," he intoned gravely in his *General Theory of Population*, bringing an "atrophy" that "affected the will to create and build." Indeed, "demographic stagnation brings a country to a moral and material crisis that is never foreseen in economic analysis" (Sauvy 1969, pp. 261, 269).

In addition to his concerns about production and productivity, Sauvy saw what might be termed the public-choice problem of aging, although he perceived it as a psychological issue. The tax burden of the unproductive elderly would, he felt, be a growing cost to the economy, but also, in a society increasingly dominated by the preferences of the elderly, "the young, being a minority, are condemned to suffer from the aging of society and cannot contribute all their vitality, or shake the burden of idleness from above them" (ibid., p. 318). Thus, economically, socially, and psychologically, an aging population was, in Sauvy's view, a cause of national economic atrophy and decline.

It is easy to mock some of these ideas. Economists generally eschew this type of generalization, and anyone might question the amateur sociology and psychology. Even if Sauvy were wholly correct as to the dangers of an aging population, it might be argued in a global cost-benefit analysis that the problems of economic and social organization stemming from population limitation are easier to solve than those of the potential global and environmental entropy that might stem from uninhibited population expansion. Nevertheless, looking at the past performance of the relatively affluent industrialized countries, it is facile to pretend that major social and economic problems, such as drug abuse, urban squalor, and rural poverty, are easy to solve. Exhortations as to the "joy of aging" coupled with a reliance on the growing affluence of the elderly are not sufficient to avoid the problem. Explicitly or implicitly, Sauvy points to the many potential problems of aging, including the growing pension burden, the possibility of dynamic inconsistency between generational temporal consumption allocations and capital accumulation, the impact of age composition on productivity, and the public-choice aspects of tax and expenditure allocation decisions—all of which merit further detailed investigation.

Baby Boom and Baby Bust?

If Sauvy erred on the side of "aging pessimism," other authors have focused on the potential social and economic dislocations associated with the postwar baby-boom generation. The most influential analysis has been that of Easterlin (1968, 1980), who argues that the size of the baby-boom cohort contributed to relatively adverse economic conditions for its members, which in turn induce wider adverse social effects, such as crime, illegitimacy, and divorce. There is evidence that baby-boomers face depressed lifetime earnings and reduced promotion prospects (see chapter 6 below). This expectation of lower incomes has led them, according to Easterlin, to hesitate to marry and to defer having children, at least in wedlock. So a baby boom generates a baby bust and the cycle is renewed.

In addition, the reduced economic circumstances of the baby-boom generation lead to higher unemployment and increased competition in the workforce as younger women, having postponed child rearing and with lower prospective household incomes, enter the labor market. Nor does retirement look rosy. The prospect of sizable bequests is reduced because parents will spread their transfers more thinly over the larger succeeding generation, and cutbacks in social security also seem likely as social security programs are stretched.

Many of these assertions rely on testable propositions as to the relationship between economic variables and cohort size. As we shall see, there is support for some while others are found wanting (or at least the evidence is sufficiently opaque as to cast doubt on the strength of the pure boom-bust hypothesis). But in showing that "demographic pessimism" can work both ways, and that baby booms may prove a mixed blessing, Easterlin has made an important point.

A Brief Demographic Description

Despite the previous discussion, this is not a book about demography, or even demographic economics. There is no theory here as to why populations grow or decline, or as to how economists or statisticians model fertility or mortality rates. There is no discussion of whether migration can offset demographic patterns, or of its economic and social benefits and costs. These are issues worthy of books in themselves.[2] The present book takes past and projected demographic trends as given. However, it is useful first to present some illustrations of the demographic trends that underpin the rest of the discussion.

Figure 1.1 depicts the dramatic drop in fertility rates (number of births per woman) in North America,[3] Northern Europe,[4] Western Europe,[5] and Southern Europe[6] (see UN 1991). From an average of almost 3.5 in North America in 1950, and 2.3–2.7 in Europe in 1950, the fertility rate has converged to just below replacement, at 1.8–1.9. Similar trends are noticeable in Japan (from 2.75 to 1.8 projected over the same period) and in Australia and New Zealand. In addition, life expectancy at birth has increased in all these countries from 63–69 years in 1950 to around 77 years in the early 1990s (figure 1.2). A further improvement of 2 years is projected in the next 30 years. Coupled with the continued effect of higher past fertility, population continues to grow for the next 25 years, albeit slowly in European countries. Thereafter, population stabilizes and indeed begins to fall in some countries as the decline in fertility outweighs the slower improvement in longevity (figure 1.3). In some countries, more precipitous declines are projected; for example, the current fertility rates in Italy and Denmark are only 1.34 and 1.50 respectively. Other low fertility rates may be offset by political changes, such as the unification of the Federal Republic of

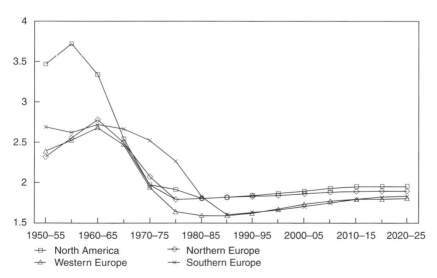

Figure 1.1
Total fertility rate per woman (medium variant).

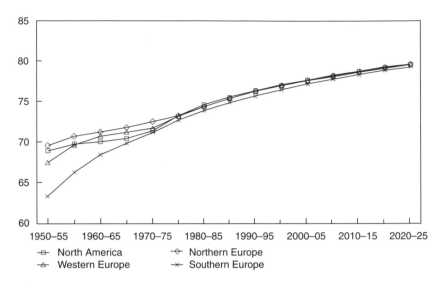

Figure 1.2
Life expectancy at birth (years).

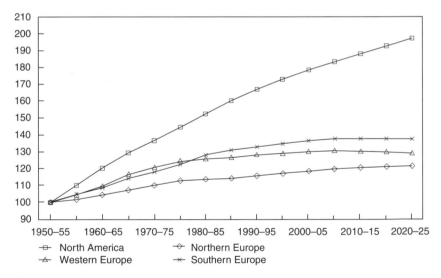

Figure 1.3
Total population (1950 = 100).

Germany (1985 fertility rate: 1.42) and the German Democratic Republic (1985 fertility rate: 1.75). When there are major changes in economic expectations, such as the German unification, fertility itself may be affected.

Figures 1.4 and 1.5 illustrate the implications of these demographic trends for the changing age structure of industrialized countries. For four representative countries, age profiles are depicted for 1950 and 1990, and then as projected to 2025 by the UN (1991), disaggregated into children, "young workforce" (ages 15–24), "prime age," and "elderly workers/retired" (ages 60+).

In France, which is representative of the countries of western and northern Europe, the *proportion* of the population aged 25–59 remains roughly constant between 1950 and 2025, but whereas the total numbers in this age group rose by 6 million from 1950 to 1990, the numbers remain stable from 1990 to 2025. The proportion aged under 25 peaks around 1990; however, the most significant change is among those aged 60+, which rises by around 4 million between 1950 and 1990 and by almost another 6 million between 1990 and 2025. Thus, while the total population of working age roughly kept pace with the growing numbers of elderly from 1950 to 1990, the ratio of potential workers to the elderly declines steadily thereafter.

In Italy the change is more dramatic. With a high fertility rate in 1950, the number of children was over twice the number of people aged 60+. But the number of children declined by 3 million by 1990, and, even with a projected recovery in the fertility rate, a further decline is predicted between 1990 and 2025. The population of working age (15–59) rises by 7 million from 1950 to 1990, but falls by about the same absolute number between 1990 and 2025. Meanwhile, the number of people aged 60+ is projected to rise by 5 million from 1990 to 2025, having also risen by 5 million from 1950 to 1990. Thus, Italy faces the prospect of both aging and a declining population. An improvement in fertility would of course "improve" the demographic structure, but only at the expense of a worsened total demographic dependency ratio (ratio of children and elderly to people of working age) in the short run.

The United States offers yet another trend and another prospect (figure 1.5). From the basis of a younger population and a relative high fertility rate after World War II, the postwar period saw a maturation of the population age structure: a significant increase in the population of prime age (24–59) and a doubling of the 60+ population. From 1990

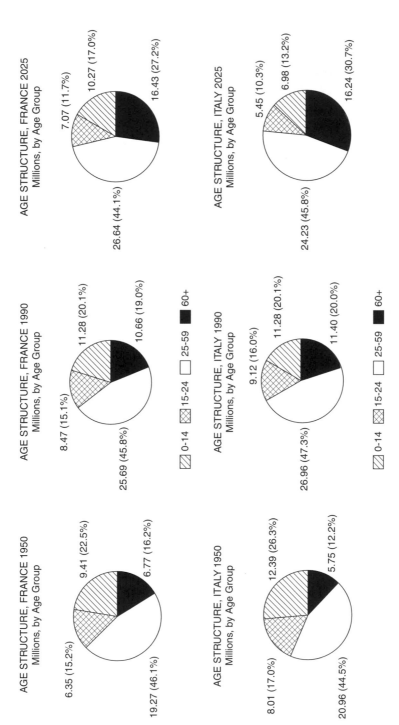

AGE STRUCTURE, FRANCE 2025
Millions, by Age Group

7.07 (11.7%)
10.27 (17.0%)
16.43 (27.2%)
26.64 (44.1%)

AGE STRUCTURE, ITALY 2025
Millions, by Age Group

5.45 (10.3%)
6.98 (13.2%)
16.24 (30.7%)
24.23 (45.8%)

AGE STRUCTURE, FRANCE 1990
Millions, by Age Group

8.47 (15.1%)
11.28 (20.1%)
10.66 (19.0%)
25.69 (45.8%)

0-14   15-24   25-59   60+

AGE STRUCTURE, ITALY 1990
Millions, by Age Group

9.12 (16.0%)
11.28 (20.1%)
11.40 (20.0%)
26.96 (47.3%)

0-14   15-24   25-59   60+

AGE STRUCTURE, FRANCE 1950
Millions, by Age Group

6.35 (15.2%)
9.41 (22.5%)
6.77 (16.2%)
19.27 (46.1%)

AGE STRUCTURE, ITALY 1950
Millions, by Age Group

8.01 (17.0%)
12.39 (26.3%)
5.75 (12.2%)
20.96 (44.5%)

Figure 1.4
Age structure, France and Italy.

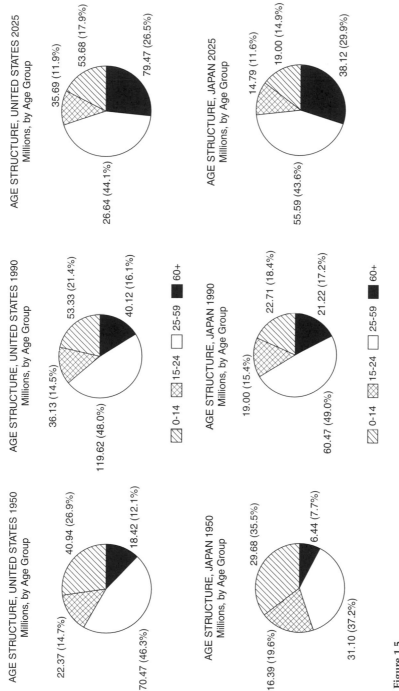

Figure 1.5
Age structure, United States and Japan.

to 2025, the working population is predicted to grow, albeit slowly (an increase of just under 12 million), but this is swamped by an increase of almost 40 million in the 60+ age group. Nevertheless, the number of children is projected to remain constant (unlike Italy), so the population is projected to grow until 2025, albeit at a declining rate.

Japan offers a scenario of rapid aging. The population in 1950 was very youthful, with a high proportion of children and younger workers. There were very few elderly. As the youthful "bulge" works it way through the age structure, the proportion aged 60+ rises rapidly. In 1950 the population aged 60+, at 8 million, accounted for less than 8 percent of the population. Between 1950 and 1990, the share and numeric size of the elderly population more than doubled. By 2025 Japan will have one of the largest shares of elderly people (almost 30 percent) after a further increase of 17 million in the numbers aged 60+. The number of children is projected to fall slightly, but of more significance is a fall of almost 10 million in the size of the 15–59 age group. The population will continue to increase, but this will be due almost entirely to the longevity of Japan's elderly; thus, dependency and retirement policy have great significance in that country.

Figures 1.4 and 1.5 illustrate that an aging population is a common phenomenon in developed industrialized countries, but that the form of this aging "problem" differs among them. In Japan and the United States, it is the demographic transition of a substantial postwar bulge that determines the trend in age structure over time, although with slightly different projected trends in fertility. In other countries, and notably Italy, a significant fall in fertility coexists with greater longevity to generate the likely possibility of a significant population decline. In the countries of northern and western Europe, aging is a more gradual process, notwithstanding demographic cycles such as the postwar baby boom; indeed, there is already some experience of population aging there on which to base social and economic policies.

Prospects for the Elderly

So far, the macroeconomic problem of aging has been considered and illustrated. These macroeconomic consequences—for such economic issues as productivity growth, national savings rates, and the viability of social security programs—form a major theme of the book. But, as the title of the book indicates, aging is also a potential microeconomic problem. People can expect to live longer and to spend a significant part of their later life in economic inactivity. What are their income prospects? If there is a trend toward increasing affluence among elderly people, on what will they spend the money? What about those who wish to continue to work: what are their employment prospects, given the greater number of elderly people, the declining numbers of young, and women's growing participation in the labor force? These topics also form the themes of succeeding chapters.[7]

One important trend is the apparently growing affluence of the elderly and their increased propensity to live on unearned income from owned assets, pensions, and social security rather than continuing to work. These facets, discussed in greater detail later, merit brief illustration at this point. In the United States, elderly households have gained relative to younger households. According to the US Census, the mean income of households with head aged 65+ rose from 54 percent of the average in 1970 to 63 percent in 1987 (Hurd 1990, table 4). Indeed, allowing for benefits in cash and kind, normalizing for household size, and adjusting for tax payments, many elderly households may on average be better off in retirement than during their earlier, working life.[8] In similar vein, Dilnot et al. (1994) show that pensioners' real incomes rose on average by 44 percent between 1979 and 1991 in the United Kingdom—somewhat higher than the increase for the population as a whole (ibid., table 2.6), with income from private pensions rising by 98 percent and investment income by 171% (outweighing a small increase in real social security payments and a decline in income from current earnings). Similar patterns are observed in other OECD countries.

Nevertheless, the perception of growing affluence among the elderly should not conceal the potential for poverty in old age. Growing *average* incomes of the elderly have concealed an increase in income *inequality* among the elderly in the 1980s. In the United Kingdom, the median income in the top quintile of the pensioner income distribution is 4 times that in the bottom quintile. Furthermore, the incomes of the former increased by 50 percent from 1979 to 1991, while the incomes of the latter increased by only 11 percent (ibid., table 2.7). Although there are issues concerning measurement, Hurd (1990) in general confirms that the income distribution of the elderly (65+) is more unequal than that of those under 65 (ibid., table 11), and that, although poverty rates among the elderly in the United States have declined significantly, inequality began to increase in the early 1980s (ibid., table 9).

In general, increases in social security payments tend both to improve the position of the elderly relative to the rest of the population and to reduce inequality among the elderly, whereas greater private pensions and high real rates of return tend to improve the position of the better-off elderly disproportionately. Insofar as population aging affects the functioning of social security, private pension schemes, and capital markets, its potential impact on these trends in absolute and relative living standards is clear. Consequently, these issues are discussed extensively here.

Methodology: On Overlapping Generations and the Life-Cycle Hypothesis

The economics of aging raises the macroeconomic issue of the impact on the economy as a whole and the microeconomic issue of individual prospects for consumption and income over the life cycle associated with greater longevity and lower fertility (fewer descendants). In order to motivate and link these concerns, a methodology is required.

It is common in policy discussions of the issue, and in conventional approaches to the "economics of aging," to discuss aging as a *burden of dependency* using static (within-period) measures of the burden, calculated with varying degrees of sophistication. Such models generally examine the interaction between the ratio of economically active to inactive people, the level of transfers, and tax rates. Behavioral responses (for example, the effects on labor-market participation of a growing financing burden of a social security program) can be incorporated by using comparative statics. Some mileage can be gained from such an approach, if the degree of complexity is reasonably realistic, in discussing for example the incidence of redistributive policies (chapter 2) and in appraising "generational strategies" designed to maximize resource shares (chapter 10).

Quite apart from the tendency of such models to oversimplify the redistributive process, however, there are limitations to this general approach of analyzing within-period generational transfers. Static models wholly focus on the "transfer burden" of providing income from the economically active for the elderly inactive, ignoring any behavioral response over time to the prospective "burdens" and consequent behavior of successive generations. Expectations are not formed in the model and by inference all participants are myopic. However, since the amount of income to be divided in any period is the outcome of dynamic (or life-cycle) behavior, it is not unreasonable to expect that people adopt a non-myopic, forward-looking perspective. For example, labor-market entrants in a large cohort may perceive the impact of cohort size on their current earnings and employability and attempt to acquire extra skills (for example, by entering college rather than entering the labor market). Or individuals who are part of a large generation nearing retirement may increase their savings rate because they fear a cutback in the generosity of the social security program given the greater potential tax burden. Each of these decisions will have microeconomic and macroeconomic effects.

It is not necessary to believe that expectations are formed rationally in such circumstances (they may be extrapolative or adaptive); the approach merely considers individuals in any generation who are passing through the stages of childhood, economic activity, and retirement as adopting a *life-cycle perspective* in their consumption, participation, and production decisions (chapters 3 and 5–8). Thus, within any period, there exist a set of *overlapping generations,* some at the largely economically active stage of their life cycle and others at the stage of economic inactivity. Within-period transfers are *generational transactions,* which may include redistributive tax-and-transfer systems, bequests, and charity to the elderly and which may encompass a variety of behavioral forms (coercive, altruistic, and strategic).

A second weakness in the application of the static redistributive framework to the problem of aging is in its implicit concept of optimality. For example, in answering (or indeed asking) the question "How much money should be taken from the economically inactive and given to the elderly inactive?" it is hard to avoid a *utilitarian* perspective, which involves explicit interpersonal comparisons of the marginal utility of income or consumption to different individuals, households, or generations. But, as chapter 10 argues, no existing agency is able to evaluate and compare individuals' utilities in the required way—quite apart from the fact that many interpersonal (or intergenerational) transactions are probably motivated by behavior more selfish than maximizing the sum of (within-period) human satisfaction.

Much of modern economics is motivated by a dynamic concept of optimality, explored and popularized by many authors, notably Samuelson, stemming from the individual allocation of time between work and leisure and of consumption across goods and over time. If we are prepared to make the strong (but in principle testable) assumption that individuals operate in an environment that allows them to optimize intertemporally, then a concept of optimality exists that does not require the use of interpersonal comparisons. "Optimality" here is used in a different sense; the question is not whether outcomes are "fair" in the utilitarian sense but whether they maximize individual utility (or would be chosen over any other alternative) within the lifetime budget constraint.

In some respects this is a more limited perspective within which to view distributional outcomes: by eschewing interpersonal (and intergenerational) welfare comparisons, economists cannot provide clear answers as to what policies are "best" for society. But an individual concept of optimality has a powerful attraction when one is considering the economics of aging: it provides a unifying theme for the analysis of the many facets of economic activity on which aging impinges. These include equilibrium in the pay-as-you-go social security system (chapter 3), the motives underlying provision of private pension schemes (chapter 5), the lifetime labor-supply decision and especially retirement (chapter 7), consumption and savings behavior (chapter 8), and even generational voting strategies in repeated games (chapter 10). There is a variety of literature that implicitly utilizes this perspective in order to examine the consequences of aging in the context of particular economic issues, and a primary task of the present book is to draw these illustrations together.

Thus, there is a good deal of emphasis here on overlapping generations, on intertemporal optimization, and in particular on the application of the life-cycle hypothesis of consumption and saving. Of necessity this perspective, which forms the basis of modern macroeconomics (see, e.g., Blanchard and Fischer 1989) is not engaged in great technical detail. The object, for those interested in the economics of aging, is to show that this perspective is a useful and relevant tool of analysis. For mainstream economists, the intention is to show that a literature is now available that brings such techniques to bear on the economics of aging, and that some of the conclusions of this literature deserve wider attention in other fields.

Reading the Book

There is no particular need to follow the chapters in the book in chronological order, although there is a logical sequence (at least, in the eyes of the author). Chapters 2 and 3 introduce the "traditional" and "LCH/OLG" approaches to aging. Chapter 2 considers static redistributive models of the aging "burden," although a non-stationary model in terms of growth rates is also considered. Chapter 3 describes an overlapping-generations perspective and a lifetime concept of optimality, then looks at the rationale for social security programs in such a framework and at the problems posed for that rationale by an aging population.

A natural first step, in view of the literature on aging, is to consider the dynamics of social security programs. Chapter 4 presents five case studies of social security pension programs and considers how the differing programs of the United States, the United Kingdom, Italy, Australia, and Japan cope with aging populations. It illustrates the problem of excessive pre-commitment of future transfers that is endemic to pay-as-you-go social insurance schemes.

In chapter 5 I turn my attention to privately provided pension schemes, which seem likely to play an increased role in supporting the growing number of elderly people in the future. Private pensions are part of the remuneration structure offered by companies, and their implementation is bound up with the lifetime productivity of workers and with other components of the pay package. Chapter 6 examines how workforce aging is related to lifetime productivity, to pay levels, and to educational attainment. The macroeconomic issue of whether aged workforces are less productive can then be examined. Chapter 7 looks at retirement, focusing on the impact of aging on labor-force participation.

Chapter 8 examines savings and consumption, describing, at the macroeconomic level, the relationship between population growth and the ratio of active to economically inactive people (on the one hand) and savings, investment, and growth (on the other). The microeconomic evidence on the validity of the life-cycle hypothesis of saving is surveyed, and the impacts of aging on the saving of the young and the elderly and on the bequest motive are predicted. Changes in individual expenditure patterns are also discussed, with particular focus on the demand for housing and health care. The latter is the topic of chapter 9.

Chapter 10 considers the public-choice perspective on aging: how a larger proportion of elderly individuals in the population will affect voting behavior in regard to the allocation of resources, particularly government expenditures. In that chapter I show how fluctuations in cohort size may generate instability in public expenditures and may make intergenerational transfers suboptimal. In the last section I speculate on whether a long-run social contract between generations that might restore an optimal intergenerational allocation of resources could be constructed.

A Burden Of Dependency? Social Security Programs and Intergenerational Redistribution

Most people do not engage in paid work after entering their mid sixties. Why this is the case will be discussed in subsequent chapters, especially chapter 7. From an economic point of view, a person who has retired from the labor market is a "burden" on society in the specific sense that his current consumption expenditure outweighs his current contribution to the total marketable output. Consequently, there must be a social mechanism permitting the transfer of consumption availability—that is, a process by which some goods and services produced by the economically active young are reallocated to the old. This process can be termed an *intergenerational resource redistribution.*

The traditional redistribution mechanism in society was the extended family, which provided income sharing for all its members. Traditional societies had imperfectly developed capital markets and incomplete or nonexistent social security programs. In addition, strong behavioral norms underpinned intrafamily transfer mechanisms. However, alternative modes of income transfer have been stimulated by the development of financial markets and public finance. These developments have underpinned changes in social and economic mores, so that family structures have typically declined in importance in Western industrialized countries as providers of economic support to the elderly.[1] As a consequence, intergenerational support has become indirect; it now rests on the ownership of claims on resources *within the market economy* by the elderly.

Many elderly people have accumulated savings or entitlements to public or private pensions and, upon retiring, derive income from these sources.[2] During his or her working life, an individual with foresight will save and will invest in financial assets (such as stocks and bonds) or in physical assets (such as housing). These financial assets will yield dividends (prior claims on the profits of companies) and interest payments (prior claims on the tax revenues of the government). When an individual is myopic and fails to invest in order to guarantee a secure future stream of income, or is simply poor, the implicit redistribution becomes explicit, with income support derived from the family, from charity, or from public transfers such as social security programs.

The redistributive mechanisms associated with an aging population become blurred in social security schemes based on "pseudo-insurance"—that is, schemes in which entitlements to pensions are built up over an individual's lifetime by tax payments to an earmarked "insurance" fund and pensions are paid upon retirement according to the legislation in force at the time. Such schemes are rarely fully funded in practice; retired individuals are not living on public annuities derived from their own investments (and, even if they were, the realized claim would still be a transfer in the sense described above). In fact, social security programs are usually "pay-as-you-go" (PAYG) schemes, in which current pension entitlements are financed out of current tax receipts, whether from general taxes or from hypothecated taxes such as the National Insurance Contribution in the United Kingdom. In any event, social security pensions paid rarely bear any relation to underlying individual contributions or tax payments (see chapter 4 below and Wilson and Wilson 1982).

Why do social security pension programs contain this pseudo-insurance component? The assertion that "willingness to pay" rests on such a procedure is unproven, as interviews generally show that people are understandably confused as to the financing method or the sources of hypothecation.[3] It seems more likely that such schemes function to defer social security commitments into the future, when full contribution entitlements will have been satisfied, while limiting the extent of current intergenerational transfers of resources to the elderly. Present workers may thereby attempt to commit future generations of workers to pay them social security pensions at considerably more generous levels than they themselves paid to the previous generation, or, at the very least, to the most favorable terms on which they were paid to the earliest members of the PAYG scheme (see chapter 10). Whether such intergenerational social contracts are sustainable is discussed in the next chapter in the context of Paul Samuelson's well-known 1958 model, but it is apparent that persuading generations not yet in the labor market (or perhaps not even born) to agree to a contract of this type made on their behalf is problematic.

As a preliminary to these intertemporal considerations, the present chapter addresses some of the issues stemming from intergenerational redistribution, and in particular its explicit nature within the operation of PAYG social security programs. The focus in this chapter is on within-period distributive transfers and pensions, although in section 2.3 comparative statics will be used to examine an extension of the basic model in which key variables may grow proportionately over time. Interperiod redistributive mechanisms in the context of a series of overlapping generations will be considered in the next chapter.

The first question to be considered here is whether, from the social point of view, there is an optimal degree of within-period resource redistribution from the young to the elderly when only the young are producers. We will examine an approach (based on cardinal utility functions) that, although generally out of favor with economic theorists these days, still implicitly underpins the way the "burden of the elderly" is often considered. Some measures of the "burden" are then constructed in the context of a simple tax-and-transfer program. Data are presented describing the within-period (or "static") burdens of social security pensions for several countries over various time intervals.

Having illustrated the static comparisons, I then present some simple arithmetic showing how the tax burden is affected by generation size and how (in steady-state comparisons) demographic trends can be offset by utilizing a range of tax instruments and tax structures. The model is then extended to the case where key variables (such as rate of participation in the labor force) are changing. The conclusion of the last section suggests that simple predictions of the "burden of the elderly" based on demographic predictions give little guidance as to outcomes (specifically, as to required changes in tax rates).

2.1 Is There a Socially Optimal Level of Redistribution from Workers to Pensioners?

At first glance there seems to be a straightforward practical answer to this question. Most countries have some kind of official minimum income standard, and most people would desire to provide at least this standard to all, including pensioners. But this view, although eminently sensible, fails to explain why social insurance systems are constructed in the way they are—and, in particular, why in most cases they offer benefits (in the future, at least) well in excess of established poverty minimum standards. An important point, considered more

This analysis presupposes measurable utility, but it was precisely the conceptual difficulty of doing so that led microeconomists toward the ideas of ordinal utility and revealed preference (although an expected utility approach might provide some insight in this context). Furthermore, the partition of the sources of the consumption of the dependent in figure 2.1 ignores the real possibility that some sources of income may substitute for others; in particular, the existence of a state levy in the form of a social security program will almost certainly have adverse effects on the extent of private asset holding, on the incentive to maximize returns on assets (or type of asset holding), and on the willingness of individuals to engage in voluntary transfers of the type described here. These important issues will be discussed in due course.

This static approach has one advantage: it permits various measures of the "burden" of elderly dependents on the total income or output of society to be calculated. It is immediately apparent that a number of measures can be derived from the algebraic formulation; some of the more obvious ones are listed here:

(i) The total resources devoted to dependents as a fraction of available resources: $(rk + g + p)/(rk + w)$.

(ii) The public burden of pension costs. This can be defined as $p/(w + rk)$, the share of pensions in total income. If some fraction q of the assets held by dependents takes the form of government bonds, the total burden on the public sector, $(p + qrk)/(w + rk)$, is somewhat higher; the corresponding tax rate on wages needed to finance this burden, $t'' = (p + qrk)/w$, is also higher.

(iii) The "replacement ratio" of the social security pension as a fraction of the wage bill. This can be defined in two ways. Before tax the ratio is simply p/w; after tax it is $p/(1 - t)w$. This, of course, assumes that pensioners pay no taxes, which is generally not the case; most countries levy indirect taxes and excise duties on expenditures on goods and services.

(iv) The burden of the dependent on the worker. The involuntary burden can be defined as in (iii), or, if part of the interest on public debt must be paid out of taxes, as $(p + qrk)/w$, and, after tax, as $(p + qrk)/(1 - t'')w$. The total burden, including voluntary gifts, is $(p + g)/w$ in the simple case; in the other cases g is added to the numerator.

In table 2.1 values of these measures are calculated for a set of plausible numerical assumptions; for example, the basic social security

Table 2.1
Illustrative calculations of social security burden.

Assumptions
$Y=1$
$w=0.9$
$rk=0.1$
$q=0.5$
$g=0.1$
$p=0.3$
Measures of burden[a]
(i) 0.5
(ii) 0.3–0.39
(iii) 0.33–0.5
(iv) 0.39–0.74
Tax rates on wage
$t=0.33$
$t'=0.38$
$t''=0.39$

a. Numerals i–iv correspond to items listed in text.

pension is set at 30 percent of total income (and one-third of the wage) and so on. The range of magnitudes of the "burden" is rather wide, from one extreme of 0.3 (the social security pension as a proportion of income) to 0.74 (the cost of all private and state-financed transfers to the elderly dependent as a proportion of the wage, net of tax). The tax rates on wages needed to finance the public cost of supporting the elderly lie in a narrower range, with the basic rate of 0.33 rising to 0.38 on taxable income (where gifts are tax-exempt) and 0.39 (where the costs of public debt finance are included). Thus, a number of measures exist, although the most frequently used are generally versions of (ii) and (iii). It is immediately apparent that the "burden of intergenerational transfers" can be quantified in a number of ways, even in this simplified and static context. Intertemporal and intercountry comparisons are often highly misleading.[7]

2.2 The "Burden" of Dependency

A logical extension of the preceding analysis is to consider the dependency burden when there are different numbers of dependents and workers. This allows a comparative-static way of comparing populations "before" and "after" the demographic transition to an aged society. The standard approach (Clark and Spengler 1980, p. 157ff; Creedy and Disney 1989a; Schulz 1992) focuses on the burden to a PAYG social security program paying an untaxed pension per dependent, p. Pensions are financed by a proportional tax, t (the percentage tax rate is $100t$). The average wage of the labor force, L, is w, and the number of pensioners (dependents) is D. Balancing the public budget requires that

$$pD = twL, \tag{2.1}$$

and simple rearrangement yields the basic formula:

$$t = \frac{p/w}{L/D}. \tag{2.2}$$

The replacement ratio p/w has already been encountered. The other key ratio is the reciprocal of the aged dependency ratio (ADR) D/L, which shows how many dependent pensioners there are per worker. If we take an order of magnitude typical of trends in several Western European countries in the next 30 years or so (see table 2.2), with a replacement ratio of 60 percent and a fall in the "support ratio" L/D from 4 to 2.5, the tax rate needed to finance the scheme will rise from 15 percent to 24 percent of income. Thus, in this simple simulation an adverse demographic trend has severe effects on the government budget.

Although changes in the ratio L/D are clearly underpinned by demographic trends, actual dependency ratios may be driven by other factors. An illustration can be drawn from the work of Falkingham (1989), who focuses on recent trends in dependency in Britain, using various definitions of dependency. Some of Falkingham's results are adapted in table 2.3. Falkingham defines "demographic" as the ratio

$$\frac{\text{Population under 20 + Men over 65 and women over 60}}{\text{Men 20–64 and women 20–59}}.$$

"Economic" dependency is measured in two ways. One (series A) multiplies the population in five-year age intervals by economic activity rates. The other (series B) adjusts the economic activity rates by age band-specific unemployment and sickness rates. For example, table 2.3 shows that for every person of working age in 1951 there were 0.73 young or old dependents. However, when account is taken of less than 100 percent activity rates, the ratio rises to 1.18. Adjusting again to take

Table 2.2
Ratio of age group 20-64 to age group 65+ in selected countries. Sources: Kelley 1988, chart C; for United States, Pitts 1978.

	1980	2020
United Kingdom	3.7	3.2
Germany	3.7[a]	2.6
Sweden	4.3	2.6
Japan	6.7	2.7
United States	5.2	3.7

a. Former Federal Republic only.

Table 2.3
Measuring the burden of dependency in Britain. Source: Falkingham 1989.

Measure of dependency	1951	1961	1971	1981
Demographic	0.73	0.81	0.88	0.86
Economic				
Series A	1.18	1.18	1.17	1.11
Series B	1.21	1.22	1.27	1.34

account of sickness and unemployment, the ratio of dependents rises to 1.21 in the young and old categories per active worker. Note too the difference in the trends over time: whereas there is a steady increase in the ratio of demographic dependency until 1971 (thereafter the fall in the number of under-20s outweighs the rise in the numbers of the elderly), the ratio of activity-rate-adjusted dependents is stable until 1971 (largely reflecting increased female participation). Series B, adjusted for unemployment rates, rises sharply between 1961 and 1981 notwithstanding the decline in the other ratios in the decade 1971–1981. The obvious conclusion is that demographic trends need not drive trends in economic dependency—a result replicated in a nonstationary framework in section 2.3 below.

In fact the driving factor in raising the burden of social security pensions in many Western countries is not the trend in dependency so much as the trend in the real value of social security. Many governments are committed to increasing the replacement ratio for pensioners, p/w, over time. As table 2.4 shows, the projected growth of real expenditure per pensioner is dramatic in several countries, such as Italy and Japan, and, with the exception of North America, is the major factor in the growth of total pension expenditures.[8]

Table 2.4
Indices of growth of pension expenditure, 1980–2025 (1980 = 100). Source: calculated
from Heller et al. 1986, tables 4 and 5.

	Index of number of retirement pensioners	Index of growth of real expenditure per pensioner
Canada	272	117
France	150	217
Germany[a]	170	176
Italy	144	346
Japan	215	611
United Kingdom	130	223
United States	215	142

a. Former Federal Republic only.

Together, worsening aged dependency ratios (table 2.2) and rising
replacement ratios (table 2.4) form the basis for concern about the future macroeconomic costs of aging, and particularly the costs of social
security programs. These trends have been the subjects of numerous
study groups, of reports from international agencies, such as the IMF,
the World Bank (e.g. 1994), the OECD (e.g. 1988a), the ILO, and the
European Commission, and of legislative changes in many Western
industrialized countries designed to reduce the buildup of public pension obligations. Nevertheless, the model in equations 2.1 and 2.2 is
naive and the arithmetic simplistic. Adding a dose of realism to the
comparison of "steady states" implicit in these equations suggests that
the trends are not inexorable and that a number of instruments of policy flexibility are available which can be, and indeed are being, used
by governments to offset these trends.

The facets of this potential policy flexibility include the following:

(i) The method of indexation. It is implicitly assumed in equations 2.1
and 2.2 that social security benefits are indexed to the growth of wages.
Pensioners share in real output growth. However, in a number of countries pre-retirement calculation of entitlements and post-retirement
benefits use alternative indexation measures. In both the United Kingdom and the United States, for example, initial pension entitlements
at retirement are calculated according to a formula that takes explicit
account of growth in real earnings until retirement. Thereafter, benefits
are indexed to *price* inflation.[9] Similar arrangements are in force in Can-

ada and Japan. France indexed post-retirement benefits to earnings and Italy to a combination of price inflation and earnings inflation (see Heller et al. 1986 and chapter 4 below). Moreover, full exploration of the consequence for the social security burden of indexing post-retirement benefits to prices where there is real-earnings growth requires a model of the type considered in section 2.3 below.

(ii) In equation 2.2, the "target" replacement ratio is based on pre-tax wages. However, in Germany post-retirement indexation of benefits has become related to movements in *post-tax* wages. Indeed, a logical extension is to base the target value of the pension on post-tax wages. If R^* is therefore defined as the desired replacement ratio (p/w), the post-tax definition implies that $R^* = p/w(1 - t - \tau)$, where τ is the tax rate levied to pay for other government expenditure, and the pension becomes $R^*w(1 - t - \tau)$. From equation 2.1,

$$R^*w(1 - t - \tau)D = twL \tag{2.3}$$

and

$$R^* = [t/(1 - t - \tau)](L/D). \tag{2.4}$$

When the target replacement ratio of 60 percent is defined in terms of post-tax wages, the tax rate is just over 9 percent when $L/D = 4$ and $\tau = 0.25$, rising to just under 15 percent when L/D falls to 2. 5. The tax rate is proportionately more sensitive to demographic changes, but of course it starts from a lower base when a net-of-tax definition of R^* is used.[10]

(iii) Although basic state pensions are themselves often tax exempt, or pensioners are given a tax allowance equal to at least the value of the basic state pension, the expenditure of pensioners is generally subject to indirect taxes, such as the Value Added Tax in the states of the European Union. Assume that pensioners consume all their income, and express the expenditure tax rate of $100v$ on the tax exclusive price as a proportion $v/(1 + v)$ of the tax inclusive price. Then equation 2.1 becomes

$$p[1 - v/(1 + v)]D = w[t + (1 - t)v/(1 + v)]L, \tag{2.5}$$

which simplifies to

$$p/w = (v + t)L/D \tag{2.6}$$

or, when the value of the pension is determined by after-tax income,

$$R^* = [(v + t)/(1 - t - \tau)]L/D. \tag{2.7}$$

In this case, if $v = 0.15$ and $t = 0.25$, no income tax at all is needed to finance pensions when L/D is 4, although when L/D falls to 2.5 an income tax rate of 2.5 percent becomes necessary. Of course, if pensioners are dissaving their existing assets, and spending more than the basic state pension, the "clawback" of tax revenue from pensioners is even greater.

(iv) In general, tax and benefit schedules are complex. For example, in Australia the public pension is means-tested in respect of both wages and assets. A highly nonlinear budget constraint derives from this scheme (see chapter 4). Australia is unusual in means-testing the basic pension, but all Western economies exhibit nonlinear income tax schedules (generally with a tax allowance and some rate progressivity), exemptions of certain kinds of expenditure from indirect taxes, differential taxes on pensioners and workers' income, and so on. Modeling the outcome of such a system for the social security burden requires knowledge of the distribution of income, and of wages in particular; the ramifications are explored in Creedy and Disney 1992.

This section has therefore suggested that, even in the "static" model of transfers from workers to pensioners within a single period, various measures of the "burden" can be constructed. The trend in the burden of social security pensions is driven as much by changes in participation rates, in unemployment, or in real pension levels as by underlying demographic factors. Moreover, once the scope for flexibility in tax policy is taken into account, the underlying upward trend in the public burden looks far from inevitable.

2.3   A Nonstationary Model of Financing Social Security

Social security programs are rarely in a static "steady state," with constant dependency ratios and replacement ratios. Over time, the relative rates of compound growth of key variables have major effects on pension finance and on the trend in the "burden of dependency." Indeed, compound growth rates underpin models of dynamic equilibrium in an overlapping-generations context, which are explored in the next chapter. Even within the essentially static framework of the previous section, however, it is possible to look at the consequences of compound growth rates on the financing model, with nonstationarity an important influence on social security tax rates over long periods of time. Such a model is developed here.[11]

The object, as in section 2.2, is to find the tax rate, t, needed to finance the social security pension. As before, it is useful to work in terms of "generations" of workers and retirees (dependents). In the present case, the relationship between current dependents, D, and current workers in employment, E, is driven by two parameters. The first, μ, is a survival parameter governed by the expected average duration of retirement for each successive cohort. The second, θ, is the proportion of the labor force, L, that participates in paid work. It is assumed that the retirement age is not a decision variable, and that no one works beyond retirement age. It is straightforward to vary the overall retirement age (here equal to the pension age) in the model, or to postulate that some fraction of workers continue to work after this notional retirement age. It is less straightforward to postulate an endogenous retirement age or a retirement (optimal stopping) rule in this model.

Using notation in which the current "generation" is not subscripted and the previous "generation" is indexed -1, these relationships can be written as

$$D = \mu L_{-1} \tag{2.8}$$

and

$$E = \theta L. \tag{2.9}$$

The sizes of the current and previous generations of the labor force, L and $L_{-1,}$ are linked by the rate of population growth, η, so that $L = (1 + \eta)L_{-1}$. Using this expression and equation 2.9 lagged one period gives

$$E = (1 + \varepsilon)(1 + \eta)E_{-1}, \tag{2.10}$$

where $1+\varepsilon$ denotes θ/θ_{-1} and where ε is therefore the growth of the labor-force participation rate. Equation 2.10 therefore states that the growth of employment is (approximately) the sum of the population and participation growth rates. By similar substitution, equation 2.8 can be written as

$$D = (\mu/\theta_{-1})E_{-1}. \tag{2.11}$$

Then, dividing equation 2.11 by equation 2.10, we get

$$\frac{D}{E} = \frac{\mu/\theta_{-1}}{(1 + \varepsilon)(1 + \eta)}. \tag{2.12}$$

Equation 2.12 contains the appropriate measure of economic dependency, rather than the demographically defined measure in equation 2.1. Current economic dependency is conditioned on the time-dated participation rate, and on the (non-time-dated) survival rate of dependents (longevity) and the rates of growth of population and participation.[12]

The components of the replacement ratio, p and w, are also related. Suppose that the benefit, p, is set as a proportion β of the wage earned by the retirees in their working life, w. Then

$$p = \beta w_{-1}. \tag{2.13}$$

The average wages of the current and previous generations are also linked by the rate of growth of real wages, ω, we have

$$w = (1 + \omega)w_{-1}. \tag{2.14}$$

Dividing equation 2.13 by equation 2.14 gives the replacement ratio in terms of β and the growth of real earnings:

$$\frac{p}{w} = \frac{\beta}{1 + \omega}. \tag{2.15}$$

The expression for the tax rate needed to finance pensions is given by combining equation 2.12 and equation 2.15, which is the dynamic analogue of equation 2.2:

$$t = \frac{\beta(\mu/\theta_{-1})}{(1 + \eta)(1 + \omega)(1 + \varepsilon)}. \tag{2.16}$$

This formula has an intuitive rationale. The average tax rate needed to finance pensions is determined by the fraction of earnings replaced, β, and by the ratio of survivors to previous workers (μ/θ_{-1}). Clearly, the higher either of these two ratios, the higher the tax rate needed to finance current pensions.

Starting from any given participation rate, the tax rate is reduced steadily over time if any of the three growth rates in the denominator is positive. Of course, some of these growth rates face upper bounds (for example, $\varepsilon = 0$ where $E = L$). Furthermore, in steady state a growth in participation may ultimately lead to an increase in social security commitments, especially where lower pensions (or no pensions at all: see note 12) are paid to elderly dependents who were inactive in the labor market earlier in life. Other growth rates within the model are sustainable in the long term, however, and it can be argued that many of the issues concerning social security provision that arise are better suited to this framework than to the commonly used static framework of section 2.2.

Another simplifying assumption is as follows: If benefits are wholly indexed to earnings,[13] $(1 + \omega)$ drops out of the denominator and one degree of policy flexibility is lost. The derivation of more complicated indexation formulas in the context of a somewhat simpler version of the model in equations 2.8–2.16 is pursued in Rosen 1984.

One of the most interesting issues stemming from this dynamic model is the interdependence of the growth rates η, ε, and ω. For example, the growth rates of the labor force and productivity may be interdependent, although the form of this relationship is not clear *a priori*. Furthermore, the growth of labor-force participation may be positively related to the growth in real wages, especially among married women. On the other hand, faster population growth may reduce labor-force participation, especially among women of childbearing age.

A "virtuous circle" stemming from slower population growth may emerge if an aging population is associated with higher human capital per capita, and therefore higher wages. Both the fall in the number of children and the rising real wages may induce an increase in participation rates, so that the growth rates combine to offset the effects on the pension burden of the rising dependency ratio. But it is possible that these factors may offset each other, or also cause a "vicious circle" of decreasing growth in real wages, a falling population, and declining labor-force participation.

Numerical Examples of Nonstationary Model of Social Security Finance

To illustrate the magnitudes involved, this subsection presents some numerical examples. The growth rates in equation 2.16 are defined over a period or "generation" without any specification of duration. Suppose that the working life is 40 years and the expected average duration of retirement is 15 years. This gives the survival parameter, μ. It is also assumed that all the men and half the women in the labor force are employed, which gives θ. These assumptions, and other starting values, are listed in table 2.5.

Table 2.5
Initial assumptions in nonstationary model.

$\mu = 0.375$
$\beta = 0.5$
$\theta = 0.75$
$\eta = 0.01^{15}$
$\omega = 0.02^{15}$
$\varepsilon = 0.00^{15}$
$\therefore t = 0.16$

Given positive population growth (assumed to be due to labor-force entry, not to greater longevity of the retired population) and growing real wages, the tax rate needed to finance the retirement of a given generation declines exponentially. The "length" of the retired duration can be considered as the expected duration of retirement, which is 15 years in this example. Thus, the growth rates of population and real wages over 15 years are inserted in equation 2.16 in order to derive the expected average tax rate needed to fund the social security pensions of this retired generation. For these numerical parameters, the tax rate is calculated to be 16 percent, which is equivalent to that obtained from an overlapping-generations model in steady-state growth where the size of the cohort does not enter equation 2.16 directly. The tax rate will vary out of steady state as changes in the rate of population growth work their way through the age distribution of working life and retirement.

An interesting result is that a change in the survival parameter, μ, affects both the numerator and the denominator of equation 2.16. A rise in the expected duration of retirement, say from 15 to 20 years, raises the tax rate needed to finance the scheme through the change in the numerator, but lowers it through the denominator, since the growth rates are now compounded over a longer period. With the numerical values in table 2.5, the former effect dominates, and the tax rate rises from 16 percent to 18.4 percent, but the relationship between the tax rate and increased longevity is nonlinear for the simple reason that the longevity occurs at the end of the life! In contrast, changes in β have a linear impact on the tax rate. Figure 2.2 illustrates this point. It shows the impact on t (the tax rate) of variations in μ (the survival parameter) and β (the replacement rate). The nonlinearity of the response to changes in μ and the linearity of the response to changes in β (the shift factor) are clearly illustrated. Similar results

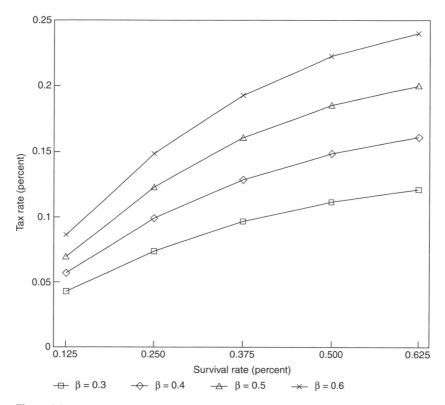

Figure 2.2
Effects of variation in expected duration of retirement and replacement ratio on tax rates.

would be obtained from varying the length of the working life via changes in the (state) pensionable age or in the mandatory retirement age.

Finally, it is useful to consider the case where the growth rates are interdependent. Suppose that η, the population growth rate, falls by one percentage point, to zero growth. Assume also that the elasticity of productivity growth with respect to population growth is -1, that of participation with respect to population growth is -2, and that of participation with respect of productivity growth is $+1$. (This is the "virtuous circle" case described above.) The reduction in population growth reduces the tax rate needed to finance social security pensions by stimulating productivity growth and increasing the rate of labor-force participation. The consequent average tax rate in the base-line case (table 2.5) is 10.2 percent.

In contrast, consider the case where the elasticity of productivity growth with respect to population growth is +1, with other elasticities as before. Although this is not a pure "vicious circle" of slowing population growth, the tax rate rises to 18.6 percent. Given the sensitivity of the tax rate to these interrelationships, the case for empirical analysis is heightened.

3 Overlapping-Generations Models, Feasible Pension Schemes, and Aging Populations

Chapter 2 provided a simple within-period or static view of the "burden" of a growing proportion of aged dependents. Within that framework, the degree of generosity of transfers to the elderly depended on the relative marginal utilities of consumption of the young and the old at all consumption levels, on the degree of altruism of the young, and on the scope for redistributive transfers within the tax system. One simple inference from such a model is that, given a declining marginal utility of consumption, so long as real income per capita is rising faster than the rate of growth of dependents, the real level of transfers can be maintained for a given degree of altruism and a specific tax structure. This is about the only "rule" that comes out of the model, although sections 2.3 and 2.4 showed that the extent of the transfer burden was sensitive to a range of other variables.

Nevertheless, the analysis of chapter 2 is limited in several respects. The structure of transfers ultimately depends on some degree of altruism among the young. The strongest reason why the young might be altruistic is that they themselves will be old one day. But the static structure of the model (the within-period comparison) is consistent only with models in which individuals are myopic in their behavior. This is a contradiction and it is natural to ask whether some kind of "contract" could be established between generations to account for the fact that every individual can expect to pass through both the worker stage and the dependent stage. Workers might find transfers to dependents acceptable if they themselves believe that such transfers will be available to them when they become dependents. This issue motivated a famous article by Samuelson (1958) which forms the basis of much of the discussion in this chapter.

This model of sequences of worker-dependents, or *overlapping generations,* underpins much modern analysis, not just of pension provision, but also of macroeconomic theory, and especially of saving and consumption. Modern consumption theory is underpinned by the life cycle of consumer behavior, which implies sequential periods of saving and dissaving during the lifetime. Changes in the age composition of the population should thereby imply different measured savings ratios, although such effects are mediated by cohort-specific expectations as to "permanent" or normal income. But, in addition, consumption behavior is affected by initial asset conditions, bequest motives, and the macroeconomic policies of the government. Population aging impinges on all these issues, and OLG models provide a unifying structure within which to examine them.

Section 3.1 lays out the basic Samuelson consumption loan model and shows how, under certain demographic conditions, intergenerational transfers may be preferred by successive generations to a strategy of each generation's saving durable resources for its own retirement. Altruism is not required in this simple model. However, slowing growth of the population poses significant problems for the sustainability of the "social contract" implied by the Samuelson model. Various extensions of the model are then considered, and these suggest that the rate of population growth will also have implications for the size and the nature of the capital stock. Myopic behavior and altruism are introduced. Both raise problems of the enforceability of the contract and of possible instability in public transfer programs—issues that will be considered again in later chapters in the context of actual pension programs and in the context of public-choice theories of resource transfers.

3.1 Overlapping Generations and Provision of Pensions

The basis of the now-extensive literature on overlapping-generations models, and indeed of much of recent consumption theory, is Samuelson 1958. The issues raised in that paper underpin much of the ensuing discussion, and it is useful to commence by examining the model devised by Samuelson and some possible solutions to problems that emerge in his framework. The model concerns not just the optimal allocation of consumption between generations *within* a period but also the optimal division of consumption by an individual *between* periods: the intertemporal allocation of consumption. Consideration of the latter may suggest a different allocation of the former than was implied in the preceding chapter.

To implement the model, four assumptions were made:

(i) No goods can be stored between time periods.

(ii) Claims on consumption are discounted at a parametric interest rate, i.[1]

(iii) Individuals are forward looking (not myopic) and do not change their preferences over time; that is, individuals make intertemporal plans at the start of their working lives, and those plans are ratified by subsequent actions.[2]

(iv) Each generation has the same preferences.

In this framework, suppose each individual's life has three periods, with the utility function in consumption defined over periods indexed $j=1,2,3$,

$$U = U(c_1, c_2, c_3),\tag{3.1}$$

and with lower-case letters denoting per-capita quantities. A key point of the model is that in period 3 workers produce less than they consume. To simplify, normalize output in period 1; then, by setting output in period 2 equal to 1 and output in period 3 equal to 0, we obtain an individual output profile (1,1,0). The point of assumption i is now clear: the worker cannot accumulate or store goods in periods 1 and 2 for consumption in period 3; he or she must utilize the capital market in order to acquire the claim on resources in period 3, which can be transformed into consumption, or else must benefit from some other form of within-period transfer.

Assume that individuals discount the future at a constant interest rate i, where $R = 1/(1 + i)$. Then the allocation of consumption by an individual to each period of his working life is determined by his preferences and by the discount rate:

$$c_j = c_j(i),$$
$$s_j \equiv 1 - c_j(i),\tag{3.2}$$

where s is individual saving, subject to the intertemporal budget constraint (given the time profile of production above):

$$c_1 + Rc_2 + R^2c_3 = 1 + R1.\tag{3.3}$$

In addition,

$$s_1(i) + Rs_2 + R^2s_3(i) = 0,\tag{3.4}$$

which simply states that at the end of the life all claims on consumption are exhausted: the discounted (dis)saving in period 3 equals the discounted saving in periods 1 and 2.[3]

The solution to equations 3.1–3.4 depends on the utility function (preferences) and the interest rate. Suppose $i = 0$ ($R = 1$). Then the solution is

$$\frac{\partial u / \partial c_2}{\partial u / \partial c_1} = \frac{\partial u / \partial c_3}{\partial u / \partial c_1}. \tag{3.5}$$

This states that individual intertemporal equilibrium is obtained where the marginal utility of consumption is equated across time periods. Where the discount rate is not zero, we have to make some assumption about the form of equation 3.1. However, if preferences are additively (log) separable,

$$\frac{\partial u / \partial c_2}{\partial u / \partial c_1} = (i + i) = R^{-1}$$

and   (3.5′)

$$\frac{\partial u / \partial c_3}{\partial u / \partial c_1} = (R^2)^{-1}.$$

By analogy with equation 3.5, equation 3.5′ states that *discounted* marginal utilities of consumption are equated across periods.[4]

At the same time, the model requires a within-period equilibrium: the *net* savings of the three generations alive in any given period must be zero under the initial assumptions. Clearly there must be a presumption that the saving of the two younger generations alive in any period will match the dissaving of the oldest generation. Denoting *total* saving and consumption of each generation by upper-case letters (i.e. saving/consumption per head × generation size), assume that the size of each generation is determined by the population birth rate η, which can be positive, zero, or negative. Each generation can be indexed by its size, so that if the youngest generation alive is normalized at 1 the size of the previous generation is $1/(1 + \eta)$ and so on. Thus, within-period saving equilibrium requires that

$$S_1(i) + (1 + \eta)^{-1}S_2(i) + [(1 + \eta)^2]^{-1}S_3(i) = 0. \tag{3.6}$$

Two questions emerge in this framework: Does an equilibrium rate (or rates) of interest exist? Is this interest rate a socially optimal one?

In answer to the first question, if we compare equations 3.4 and 3.6, and so long as all individuals are identical, it is apparent that one solution in which the individual intertemporal equilibrium and the within-period equilibrium are consistent is where $i = \eta$. In this economy (which Samuelson terms a *consumption loan economy*), one equilibrium market rate of interest equals the population growth rate. The intuition is simple: if we suppose η to be positive, each successive generation is larger, and this allows a rate of return η to be paid on the savings of the preceding generation. Thus, if the economy is on this equilibrium path, positive interest stems from positive population growth and not from, say, positive capital productivity (or, indeed, an explicit rate of time preference).

The second question is also answered: this solution is socially optimal in the specific sense that the sum of individual lifetime utility is maximized because it satisfies equations 3.5 and 3.5'. Consumption is allocated among the three age groups alive in any one period in the following proportions (Samuelson 1958, p. 472):

$$C_1 + (1 + \eta)^{-1}C_2 + [(1 + \eta)^2]^{-1}C_3. \tag{3.7}$$

Note that equation 3.5 gives a different definition of the social optimum from that employed in chapter 2, where the social optimum equated the marginal utility of different individuals within a given time period. As the exchange between Lerner (1959) and Samuelson (1959) made clear, individual intertemporal utility maximization of the Samuelson form would normally imply inequality of marginal utilities of consumption among individuals from different generations within a given time period (unless population growth was zero). In contrast, the within-period social optimum favored by Lerner would not generate individual intertemporal equilibrium (i.e. where discounted marginal utilities of consumption were equated) where population growth was nonzero.

Unfortunately $i = \eta$ is not the only solution to equations 3.4 and 3.6. An equilibrium can also be obtained where $i = -1$ (or $R = +\infty$). The practical interpretation of this result is that the oldest generation, bereft of income from production in the final period of its life, is prepared to pay up to all its previous resources to persuade successive generations to support it in its retirement. But since one of the generations with whom this retired generation needs to negotiate is not even alive (in the workforce) during this final period, how is this "social contract" to be arranged? Samuelson shows by various numerical examples of actual utility functions with nonstationary populations and nonzero discount rates that large negative rates of interest are possible solutions to the model—solutions which imply that the old have to lose substantial amounts on their retirement loans in order to retain a subsistence income in that last period. What Samuelson (1958, p. 480) felt was needed was a "Hobbesian contract" by which "the young are assured of their retirement subsistence if they will today support the aged, such support to be guaranteed by a draft on the yet-unborn."

Samuelson himself suggested that the function of money as a store of value might do the trick. If the total money supply was constant, with population growing at rate η, prices would also fall at rate η, giving a real return on money, i, equal to η. However, to assume that prices, and indeed the money supply, would behave in the manner required is asking a lot of the economy.

An alternative, more appropriate to the present context, is to legislate a pay-as-you-go social security program through which present workers would be prepared to finance the retirement pensions of a past generation if they felt that the "social contract" contained in the social security program would guarantee that future generations would themselves support current workers in their retirement. Indeed, the Samuelson model implies a good reason why this approach might work, so long as population growth was positive. The "burden" of each previous generation on each successive generation would be reduced over time, because each successive generation is larger than the previous one. Indeed, the positive rate of interest *implies* that the marginal utility of consumption of the older retired person in any period is higher than that of the younger worker in Samuelson's social optimum. The only losers in this scenario are the "last" generation, who would find no generation to support their retirement. For every preceding generation, however, an arrangement such as a social security program that offered a return at least equal to the population growth rate would be optimal.

This analysis is the basis of the "social insurance paradox" (see Aaron 1966 and the discussion below), but it is of course immediately apparent that a decline in the rate of growth of the population makes continuation of this social contract, or open-ended game, more problematic. In such circumstances, some generation will have to accept a lower (even negative) return, but it is tempted to carry on with unsustainable pension commitments. In turn, the next generations, who bear the burden of these "excess" commitments may be tempted to pass them on to subsequent generations by legislating still higher social security. Such an explosive (Ponzi-scheme or chain-letter) game is not an equilibrium in the Samuelsonian sense; it is an attempt to pre-commit future generations so as to obtain "excessive" return on one's contributions. This type of issue is central to the literature on public choice.

All this abstracts from population growth induced by greater longevity of generations. If, say, each generation now lives for four periods, of which two are "in retirement," satisfying equation 3.5 requires that absolute consumption in all four periods is lower. However, the Samuelsonian "social contract" again becomes problematic. Although the size of the generations is no longer affected solely by the birth rate h, the equilibrium rate of interest can still be determined. It will be lower than in the case discussed here; indeed, if the increasing longevity of the population outweighs the birth rate of new producers (with fixed participation and retirement behavior) it will probably be negative. This is the "penalty" that the younger generations exact for having to support the increasing size of the older generation. Evidence from chapter 4 suggests that in many social security programs a significant proportion of each future generation may indeed face negative actual returns on their social security contributions, raising the issue of whether reliance on funded pensions earning positive returns may not be superior to "social insurance" arrangements.

3.2   Extensions of Samuelson's Overlapping-Generations Model

The Samuelson consumption loan model, of course, contains a number of highly restrictive assumptions. These include the assumption of consistent lifetime preferences (no myopia), no changes in output (productivity) with each generation, and no storable output (capital stock) left as a legacy by each generation. The succeeding literature has attempted to address all these issues and has refined the model considerably.

Myopia and Forced Saving
The possibility that younger generations would not save to maintain older generations because they could not guarantee that future

generations would treat them in an identical manner was explored by Samuelson. The possibility that younger generations would not *care* about the future until they themselves had aged was, however, ruled out by assumption. The problem of myopia, or lifetime inconsistent preferences, would seem to be central to the problem of optimal saving. However, such behavior merely strengthens the rationale for public pension provision of some kind. Diamond (1977) has argued that myopia is pervasive in saving behavior, pointing to the empirical inconsistency in people's behavior when it comes to investing in private savings and insurance plans. In a revised model where the possibility of preference change is allowed, a PAYG social security program therefore provides not just the bridge between generations: the "social contract" but also the bridge between age-specific preferences, guaranteeing that individual saving will be consistent with the saving undertaken had individual preferences been lifetime consistent.

There are two reservations concerning the "forced saving" or paternalist argument for public pension provision. The first is that the existence of a social security program changes individual saving behavior toward other assets: we do not know what private saving would have been in the absence of the public program, and therefore we do not know whether such saving would have been "optimal." Proponents of the paternalist argument might well counter that, although a public pension program might affect the magnitude of private saving, it should not lead to inconsistency in private behavior (for example, starting insurance contracts and then allowing them to default before maturity or even before benefits are vested). The second reservation is as follows: though the paternalist argument provides a case for public provision, it does not guarantee that the public provision that emerges is in any sense optimal to the individual, as witnessed by the dispute concerning the introduction of earnings-related pension benefits in Britain (Wilson and Wilson 1982) and the constant changes to its social security program, and the pension component in particular, in the last two decades (Creedy and Disney 1985, 1988). Indeed, if the social security program is the subject of great uncertainty, or if different individuals hold various expectations as to the future trend in social security, the scope for apparently inconsistent *private* saving behavior becomes that much greater. Credibility is as important in social security policy as it is in other facets of macroeconomic policy, and public concern as to the "burden" of future pension commitments merely heightens this sense of individual insecurity. Thus, the possibility of myopia strengthens the link between the OLG model and the existence of a social security program while at the same time raising a host of other important issues.

Growth in Productivity and Real Wages

Another simplification of the Samuelson model has also been examined and a more general result established. This concerns the assumption of constant productivity (real wages) of each generation. However, Aaron (1966) provided a more general result, which can be stated in the notation of equations 3.1–3.6 as follows[5]: Suppose each generation is more productive than the last, with the productivity (real-wage rate) of each generation growing at a rate ω. Assuming a proportionate savings function, the per-capita saving of the current generation can be indexed as before as s, with the previous generation saving $s/(1 + \omega)$, and so on recursively. Using the notation of equation 3.6, we can write within-period equilibrium in the three-generation model as

$$S_1(i) + (1 + \eta)^{-1}S_2(1 + \omega)^{-1}(i) + [(1 + \eta)^2]^{-1}S_3[(1 + \omega)^2]^{-1}(i) = 0. \quad (3.8)$$

It is apparent, comparing equation 3.8 with equation 3.6, that a result parallel to that of Samuelson can be obtained where (ignoring the cross-products) $i = \eta + \omega$. As Aaron (1966, p. 472) states, "social insurance can increase the welfare of each person if the sum of the rates of growth of population and real wages exceeds the rate of interest." This is simply an extension of the $i = \eta$ result obtained by Samuelson.

Aaron also emphasizes the "paradox" implicit in Samuelson's consumption loan model, by comparing explicitly the rate of return to an individual belonging to an (unfunded) PAYG scheme with that accruing to a fully or partially funded social security program (i.e., one in which a "social insurance fund" is accumulated). The "paradox" is that if a person saves in a funded scheme, the present value of his pension (benefits net of contributions) will be lower than if he belonged to a PAYG scheme at any given interest rate. Thus, to gain a given pension, one can save less in a PAYG scheme and still receive a greater pension in the end! The reason is, of course, that in a funded scheme individuals are saving as members of a larger generation, so that the "generationally neutral" contribution rate is higher than in a scheme where they are funding the identically valued pensions of the existing, smaller retired generation. The present values would be identical if the two schemes were discounted at the "appropriate" discount rates. The appropriate discount rate for a funded scheme would be $i = 0$ in the Lerner case and $i = \eta + \omega$ for the extended Samuelson model. Again, the "chain letter" aspect shows up in the fact that each generation is content to rely on its "social contract," as each successive generation is larger than the previous one.

However, two problems arise in this context. First, as suggested previously, where population growth starts to slacken and the population ages, the pressure from younger generations to renege on the implicit contract becomes greater. Second, where positive utility is attached to a higher *total* saving rate of the community, the introduction of an unfunded social security program may reduce total savings by depressing savings in the form of privately funded assets. Since, *ceteris paribus*, the amount of savings required to accumulate a given pension entitlement in the form of funded assets is lower than in the unfunded case, then with a sufficiently large elasticity of substitution between public and private saving, total savings may fall. This important question, which lies at the heart of much of Martin Feldstein's work (see, e.g., Feldstein 1974a,b), will be considered in later chapters in the context of privately funded pensions and of the impact of aging on aggregate consumption and saving.

Durable Capital Goods in OLG Models

So far, the analysis has assumed that no capital stock is passed on from generation to generation. Much effort has been expended in the literature in removing this highly restrictive simplification. The general starting point in considering the accumulation of capital stock is the neoclassical growth model, developed by Robert Solow (1956) and others. In this model, in equilibrium growth, with the capital stock and the labor force growing at the same rate, steady-state per-capita magnitudes will be in the relationship

$$c = f(k) - \eta k, \tag{3.9}$$

where C is consumption, K is the capital stock, and $F(\cdot)$ denotes the aggregate production function (which satisfies the standard Inada conditions). Here again lower-case letters are used to denote per-worker magnitudes of the variables. Thus, equation 3.9 states that, in a steady state, per-capita consumption is based on per-worker output (from the per-worker production function) less the amount of output needed to maintain the capital-labor rate, k, in the face of population growth. In equilibrium k is unchanged, and in this model the saving rate does not affect the rate of growth; it merely affects the value of k.[6]

Phelps (1961), among others, further established the "Golden Rule of Accumulation," determining the maximum rate of c, given η, as being where the profit rate π (in competitive conditions, equal to the marginal product of capital) equals the population growth rate:

$$f'(k) = \pi = \eta. \tag{3.10}$$

A consequence of this model, as Samuelson (1975) points out, is that a *lower* rate of population growth is beneficial, because a higher level of consumption can be sustained as less capital must be set aside to maintain the capital stock (see equation 3.9). However, at first sight this contradicts the implication of the consumption loan model, where a *higher* rate of growth of population permits a greater level of consumption when retired.

The Samuelson consumption loan model and neoclassical growth theory can be synthesized by decomposing consumption in equation 3.9 into the consumption of successive generations. For simplicity, assume that only two generations are alive in any period: the old, indexed A, and the young, indexed B (Diamond 1965; Samuelson 1975a,b). Denote their per-capita consumptions as c_A and c_B. Then it can be shown (see the appendix to this chapter) that the new equilibrium is

$$\frac{c_A}{1 + \eta} + c_B = f(k) - \eta k. \tag{3.11}$$

The question now arises as to whether there is an equilibrium in the model. With no time preference, and assuming no technical progress (productivity change), the Samuelson consumption loan model specified that $i = \eta$ solved the problem of life-cycle consumption allocation, and it is straightforward to extend the result, as we have seen, to positive productivity growth (Aaron 1966) and also to positive time preference (Blanchard and Fischer 1989). Furthermore, from equation 3.10, the Golden Rule of Accumulation suggests that η should equal the profit rate. Thus, it is apparent that a potential equilibrium exists where $i = \eta = \pi$, where π is the profit rate.

This solution is intuitive, but is it feasible? Consider the two sides of equation 3.11. The left-hand side represents the optimal life-cycle allocation of consumption by individuals. The right-hand side represents the optimal allocation of production between "capital widening" (investment to maintain the capital-labor ratio given the population growth rate) and output of consumption goods. Saving must be just sufficient both to satisfy individual life-cycle plans and (in the absence of an exogenous investment function) to permit enough investment to maintain the capital stock. Rearranging equation 3.11 and substituting i for η (see Samuelson 1975b), we require that the interest rate i^* be such that

$$f(k) - i^*k - c_B = \frac{c_A}{1 + i^*} = k(1 + i^*). \tag{3.12}$$

Suppose, however, that population growth is rapid. This implies that life-cycle savings are required to be high enough to provide sufficient investment as to maintain the capital-labor ratio of the rapidly growing labor force. Given standard income and substitution effects of saving with respect to the interest rate, we cannot guarantee that there is an interest rate that will yield the requisite savings (Diamond 1965). Indeed, the Ponzi-scheme process underlying the consumption loan model implies that in such circumstances, with ever-larger generations, there is strong resistance among the younger generations to making the sacrifice in current consumption required to sustain the capital stock of future generations. The result may be a declining capital stock and no long-run economically meaningful equilibrium.

Under competitive conditions, a declining capital stock per worker, and therefore a rising marginal product of capital, implies a rising rate of profit. In equilibrium, this in turn implies a rising rate of interest. If the substitution effect of the interest-rate increase outweighs the income effect, then savings and investment will rise and the decline in the capital stock may be halted or even reversed. But again, the net effect of an interest-rate change on saving may not be in the required direction, and the decline in capital per worker will be intensified. A similar unstable outcome may emerge in the reverse case, where population growth slows and there is oversaving, leading to a per-worker capital stock that is "too high." Thus, plausible mechanisms may not guarantee the emergence of a satisfactory solution to equation 3.12.

The existence of a social security system may provide an answer to the problem by allowing the possibility of underfunding (or, indeed, overfunding) of pensions (Samuelson 1975b). To illustrate this point, suppose as before that the government provides a pension per dependent, p. With a little more generality than equation 2.1, however, assume that this pension is financed by some combination of a tax on workers, levied at a rate τ per worker (which might, for example, be tw, as in equation 2.1), and the return, r, on a part of the capital stock held as a social security fund K_S. The steady-state budget identity of the social security program is

$$pD = \tau L + rK_S \qquad (3.13a)$$

in the notation of equation 2.1, or

$$pL_A = \tau L_B + rk_S L_B \qquad (3.13b)$$

in the notation of this chapter. Assuming, as before, that L grows at rate η, equation 3.13 can be written as

$$\frac{p}{1 + \eta} = \tau + rk_S - \eta k_S. \qquad (3.14)$$

The last term in equation 3.14 indicates that a proportion of the return on the fund must be set aside in order to maintain the fund per worker in the face of population growth. There are clearly a number of special cases of equation 3.14. Where no fund is held, the terms in k_S drop out and we revert to the model in chapter 2. When the return on the fund is equal to the rate of population growth, $r = \eta$, a constant proportion of the capital stock per capita is held in perpetuity by the social security fund, with current outgoings financed by taxes.

In the case of a fully funded scheme, where enough revenue is put aside to support the existing working generation in its own retirement, the analysis is considerably simplified. In the context of equations 3.13 and 3.14, the tax rate levied on the working generation must be such as to maintain a fund sufficient to yield a return sufficient to support their own retirement; that is,

$$pL_A = \tau L_A(1 + r) = k_S L_B(1 + r), \qquad (3.15)$$

or, substituting and rearranging,

$$\frac{p}{1 + r} = \tau = k_S(1 + g), \qquad (3.16)$$

as in Samuelson 1975b (p. 542), where g is the rate of growth of the social security fund. Comparison of equations 3.12 and 3.16 suggests that this scheme merely imitates private-sector equilibrium, with the return on the social security fund mirroring the optimal interest rate. All the social security system does in a fully funded system is use the tax rate to create a fund to finance pensions, leaving $k - k_s$ of private-sector capital per capita to finance other retirement consumption. If i^* in equation 3.12 equals r in equation 3.16, there is a pure transfer of savings from the private to the public sector, leaving everything else unchanged. Fully funded social security, therefore, cannot function as an additional policy instrument where the conditions underlying equation 3.12 in the private market are not satisfied.

This contrasts with the case where social security is not fully funded. Equations 3.13 and 3.14 can be added to equation 3.11 to examine private-sector equilibrium where a partially funded scheme exists:

$$c_B + \frac{c_A}{1 + \eta} - \frac{p}{1 + \eta} = f(k) - \eta k - \tau + (r - \eta)k_s. \tag{3.17}$$

This can be rearranged as

$$c_B + \frac{c_A}{1 + \eta} = f(k) - \eta(k - k_s) - \tau + rk_s + \frac{p}{1 + \eta}. \tag{3.18}$$

Equation 3.18 shows that private consumption in retirement is supplemented by the social security pension. The total product requires a deduction to maintain the private stock of capital, and to finance the pension and social security fund, less any return on the latter. In the case where $\eta = r$, the social security fund is self-sustaining and a result analogous to equation 3.12 can be obtained (ibid., p. 541):

$$\frac{c_A}{1 + \eta} = \tau + (1 + \eta)(k - k_s). \tag{3.19}$$

In essence, the introduction of social security into the picture allows one further degree of policy freedom into the consumption loan interest model with capital accumulation. Suppose that, with high population growth, not enough savings are being generated to support the stock of capital per worker needed to maintain the growing labor force. Then $\dot{k}_s$ must be positive, which requires a tax rate greater than that needed solely to fund the existing retired generation. Note, however, that this enhanced social security fund must be invested in capital. (Whether the investment is private or public presumably does not matter.) The United States has failed to follow this precept in its transition to a fully funded pension scheme.

Conversely, if the rate of population growth slows, and the overall capital stock is too high, then $\dot{k}_s$ must be negative, which might be achieved gradually by moving toward "pure" pay-as-you-go social security with no public social security fund at all. However, this would seem to contrast with the view of those advocating a shift to more fully funded social security as a means of dealing with the aging of the population. Indeed, a policy of depleting the social security fund as population growth slows would not be optimal where the growth in P, total expenditure on pensions, and τ over time may displace private capital accumulation and so reduce $k - k_s$, as mentioned previously.

Social Security in OLG Models: An Overview

The literature on overlapping generations provides a more general framework within which to analyze the transfer of resources between generations than the simple "static" model of dependency. This is not to say that OLG models describe all the facets of intertemporal economic processes. For example, the underlying model of capital accumulation is of most value in defining steady-state equilibria. Whether such equilibria are attainable when, for example, capital investment is driven by other autonomous factors is open to doubt (Sen 1970), and the analysis of disequilibria and stability properties can get extremely complex.[7]

It is apparent that social security plays a number of potentially important roles in these models as a source of attaining intertemporal equilibrium. Before moving on, it is useful to summarize the main insights stemming from the introduction of social security:

(i) In Samuelson's (1958) model, the existence of a social security system may provide the means by which a "social contract" can be established between generations, so that present workers will be prepared to finance the consumption of existing pensioners in the belief that the social security system will guarantee similar treatment of them by future workers. It may then be possible to attain the desirable equilibrium where the interest rate equals the population growth rate. However, the feasibility of this as a strategy is weakened when declining population growth reduces the likelihood that the social contract can be maintained in the future.

(ii) The existence of social security as a form of forced saving permits myopic individuals to save according to lifetime-consistent plans.

(iii) The Samuelson-Aaron paradox of social insurance shows that social security need not be fully funded; indeed, Samuelson (1975b) suggests that fully funded social security is merely a transfer of resources from private to public accumulation. The paradox shows that where there is positive population growth each generation will gain (in the sense of a higher present value of net benefits and therefore higher welfare) by adopting a pay-as-you-go scheme rather than a fully funded scheme, so long as the return on social security is at least equal to the sum of population growth and real productivity growth rates. The paradox also shows that a slowing of population growth may render the PAYG scheme less attractive, particularly if some kind of funded scheme would yield higher returns.

(iv) When capital accumulation is brought into the picture, the conditions for overall equilibrium between intertemporal consumption decisions and the allocation of resources between current consumption and maintaining the capital stock become more stringent. Plausible cases were described in which cumulative movements away from optimal equilibria arise. Public intervention, through policy toward government debt (Diamond 1965) or partially funded social security (Samuelson 1975b), adds another policy instrument to the government's armory. In particular, the government could build up a public social security fund (overfunding) where the capital stock was insufficient to sustain the level of population growth. Perhaps surprisingly, it is not always the case that declining population growth enhances the need for greater funding of public social security. But if rising pension costs and, therefore, rising personal tax rates have extremely strong adverse effects on private capital accumulation, a move toward funding may be desirable.

3.3   Contract Enforcement and Altruism

Whereas chapter 2 considered intergenerational transfers purely as altruistic behavior, the basic Samuelson model of this chapter raises the question of what intertemporal "terms of trade" can be established through an intergenerational social contract so that older people are supported by consumption transfers, when there is no possibility of storing goods across time periods. The model was extended to the case where durable goods existed, and where the rate of interest was required to maintain an adequate capital stock in the face of population growth or decline. A rationale for social security (not necessarily fully funded) might be to equate the rate of return on capital to the consumption loan rate of interest where this could not be achieved in the market.

The model with durable capital goods allows both planned interperiod transfers (life-cycle saving) and within-period intergenerational transfers (gifts, or pay-as-you-go social security). But there has been little consideration so far either of the optimal form of social security financing (whether fully funded or PAYG) or of the behavioral consequences of whatever contractual arrangements are in force. One consideration is whether the reintroduction of altruism into the analysis affects the viability of whatever contractual mix of savings and transfers has been agreed upon between generations. Specifically, it has been argued that altruism allows strategic behavior by generations that renders certain intergenerational social contracts inoperable.

As an illustration of the point, assume again that there are two periods, indexed 1 and 2. Within each period, two generations are alive. Generation B is working in 1 and retired in 2, whereas generation A is only observed retired in period 1 and generation C impinges as workers in period 2. Assume also that within-period altruism is one-way, from young to old (there are no bequests). Out of income Y in the working period, a generation is prepared to transfer a gift G to the previous generation, the remainder of their income being consumed or saved. Assume that savings and gifts are proportional to income, that the rate of return is r, and that the population (as a result of changes in the birth rate) grows at a rate η.

The altruism postulate suggests that a given generation value its own consumption and that of its parents. For generation B we have[8]

$$U^B = u(C_1^B, C_2^B, C_{-1}^A).\tag{3.20}$$

The effective lifetime budget constraint of generation B can be constructed from table 3.1, which describes the allocations available to that generation. Generation B can make gifts in period 1 and receive them in period 2. Period-2 consumption by generation B depends on savings and on the net acquisition of gifts. In contrast with the table, there

Table 3.1

Period	Income	Gifts	Saving	Consumption
1	Y_1	g_1^B (given)	$Y_1(1 - c_1 - g_1)$	C_1
2	0	$(1 + \eta)g_2^C$ (received)	0	$(1 + r)Y_1(1 - c_1 - g_1) + (1 + \eta)g_2$

are more productive and can therefore support a growing elderly population. This is an attractive result, but it is not necessarily intuitive.

Finally, is there practical evidence that generations are linked by altruism? If they are not, then switching strategies of the type examined here are just not feasible. Hansson and Stuart (1989) produce some pieces of evidence, but these provide little direct corroboration of the hypothesis. For example, the evidence that private charity existed before social security is certainly correct, but the manifest inadequacy of such arrangements in providing even a minimum subsistence income was one reason why private schemes of insurance against labor-market and health risks developed so early in Britain, well before the development of national public-transfer schemes (Creedy and Disney 1985). Kotlikoff and Morris (1989) also found little evidence of general intergenerational transfers.[9] (Remember, we are looking here not for bequests but for child-to-parent transfers.)

Altonji et al. (1992) also found little support for intergenerational altruism in consumption strategies. Following parent-child pairs in the US Panel Survey of Income Dynamics (PSID), they tested whether, in a fixed-effects model (to control for preference heterogeneity), the *individual* incomes of parents and children affected their own food consumption (the only expenditure category defined in the PSID). Altonji et al. inferred that in an extended-family income-sharing arrangement consumption would be independent of the income allocation between family members, whereas in a pure life-cycle (non-altruistic) consumption model only own income would be significant. Although their results are open to other interpretations,[10] there is strong evidence from their econometrics that the income division between members of the extended family affects the consumption of households within the family, and that "pure altruism" (extended-family income sharing) is limited.[11]

Taken at face value, such a result limits the feasibility of the reneging strategy, in which a single generation spends its income in the first period in order to encourage gifts in the second period. Nevertheless, in the presence of social security it is hard to establish in empirical work whether such a strategy ever would be effective in attracting altruistic behavior from a succeeding generation. Furthermore, there is evidence that where social security is income-tested (that is, transfers are given only to those below a certain income threshold) individuals will alter their lifetime consumption plans in order to benefit from transfers (see Hubbard et al. 1995 and chapter 8 below). In similar vein, a rise in income from work may induce a fall in consumption, since a savings strategy, rather than reliance on public transfers in the future, thereby becomes feasible. These forms of strategic behavior might be reproduced in a non-social-security altruistic environment, and they certainly cast doubts on proposals to move toward a means-tested framework for pension benefits. They are also consistent with the frequently observed dichotomy between the better-off elderly, living primarily on their own assets, and those relying wholly on state benefits.

Funded or PAYG Pensions with an Aging Population?

Aaron (1966) and Samuelson (1975a) raised the question of the funding of social security. It is important to ask whether the optimal method of finance is affected by population aging. Intuition suggests that a move away from PAYG funding is optimal, but the varied experiences of social security programs in the recent past suggest that this view is not always taken by governments.

Consider first the consequences of fully funding social security—that is, of establishing a pension fund that covers all future discounted liabilities, and in which the discharge of liabilities (pension payments) is matched in each period by an addition to the fund in line with additional pension accruals. If the government and the private sector face identical transformation possibilities, this simply means that a fraction of the nation's capital is held as institutional debt, and that there is no net effect on the economy. However, when compared with partial funding or PAYG social security, the capital stock per worker is higher and, subject to a neoclassical or "well-behaved" production function, the rate of profit is lower and the wage rate higher. So long as the optimal capital-labor ratio is feasible, and the current capital stock is below this level, a transition to full funding can be welfare improving in comparative statics (Feldstein 1974b). But it is apparent that early generations, who bear the brunt of the "transition cost" of higher payments into the fund, will lose from this transition (Burbidge 1983a).

In considering a PAYG scheme, the standard Aaron result, for a given rate of real-wage growth, suggests that a declining rate of population growth makes PAYG less attractive. In a PAYG scheme, capital per capita is lower (Feldstein 1974a), and the profit rate is correspondingly higher and the wage rate lower. The main beneficiaries from PAYG funding are those who are in at the inception, as such schemes typically treat early generations more favorably than would be consistent with actuarially fair social insurance. This comparison of PAYG and full or partial funding in the context of demographic changes therefore illustrates the potential for generational conflict.

The time path of debt in the transition, and in different types of equilibria, has been the subject of extensive discussion since Diamond's 1965 paper (see Burbidge 1983a,b). Where the real rate of return is less than the rate of population growth (as it is when there is high inflation), the real value of institutional debt may fall, allowing successive generations to benefit in real terms from debt-financed transfers.[12] This ignores altruism, and in particular a bequest motive, but even with bequests a lower capital stock is likely.[13] When the rate of return is greater than the rate of population growth, as it has certainly been since the early 1980s, the real value of institutional debt will rise, and financing it may become difficult. Allowing transfer payments such as pension payments to grow, unmatched by an accumulation of private or institutional assets is an "infeasible" strategy (Burbidge 1983a), as ultimately the net capital stock will be driven down to zero. Infeasible or not, some governments have apparently followed just such a strategy in recent years.

To put the comparison in its simplest terms: A fully funded strategy pays pensions from the return on capital, whereas a pay-as-you-go scheme pays pensions from a tax on labor. Population aging implies a potential for intergenerational conflict, and it seems intuitive that pension schemes that are explicit in imposing a dependency burden on the earnings of current workers fan the flames of this conflict. Full funding of pensions therefore seems the more attractive option in an aging society—a result that replicates the earlier discussion of life-cycle saving versus altruistic gifts. Unfortunately, the funding transition exacerbates the dependency burden; workers in the transition generations must bear both the cost of higher dependency and the cost of creating a fund from which to finance their own pensions in the future. How aging societies can make this transition to a social optimum is far from clear. The next two chapters therefore consider the recent experiences of some countries in providing for a growing number of elderly by public and by private means.

Appendix

Derivation of Equation 3.9
Given the national income identity

$$Y \equiv C + I \tag{A3.1}$$

and

$$I \equiv \dot{K} \tag{A3.2}$$

(i.e., that investment equals the change in the capital stock), define the production function

$$Y = F(K,L), \tag{A3.3}$$

or, in per-worker magnitudes,

$$y = f(k). \tag{A3.4}$$

The change in the ratio of capital to labor over time is

$$\frac{\dot{K/L}}{K/L} = \frac{\dot{k}}{k} = \frac{\dot{K}}{K} - \frac{\dot{L}}{L} = \frac{\dot{K}}{K} - \eta. \tag{A3.5}$$

Multiply both sides of equation A3.5 by $k = K/L$:

$$\dot{k} = \frac{\dot{K}}{L} - \eta k. \tag{A3.6}$$

But

$$\frac{\dot{K}}{L} = \frac{I}{L} = f(k) - c; \tag{A3.7}$$

therefore,

$$\dot{k} = f(k) - c - \eta k; \tag{A3.8}$$

therefore,

$$c = f(k) - \eta k - \dot{k}. \tag{A3.9}$$

However, in steady state, $\dot{k} = 0$. Therefore, in steady state, equation 3.6 holds.

Derivation of Equation 3.1
Generalize equation A3.1:

$$Y \equiv C_A + C_B + I, \tag{A3.10}$$

where C_A is the consumption of the old and C_B is the consumption of the young. There are L_A old people and L_B young. Therefore,

$$C_A = \frac{C_A}{L_A} \cdot L_A = c_A \cdot L_A \tag{A3.11a}$$

and

$$C_B = \frac{C_B}{L_B} \cdot L_B = c_B \cdot L_B. \tag{A3.11b}$$

But

$$\frac{L_B - L_A}{L_B} = \eta; \tag{A3.12}$$

therefore,

$$c = c_B = c_A(1 + \eta)^{-1}. \tag{A3.13}$$

The rest follows from the derivation of equation 3.9.

4 Social Security: Paying for Past Pension Promises

Every developed Westernized country operates some form of publicly provided social security program of pension provision. This chapter focuses on a number of case studies of social security provision, describing five countries in all. Typically, social security programs are operated as pay-as-you-go (PAYG) "social insurance" schemes, in which current contributors build up future pension entitlements but current contribution revenues pay for current pension commitments. A few countries initially attempted to advance fund at least a portion of their social security program, so that tax or contribution increases could be softened as the pension component reached maturity. But accumulated reserves were often run down well before maturity was reached; therefore, social security programs have had to respond to the aging of the population, and the growing dependency ratio, by raising contribution rates (see World Bank 1994, figure 4.2).

Some countries, notably the United States, have responded to a greater dependency ratio by reverting to partially funded social security. If this shift in the method of finance is to be more than merely a notional shift in the form of government debt, it will generate a significant intergenerational redistribution. However, in a country running a substantial budget deficit (stemming in part from other consequences of aging, such as rising disability and health-care payments), the temptation to utilize surpluses in a funded social security program for other purposes is considerable. In chapter 3 it was suggested that a shift to full or partial funding in the face of population aging might be utilized to maintain or deepen the capital stock in the face of a decline in or slower growth of the working population; however, governments have rarely had the long-term view or the political ability to resist shorter-term objectives, and may use social security surpluses as an alternative to tax rises.

In the United States, much as in Italy, political difficulties and the inability of Congress to pass budgetary measures have contributed to the financial problems of the social security program in recent years. In the United Kingdom, in contrast, measures designed to offset potential short-run funding crises can generally be passed through Parliament with a minimum of fuss. Nevertheless, detailed long-run forecasts have created a good deal of political alarm there, inducing oscillations in the public's fervor for legislation and a series of "reforms" of pension provision in the last two decades. This has resulted in a significant decline in the projected value of social insurance benefits relative to earnings, a rapid growth in private pension provision, and, as in the United States, a significant redistribution away from younger generations within the social security program.[1] Although much of the controversy surrounding reform of the program in the United Kingdom has focused on its redistributive aspect, the redistributive potential of the scheme has rarely been correctly measured. The complexity of the indexation procedures has been a particular source of confusion among politicians and among analysts.

The Italian experience is a particularly revealing example of how premature rundown of the funding basis before maturity can generate a significant crisis in social security provision before the impact of aging is really felt. Nevertheless, in a country with Western Europe's lowest birth rate and with a social security program in crisis, Italian administrations have broken with tradition and introduced major reforms in recent years. Other countries bordering the Mediterranean, such as Greece and Turkey, have contrived to generate major crises of social security finance even before aging sets in. Instead of a "social contract" that can be adjusted to the sizes of generations, these countries illustrate that unsustainable Ponzi-scheme outcomes can be generated, especially before maturity. As in Italy, the crises so generated may have social and political consequences well beyond the social security program.

Australia offers a different model, one more akin to the model of within-period redistribution described in chapter 2. Here, social security program expenditures have always been tightly controlled by income and capital tests on program participants. Income testing, which has divided the political parties in the United Kingdom, has gained greater support in Australia and is an alternative to the benefit cutbacks and the privatization programs followed in other countries. Yet income testing is not without its costs; in particular, the Australian market for private-sector saving is highly distorted by the structure of income testing (and by subsidies to other assets, notably housing). Thus, the Australian government has periodically exhibited doubt as to the form of its social security program, and the model may not prove as durable as it might appear.

The case study of Japan offers an economic success story against a background of relatively favorable demographic and social trends. As these trends reverse, the viability of the social security program, and with it some aspects of the Japanese "economic miracle," may be called into question. However, it would be a brave man who would bet against the ability of the Japanese economy to transcend these difficulties.

4.1 The United States: Redistribution between Generations

The scope of the United States' program of old-age social insurance has gradually broadened since its inception in the Social Security Act of 1935. Over 90 percent of civilian workers now belong to the OASDI (Old-Age, Survivors, and Disability Insurance) scheme. The main exclusions are many public-sector workers, although since January 1984 new federal employees belong to OASDI (Aaron et al. 1989), as do new state and local government employees since July 1991. As in other countries with coexisting programs, it has been argued that there are inequities stemming from incomplete coverage: although workers uncovered by OASDI generally belong to other retirement programs, their treatment in such programs is not always identical to that in OASDI. Furthermore, workers can spend periods in uncovered jobs as well as periods in covered work and still receive a better OASDI benefit to contribution ratio than those remaining covered throughout life. The annual cost of these contribution gaps and benefit "windfalls" was put at US$2 billion in 1981 (Schieber 1984), but the real cost will presumably decline as coverage gradually extends to all government employees.

OASDI benefits are financed by a payroll tax notionally levied on covered workers and their employers. Tax rates rose by more than 600 percent from 1945 to 1990, reflecting the PAYG aspect of the scheme: in the early years there were few beneficiaries, but as increasing numbers of covered individuals retired the number of beneficiaries rose (almost tenfold between 1945 and 1985). Table 4.1 illustrates some of the salient features of the growth of the OASDI scheme. Figure 4.1

Table 4.1
Growth of the OASDI scheme in the United States. Source: Compiled from tables 2-2–2-4 of Aaron et al. 1989.

	Thousands of benefit recipients	Total expenditure[a]	Total income[a]	of which interest and tax receipts	Trust fund reserve[a]	Average replacement ratio
1950	2,326	961	2,928	257	13,721	30.0
1960	10,599	11,245	12,445	569	22,613	33.3
1970	17,096	31,884	36,993	1,791	38,068	34.3
1980	23,336	120,598	119,712	2,330	26,453	51.1
1990	26,970[b]	246,374	309,527	20,926	211,932	42.3

a. Millions of US dollars.
b. For 1987.

reports past payroll-tax rates and the rates that would give PAYG balance with the income and expenditure totals in table 4.1. After the rapid growth in the number of beneficiaries in the first two decades as increasing numbers of workers became eligible for benefits, the rate of increase declined. The numbers of beneficiaries has since been driven largely by underlying trends in participation and demography and by the extension of coverage in the 1980s.

The columns in table 4.1 describing the growth of income and expenditures (which are in nominal terms) show how the sources of income have changed, as reflected in the size of the OASDI trust fund. In the 1950s and the 1960s, the relatively small number of beneficiaries meant that receipts exceeded expenditure, and a small fund was accumulated. However, outgoings rose sharply in the 1970s, because replacement rates rose (see the last column of table 4.1), as did the rate of inflation and the number of recipients of disability benefits (Levy 1984). The real value of the trust fund was eroded at the end of the 1960s and at the end of the 1970s. This precipitated a series of funding crises.

Congress was forced to address the rapid depletion of the trust fund in the 1970s, and in 1977 it responded by raising payroll-tax rates and by changing the benefit formula. Levy (1984, p. 9) quotes the acting commissioner of social security as saying "the Congress and the president have assured the financial soundness of the social security program for the next 50 years." In the next few years, however, it became apparent that the these measures were not sufficient to guarantee the short-term viability of the OASDI trust fund, in view of the slowing

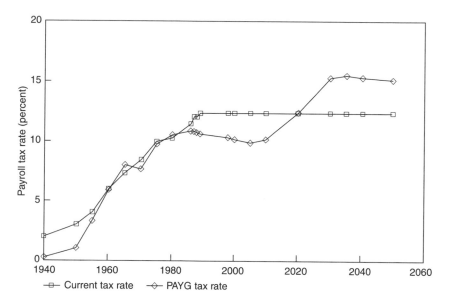

Figure 4.1
Past and future OASDI payroll-tax rates, United States. Source: Aaron et al. 1989, tables 2.1 and 2.2 and figure 3-3; combined employee and employer rates.

growth of real wages and the high unemployment at that time. In addition, little attention had been paid to long-term trends in dependency and to the future net expenditures of the trust fund.

Another major rethink in the early 1980s (an era of "fiscal conservatism") culminated in a more radical retrenchment of OASDI benefits. The Social Security Amendment of 1983 increased the retirement age on full benefits from 65 to 66 in 2009 and 67 in 2027 and, from 1984, ensured that up to half of OASDI benefits were to be treated as taxable income (Heller et al. 1986; Aaron et al. 1989). Changes have also been introduced in the "retirement credit" (the proportionate increase in social security benefits obtained from deferring retirement beyond the earliest possible age of 62) and in the method of averaging (revaluing) lifetime earnings. With the combined payroll tax rate also exceeding the "current" PAYG tax rate, the fund is projected to accrue a substantial surplus, as table 4.1 and figure 4.1 show.

From PAYG to Partial Funding

With the 1977 and 1983 Social Security Amendments, the financial future of the OASDI scheme might seem secure. Using 1988 projections (based primarily on Social Security Administration 1987), Aaron et al.

(1989) calculate that OASDI trust funds will grow until the year 2031, outstripping government budget deficits on other accounts and indeed outstripping the total government debt for some periods. Figure 4.1 shows that the current OASDI tax rate exceeds the forecast PAYG tax rate in all periods until 2020. In notional terms, the US pension scheme has moved from a "pure" PAYG scheme toward a partially funded scheme.

The discussion in section 3.2, where capital accumulation was introduced into the overlapping-generations model, suggested that overfunding of public social security, or at least a shift away from "pure" PAYG funding, could be a means of reconciling the conflicting intertemporal plans of consumers and the need for an increased rate of capital accumulation. This might seem especially desirable where population growth was rapid, and where current workers relied on the Ponzi-scheme aspect of the larger sizes of future generations to provide high pensions in their retirement. In such circumstances, saving might not be sufficient to generate the requisite capital accumulation.

Table 2.4 suggested that the growth in the number of retirement pensioners in the United States was above the average for the cited countries, with a doubling of numbers between 1980 and 2025. However, the total pension bill is not projected to increase particularly rapidly, as the US scheme appears to be closer to maturity and has cut back insurance benefits. The rationale for moving to partial funding was that the social security fund would be used to enhance capital accumulation. Nevertheless, Aaron et al. point out that the main function of the accumulated OASDI trust fund so far has been to offset public *consumption:* it is used to finance part of the federal budget deficit, since by law the trust fund must hold its funds in US Treasury bonds. Thus, the fund is financing an intragenerational reallocation of consumption and is not contributing directly to the intergenerational redistribution problem posed at the beginning of this chapter. It is therefore often argued that the OASDI fund surplus should be separated out from the underlying budget in order to make this transparent. However, the legal restriction on the fund's autonomy (particularly its investment strategy) seems to be the pertinent issue. Furthermore, Kotlikoff (1992) has trenchantly argued that this whole debate is largely misleading; the relevant calculation (and the basis of any intergenerational comparison) is to measure correctly the net tax burden on each current and prospective generation of the government's activities. Only by this "generational accounting" can the fiscal burden to each generation be made explicit.

The US pension scheme therefore appears to illustrate the application of a policy measure (partial funding) in order to resolve the dilemma of establishing an intergenerational social contract in the face of growing dependency. Further investigation of the reforms and of the uses of the funds generated by them suggests that the view of section 3.1 must be qualified. Policy measures in the United States have been driven by short-run considerations for a long period, and funds have been utilized for reallocations that are not consistent with the underlying economic theory. Whether more rational outcomes are politically feasible would seem to rest on an examination of the political-economic, or public-choice, aspects of aging.

Benefits and Public and Private Replacement Ratios

The adequacy of benefits and the various measures of the replacement ratio were discussed at some length in chapter 2. The discussion there distinguished between income replacement provided by social security and the full within-period intergenerational transfer (which takes account of all sources of income to the elderly). The preceding subsection also suggested that *rates of return* to successive generations would illustrate the extent of intergenerational redistribution embodied in the program.

Table 4.1 depicted the average replacement ratio, which rose sharply in the 1970s and which is projected to fall back to little above the 1970 ratio by the middle of the next century. However, individual replacement ratios vary, because social security entitlements, although earnings-related, are not wholly proportional to earnings. The basic social security calculation determines benefits as a multiple of the best 35 years' earnings, with all earnings revalued at retirement by an economy-wide earnings index so as to normalize for real productivity growth. The "weighted benefit formula" determines the entitlement by a progressive formula whereby the accrual rate attached to higher "slices" of average earnings tapers off substantially.[2]

As in the United Kingdom, the revaluation of earnings at retirement attaches a greater weight to economy-wide real earnings growth in the years just before retirement than it does to notional earnings (and, therefore, insurance contributions) in earlier years. This implies an arbitrary degree of *ex post* redistribution according to earnings profiles and differential real-wage growth across decades. Furthermore, care is needed in indexing earnings, bend points, and accrual rates consistently; mistakes in so doing led to the overindexation of benefits in the 1970s, which played a part in the first major funding crisis in the 1970s

(Diamond 1977; Levy 1984; Rosen 1984), although consistent index-ation was implemented in the 1977 Social Security Amendment.

Other salient features of the benefit structure under the OASDI scheme include: the revaluation of benefits after retirement in line with prices rather than earnings, a retirement test by which benefits are reduced for the first five years after retirement for earned income above a certain level, the treatment of OASDI benefits in part as taxable income from 1984 on, and the payment of dependents' and survivors' benefits. These fairly standard procedures, like the progressivity of the benefit formula and the revaluation of earnings to retirement, guaran-tee that the "returns" paid to different members of the same "genera-tion," and indeed to generations retiring at different times, are not identical.

A number of studies have calculated and compared intergenera-tional and intragenerational rates of return, both in the United States and elsewhere. The typical methodology, evaluated by Aaron (1985), requires certain caveats. In particular, when mortality is unknown *ex ante* and when the possibility of additional social security (such as sur-vivor benefits) and medical benefits generate further divergences in returns *ex post*, individual returns may diverge widely from the simu-lated returns. Indeed, given that pensions generally are insurance against longevity risk, *ex post* individual returns would be expected to diverge from the calculated return. However, the argument for such studies is that they provide evidence of *systematic* divergences in re-turns, associated with, say, cohort size and timing, social class, gender (where there is differential mortality), and the pension benefit formula. As such, they provide useful information on the operation and the implications of the program.[3]

A representative study in the US context is that of Hurd and Shoven (1985). In their simulations of "average" profiles for various age co-horts and household types, they utilize "backward-looking" data on median annual earnings, assume projected growth rates of earnings from 1978 on, and thereby calculate the internal rate of return on public social security benefits less contributions for different households. Some of their results are illustrated in table 4.2. The differences in re-turns between household types indicate the degree of progressivity built into the benefit formula: women earn less than men and thereby obtain a higher return. Similarly, the presence of pension allowances for dependents imply that married couples obtain a greater return than single people.

Table 4.2
Rates of return to US Social Security. Source: Hurd and Shoven 1985, table 7.11.

Household type	Earnings profile	Year in which household head is 65			
		1970	1980	1990	2020
Single man	Median	6.3	4.5	2.4	2.1
Single woman	Median	9.1	6.6	4.6	3.3
Married couple	Median/zero[a]	8.5	6.7	4.5	3.2
Married couple	Median/low[b]	7.7	6.0	3.9	2.6

a. Man earns median of single man; woman has no earnings.
b. Woman earns half median earnings of single woman.

The decline in returns over time illustrates that successive cohorts are obtaining lower returns on their social security contributions (see also Boskin et al. 1987). The reasons for the decline are the abnormal gains to the first cohort (retiring in 1970) stemming from their shortened period of tax payments, as the scheme was only introduced in 1935. Members of the startup cohort within a pension scheme usually gain in this manner because they are not contributors throughout their whole working life. The 1980 cohort and (to a lesser extent) the 1990 cohort benefit from the low contribution rates in the 1950s and the 1960s (see table 4.1). Of the cohorts in table 4.2, only the 2020 cohort fails to benefit from these aspects of the scheme, and its rate of return is very much lower than those of the earlier cohorts. The lower rate of return for this last cohort also illustrates the consequences of the shift from "pure" pay-as-you-go to partial funding of the pension scheme. Special factors such as these override the Samuelsonian "social contract" and the Ponzi-scheme aspect of pension finance in the face of generations of increasing size.

Another issue raised in chapter 2 was the appropriate measure of dependency. Evidence in the United States of replacement ratios, taking into account both public and private means of support in retirement, as well as measures of both net and gross earnings, was provided by Boskin and Shoven (1987). Using the Retirement History Survey for the years 1971–1979, they computed a variety of replacement ratios, of which several are illustrated for the 1979 sample in table 4.3. Official calculations typically define replacement ratios (RRs) by relating social security benefits to highest earnings in recent years, and table 4.3 shows that calculated RRs on this basis are rather low at 44 percent for low earners and 19 percent for high earners. The lower

Table 4.3
Various replacement ratios for married couples from 1979 Retirement History Survey.
Source: Boskin and Shoven 1987, tables 5.3, 5.5, 5.9, and 5.12.

	Career average earnings	Best 3 years' earnings	Career average adjusted for taxes and child costs[c]
Low earners[a] (%)			
Social Security	65.4	44.4	90.4
SS and pension	78.5	52.8	107.9
Total income	116.3	76.3	157.2
High earners[b] (%)			
Social security	25.6	19.4	41.3
SS and pension	48.2	35.8	74.1
Total income	69.9	54.4	106.0

a. Career earnings: US$7500–12,500
b. Career earnings: US$30,000–50,000
c. Child costs reduce denominator of replacement ratio by 20%.

rate for high earners, of course, reflects the progressivity built into the benefit structure.

Various adjustments to the RR formula are suggested by Boskin and Shoven. For example, comparing social security benefits with average career earnings from 1951 to 1974 raises the calculated RRs significantly. Adjusting the RRs to take account of *net* career earnings by deductions for taxes and child care costs raises the RR for low earners to 90 percent when only social security benefits are taken into account. Introducing average private pension benefits raises the RRs of low earners by around 25 percent, and including other income (returns on investments, housing, and so on) raises them significantly more. Unsurprisingly, incorporating private sources of income in addition to social security raises the RRs of high earners disproportionately. Consequently, the RR (defined as total income in retirement divided by career earnings net of taxes and child-care costs) exceeds 100 percent even for high earners.

It is apparent that further refinements could be introduced into the analysis—for example, replacement ratios that take account of payment of indirect and other taxes. Nevertheless, it is apparent from table 4.3 that, even when measured official replacement ratios are rather low, effective RRs (which take account of other sources of income) indicate that elderly people in the United States can be significantly better off in retirement than they were when working (see also Hurd 1990). This, is of course, especially true when they were low earners while working. For better-off earners, table 4.3 illustrates the other salient fact: that access to other private income, such as private pension benefits, makes a major contribution to retirement consumption. And even if we allow for the retrenchment of the social insurance program in recent years (stemming in part from the perceived "burden" of an aging population), poverty in old age tends to stem from poverty in the working life, not from the structure of the old-age income maintenance program.

4.2   The United Kingdom: The Rise and Fall of Social Insurance

State pension provision has a long history in the United Kingdom, a means-tested pension having been introduced in 1908. A PAYG social insurance scheme with flat-rate (lump-sum) contributions and benefits was introduced in 1911. Social security coverage was gradually extended in the interwar years, with almost-universal coverage attained as a result of the 1946 National Insurance Act. However, it should not be inferred from this longevity that the UK social security program has now attained maturity. In the post-1945 years, against a background of the development of a private (occupational) pension sector, there was constant political pressure to extend earnings-related pensions to all workers, either through some form of compulsory private supplementary scheme or (for those without private pensions) through an additional state earnings-related social security pension. Furthermore, the perceived regressivity of the flat-rate National Insurance contribution placed a limit on the contribution rate, which soon proved inadequate to deal with the steady growth in the number of pensioners and level of real benefits in the 1950s and the 1960s.

After several legislative false starts, the route of an additional "state earnings-related pension scheme" was chosen, and such a scheme, known by the acronym SERPS, came into operation in 1978 under the auspices of the Social Security Pensions Act of 1975. This new two-tier scheme, like the wholly flat-rate scheme that preceded it, was financed by a payroll tax, the National Insurance contribution, and operated on a PAYG basis.[4] Contributions to the scheme were explicitly related to earnings within a certain range. Companies and institutions that operated an approved (defined benefit) private pension scheme could opt to "contract out" of SERPS, and in compensation they and their employees would pay a lower contracted-out rate of the National Insurance (NI) contribution.

The SERPS benefit formula introduced in the 1975 act was ingenious but expensive. For those who remained contracted in, earnings up to the upper earnings limit were revalued by an earnings index to retirement, and benefits were based on 25 percent of average earnings derived from the "20 best years" of the revalued earnings minus the lower earnings limit at the state pensionable age (which was 65 for men and 60 for women). Conveniently, the lower earnings limit was set at the level of the basic flat-rate social security pension, which was payable to contracted-in and contracted-out individuals alike. Thus, there was a degree of progressivity built into the benefit formula, via the two-tier formula of a flat-rate pension plus an earnings-related component (Creedy 1982; Creedy and Disney 1985). In addition, there were generous provisions for widows (and, subsequently, widowers), who could take over the whole of the deceased spouse's pension, and the state agreed to inflation-proof future contracted-out private pensions in payment.

The official actuarial forecasts as to the future costs of SERPS in 1975 appear to have been rather rushed, and it was not until the costs were projected into the second quarter of the next century that concern arose about the financial commitments implied by the introduction of SERPS. The 1975 forecasts had suggested that a rise in contribution rates of 3–4 percent of qualifying earnings would be sufficient to fund SERPS for the next 30 years. As table 4.4 shows, this was not an unfavorable period demographically. However, an influential analysis by Hemming and Kay (1982) suggested a rise of 4 or 5 times that amount in the contribution rate would be needed to fund SERPS in "steady state" from 2025 on. A subsequent analysis by the government (DHSS 1984, republished in HMSO 1985a, Cmnd 9519, Paper 2) confirmed this general conclusion. Consequently, in 1985 the government proposed yet another change to pension provision (HMSO 1985a), this time reverting to the other model of supplementary pension provision: a form of compulsory private insurance. This too failed to gain support, and the final legislation as implemented retained a residual SERPS scheme while giving individuals a greater incentive to contract out into existing occupational pension schemes and into "money purchase schemes" such as group and individual savings accounts (HMSO 1985b).

Table 4.4
Future trends in UK support ratio, social security expenditure and contribution rates (£billion at 1994–95 prices). Source: HMSO 1994, tables 1 and 3 and appendix D.

	1994–95	2000–01	2010–11	2030–31	2050–51
Pre-1995 scheme					
Basic pension	26.9	29.8	33.7	46.9	46.6
SERPS	1.8	4.2	9.2	18.7	19.3
Incapacity benefits	6.3	5.7	6.3	6.3	6.0
Other benefits[a]	2.5	2.6	2.4	2.4	2.4
Total	39.9	42.2	51.7	74.2	74.2
Contribution rate[b]	18.3%	17.6%	17.6%	20.0%	16.8%
No. of pensioners[c]	10.6	11.0	12.5	16.9	16.8
No. of contributors[c]	22.0	22.7	24.0	23.1	22.2
Support ratio	2.06	2.06	1.92	1.37	1.32
Post-1995 scheme					
Basic pension	26.9	29.8	33.6	41.9	42.3
SERPS	1.8	4.2	8.4	12.0	9.9
Incapacity benefits	6.3	5.7	6.3	6.9	6.5
Other benefits[a]	2.5	2.6	2.4	3.0	2.9
Total	39.9	42.2	50.8	63.8	61.7
Contribution rate[b]	18.3%	17.9%[d]	17.5%	17.4%	14.1%
No. of pensioners[c]	10.6	11.0	12.4	14.7	14.9
No. of contributors[c]	22.0	22.7	24.0	23.9	22.9
Support ratio	2.06	2.06	1.94	1.63	1.54

a. Including widow's benefits and other benefits.
b. Joint contribution for contracted-in employees.
c. In millions.
d. Assumed contracted-out rebate for 1997–98 to 2001–02 is 4.95%.

Pension Provision after the 1986 and 1995 Reforms

The reformed SERPS scheme, introduced in the Social Security Act of 1986, downgraded SERPS benefits significantly. Entitlement was to be based on the formula of a maximum of 20 percent of average lifetime revalued earnings, rather than 25 percent of "20 best years" as before. The provision for widows and widowers to take over their partner's SERPS entitlement was halved in value. Private pension schemes were required to inflation-proof pensions in payment up to 3 percent inflation (Creedy and Disney 1988). In addition, members of the National Insurance scheme not only had the right to "contract out" of the SERPS tier into a standard defined benefit company scheme; alternatively, they could "contract out" into a group or individual savings account (defined contribution plan). Individual accounts, known as Personal Pensions, have proved extremely popular. However, individuals retain the right to re-contract in to SERPS later, and with a uniform contracted-out rebate it would almost always have been optimal to do so.

The Pensions Act of 1995 made yet more substantive and technical changes. Some of the important issues addressed by that act concerned private pensions—in particular, the introduction of a new regulatory structure in the wake of the Maxwell fraud and the introduction of age-related contracted-out rebates for defined contribution pension plans such as Personal Pensions. Of more immediate relevance to the social security pension was the decision to equalize the pensionable age for men and women at 65 (previously women could obtain the state pension at age 60) in stages between the years 2010 and 2020, saving £5.6 billion per annum in steady state. A further, largely unreported technical change to the indexation procedures produces an even larger saving of up to £7 billion, a substantial part of the budget. This change can be explained briefly by means of a simplified algebraic description of the post-1986, pre-1995 formula for calculating SERPS benefits:

$$P_{\text{SERPS}} = \sum_{t}^{R} \left(W_t \frac{E_R}{E_t} - \text{LEL}_{R-1} \right) x_{Rt}. \tag{4.1}$$

The SERPS pension is calculated by summing eligible individual earnings W to retirement R, revalued by an index of average earnings, E. The value of the lower earnings limit LEL (basic flat-rate pension) *in the year prior to attaining pensionable age* is then deducted before the accrual factor specific to the year of retirement is applied.

The new method of calculating SERPS will be introduced for new awards commencing in the financial year 2000–01; that is, the revised formula will apply to the whole period of accrual for these awards rather than only the post-1995 period. The new formula introduces a simple change: the contemporaneous LEL will be applied before revaluation of earnings for each year, instead of applying the LEL in the year before retirement after revaluation. This changed formula is as follows:

$$P_{\text{SERPS}} = \sum_{t}^{R} \left(W_t - \text{LEL}_t \frac{E_R}{E_t} \right) x_{Rt}. \tag{4.2}$$

The financial saving arises because the LEL (the basic pension) is indexed to prices, whereas eligible earnings are revalued in line with average earnings growth. Since real earnings growth has averaged around 2 percent per annum, the changed formula involves subtracting a larger real value from the SERPS calculation when the LEL is deducted. Given compounding and the retrospective application of the procedure, the savings are substantial; however, because of the technicalities of the differential indexation procedures, the consequences have been little understood.[5] Fundamental changes to the generosity of social security provision have been made over the last 15 years with little public hostility, not least as a result of this procedural complexity.

Trends in Pension Costs and Dependency
The most recent estimates of the future costs of pension provision, from the Government Actuary's Department (HMSO 1994, 1995), are given in table 4.4. Since the scheme is fully PAYG, and is projected to remain so, the fund's balance will remain roughly constant as a proportion of real benefit expenditure (at roughly two months' expenditure). It can be seen from table 4.4 that the number of contributors keeps pace in the 1990s with the number of pensioners. Thereafter, the sharper increase in the number of pensioners as the baby-boom generation retires, and a decline in the number of economically active persons cause a steady rise in the economic-dependency ratio and a decline in the number of workers per pensioner from a peak of 2.1 in the year 2000–01 to 1.5 in 2050–51. The effect of equalizing the state pensionable age is to raise this support ratio by 0.2 from the previously projected 1.3, and thereby to reduce the growth of expenditure on the basic state pension after 2020–21.

Expenditure on flat-rate pensions is affected by these demographic factors, by the equalization of the pensionable age (which can be seen from the pre-1995-vs.-post-1995 comparison) and by the slow improvement in longevity. Real earnings growth is positive; this is a significant factor in keeping costs down, given the post-retirement indexation of benefits to inflation. Indeed, once the baby-boom generation has passed through the system the contribution rate drops sharply—compare the figures for 2030–31 and 2050–51. The new projected joint contribution rate of just over 14 percent at the end of the period (on only a segment of earnings) contrasts sharply with the more alarmist scenarios for other OECD countries.

Some commentators have indeed suggested that the United Kingdom could afford to index the basic flat-rate social security pension to earnings rather than to prices. But with real earnings growth projected by the Government Actuary at 1.5 percent per annum, this would more than double expenditure on the basic state pension by 2050–51, raising the required contribution rate by 11 percentage points (HMSO 1995). And without further adjustments such a strategy would have some perverse redistributional effects. Expenditure on "other benefits" remains roughly constant in real terms, and the most noticeable change on the benefit side is the rapid rise in expenditure on SERPS, although this rise is considerably dampened after 2010–11 as a result of the 1995 legislation.

There is an important addendum to this analysis. In addition to social insurance benefits, pensioners may also be entitled to various forms of means-tested (income-tested) benefits, notably assistance with housing costs and direct cash payments (currently known as Income Support). These benefits, financed out of general tax revenues, act as "passport benefits" to other entitlements such as domiciliary care, although many such benefits (e.g., exemption from medical charges) are contingency rather than income-linked. The basic pension has declined as a fraction of earnings in recent years. The different basis of calculation of income-tested benefits has meant that a growing number of relatively poor pensioners have become eligible for such benefits in addition to National Insurance benefits. Consequently, the share of income-tested benefits in total expenditure on pensioners has increased from 10 percent to over 20 percent in the past 15 years.

There are conflicting trends at work. The growing affluence of pensioners on average and, ultimately, the maturation of SERPS should "float" pensioners off income-tested benefits, but the relative decline in the value of social insurance benefits has had an offsetting effect. Roughly £11 billion is current spent on additional income-tested benefits for pensioners, in addition to the £29 billion spent on social insurance, and those benefits are received by over a third of pensioners (Dilnot et al. 1994). Consequently, reform proposals for the "basic" pension tier of the social security system are increasingly focusing not on raising the basic pension but on integrating the income-tested and social insurance sectors, perhaps to construct some form of minimum pension "guarantee." Whether this ultimately looks like a guaranteed income "floor" for all pensioners or like some form of negative income

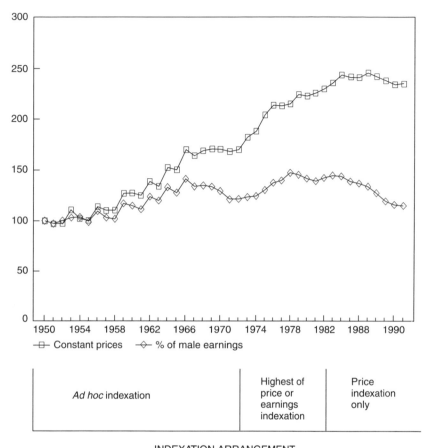

Figure 4.2
Value of basic pension: married couple, United Kingdom (1950 = 100).

tax or income credit, it is likely that a greater degree of income testing, whether implicitly or explicitly, will underlie provision of the basic social security pension.

Replacement Ratios and Rates of Return

Because the social security benefits of retiring pensioners have been largely flat-rate (lump-sum), it is to be expected that replacement ratios are negatively related to lifetime earnings levels, and that changes in the average replacement ratio over time would vary in accordance with indexation procedures when real earnings are growing. This is confirmed by figure 4.2, which illustrates how the basic pension has varied in the postwar period relative to prices and to average male earnings in the United Kingdom. Between 1950 and 1973, benefits were raised in an *ad hoc* manner. It is apparent that until the mid 1960s this resulted in a real increase in benefit levels, whether deflated by earnings or by prices.

The decline in real benefits in the late 1970s as inflation peaked led to a reappraisal. When SERPS was introduced, a relatively generous provision (particularly in view of the state of the economy after the oil shocks) of overindexation was implemented, by which the basic state pension and the earnings limits were indexed to the higher of price inflation and earnings growth. As a result, real benefits went up sharply in the late 1970s. After 1980 there was yet another change in the method of indexation, to price inflation only. The 1980s proved to be a period of particularly rapid earnings growth, despite high unemployment, and it is interesting to note how rapidly the real value of the basic pension declined relative to average earnings in that period.[6] In 1979 a married couple's flat-rate pension was 31.5 percent of average male earnings. By 1991 the replacement ratio had fallen to 24.7 percent, having gone down 5 percentage points since 1984. The RR was fast approaching its 1950 starting point of 21.9 percent, although the real value of the pension in terms of prices had more than doubled in the same 40-year period. It should be borne in mind, of course, that replacement ratios for low earners are considerably higher not least because, in the absence of income from other assets such as private pension benefits, their incomes will be supplemented by the income-tested benefits described previously.

Recent official forecasts provide an estimate of the impact of SERPS on future replacement ratios. With continued price indexation, and with real earnings growth of 1.5 percent per annum, the Government Actuary forecasts a value of the basic pension for married couples relative to earnings of 22 percent in the year 2000, 14 percent in 2030, and just around 11 percent in 2050. However, these will be supplemented by SERPS entitlements worth, pre-1995, around an additional 12 percent in 1990, 21 percent in 2000, 16 percent in 2030, and 13 percent in 2050. The 1995 changes in indexation procedures will reduce these SERPS entitlements by, on average, about 2 percentage points after the year 2000. Thus total replacement ratios for individuals wholly dependent on social security pensions will peak at an average of 43 percent in the year 2000 and will then decline to 24 percent in 2040. Single people will have lower replacement ratios, reaching a peak of 35 percent in the year 2000 for men and 40 percent for women before declining proportionately.

With these trends, it is not surprising that, as in the United States, rates of return to successive cohorts from the social security pension scheme are steadily declining in the United Kingdom. Some calculations of rates of return for samples of successive cohorts of men under the pre-1995 rules have been undertaken (Disney and Whitehouse 1993c). It is assumed that there is no contracting out, that widows' and dependents' benefits are ignored, that the retirement age is 65, and that the projections by the Government Actuary give accurate estimates of the future contribution rates in the PAYG scheme. Uniform projections of real productivity growth and occupation-specific mortality rates are applied to occupation-specific and industry-specific age-earnings equations. Real internal rates of return to individual members of each cohort are then calculated, differentiated by their earnings within cohorts.

One crucial factor driving the relative returns is the decline in SERPS accrual rates for successive retiring cohorts. Under accelerated accrual procedures, the first cohort to participate in the scheme (men aged 45 in 1978) could retire on full benefits after 20 years (i.e., in 1998) with 25 percent of their average earnings. The next "cohort" to retire therefore would not benefit from the extra year of contributions, but it could drop the worst year from the "20 best years" calculation. Successive cohorts face reduced accruals from the diminution of the impact of accelerated accrual, from lifetime averaging rather than "20 best years" for accruals after 1986, and from the reduction in the underlying replacement ratio from 25 percent to 20 percent of the appropriate earnings after 1986. Thus, the accrual fraction for a person retiring in 1995–96 is 25/20 (i.e., 1.25) percent; that for a person retiring after 2027 is 20/49 (i.e. 0.41) percent. Add to this the 1995 change in the procedure for deducting the lower earnings limit, and the price indexation of the basic pension, and the declines in returns observed in table 4.4 are not surprising.

Table 4.5 suggests that, with differential mortality and price indexation, real rates of return are generally negative for younger cohorts (born in 1955 and 1960 and retiring in 2020 and 2025), and barely positive for older cohorts. For uniform mortality the returns are scarcely more impressive, and they exhibit the same decline with youthfulness of cohort. With indexation of the basic pension to earnings, real returns are improved but even so decline over time. There is some evidence of

Table 4.5
Intergenerational rates of return to UK social security program. Source: Disney and
Whitehouse 1993b.

Cohort[a] and assumptions	Rate of return (%)					Average lifetime earnings[d]	
	Mean	s.d.[b]	d2[c]	Median	d8	Mean	s.d.
Price index							
uniform mortality							
c2000	2.4	1.1	3.3	2.5	2.1	234	122
c2010	0.4	1.0	1.2	0.6	−0.1	277	129
c2020	−0.2	0.8	0.3	−0.1	−0.5	313	126
c2025	−0.3	0.8	0.4	−0.2	−0.7	286	107
differential mortality							
c2000	1.0	3.1	0.5	0.0	2.2		
c2010	0.2	2.6	−0.1	0.1	0.5	as above	
c2020	−0.9	2.6	−1.0	−1.2	−0.5		
c2025	−0.7	1.9	−0.5	−0.9	−0.8		
Earnings index							
uniform mortality							
c2000	4.0	1.2	5.1	4.2	3.4		
c2010	1.7	1.1	2.9	1.9	1.1	as above	
c2020	0.9	1.0	1.8	1.0	0.2		
c2025	0.8	0.9	1.7	0.9	0.2		
differential mortality							
c2000	3.6	3.0	3.7	3.3	3.5		
c2010	1.6	2.5	1.7	1.5	1.7	as above	
c2020	0.2	2.7	0.3	−0.1	0.4		
c2025	0.4	2.0	0.7	0.1	0.0		

a. For example, c2000 refers to cohort retiring in 2000.
b. Standard deviation.
c. For example, dx refers to xth decile (d1 is lowest).
d. Pounds per week at 1990 levels.

progressivity *within* generations: the second decile generally does better than the eighth decile, but it is not clear-cut. Indeed, the full inter-
decile comparisons of Disney and Whitehouse (1993c) confirm that
there is no clear relationship between within-cohort earnings and internal rate of return by cohort. It should be noted also that women will
typically earn positive returns, given the various redistributive components of the social security scheme in the United Kingdom, their earlier
retirement age until 2020–21, and their greater longevity on average.
These results illustrate clearly how a PAYG scheme tends to redistribute to earlier generations, swamping any cycles associated with cohort
size and any intragenerational redistribution.

Microsimulation studies of intragenerational redistribution (that is, of differences in returns between individuals within a generation) have produced more complex results. In the work of Creedy (1982), estimates of benefit-cost ratios associated with various pension schemes for males, at different discount rates and real earnings growth rates, are calculated across distributions of lifetime earnings. The cohort earnings profiles are calculated from actually observed National Insurance longitudinal earnings data, and account is taken of differential mortality rates among various socio-economic groups. The findings of this and subsequent studies include the following:

• Where benefits are related to earnings, pension-contribution ratios for men are most regressive (that is, highest for those with high lifetime earnings) where pensions are related to the last 3 years of earnings, and just regressive when pensions are related to average lifetime earnings (Creedy 1982). This residual regressivity in the case of average lifetime earnings case is due to differential mortality by income group.

• When account is taken of the flat-rate pension component, to generate a two-tier system analogous to the current UK system of a flat-rate component plus SERPS, the pension-contribution ratio for men is insignificantly progressive. For example, in an approximation to the present UK system, where the upper earnings limit is 7 times the lower earnings limit, and where benefits comprise a flat-rate component and an element related to average lifetime earnings, the regression coefficient of pension-contribution ratio on lifetime earnings is -0.013 (s.e. 0.011 and R2 = 0.009; Creedy 1982, table 5.2). Again the progressivity in the benefit schedule stemming from the flat-rate component is almost outweighed by differential mortality.

• Pension-contribution ratios, and the dispersions of post-pension and contribution incomes relative to pre-contribution earnings, are highly sensitive to the indexation assumptions. Only the combination of a pure earnings-related contribution and a flat-rate pension scheme unambiguously reduces the inequality of the male income distribution net of social security contributions and receipt of pensions (Creedy and Disney 1985, table 5.3). Attempting to index the basic flat-rate (lump-sum) pension in payment and the floors and ceilings for SERPS contributions and benefit entitlements to earnings growth rather than to price inflation generates quite complex intragenerational redistribution, which is barely progressive but which almost doubles the contribution rate in steady state (Creedy et al. 1993; see also Disney and Whitehouse 1991 and the next subsection).

• The SERPS scheme introduced in 1978 was highly redistributive toward women. Women were calculated to receive about 6 times as much benefit per pound contributed as men (Hemming and Kay 1982, p. 304). The elimination of the "20 best years" rule, the halving of widows' benefits under SERPS, and the equalization of pensionable age will ultimately reduce but not eliminate this disparity. Differential longevity of men and women and the implementation of "Home Responsibility Protection" (by which carers will in effect get contribution credits toward their social insurance benefits) will preserve a residual redistributive effect.

The final issue of interest concerning replacement ratios is the contribution of various income sources to total replacement ratios for people of pensionable age. Figure 4.3 shows that the contribution of social security to income shares rose systematically in the 1970s, when real benefits rose sharply (see figure 4.2), and declined in the 1980s. There has been an inexorable downward trend in income from employment, matched by a steady rise after the late 1970s in the share accruing

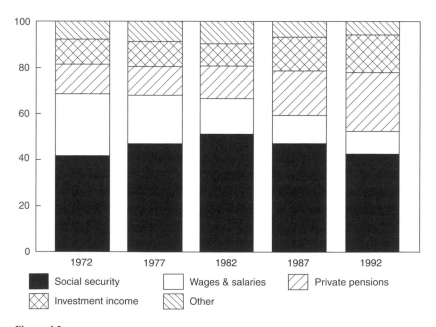

Figure 4.3
Average shares in pensioner income (percentages, United Kingdom, various years). Source: Family Expenditure Survey (Central Statistical Office, various years). "Other" sources include income from self-employment.

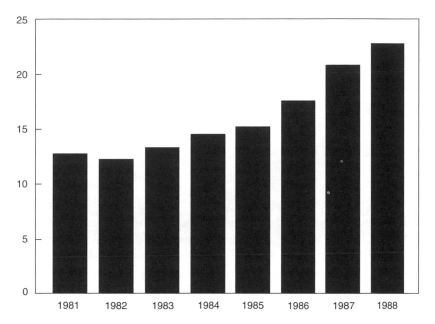

Figure 4.4
Percentage of male earners above UEL.

from private pensions and, latterly, from income on other investments. Income from self-employment and other sources shows no
clear trend.

An Anomaly in Calculating SERPS Entitlements
SERPS entitlements are determined by the value of National Insurance
contributions on earnings between the Lower and Upper Earnings
Limits (LEL and UEL). The value of the LEL itself is determined by
the value of the basic state pension, which is indexed to price inflation.
The UEL is a multiple of roughly 7.5 times the LEL.

One consequence of the indexation method is that the contribution
base was eroded by real earnings growth in the 1980s (figure 4.4).

The proportion of males earning above the UEL almost doubled in
8 years. As a result, the upper part of the earnings distribution will
steadily be removed from the contribution base over time.

In contrast, lower-paid workers such as part-timers become eligible
for SERPS pensions as the value of the LEL declines, although the revenue from their contributions will not replace the loss from higher
earners.

A further complication in calculating SERPS entitlement is that the earnings themselves are revalued using an index of economy-wide average earnings. The annual value of the LEL is then deducted from this revalued total (this being the value of the basic state pension) in order to calculate SERPS entitlements. Although the problem is less acute since the 1995 changes, equation 4.1 can be used to illustrate the post–1986 calculation:

$$P_{SERPS} = \sum[W_t(E_R/E_t) - LEL_{-1}]x_{Rt} \ \forall \ w_t < UEL_t$$
$$= \sum[UEL_t \ (E_R/E_t) - LEL_{R-1}]x_{Rt} \ \forall \ w_t \geq UEL_t,$$

where R is the date of retirement, x is the accrual factor specific to that date, W is actual earnings, and Y is average earnings. Whereas the UEL is applied in each year, the LEL is applied only in the year of retirement.

Indexing the earnings limits to average earnings in order to preserve the tax base has perverse redistributive effects: it brings a greater proportion of higher earnings into SERPS entitlements at the expense of the lower-paid, some of whom will lose any entitlement to social insurance benefits.

Widening the base still further by abolishing the UEL would not generate losers, but the highest pension gains would go to the highest paid. The 1995 changes apply the LEL and UEL in a temporally consistent sense, but the distributional paradox of raising the basic flat-rate pension remains (figure 4.5).

Figure 4.6 illustrates the observation that well-off (and younger) pensioners typically have a disproportionate share of income from private pensions and investments, whereas poorer pensioners rely largely on social security. Thus, inequality among pensioners decreased in the 1970s, when social security benefits were rising, and increased sharply in the 1980s and early 1990s, when private incomes grew sharply while social security stagnated in real terms. As was mentioned in chapter 1, in the period 1979–1991, for example, social security benefits to pensioners rose by 17 percent in real terms, whereas private pensions rose by 98 percent and investment income by 171 percent (Dilnot et al. 1994). Income from employment *fell* by 8 percent, indicating a trend toward earlier retirement. As successive cohorts will tend to retire with greater private assets, such as pension wealth and housing, these trends toward greater affluence among a large proportion of pensioners and growing disparities among pensioners seem set to continue.

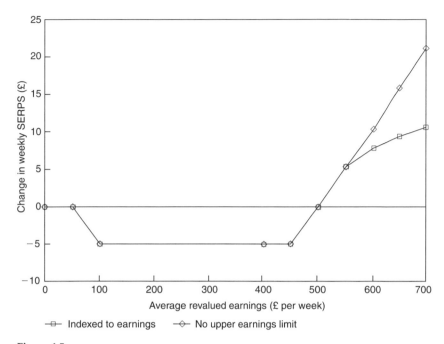

Figure 4.5
Alternative SERPS indexation

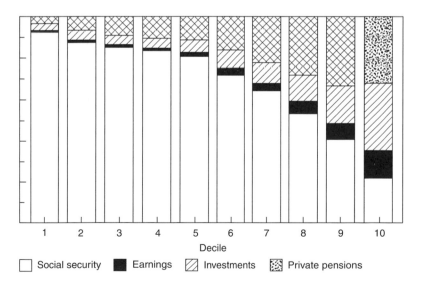

Figure 4.6
Shares of pensioner income by source, 1992–93, United Kingdom. Source: CSO: Family
Expenditure Survey, 1993.

Summary

The continued revisions to the social security program in the United Kingdom seem to illustrate an awareness of the implications of long-run trends in dependency ratios and replacement ratios for the "social contract" between generations. In contrast with the United States, where short-run funding crises have driven pension reform, at first sight the UK debate would seem to have been driven by consideration of intergenerational issues. However, this would be a misleading view: public awareness as to the implications of SERPS has been quite limited, and much of the debate stemmed from a somewhat myopic planning process in the early days of SERPS.

Although SERPS was seen in the 1970s as the future centerpiece of state provision of pensions in the United Kingdom, the importance of social insurance has been steadily eroded. Projected benefits from SERPS are now considerably less generous than appeared likely when SERPS was introduced in 1978. Furthermore, the majority of employees have opted out of SERPS by contracting out into a company-based occupational pension scheme or into a Personal Pension.

Moreover, for individuals retiring during the transition to a mature SERPS or a contracted-out scheme, the fall in the value of the flat-rate (lump-sum) pension relative to earnings means that a diminishing share of pensioner resources will come from the social security program (as was shown in figure 4.3). For those without other resources, income-tested benefits such as Income Support are becoming an important component of state provision. Thus, the trend toward income-tested pensions for low-income pensioners and toward greater private provision for higher-income pensioners suggests that "traditional" UK social insurance, enacted as a result of the Beveridge Report of 1942, is in terminal decline and is being replaced by a mixture of income testing (akin to the Australian social security program) and private provision. This is the prospect facing the gradually aging population in the United Kingdom.

4.3   Italy: Crisis and Reform in Pension Provision

Italy, in common with other countries bordering the Mediterranean, has experienced severe difficulties in financing its social security program in recent years. Commitments built up in the early years of the schemes have had to be redeemed in the context of a rapidly aging population and of macroeconomic instability. According to the United

Nations (1991), the Italian aged dependency ratio (i.e., 65+ population as a percentage of working-age population) rose from 12.6 percent in 1950 to 20.4 percent in 1980, while the crude birth rate fell from 18.3 per 1000 to 10.7 over the same period (compared to a European average for 1980–1985 of 13.4).

Nevertheless, Italy's social security program, which had been jealously protected by politicians and workers, did not prove susceptible to reform until the political elite of the previous 45 years lost power in 1992. The lesson of Italy's experience (repeated in adjacent countries, including Greece, Portugal, Spain, and Turkey) is that pension benefits voted in the early years of PAYG schemes can rapidly become unsustainable. A demographic transition to an aged society need not be a prerequisite for a social security crisis. Indeed, rapid aging may draw enough attention to the issue to generate a reform process.[7]

The basic Italian social security program evolved after 1945 as pension coverage was extended from wage earners to most of the working population. Although initially funded, the system gradually moved toward a PAYG basis of financing benefits, which was formalized in 1969. There are currently several schemes, covering different categories of workers and the self-employed, although the majority of salaried and waged workers belong to the Istituto Nazionale della Providenzia Sociale (INPS). Each Istituto has a management board, composed of government representatives, employers, and employees. From the outset, the social security program promised extremely high replacement ratios. Indeed, the Italian Constitution had set the goal that pensioners' standard of living should be similar to what they had when they were working.

The main features of the pre-1992 social security system, as applied to INPS, were as follows:

• A normal retirement age of 60 for men and 55 for women, with a minimum period for entitlement of 15 years of contributions and a maximum of 40 years. However, this provision was supplemented by a seniority pension, drawable after 35 years of contributions, by provision for income support, and by generous disability pensions.

• The pension calculation involved revaluation of earnings in line with average earnings growth, with benefits determined by the last 5 years' revalued earnings. The base accrual rate in the pension calculation is 2 percent on earnings up to a maximum earnings level (in 1993, 53.5 million lire—roughly US$35,000), but from 1989 accruals were allowed on higher earnings (albeit at rates of less than 2 percent and declining with earnings level). Overall, a full contributions history of 40 years would generate a maximum replacement ratio of 80 percent of earnings, above a minimum pension level which must be 100 percent covered.

• Since the 1970s, indexation of post-retirement pension benefits to earnings. By 1992 the system involved a mixture of price and earnings indexation.

• Survivors' pensions, composed of 60 percent of the pension payable to the spouse and a further 20 percent for orphans.

Other sectors permitted still more generous provisions. Public employees could receive seniority pensions after 15–20 years, and the pension calculations were based on the final month's salary. In such multiple-scheme systems, there is every incentive for an employee to retire in whichever sector guarantees the most favorable benefits.

In addition to these social security benefits, companies were liable to pay termination indemnities (TFRs) to employees (or their survivors) who left their jobs for reasons of retirement, death, disability, or redundancy. Since 1982, the annual TFR accrual is calculated at just over 7 percent of annual pay per annum, with past accruals revalued at 75 percent of the change in prices plus 1.5 percent per annum. With inflation at 10 percent, an individual retiring after 40 years' service would receive an additional lump sum of approximately 2.5 times his final salary, financed from the reserves of the companies involved (which are substantial, valued at 10.5 percent of GDP in 1988). However, with incomplete indexation, and with the transfer from the wage fund to the TFR reserve assumed to be ultimately borne by workers, the real return to the employee is negative (Jappelli and Pagano 1994).[8]

As the social security program matured from the late 1970s, its financial situation deteriorated. The number of pensions paid rose from 3.2 million in 1949 to 17.9 million—roughly 30 percent of the population—in 1989. Total pension expenditure as a share of GDP in 1980 was 16.9 percent compared to 8.1 percent in the United States and 7.7 percent in the United Kingdom. Expenditure on state retirement benefits was 13.9 percent of GDP in 1990 (Jappelli and Pagano 1994). In the context of the lowest fertility rate in Europe, and macroeconomic setbacks culminating in a serious public budget deficit, these social security expenditures were unsustainable.

Table 4.6
Projections of INPS pension scheme in Italy before 1992 reforms.

	Total expenditure		Contributions		Budgeted fiscal	Uncovered expenditure	
	million lire[a]	as % of earnings	million lire[a]	as % of earnings	transfers (million lire)	million lire[a]	as % of earnings
1993	116,043	43.44	67,235	25.19	15,626	33,132	12.40
1995	122,352	44.31	69,612	25.21	15,360	37,380	13.54
2000	136,028	43.70	78,605	25.25	14,164	43,259	13.90
2005	162,466	46.01	89,301	25.29	13,726	59,439	16.83
2010	197,691	50.08	99,956	25.32	13,120	84,615	21.44
2015	240,949	54.76	111,496	25.34	13,831	115,622	26.28
2020	288,884	58.49	125,249	25.36	13,969	149,667	30.30
2025	335,452	59.64	142,636	25.36	13,156	179,660	31.94

a. 1992 prices.

Total contribution rates for all social security benefits, across employers and employees, are currently around 35 percent of liable earnings. Retirement, survivors', and disability pensions alone account for just over 28 percent. There is now no ceiling on earnings to which contributions are applied and on which benefits are determined (although the benefit formula is slightly progressive in that the accrual rate declines with earnings level). Table 4.6 gives projections of expenditure for INPS to 2025 on the basis of the pre-1992 arrangements, and payroll costs on the assumption that the contribution rate for pension and survivors' benefits remained near its current level. As is apparent from the table, INPS was already in deficit in 1993, with uncovered expenditure equivalent to 12.4 percent of payroll. However, the situation deteriorates steadily, so that the uncovered component of pension costs exceeds the contribution rate after 2015, and an aggregate payroll cost of 60 percent emerges by the year 2025. This would be the combined contribution rate need to operate the scheme on a PAYG basis by that year, which is clearly infeasible in the Italian economic context.

The Pension Reforms of 1992–93

The economic and political crisis of 1992 led to a severe retrenchment of the Italian pension scheme, which occurred in three stages. In November 1992, Law 438 abolished the seniority provision and temporarily froze the nominal value of the pension, giving a temporary and partial breathing space. The more radical reform proposals of December 1992 have tackled some of the main eligibility conditions of the Italian scheme, albeit to a more medium-term horizon than has been warranted by the state of public finances (here, again, we focus on INPS):

• The retirement age is to be raised over the next decade by five years, to 65 for men and 60 for women.

• The "minimum service" criterion is to be raised over a decade from 15 to 20 years.

• Pension entitlements will be determined, not by the last 5 years of earnings revalued in line with average earnings, but by average career earnings in line with price inflation plus 1 percent per annum.

• Pensions in payment will normally be indexed to prices, not to earnings (although the discretion of earnings indexation is still permitted).

• Accrual rates have been reduced for higher earners.

• Criteria for the minimum pension and income support payments were tightened.

The consequences of these changes are illustrated in table 4.7, which shows how each of the measures is projected to affect pension costs. Clearly the effect of the November measures (L438) decays over time (the date are in real terms); in the long run, the rise in the retirement age and the shift to an average earnings basis and price revaluation in the benefit formula account for the bulk of the 5.8 percent cut in payroll costs projected by 2025. Even so, without the removal of earnings indexation post-retirement, the revenue cuts are not large enough; as in the United Kingdom, it is the removal of real earnings growth from post-retirement indexation that generates significant savings. Moreover, by adding the last two columns, it can be seen that only 23 percent of the 32 percent deficit is eliminated despite a cut in average replacement ratios of some 20 percentage points and a total annuity value cut (given later retirement) of more than 50 percent. This underlying deterioration, which in part reflects the demographic transition, precipitated further measures to reduce costs.

Early in 1993 measures were introduced to encourage private pension development and to facilitate integration of TFR accounts into a funded basis of annuity provision. Providers would be able to operate either defined benefit or defined contribution schemes, on a group or

Table 4.7
Impact of 1992 reforms on INPS finances.

	Impact[b] of							Total impact on payroll tax burden (%)	Further impact of price indexation only (%)
	Expenditure[a,b]	L438	Raising age of retirement	Pension benefit calculation	Raising minimum period	Changing accrual rates	Interaction		
1993	100,417	−5,761	0	−1	−120	0	0	−2.2	0
1995	106,992	−4,288	−1,467	−12	−433	−846	+262	−2.5	− 0.8
2000	121,664	−4,009	−5,729	−145	−1,532	−922	+1,336	−3.5	− 3.0
2005	148,740	−3,885	−9,498	−566	−2,623	−1,101	+2,643	−4.3	− 7.0
2010	184,571	−3,738	−11,122	−1,589	−3,073	−1,340	+3,186	−4.4	−10.2
2015	227,116	−3,614	−11,704	−4,436	−3,550	−1,637	+3,625	−4.9	−13.0
2020	274,915	−3,550	−11,151	−10,249	−3,308	−1,958	+3,202	−5.5	−15.5
2025	322,296	−3,576	−8,768	−17,469	−2,671	−2,274	+2,107	−5.8	−17.3

a. Expenditure from contributions and uncovered expenditures only.
b. Million lire, 1992 prices.

individual basis. It was intended that such funded schemes might ultimately make up some of the cut in replacement ratios induced by the
measures of late 1992. The imposition of a 15 percent withholding tax
(a tax on fund capital gains) in order to reduce the fiscal deficit has
been seen as a disincentive to new providers, and existing pension
schemes (such as those offered by banks) have opted to stay out of the
new scheme.[9]

The incoming Dini administration introduced another package of
measures in July 1995 after the fall of at least one administration which
had endeavored to accelerate the timetable for the retrenchment of the
social security program. The 1995 measures promise an accelerated
timetable for the new retirement age, the phasing out of "seniority
pensions," and a recalculation of pension accruals to make benefits
"contribution based," and integration of the various schemes' eligibility conditions. The intention to enhance the private component of the
scheme was also announced, but it is not yet clear how this sector
will evolve.

Appraisal
The Italian experience shows how overgenerous benefit formulas and
eligibility conditions at the inception of PAYG social insurance, and in
particular the failure to take account subsequently of enhanced longevity, can precipitate crises and a severe retrenchment of the program.
Such a history generates significant differences in rates of return to
social security across generations; redistribution toward those who
first retire in pension schemes followed by low or even negative real
returns to ensuing generations reflects the pattern already observed in
the United States and the United Kingdom. Indeed, these redistributions across generations induced by "set-up" provisions have dominated differences in returns predicted by fluctuations in cohort size
(Castellino 1995; Cozzolino and Schioppa Kostoris 1995). There is also
evidence that intragenerational redistributions tend to be from low
earners to high earners—a redistribution arising, again, from differential mortality, from the final salary basis of schemes before the reform
process of 1992 on, and from the availability of "seniority" pensions
(Schioppa 1990).

Looking at the situation dispassionately, it might seem surprising
that such a costly pension scheme was able to survive into the early
1990s; the coalition of interests that governed Italy since 1945 appears
to have caused this inertia. Yet PAYG financing was able to imbue

social-insurance-scheme participants with an entirely misplaced sense of security. This is illustrated in an interesting study in which Jappelli and Pagano (1993) used the 1989 Survey of Household Income and Wealth (SHIW) conducted by the Central Bank of Italy. This survey asked the followed question: "Considering the moment when you retire, and setting your final monthly income before retirement equal to 100, what do you expect your first monthly pension to be?" This question, designed to elicit a subjective projected replacement ratio, revealed that across all income classes bar the lowest decile, expected replacement ratios were in the region of 75–80 percent. This exceeded *actual* replacement ratios, which showed greater variance in a range of 65–80 percent. Astonishingly, the youngest age groups projected the highest replacement ratios, predicting over 80 percent for 25-year-olds and with no group until age 65 slipping below a projection of 75 percent of final earnings. The dangers of the Ponzi-scheme nature of PAYG financing are well illustrated by this survey, undertaken at a time when the fiscal strains to the Italian system were already evident. Indeed, there is evidence, cited by Jappelli and Pagano (1994), that these overoptimistic perceptions have contributed to the macroeconomic problems in Italy; some commentators have argued that the sharp increase in net social security wealth may have led to a cut in private savings rates[10]. The obvious counterargument, advanced by Brugiavini (1987), is that if such pension benefits are perceived as unsustainable then little substitutability will be revealed between social security and private saving. The survey evidence cited above casts doubt on this proposition, but the crisis and the reforms since 1992 may well generate just such a revision of expectations, with a consequent rise in private savings.

4.4   Australia: Income Testing—An Alternative Route?

The Australian social security program is unlike the others studied here two important respects. First, in view of the relative youth of the population and the continued immigration, growth in the "dependency burden" is not yet a major political concern. Second, the Australian program is financed out of general revenue, with basic benefits flat-rate, taxable, and means-tested with a significant taper. The combination of these two facts means that financing future social security entitlements has not been a major issue in Australia. But the structure of the program is of interest to countries where the burden of the demographic transition is more imminent.

Projections of the number of pensioners in Australia indicate steady growth, but from a rather low starting point. In 1981 there were 1.5 million pensioners and 8.4 million people of ages 20–64, a ratio comparable to Canada that in or Japan. The number of pensioners rises to 2.3 million by the year 2001 and doubles again by 2040. However, the aged dependency ratio rises very slowly from 1980 to 2000, picking up more significantly in the second quarter of the 21st century (Ford 1986; UN 1991). Even so, the aged dependency ratio lies below those of all the major OECD countries until 2050 (OECD 1988a). Forecasts of pension expenditure suggest steady rather than dramatic growth, with eligibility in the light of means testing of other income the key parameter.

The demographic transition has therefore induced only muted concern in Australia. In contrast, the structure of the state pension program, and particularly its means-tested aspect, have created some controversy. The debate has concerned the effect of the program on other forms of saving, and, in particular, the incentives within the scheme to dissipate other forms of wealth in order to minimize the impact of means testing of income and assets in retirement. A comprehensive survey of the pension program was undertaken in the late 1980s in the context of a reappraisal of the social security system as a whole (Foster 1988). In 1992 the decision to introduce compulsory supplementary private pension provision and to amend the tax treatment of annuities signaled that the state pension would continue to function as a residual mechanism of redistribution.

Benefit Entitlement in the Social Security Program
The Australian social security pension is flat-rate (lump-sum), with a higher rate for married couples. It is treated as taxable income, although single pensioners receive a tax allowance approximately equal to the value of the pension and couples an allowance slightly in excess of the value of the pension. The pension is subject to an income test: all income above Aus$40 per week for a single person and Aus$70 for a married couple in 1988 prices (these values are moved up regularly but not automatically) reduces the basic pension by 50 cents per dollar of earned income.[11] There is also an asset test, which treats owner-occupied housing more leniently than it treats other assets. Whichever of the two tests actually applies is the one that results in the lower basic pension, and for a stylized simulation this is normally the income test (Creedy and Disney 1989a). However, the 1992 reforms complicate this argument slightly (Bateman et al. 1993). Elderly people are also

eligible for other means-tested benefits, such as the pensioner health benefits card. The structure of withdrawal rates is slightly different for these other benefits, and this complicates the effective budget constraint.

By 1987 around 40 percent of wage and salary earners also belonged to company-based superannuation schemes, which provide pension benefits on retirement and which obtain significant tax concessions during accrual. These private pension benefits in principle count toward the income test and are therefore typically taken as a lump sum in order to pay off outstanding debts, notably mortgages on property. Measurement of replacement ratios is therefore a complex task, as the tax and benefit structure has as one consequence the distortion of the asset structure and a diminution of the market in "free-standing" pension annuities (see below). Calculations from Foster (1988) suggest that up to one-fourth of single individuals and up to one-sixth of married couples among pensioners are directly affected by the income and asset tests (primarily the former). Indeed, Aaron (1984) suggests that up to a third of individuals may have been affected by the tests in 1981–82.

An example of the effective marginal tax rate structure, for an aged couple under 70 years old, with private income split equally, is given in figure 4.7. The extreme nonlinearity of the structure of marginal tax rates is apparent; indeed, it is surprising that so many individuals are subject to the income and asset tests when the effective rates are so high over a significant part of the budget constraint. In fact, distributions of income for the elderly suggest a pronounced bunching of total income around the basic pension, and of other sources of income below the (low) income test threshold (see, e.g., Creedy and Disney 1989a, figures 3 and 4). The consequences for savings rates *before* retirement are also apparent, other than in specialized assets such as home ownership. Figure 4.8 illustrates the effective net-of-tax rate of return (as a fraction of the nominal return) on saving for retirement in a financial asset under the somewhat stylized budget constraint modeled in Creedy and Disney 1989a, and again the disincentive effects of the income tests are clear.

The adverse effects of these tests on the structure and the level of capital accumulation and on the labor-force participation of the elderly have been pointed out by a number of authorities, including Aaron (1984). In defense of this structure, it has been argued that it targets social security effectively; and it is commonly asserted that

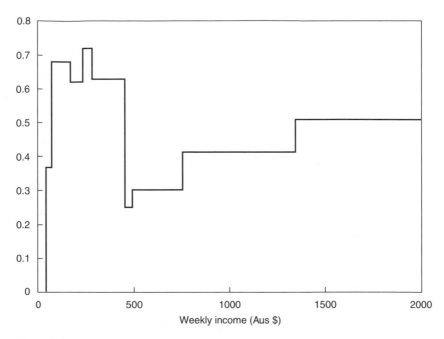

Figure 4.7
Effective marginal tax rates on income for aged couple under 70, Australia, 1987. Source: Foster 1988.

superannuation scheme members have obtained tax concessions during their working lives which offset the adverse effects of later income tests on retirement income. Nevertheless, "double dipping" (i.e., taking superannuation in the form of a lump sum and then obtaining full entitlement to the social security pension) has been observed as a rational but unattractive feature of the scheme. Furthermore, the frequent changes that have been made to the income and asset tests (often to block loopholes and distortions that have emerged as a result of existing tests) mean that it is difficult to adopt the *ceteris paribus* assumption in forecasting future benefit coverage and likely replacement ratios.

Replacement Ratios
In calculating various values of the replacement ratio, whether for social security benefits only or for total transfers, the asset and income tests must be taken into account. An illustration of the complexity of this calculation can be gleaned from Foster 1988, in which alternative

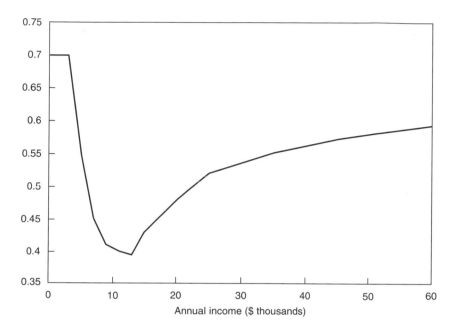

Figure 4.8
After tax return on savings (net return as percentage of gross return) for single person of pensionable age, Australia, 1988. Source: Creedy and Disney 1989a.

replacement ratios are calculated for the basic social security pension plus the benefits derived from superannuation, the alternatives depending on the way in which the private benefits are utilized upon retirement (see also Bateman et al. 1990, 1993).

In table 4.8, a single male pensioner is taken as the example. He has accumulated 40 years' contributions into a superannuation scheme, and the tabulation describes his replacement ratio of pension benefits as a fraction of average economy-wide weekly earnings (AWE) for different final salaries, by how his superannuation is utilized. In the "dissipated" column, where the lump sum is fully spent (for example, in paying off a mortgage), no annuity is derived. Consequently, the RR reflects only the social security pension. Being a flat-rate pension, the RR falls proportionately with the earnings level. In the "partially dissipated" case, a fraction of the pension is spent at retirement and the rest converted into an annuity, and the RR is raised (especially for an individual with a higher final salary), although the residual fall in the RR with earnings illustrates the progressivity of the flat-rate pension formula. The rightmost two columns of the table illustrate two

Table 4.8
Replacement ratios (income stream in retirement divided by final salary) from pension and superannuation. Source: Foster 1988, table 50.

Final salary as multiple of AWE[a]	Use of lump sum			
	Dissipated[b]	Partially dissipated[c]	Rolled over[d]	Invested[e]
0.50 AWE	0.50	0.60	0.82	0.84
0.75 AWE	0.33	0.50	0.63	0.64
1.00 AWE	0.25	0.44	0.53	0.53
2.00 AWE	0.12	0.38	0.48	0.47
3.00 AWE	0.08	0.41	0.48	0.46

a. Average weekly earnings (economy-wide).
b. The lump-sum tax is paid; the rest is spent in ways not affecting income test or taxes.
c. Aus$50,000 is dissipated; the rest is rolled over into an annuity.
d. The entire sum is converted into an annuity.
e. A lump-sum tax is paid; the balance is used to produce income, which is assessed for tax.

alternative methods of converting the lump sum into a stream of income: by transforming the whole sum into an annuity, and by investing it in a taxable asset. The slight differences in returns by income suggest that this choice is not neutral from the point of view of gross and net return; this is due to differential tax treatment. The progressivity of the flat-rate (lump-sum) social security pension benefit is still revealed, however.

The 1992 "Superannuation Guarantee Charge"

An important change to the pension program was introduced in 1992. In view of the function of the state pension as a "backstop" mechanism and the strong incentives to underannuitize savings, the reform was two-pronged. First, for those employees not covered by "traditional" defined benefit superannuation schemes, membership of a defined contribution private pension becomes compulsory. Eight percent of salary (5 percent by the employee, 3 percent by the employer) must be contributed to the fund, rising to 12 percent by the turn of the century. This is in essence a forced saving scheme, since the annuities are not paid from the funds themselves (Davies 1995). Contributions to these funds will increasingly be part of the national bargaining over pay rates and other remuneration.

Annuitization does not appear to be compulsory; instead, tax incentives were introduced in parallel to persuade individuals to annuitize rather than to take private fund proceeds in the form of lump sums. Specifically, there was a 15 percent tax on lump sums coupled with a rebate of the 15 percent tax on employee contributions for those opting to annuitize. It is not evident, however, that this changed tax treatment is sufficient to encourage annuitization: as Bateman et al. (1993) point out, a large proportion of the value of an annuitizable pension fund arises from the return on contributions rather than from the value of the contributions themselves, especially if nominal returns (and inflation) are high. So this tax treatment is not inflation neutral. Furthermore, the asset and income tests on social security will still come into play upon retirement, and the relative efficacy of annuitizing (thereby incurring the social security test) versus rolling up into a lump sum (thereby failing to attain the tax rebate) is not clear cut. However, these tax-treatment issues seem in principle to be resolvable.[12]

Intergenerational Redistribution
The clear interpretation of the income and asset tests in the Australian social security program concerns the overriding influence of within-period redistribution in public pension policy. The Australian state pension is effectively targeted on alleviating poverty, and this is consistent with the socially optimal redistribution model described in chapter 2. The lifetime (overlapping-generations) perspective appears to carry less weight because the presence of income tests drives a wedge between contributions and benefits in calculating individual rates of return.[13]

Income tests of this kind (which are used to a lesser extent in other social security programs: see Hubbard et al. 1995) do, however, have a greater impact on lifetime consumption patterns, on the pattern of labor-market activity, and on the structure of asset markets than "traditional" social insurance schemes. Whether the Australian state pension has significantly reduced total saving is open to doubt, but it has certainly encouraged the development of particular forms of asset holding: superannuation (private pensions) and private housing. That this is the "productive" investment a social security program should encourage in the context of the overlapping-generations model with capital accumulation is questionable. Nevertheless, the means-tested aspect of the Australian PAYG scheme means that it costs less than an orthodox social insurance scheme and thereby diverts less private capital. The net effect on aggregate private saving may therefore be less deleterious than some critics have suggested.

The income-tested Australian social security program has evolved in a relatively youthful society. The demographic pressures on public financing of social insurance (universal) pensions described in the other case studies here may lead to a greater interest in the Australian approach of income testing plus compulsory private provision, notwithstanding the adverse impact on incentive structures and the distortion of the capital market arising from the tax treatments of various options. Indeed, in the debate in the 1990s in the United Kingdom concerning cutbacks in social security spending there has been a clear divide between those who believe that greater private provision of pensions is the answer and those who, mindful of the transitional costs of a privatization strategy, are inclined toward a more comprehensive social security program with greater targeting of benefits on the poor. This debate has, to a large extent, superseded the older debate between social insurance and integrated tax-and-transfer schemes (such as a minimum income guarantee or a negative income tax).[14] The Australian scheme may be regarded as an embryonic version of both compulsory private provision and a negative income tax. It illustrates the great difficulty of such tax-and-transfer programs: how to strike the correct balance between the level of income transfers to the poor, the average tax burden, and the structure of marginal tax rates. Nevertheless, this is a continuing debate, in which the Australian pension scheme deserves attention for both its strengths and its weaknesses.

4.5   Japan: A Demographic Burden on the "Economic Miracle"?

Japan's "economic miracle" has been identified with high levels of saving and investment, rapid economic growth, and relative efficiency in total factor productivity. Increasingly, however, the Japanese are concerned as to whether this performance can be maintained in the face of adverse demographic trends: a decline in the size of successive "prime-age" cohorts, a fall in the participation rate of the elderly, and a rapid rise in the number of pensioners. The consequences for tax rates and for the saving rate have been debated, and it has been pointed out that the increased average age of the prime-age workforce may render unsustainable the seniority system of wage structure, bonuses, and employment security (OECD 1990; see also chapter 5 below).

Table 4.9 depicts some of the salient aspects of the Japanese case. The proportion of the population aged 65+ doubles from 1990 to 2040.

Table 4.9
Japan: some relevant statistics.

1 Percentage of population aged 65+, 1980–2040[a]

1980	1990	2000	2010	2020	2030	2040
9.1	11.4	15.2	18.6	20.9	20.0	22.7

2 Growth rate of working-age population (% per annum)[b]

	1950–70	1970–90	1990–2010	2010–30
Japan	1.9	0.9	−0.3	−0.3
OECD average	0.9	0.95	0.25	−0.4

3 Ratio of old (55+) to young (15–35) workers[a]

Males			Females		
1968	1988	2010	1968	1988	2010
0.34	0.63	1.04	0.27	0.55	0.87

4 Labor-force participation rates of individuals 65+, 1985[c]

Males		Females	
Japan	Canada[d]	Japan	United States[d]
37.0%	12.3%	15.5%	6.8%

a. Source: OECD 1988a.
b. Source: Heller et al. 1986.
c. Source: OECD 1990.
d. Next-highest OECD country.

In fact, life expectancy in Japan is the second highest among OECD countries (OECD 1988a). The significance of these facts is that Japan is in transition from having the lowest proportion of elderly and social security pension expenditure as a proportion of GDP among OECD countries in the 1980s to the highest by the turn of the second quarter of the 21st century.

Table 4.9 shows that, while expenditure on the elderly is increasing, the tax base of employees in employment is declining. In the period 1950–1970, Japan benefited from a rate of growth of the workforce twice the OECD average, but from 1990 to 2010 Japan's workforce will shrink as the OECD average rises. Furthermore, there is a sharp increase in the proportion of elderly workers to young workers. Items 3 and 4 in table 4.9 reveal the change in the age structure of the workforce and highlight the large proportion of workers 65+ who continue to work in Japan. If this last number remains high, the aging of the population poses a lesser problem; however, concern will arise if the labor-force participation rate of the elderly begins to decline to the much lower levels characteristic of other OECD countries. With rising real incomes, and growing private pension entitlements among a substantial body of workers, the latter outcome remains a distinct possibility.

There is a further aspect to the financing problem of Japan's social security program. As was shown in section 4.1, the growth in pension commitments and the aging of the working population in the United States have led to measures designed to shift from a pure pay-as-you-go public pension system toward a partially funded system. Even in the United Kingdom, which operates a pure PAYG scheme, there have been reductions in intergeneration subsidies to the National Insurance scheme from general taxation. In Australia, Italy, and the United Kingdom, there are sustained efforts to encourage private funded pensions to take over responsibility from the state. These are the strategies that might be anticipated, in view of the potential breakdown of the "social contract" underlying PAYG schemes as populations age.

In contrast, the Japanese public pension scheme started as a partially funded system but has moved steadily toward PAYG status. Contribution rates have proved insufficient to maintain the scheme's reserve as well as to fund current pension entitlements. The ratio of reserves to annual expenditure is anticipated to fall from 5.8 in 1990 to 1.3 in 2020 (OECD 1990). The consequences for projected social security contribution rates are reported in the next subsection. In addition, a third of the expenditure on the "basic" first-tier pension (see below) is financed directly from the government's budget. Interpolating the tradeoff of savings rates and old-age dependency ratios constructed by the OECD (ibid., diagram 22), Japan goes from being the highest OECD saver in the 1980s, with a rate of 16 percent, to a saving rate of zero when the old-age dependency ratio and the contribution rate rise to their projected levels in 2020. Such extrapolations are risky, but they illustrate the magnitude of the potential problem of aging in Japan.

Structure of Public Pension and Potential Replacement Ratios

In many respects, the Japanese social security program of pension provision is similar to that of the United Kingdom in the period 1975–1986. There is a two-tier scheme of a basic flat-rate (lump-sum) pension, financed by a flat-rate contribution levy, which, for employees, is supplemented by some form of earnings-related pension financed by earnings-related contributions. The latter benefits are calculated as an average of lifetime earnings, with accrued entitlements revalued in line with earnings. There is an upper earnings limit on earnings to which contributions can be applied, again as in the United Kingdom (Shimono and Tachibanaki 1985). The minimum insured period is 40 years, although for the earliest cohorts 25 years sufficed.

The earnings-related pension for private-sector employees can be received at age 65, although basic flat-rate benefits will be paid in the interim from when the contributor reaches 60. In effect, the pensionable age is 60, and attempts to raise the minimum age to 65 in 1979 and 1989 were thwarted (Takayama 1992). The basic (flat-rate) pension in receipt is indexed to the cost of living, but the social security program providing earnings-related benefits for private- and public-sector workers has typically uprated benefits in line with average nominal earnings every five years (OECD 1990). As in the United Kingdom, there is a scheme of contracting out of the earnings-related social security component for employers offering their own pension schemes. Contracted-out individuals pay a lower contribution rate, and around 30 percent of private-sector employees are contracted out in this way.

Calculations in the early 1980s suggested that theoretical replacement ratios of the combined tiers of social security benefits relative to average lifetime gross earnings could rise as high as 83 percent. Indeed, historically the structure of the social security program was rather more fragmented then the simple description provided here; in particular, it was potentially possible for a retiree to receive multiple benefits under several of the earnings-related schemes. The Pension Reform Act of 1985 introduced a ceiling on pensions as a proportion of average revalued lifetime earnings of 68 percent, effectively curtailing the potential for multiple pensions by unifying the entitlements obtained among the various schemes covering different parts of the workforce. In fact, since bonuses (an important component of Japanese remuneration systems) are excluded from base earnings in the pension calculation, effective replacement ratios may be somewhat lower. On the other hand taxes on pensioners are very low in Japan, and the net-of-tax replacement ratio can be considerably higher.

The flat-rate component to benefits and the limit on earnings provide a degree of intragenerational redistribution. Using methods similar to those of Creedy (1982), Shimono and Tachibanaki (1985) calculate the variation in lifetime income without and with the pension system for different values of the upper limit on earnings. Not surprisingly, abolition of the upper limit on contributions would enhance the redistributive capabilities of the Japanese public pension system. Takayama (1992) calculates benefit-contribution ratios (BCRs) for successive cohorts and different household types, utilizing lifetime age-earnings profiles estimated by regression analysis and applied to the benefit-accrual formula.[15] For the "startup" cohorts, the calculated BCRs are enormous. A married couple with a single wage earner born between 1925 and 1929 and thus retiring after 1985 has a BCR of 5.54. This declines to 3.13 for a couple born a decade later, 1.99 for a couple born between 1945 and 1949, and 1.4 for a couple born between 1955 and 1959. The baby-boom generation can expect much lower returns, although again the startup of the scheme, rather than cycles in cohort size, seems to be the primary factor determining returns. Indeed, Takayama suggests that, with zero wage growth, internal rates of return for male cohorts born after 1960 would be negative even though these cohorts are smaller (ibid., table 4B.1).

The Major Issues in Japan

Table 4.10 sums up the immediate financial consequences for Japan of the demographic transition and the design of the social security program. It is apparent that the current support ratio is high relative to other OECD countries, but that within the next 15 years the position will deteriorate sharply. The level of the flat-rate contribution required to finance the first tier of the system more than doubles between 1990 and 2010. The much slower increase thereafter is partly attributable to the assumption that the fertility rate will rise quite sharply in the next 25 years. This may be overoptimistic. Notional contribution rates to the earnings-related tier also rise sharply. It is hard to believe that this increase will be permitted in an economy that will be increasingly exposed to international competition (particularly in the siting of new investment in South and East Asia), and a rise in the state pensionable age would seem to be an inevitable response to these projections.

It is not surprising in the light of the preceding discussion that OECD 1990 and Takayama 1992 highlight the optimal degree of intergenerational redistribution as the key issue facing Japan's social security program. Early retiring cohorts have done particularly well from the program, and it is unlikely that future cohorts will sustain rates of return anywhere close to those of these earlier cohorts. Thus, our final case study of social security pensions returns to the question that underpinned much of the analysis in earlier chapters: the intergenerational optimum.

Table 4.10
Projections of the finances of the Japanese social security program. Source: Takayama 1992, from projections by Japanese Ministry of Health and Welfare (1990).

	1990	2000	2010	2030	2050
Base (flat rate) tier					
No. of contributors[a]	65.5	67.1	64.5	63.7	60.9
No. of pensioners[a]	12.7	16.3	26.1	29.9	29.1
Support ratio	5.2	3.4	2.5	2.1	2.1
Flat-rate contribution[d]	100	167	233	253	260
Earnings-related tier[b]					
No. of contributors	29.5	30.7	29.0	29.0	28.3
No. of pensioners[a]	4.6	7.9	11.9	13.3	12.5
Support ratio	6.4	3.9	2.4	2.2	2.3
Total expenditure[e]	12.6[c]	23.4	31.4	31.7	29.6
Contribution rate	12.4[c]	19.0	27.5	31.5	31.5

a. Assumption: fertility rate (currently 1.5) reverts to 2.0 by 2025.
b. For private-sector employees.
c. 1989 figure.
d. Index: 1990 = 100.
e. Trillion yen, 1989 prices.

OECD 1990 argues that the shift from partially funded to PAYG status in Japanese public pensions has blurred the degree of intergenerational redistribution within the Japanese system, perhaps providing a cushion for the inevitable transition to an economy with higher tax rates, lower saving, and increased old-age dependency. It argues that the choice of tax rate and pension level should be made "transparent," perhaps by establishing notional "retirement accounts" parallel to IRAs in the United States and Personal Pensions in the United Kingdom. Alternatively or additionally, supplementary reforms to cap the replacement ratio should be introduced; these might include later retirement, greater encouragement to continue to work after 65,[16] and selectivity of pension provision. Greater private provision is also to be encouraged; although this may simply substitute private for public provision in the numerator of the replacement ratio, the impact on savings rates may be non-neutral. Measures to relax the earnings test in order to induce later retirement were indeed proposed in the 1994 reform bill (see Takayama 1994).

One key issue in examining the effect of high future social security contributions is the validity of the life-cycle model of saving.[17] If social security substitutes for other kinds of saving, private saving and domestic capital accumulation may be much lower. Individual behavior depends in part on whether such contribution rates and benefit levels are expected to be sustained. However, it does seem from empirical studies (e.g. Takayama 1992 and Ando et al. 1995) that the Japanese experience is particularly hard to match to the life-cycle model: in particular, the elderly do not dissave to anywhere near the extent that the life-cycle model would predict. This may signal that Japanese consumers have a high propensity to save, which may be sustained irrespective of the burden of the social security program. Indeed, growing uncertainty as to the future sustainability of the system may generate greater precautionary saving, rather than simply substituting public forced levies for private saving. In addition, high savings may mean large bequests, which may imply that younger cohorts' wealth position is sustained despite lower social security benefits. Higher bequests would also limit the net extent of intergenerational redistribution stemming from future lower returns on social security contributions. But the anticipation of higher bequests may lead to a reduction in saving.[18] Notwithstanding the reform of 1985, the demographic transition, its implications for the social security program, and its consequences for the future of Japan's economic success story continue to be topics of great interest in Japan and elsewhere.

4.6   Conclusion: Past Pension Promises and Population Aging

The lesson of all five of these case studies, with the possible exception of Australia, is that pension promises made in the early stages of social security programs are unlikely to be realized for all but the earliest participating generations. Although aging populations have rendered the task of providing generous social security benefits more difficult, it is not aging *per se* that has created many of the financing difficulties in which countries find themselves. The promise of pay-as-you-go social insurance, as described in chapter 3, was that it could provide a feasible "social contract" between generations in which (in the simplest Samuelson-Aaron model) current and future generations could maintain positive real rates of return on contributions so long as both the growth of real earnings and the growth of the population remained positive. In contrast, what seems to have happened in many countries is that the promise of "jam tomorrow" endemic to PAYG financing has led programs to make unrealistic future commitments that cannot or will not be fulfilled by future generations.

In some countries, including the United Kingdom, official or private projections of funding crises led to retrenchment before the crisis appeared. In other countries, e.g. Italy, financial crises have led to major political upheavals and drastic cuts in the benefits attached to the social security program. In still other countries, the continued pressure of demographic aging on weak program finances have yet to be addressed. It is interesting to speculate as to why PAYG social security programs have proved unable to generate stable pension schemes: it may be myopic behavior, the absence of votes of future generations, or utility-maximizing behavior by successive generations (as is suggested by public-choice theory). These questions are examined in chapter 10.

One consequence is that differences in rates of return between generations can be substantial and can be dominated by the dynamics of pension schemes out of steady state (particularly en route to maturation) rather than by differential generation size.[19,20] It may be that PAYG financing would work in a mature scheme, but few pension programs have been in existence long enough, without constant tinkering, for this hypothesis to be tested.

In contrast, differences in returns to the social security program among members of the *same* generation are often unsystematic (from a policy point of view), depending in quite complex ways on eligibility conditions, nonlinearity of benefit-contribution schedules, indexation arrangements, and differential mortality. As an agent of systematic redistribution, PAYG social insurance is generally a weak instrument (although most schemes, on balance, redistribute from men to women). Of course, systems of individual insurance, discussed in the next chapter, should provide *no* systematic redistribution, and this has led policy makers to continue to experiment with variations in the structure of social insurance programs in attempting to attain redistributive ends.

The unsatisfactory functioning of social insurance programs has led countries to examine private provision in more detail. This is examined in the next chapter, where it is suggested that, although fully funded private schemes offer the prospect of long-run financial viability (albeit with very limited scope for systematic redistribution), the transition arrangements are problematic. A second route, illustrated by Australia and to an extent by the United Kingdom, is the move toward income-tested benefits. Although such an approach appears explicitly redistributional, and has proved to be a means of limiting social security expenditure, the incentive effects again often generate arbitrary differences in rates of return (as illustrated in table 4.8) stemming from behavioral distortions. The consequences for savings and labor-supply behavior and for the structure of the capital market are often adverse.

Thus, there is thus no straightforward solution to the problem of how to finance pensions within an aging population. This change in population structure has revealed the defects of many existing social security programs in starker detail. By provoking reforms and attempts to place such schemes on a sounder financial footing, population aging may have proved a blessing in disguise.

Private Pension Plans in the Demographic Transition

Most countries have developed social security programs to replace relatively primitive private schemes of insurance (mostly against disability, as opposed to old age *per se*), but some countries (notably Canada, the United States, the United Kingdom, the Netherlands, Japan, Singapore, Australia, and New Zealand) have also developed private-company-provided pension schemes in parallel to social security. These private schemes will provide a significant and possibly predominant share of retirement income for their workforces in the future.

In the United Kingdom, benefits from employed-operated pension schemes are the primary source of income in retirement for an increasing fraction of successive retirement cohorts. Between 1979 and 1990, the amount of gross income from private pensions received by those over the state pensionable age doubled in real terms to around 25 percent of average income (half of income for covered individuals), while social security income increased by only 17 percent and income from earnings among this age group fell by 8 percent (Dilnot et al. 1994). And Fry et al. (1985) calculate that annual benefit payments by such schemes will increase fivefold to almost £40 billion (in constant 1990 prices) by the year 2024. But while pensioners will typically receive a greater share of income from such schemes, membership in company schemes among workers peaked two decades ago at around 55 percent, and is now falling, especially among younger workers.

Table 5.1 shows the total assets of private pension plans as a proportion of GDP in several countries where private-sector plans are important. The proportions vary among countries as a result of differences in tax treatment of reserves and coverage. Among those countries with large shares in GDP, the absolute size of investments is considerable: in the United Kingdom, assets of pension funds were

Table 5.1
Assets or private pension plans in selected OECD countries as percentage of GDP.
Source: Davies 1995, table 3.2 (excluding life insurance assets).

	1970	1980	1990
Australia	10	9	19
Canada	13	17	28
Denmark	5	7	15
Germany	2	2	3
Japan	0	2	5
Netherlands	29	46	77
United Kingdom	17	23	55
United States	17	24	43

worth over $US600 billion, in the Netherlands $US150 billion, and in the United States $US2900 billion by the end of 1991 (Davies 1995).

For other countries in Western Europe, and in other continents, where company-led provision has been slow to develop outside the public sector and among workers in financial institutions, there is also interest in private provision; not as a complement to social security, but as a *substitute* for it. Countries in Latin America, notably Chile but also including Mexico, Bolivia, and Colombia, are replacing "traditional" PAYG social security programs with partially or wholly privatized schemes that take the form of tax-subsidized individual retirement savings accounts (World Bank 1994). In Chile, assets of such plans accounted for a value equivalent to 40 percent of GDP in 1993.

Unlike PAYG social security programs, such savings accounts provide individual fully funded annuities, with pension levels wholly determined by the return on accumulated funds and individual characteristics (annuity rates). These *defined-contribution* (DC, or money purchase) pension accounts typically differ from company *defined-benefit* (DB) plans. In the latter, pension benefits are based on some formula related to (usually final) earnings and years of service. There is generally some cross-subsidization in DB plans from younger workers to older workers (given the accrual structure) and from lower-paid to higher-paid workers (because the latter tend to live longer)—a feature lacking in many DC plans.

Yet another trend has been observed in the United States, and increasingly in the United Kingdom: a switch within the employer-provided pension sector from DB plans to DC plans. DB-plan coverage of workers in the United States grew from 17 percent in 1940 to a peak of 52 percent in the early 1970s, but has since declined among private-sector workers (from 40 percent coverage at the peak to 31 percent in 1987). In 1975, 78 percent of pension-scheme participants were in DB plans, but by 2000, according to a study commissioned by the US Department of Labor, this proportion will have fallen to 51 percent. And whereas before 1975 two-thirds of new primary plans were of the DB form, since 1975 80 percent have been of the DC type.[1]

In the United Kingdom, only 8 percent of pension plans were of the DC type in 1987 (and many of these were secondary plans to primary DB plans). Recent evidence suggests that DC coverage may have doubled. More revealing, perhaps, was a survey, undertaken by the Confederation of British Industry in 1994, that asked top executives in companies that provided pension plans about current and future pension provision. While 81 percent of their current primary pension plans were DB plans, 80 percent of the schemes introduced since 1988 were either "pure" DC plans or hybrid DB-DC plans. Looking ahead to the year 2000, only 32 percent envisaged operating a traditional final-salary-based DB plan. The majority of the executives predicted that they would offer hybrid DB-DC or even "pure" DC plans (Disney 1995; Disney and Stears 1996).

Among the other popular DC plans are 401(k) plans in the United States (retirement savings accounts, operated at the employer level, in which employers often match employees' contributions). Canada, the United States, and the United Kingdom also have seen the development of individual retirement savings accounts, known respectively as Registered Retirement Savings Plans, Individual Retirement Accounts, and Personal Pensions. Other countries, including Italy, are actively considering such plans as a supplement to social security.

Thus, there are several trends at work: from public to private provision, from defined-benefit to defined-contribution plans, and from company-provided plans to individual plans, with the emphasis varying among countries.

Why has private provision developed so rapidly in recent years? Should such provision be in the form of defined-benefit plans, or in the form of defined-contribution plans? Can private provision handle the "demographic transition" better than state-run social security programs, and if so are company-offered DB plans or DC plans such as individual retirement savings accounts the answer? These are important and lively questions of pension policy, and they form the basis of the discussion in this chapter. A few introductory remarks should motivate the discussion in subsequent sections.

The trend toward private provision has taken place against a backdrop of continued budgetary difficulties for governments in the 1980s and social security deficits (or rising payroll-tax rates in PAYG schemes). These trends have engendered an interest in privatization or contracting out of pension provision to the private sector. Indeed, if fiscal deficits are associated with high real interest rates, the associated high returns on asset holdings makes the achievement of target replacement ratios by the private sector in retirement that much easier. However, the transition from social security to private provision is far from simple; in particular, someone, whether the taxpayer, the private sector or external funders, has to bear the cost of the transition where there are unfunded commitments to pensioners left from the previous PAYG social security program. Consequently, the short-run impact of new privately provided pension instruments on national pension saving may be adverse, even if private saving is enhanced.

The transition from DB to DC provision within the private sector raises different issues. Just as the enlargement of public social insurance programs was associated with the development of state administration and of modes of effective tax collection, so it seems that the growth of company-based private provision was associated with the desire for a stable, longer-tenured, loyal workforce (Hannah 1986; Ghilarducci 1992). However, for pensions to be an attractive "incentive device" to both firms and workers requires a minimum proportion of younger workers within the pension scheme. As the workforce ages, the cost of this particular incentive structure to the company is increased, because funded schemes with benefits calculated by reference to the tenure and the salaries of older workers become more expensive to the firm and less attractive to younger workers who face an adverse ratio of pension accruals to contributions. Consequently, younger workers, and private pension providers themselves, may find DC plans more attractive. Therefore, it is natural to look first at the incentive structure that underpins company-led private provision of DB plans. Models have been constructed which are similar to the models of intertemporal choice of consumption discussed in chapter 3 but which instead examine the role of pensions in the firm's decision process as to the optimal level and allocation of production over time and in relation to the input of effort by workers. Such models must explain what motivates employers to offer, and workers to accept, wage profiles that involve deferred pay in the form of pensions rather than simple payment of a "spot" market wage equating with the marginal productivity of labor at each point in the working life.

In the well-known model of Lazear, deferred pay is closely bound up with the issue of mandatory retirement. DB plans can also be used as an early-retirement device.[2] The linkage of pay, pensions, and retirement is explored here with a case study of wage-tenure profiles and retirement strategy in Japan. The concept of pensions as deferred pay also impinges on the question of valuing pension rights when "legal" job rights are strictly limited, and this is also briefly discussed here. Finally, the impact of an aging population on this type of pay-pension structure is examined, and it is reiterated that the incentive structure is weakened in such circumstances. This may explain the decline in company-provided DB schemes of this kind in North America and the United Kingdom.

Section 5.2 considers the more recent trend toward DC pension provision, and especially toward individually provided savings accounts. This is a more radical departure from social security than private DB plans, for where there is an insurance motive for pension provision the switch from a publicly or privately provided DB plan to a group or individual DC plan seems to involve the participant in much greater risks. A crude formulation would argue that the "demographic transition" heightens uncertainty as to the adequacy of pension provision, and that institutions (government or private) have responded by transferring the risk to individuals. But this line of reasoning may be too simplistic: although the status of previous social insurance commitments is unclear, private DB plans also suffer from uncertainties.

5.1 Company Pension Plans in the Demographic Transition

Why Have Private Plans? Defined-Benefit Schemes as an Incentive Device

A motive for pension provision by organizations arises from the enhanced productivity and social benefits of long-term contracts between employers and employees. However, the two sides are often unable to write a legal employment contract that can bind both sides to any future level of effort or productivity. Thus, the time horizon of the contracting parties will typically extend beyond the duration of the legal employment contract. Taking the extreme case where both parties assess the value of an implicit contract between the worker and the employer through to retirement at known R, and denoting the employee's wage at time t as $w(t)$ and his or her marginal value product (MVP) as $v(t)$, then the employer requires for profit maximization that

$$\int_0^R w(t)e^{-it}dt = \int_0^R v(t)e^{-it}dt, \tag{5.1}$$

i.e., that the present value (PV) of lifetime earnings at the time of hiring, 0, discounted at rate i, equal the PV of the stream of MVPs. With lifetime commitment, optimality merely requires that equation 5.1 be satisfied for the sum of all values of t from 0 to R; there is no requirement for "spot-market" equilibrium (that is, an equality of $w(t)$ to $v(t)$ for every t).

But why should the firm or organization want to deviate from spot-market equilibrium in its lifetime wage offers? In the absence of piece rates, which would guarantee spot-market equilibrium, it is argued that the labor contract cannot fully specify the productivity, or MVP, per time period of the employee. An agency problem arises: although the employee is the agent of the employer in carrying out tasks, that worker has no incentive to maximize the amount of output or effort per time period as the employer would wish with a standard per-period wage contract.

Of course the employer will attempt to monitor effort, but the main weapon at the employer's disposal is the threat of dismissal. However, if wages in all firms are equated with expected MVP in each time period, the threat attached to dismissal is minimal if the employee can obtain a job at a similar wage elsewhere. Thus, the agency problem provides a potential motivation for moving away from spot-market equilibrium in the wage contract.

What wage profile would minimize the problem of maintaining worker effort? Lazear (1979, 1981) has explored this question. Some economists have argued that posting a cash "performance bond" at the start of the contract might deter shirking during the contract (Becker and Stigler 1974). A more practical suggestion that achieves the same result is to backload pay toward the end the contract, or indeed beyond its termination, and this is the basis of Lazear's model.

To illustrate the model, define the reservation wage, denoted $\hat{\omega}$, as the minimum wage that would induce the employee to remain with that employer and that equates the marginal wage to the marginal utility of leisure (MUL). We might assume that the MUL rises with age.

For the worker to remain with the present employer, in any period t, it must be the case that

$$\int_t^R w(t)e^{-it}dt = \int_t^R \hat{\omega}(t)e^{-it}dt. \tag{5.2}$$

That is, the prospective return from remaining with the firm at any tenure interval t must outweigh any outside offer that the worker may obtain.

To further refine the model, assume also that the date of retirement, R, is the date at which the employee reaches pensionable age in the social security program. At this point, the reservation wage (MUL) jumps as the income effect of social security receipt raises the threshold level of earnings needed to induce continued participation in the labor force—especially if there is some kind of income or earnings test attached to receipt of the state pension, as described in the case studies in chapter 4 (and later in chapter 7).

A diagrammatic format illustrates how the various parts of the model come together. The top graph in figure 5.1 elaborates the basic Lazear model. It is assumed that the "true" $v(t)$ profile (without shirking) approximates a quadratic function, with productivity declining in later years. Similarly, it is assumed that the $\hat{\omega}(t)$ (MUL) profile is increasing with age, with a step at R as explained previously, reflecting a greater preference for leisure with age. Finally, the employer's choice variable, the path of $w(t)$, is assumed to be upward sloping with age.

Is this an optimal $w(t)$ profile? Certainly, if equation 5.1 is satisfied, either the strict inequality in equation 5.2 is also satisfied or else the worker would not receive a better offer from another employer paying the spot rate; $\hat{\omega}(t)$ lies above $v(t)$ for all subsequent periods. Furthermore, the cost of reduced effort, or shirking, by the employee is intensified relative to the spot-market profile. This is because the loss from being caught and dismissed is raised by the backloading of pay. The employee might be tempted to shirk only where the probability of avoiding detection is high. Thus, this profile seems to satisfy the requirements of the model.

The problem for the employer offering $w(t)$ in the top graph in figure 5.1 is somewhat different, however. At point R, the worker would prefer to continue working because the inequality in equation 5.2 is also satisfied there because $w(R) > \hat{\omega}(R)$. Note that with spot-market equilibrium at R, i.e. $w(R) = v(R)$, the worker would voluntarily retire because $v(R) < \hat{\omega}(R)$ there and in all subsequent periods. Thus, to satisfy

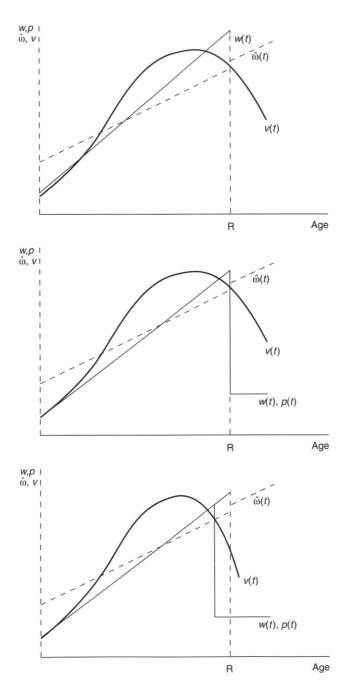

Figure 5.1
Some pay, productivity and pension profiles. Top: the basic Lazear case, mandatory retirement. Middle: pension as a supplement to an upward-sloping wage profile. Bottom:
early retirement as an option.

equation 5.1, firms with $w(\cdot)$ profiles of this type would insist on mandatory retirement at R, as Lazear (1979) argued.

Firms do not entirely backload pay, or pay a lump sum on retirement, presumably because there is an imperfect capital market, so that workers cannot borrow against future pension receipts. In addition the reputation or credibility of an employer's commitment (or indeed that of an employee's representative, such as a trade union) may be doubted. Extensive backloading of pay toward retirement gives a firm a stronger incentive to renege on the deal and dismiss an employee before the point at which severance and retirement pay are maximized. In this case it is the employer that cheats on the contract, rather than the employee. Insofar as employees are aware of this possibility (i.e., if there is a history of terminations), they will be unlikely to accept contracts promising extensive payments later in life, where there is greater uncertainty as to the reputation of the employer in holding to the implicit contract.

The pension case is illustrated by the second graph in figure 5.1, where employees receive less than their lifetime present value of the MVP during their working lifetime but receive a pension on retirement. In this case the equality that must be satisfied is

$$\int_0^R w(t)e^{-it}dt + \int_R^T p(t)e^{-it}dt = \int_0^R v(t)e^{-it}dt, \tag{5.3}$$

where $p(t)$ is the pension at time t between R (retirement) and T (death). Any combination of $w(t)$ and $p(t)$ that satisfies this formula should be satisfactory (Lazear 1985). Again, there is an equivalent concept of "spot-market equilibrium" in which the current wage *plus* the current accrued net additional pension cost to the firm is equated to the current MVP. However, evidence from the United States suggests that "spot-market equilibrium" of this form probably does not exist; there would have to be sharp discontinuities in either the MVP or the wage profile to offset observed discontinuities in pension accruals, for example at the first point at which pension benefits are vested.[3]

The profile in the middle graph is more attractive to the employer than that in the top one because the prospect of a pension enhances the propensity to retire at R. For the employee, too, the pension option is attractive. Since pension entitlements are accrued incrementally with job tenure, the employer cannot renege wholly on the pension commitment: even if the worker is dismissed before R, the pension scheme carries some obligation on the employer, usually backed by legislative protection, to retain an accumulated pension fund for that individual obtained from the return on contributions.[4]

The Aging Workforce, Pension Strategy, and Premature Retirement
Figure 5.1 is drawn so that older workers are currently less productive than their projected wages plus pension accruals require.[5] Thus, for an aging workforce there are conflicting forces at work. The gain to the firm of reneging on commitments (via premature dismissals or pre-retirement terminations) is that much greater where the number of workers with $v(R) < w(R)$ is higher. However, having already accepted a structure of pay plus deferred pay, older workers will lose current and future benefits by subsequently agreeing to another structure of pay and deferred pay, and will resist such offers by the firm. This, of course, explains why, where workforces are unionized, older workers take an active role in promoting "last in, first out" policies and the maintenance of fringe benefits such as company pension plans.[6]

One solution is for the firm to offer early retirement, either as an option within the plan or as a "window plan" (Lumsdaine et al. 1990) in periods of decreasing demand or "excessive" numbers of older workers. The last graph in figure 5.1 illustrates the case where such a provision would be desirable to the employer and chosen by the employee. Here the $v(t)$ function not only lies below the $w(t)$ function in the years approaching R; it also drops below the $\hat{\omega}(t)$ function before R. At the point where it makes this drop, both parties will prefer to terminate the employment contract in exchange for provision of a pension before the employee reaches the state pensionable age.

As drawn in the third graph, the early-retirement option is approximately actuarially fair. But there is evidence from the United States that early-retirement provisions are often advantageous to the employee: the rate of benefit reduction is often less than the real rate of return on accrued pension entitlements (Kotlikoff and Smith 1983). Although, this result seems to depend crucially on the rate of discount assumed (Kotlikoff and Wise 1985), the balance of the evidence, at least for the United States, is that "voluntary" retirement of this type, rather than mandatory retirement, is the dominant motivation for separations by older workers (see Quinn et al. 1990 and chapter 7 below).

There is, however, a danger in adopting an early-retirement strategy in the context of an aging workforce. Although individual workers approaching retirement will happily accept the offer under the conditions described in the third graph of figure 5.1, it is not apparent that such a plan is in the interests of younger workers, unless the option is offered on actuarially unfavorable rates and is thereby less attractive to potential participants: the early-retirement option, although reducing the net cost to the firm of employing these particular workers, involves a reduction in total product (if the retired workers still have a positive MVP) and a rise in the costs of the pension plan.

If the firm now hired replacement younger workers, paid them less than their current MVPs, and subsidized the early-retirement option from general cash revenues, existing younger workers would remain unaffected. But demographic trends make it hard to find new younger workers, or a higher wage may be required in order to induce them to work for the firm in the changing demographic structure. In any event, one response of the firm is likely to be to use the pension scheme itself to finance the early-retirement option, at least in part. This means that pension contribution rates will rise.

Rising contribution rates generate an intergenerational redistribution within the pension plan. All workers now face higher contribution rates, with the prospective benefit rates unchanged. For workers nearing retirement, the prospect of early retirement (if available) or the possibility of additional "windows" in the future may outweigh the cost. However, for younger workers, if future benefits are discounted, the costs of transfers to current plan members may be substantial, especially if the present early-retirement option was not foreseen.

The consequences of such plans would be alleviated if contribution rates at different ages reflected marginal benefit accruals. Typically, however, contributions are proportionate to earnings while benefit accruals are "backloaded" (that is, in general, they accrue faster to older workers). Figure 5.2 illustrates some work that calculates these pension-accrual structures by age for a large sample of workers, using data from the United Kingdom.[7]

Figure 5.2 focuses on a single case: a woman working in a clerical job who joins a defined-benefit pension scheme at the start of her career, at age 20 (the vesting period in Britain is generally a maximum of 2 years), and whose pension entitlements are based on years of service time multiplied by earnings in the last year of pension-scheme tenure. There are several possible methods of valuing pension rights (accruals) for current workers. The V^L measure in figure 5.2 is derived by the methodology of Bulow (1982), who argues that pension accruals should be calculated on the "legal" basis that job rights do not extend beyond the current period. The V^F measure is based on the converse

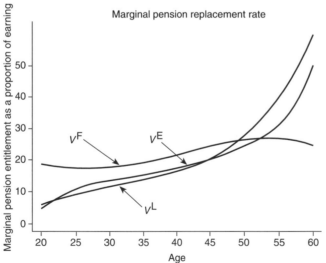

Figure 5.2
Alternative measures of pension accrual, United Kingdom. Source: Disney and
Whitehouse 1996.

expectation that the worker will survive to retirement in the same
job, and is thus the closest measure to a "lifetime implicit contract"
measure of pension tenure. Finally, the V^E measure is based on an
estimated hazard for each employee of pension-scheme termination:
the measure calculates, at each age, the expected wage and the expected probability of terminating membership of the pension scheme

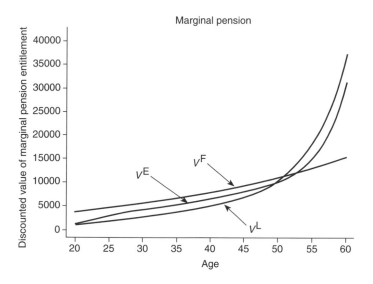

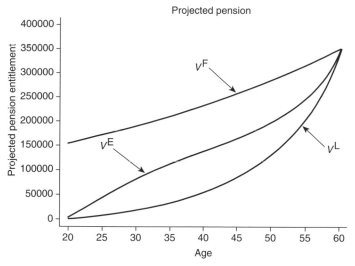

in each future period, and then weighs the period-by-period final wages by the termination probabilities to obtain an expected-value measure of the final wage.

Using the Bulow or "legal" measure, benefits are highly backloaded: each year brings longer tenure and higher "last" earnings, discounted back from retirement by one less year. Conversely, the "lifetime contract" measure is the least backloaded, because the worker is already discounting benefits at the expected final salary on retirement, which is likely to be very much higher. (In the "accrued pension" measure, final earnings are multiplied by actual years of service at each point in time, in the "projected benefit" measure by total expected years of service.) The tenure-weighted V^E measure of course lies somewhere in between, although an extra year's service, by affecting future survival probabilities, may cause the marginal accrual to lie outside the bounds of the V^L and V^F measures.

The standard summary measure described in the literature (where an explicit V^E measure is not usually calculated) is the marginal pension accrual as a fraction of current earnings: the marginal pension replacement rate depicted in the lower left panel of figure 5. 2. With a typical total contribution of 20 percent, it can be seen that the V^F measure is roughly tracked by the contribution rate: the young worker is discounting prospective benefits at her final salary, and marginal accruals roughly reflect marginal contributions. But the other measures, including the preferred V^E measure, are backloaded: the younger worker is facing a marginal contribution rate that exceeds the marginal accrual rate until (perhaps) her mid forties. Given this backloading, younger workers may perceive themselves as getting a "worse deal" in a defined-benefit scheme than older workers, especially if they share the burden of temporary early-retirement plans stemming from stochastic shocks or from the age structure of the workforce. Early-retirement measures imply transfers between generations within the pension scheme. A majority voting system within the pension scheme with an aging workforce will imply that the preferences of younger workers are discounted. However, if younger workers have the option of exiting (as in the United Kingdom, where they can buy an individual Personal Pension instead) or simply joining a firm with a younger workforce, then there may be serious problems for the viability of defined-benefit schemes when the workforce contains a growing preponderance of older workers and retirees.

This scenario may be too extreme for several obvious reasons. Younger workers will themselves be older workers one day; they may support early-retirement policies as a way of freeing senior job slots for themselves—the improved career prospects outweighing the higher pension costs. A company sponsoring a pension plan is unlikely, too, to allow a steady erosion of its younger members, and might seek to change the wage profile, the pension accrual profile, or the age structure of pension contributions. However, all these moves may erode the incentive provided by the existence of the pension scheme; hence an aging workforce may provide the impetus for significant changes in the form of company pension plans, with alternatives such as defined-contribution plans looking more attractive.

Mandatory Retirement and Pension Provision in Japan: An Illustration of the Lazear Model?

Seniority-based wage profiles and "lifetime employment"

Japan is often deemed to be the classic case of an economy in which, at least in the "core" sectors, companies have utilized a commitment to lifetime employment contracts and an age-related wage structure to achieve an above-average rate of productivity growth. There has been some dispute as to whether the origins of the Japanese system of industrial organization, known as *nenko,* are culturally specific or a postwar response to certain economic conditions (Jacoby 1979; Gordon 1985). Indeed, some commentators, such as Koike (1988), dispute the alleged uniqueness of the Japanese system. Nevertheless, the impact of aging on the Japanese economy offers a potential case study of the issues raised in the context of the Lazear model discussed here.

Do Japanese employees exhibit above-average durations of job tenure, and wage profiles based to a greater extent on seniority than other countries? What is the incidence of company pension coverage in Japan? Do Japanese companies therefore utilize mandatory retirement in the manner suggested by the Lazear model? And how is the Japanese system of work organization affected by the rapid aging of the workforce and the growing number of elderly people?

Data for the early 1970s (Koike 1988) show that Japanese companies, especially larger ones, clearly tilted their wage profiles toward older workers; at least until those workers were in their early fifties. For white-collar workers, as figure 5.3 shows, the differences in cross-section age-earnings profiles between Japan and some major European countries are not apparent. "Medium-size" Japanese companies (10–99 employees) and French companies exhibit the steeper cross-section age-wage profiles; West German and "large" Japanese companies (1000 or more employees) are little different and exhibit a slower rise in pay with age. What is perhaps significant is the much sharper fall in pay with age in the 50–60 age bracket in Japan than in the other countries.

In contrast, figure 5.4 reveals clear discrepancies between the seniority-based profiles of Japanese companies and those of the European Western countries among blue-collar workers, especially in "large" Japanese firms. For Japanese companies, cross-section earnings

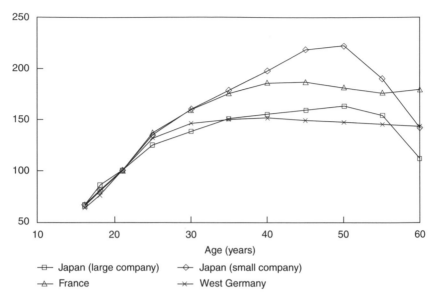

Figure 5.3
White-collar age-wage profiles (wage index, with age 21–24 = 100). Source: Koike 1988, figure 1.2.

peak some 10 years later than those for France and West Germany. Here, at least, there is strong evidence for a specific Japanese adherence to seniority-based wage profiles.

The greater use of seniority-based pay in Japan among blue-collar workers may play a part in explaining the faster growth of labor productivity, via the incentive mechanism posited by Lazear, but it is only part of the story. The sharp downturn in the cross-section age-wage profile for the 50+ age group remains to be explained in the context of the Lazear model. We also need to look at evidence as to relative job tenures, and as to provision of mandatory retirement.

Job tenure

Data in Koike 1988 suggest that average job tenures are longer in Japan than in other countries, but that this arises from a lower proportion of short spells: among blue-collar males in the 1970s, 34 percent of employees had been with their company less than 4 years, compared with 56 percent in West Germany, 52 percent in the United States, 48 percent in France, 46 percent in Germany, and 45 percent in Britain. On the other hand, there is little evidence of "lifetime jobs"; according to Gordon (1985), only 30–40 percent of those hired by Japanese companies

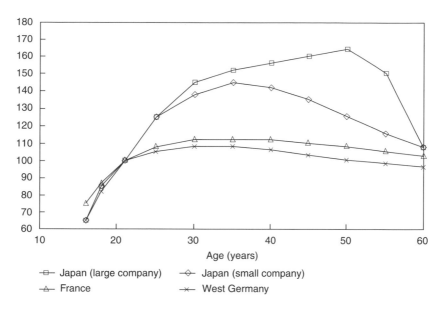

Figure 5.4
Blue-collar age-wage profiles (wage index, with age 21–24 = 100). Source: Koike 1988, figure 1.1.

were still in their posts 12 years later. The proportion in the 20+ years category of job tenure is lower in Japan than in West Germany or France (Koike 1988, table 2.1). Moreover, there have been periods in the recent past when even the largest "core" companies have utilized temporary and part-time employees on a large scale. For example, in 1960 one-third of Toshiba's workers were temporary or part-time, although by 1983 this proportion had fallen to 2.5 percent. Thus, while seniority-based wage profiles exist, evidence of prolonged job tenure in Japan is not so clear cut.

Mandatory retirement
The issue of mandatory retirement can now be considered in conjunction with the apparent breakdown of the positive age-wage relationship in Japan after age 50, as exhibited in figures 5.3 and 5.4. In fact these issues are related and at first sight appear to provide powerful support for the Lazear model of mandatory retirement. Large companies in Japan have traditionally had mandatory retirement at age 55. Koike's data for 1970 show that the separation rates among male manufacturing workers declined through the working life, but that for large companies almost half the workers departed at 55 (see figure 5.5).

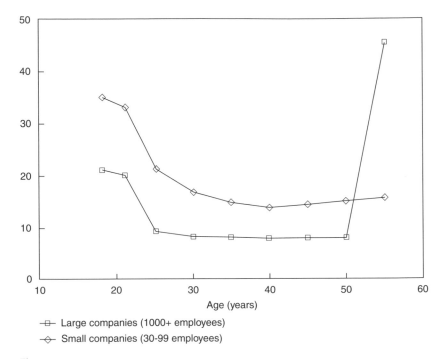

Figure 5.5
Separation rates (as percentage of age group in workforce), Japanese companies, 1970.
Source: Koike 1988, figure 2.1.

The fall in cross-section earnings from age 50 onward observed in figures 5.3 and 5.4 is not therefore a consequence of the breakdown of seniority-based pay within jobs, but is associated with workers moving to lower-paid jobs after retirement. Typically these are in other parts of the company or in companies associated with the original employer as suppliers or customers (Rebick 1993). Nevertheless, it appears that an increasing proportion of older workers have considerable difficulty obtaining jobs after separation. So involuntary separation is associated with seniority-based pay, as the Lazear model would predict, but older workers continue to participate in the labor market after mandatory retirement, either as job seekers or by working in lower-paying jobs. Indeed this is one reason why labor-force participation rates are much higher among the elderly in Japan than in other countries (see table 4.9): most people kept working well into their sixties, having been retired from their "primary" jobs in their mid fifties.

Recent trends suggest that this system of seniority-based pay and early mandatory retirement was specific to a particular historical period and to a particular age structure of the working population. As the average age of the workforce has increased, dissatisfaction has emerged with these consequences of the *nenko* system. Lower pay and higher unemployment rates among the increasing numbers of labor-force participants in their fifties and sixties enhance the prospect of greater social security burdens arising from the size of this cohort. The public debate over this in Japan has led to radical revisions in recent years. These will be described shortly, after a consideration of company pension plans in Japan (the additional incentive device posited by the Lazear model).

Company pension schemes

Several Japanese private-sector companies offer their employees company pensions in addition to seniority-based wages. As in the United Kingdom, the Japanese social security program offers both a flat-rate (lump-sum) component and an earnings-related component, with contracting out of the latter segment possible. Some Japanese companies have been content to imitate or slightly improve on the official formula for earnings-related additions in their plans, thereby gaining certain tax advantages on pension contributions. Indeed, the trend toward assimilation of company pension schemes into the overall system of social security has been especially pronounced among larger companies and in the last two decades.

Nevertheless, the traditional Japanese company pension provision has been somewhat different from the standard earnings-related indexed-annuity form taken by social security, especially among small and medium-size companies. In the late 1970s, roughly 11 million employees in the private sector were covered by company pension plans—roughly 40 percent of total private-sector employment. Of these, just under half were in "adjusted pension plans" (*Chosei-Nenkin*) which typically offered an annuity to death or a lump sum on retirement; the annuity value of the lump sum was close to that provided by the earnings-related component of the public pension scheme. Of some interest, however, were the "qualified pension plans" (*Tekikaku-Nenkin*) covering most of the remaining 11 million. These schemes offered two options: either a lump-sum retirement allowance or a fixed-term annuity, typically of 10 years but sometimes less. Only 10 percent offered an annuity to death (Yamaguchi 1981). Indeed, the lump-sum retirement allowance seems to have been the traditional mode of pension provision.

The existence of pension schemes that fail to offer a lifetime annuity is not consistent with the standard insurance rationale for pension provision, where longevity uncertainty is the primary motive for pension insurance. Presumably, however, the participant could choose to take the lump sum and invest in a variable-life annuity on the open market, although thereby incurring transaction costs and the risk of adverse selection inducing unfair annuity prices; a paternalist motive would imply that the pension provider should annuitize on behalf of the worker. The voluntary nature of such schemes and the favorable tax treatment of lump sums suggest that tax avoidance may have been one motivation for such payments, but there is also some support for the adjusted Lazear model of offering pay deferral as a means of discouraging shirking. (Opting not to take the pension would itself be a signal to the employer.)

Overall, however, it appears that the basis of the Japanese "system" in large companies, at least until the 1980s, comprised seniority-based pay, opportunities for saving at lower tax rates for a retirement lump sum through the company, and mandatory retirement at the relatively early age of 55 (albeit with widespread variation in companies' practices).

Revisions of work organization in light of labor-force aging

The proportion of the Japanese population aged 15–39 declined from 40.6 percent in 1975 to 34.7 percent in 1990; that aged 40–64 rose from 27.1 percent to 33.3 percent. Concern, especially, as to the growing number of workers aged 55+ has cast doubts on some traditional aspects of the *nenko* system. Suggestions for reform had already been voiced in the previous decade; for example, Shimada (1980) advocated (i) raising the mandatory retirement age above 55; (ii) in the light of suggestion i, flattening the age-earnings profile for workers above middle-age; and (iii) converting lump-sum retirement allowances (which had been eroded in relative value by nominal earnings growth) into standard pension annuities.

Significantly, the proportion of companies setting the age of mandatory retirement at 55 fell from 63.2 percent in 1968 to 23 percent in 1987, with 59 percent now retiring their employees at 60 or over and a further 16 percent planning to do so (Japan Institute of Labor 1988). In approximately the same period, the labor force participation rate of the over-60s has fallen by 10 percentage points, although still remaining at 36 percent for males in the 65+ category in 1988 (OECD 1990). Survey evidence also suggests some erosion of long job tenures: more workers want to change jobs, and productivity incentives are playing a greater part in the pay package.

Case studies of the process of adaptation to an aging workforce are also interesting. Inagami (1980) cites these two:

• Japanese Steel decides in 1981 to raise the mandatory retirement age to 60. They propose at the same time to extend the seniority-based wage system to employees aged 50 and over, but with a reduced seniority-based increment throughout the wage structure and with a reduced fraction of "seniority-based" to "job-related" pay in the basic wage (the ratio falling from 6:4 to 5:5). The weight of seniority (years of service) in the calculation of the retirement allowance would also be reduced.

• Matsushita Electric Industrial Co. announces in 1980 its "Ripe Old Age Plan," by which it will establish a separate "National Family Company" in which workers would work until 65, part-time if they wished. Individuals at age 55 can stay with the same job full-time until 60 (Matsushita having already increased mandatory retirement to 60 as early as 1972), move to the National Family Company, or take a retraining course.

The Matsushita example suggests that a paternalist approach to work organization in the context of workforce aging is not dead, although this particular response may be atypical. Nevertheless, the recent reaction to aging in the Japanese economy, including the reforms to the social security program described in chapter 4 and the changes in workplace organization described here, make Japan an interesting case study. In particular, it raises some doubts as to the feasibility of deferred pay as an incentive structure where workforces are aging. While the combination of a relatively youthful workforce, seniority-based wages, low quits, and early mandatory retirement from the postwar years to the mid 1970s in Japan was a prime example of the Lazear model in practice, the change in the average age of the workforce since that time cast doubt on the rationale for such incentive structures, irrespective of their financial viability, and this is illustrated by the changes described here.

Insurance Motives for Company Pension Schemes
In the simple model of equation 5.1, the employee is indifferent about his or her lifetime wage profile so long as the lifetime earnings stream can be guaranteed. However, the presence of earnings uncertainty and

the likelihood that an aging workforce is more averse to risk suggest that pensions may provide additional insurance—in this case, against earnings risk if pension calculations are based on "smoothing procedures" such as average earnings or if there are convexities in the benefit-earnings calculation (Samwick 1993).

Models that portray pensions as an incentive device, in particular some variants of the Lazear model, tend to ignore the insurance motive. An alternative view sees company pension schemes primarily as a form of saving, undertaken on behalf of the employee by the employer and giving the employee insurance against future uncertainty of income rather than as an incentive device. This might explain why defined-benefit plans sometimes contain features that are hard to reconcile with the incentive motive.[8]

The standard insurance rationale for employer-provided pensions concerns longevity risk when the market for individually purchased annuities is thin as a result of adverse selection, particularly when purchase of annuities is postponed until late in life and cannot be obtained at actuarially fare rates (Friedman and Warshasky 1988, 1990; Brugiavini 1993). Employer provision allows both pooling of risks and the lower transaction costs associated with collective provision.

But various other types of income uncertainty that might create a demand for employer-provided DB plans have been identified. Diamond and Mirrlees (1985) identify unknown future productivity of individuals as a major source of income uncertainty for both employer and employee. If later in his or her working life an employee reveals higher-than-expected productivity, there is a risk to the employer of that employee's going to another firm, whereas lower-than-expected productivity may incur unexpected income losses to both sides. Diamond and Mirrlees show that the combination of a wage less than marginal productivity in the earliest period and a pension that is (at least in part) not transferable to other employers may, in effect, provide insurance for both employers and employees.

A second type of income uncertainty stems from social security uncertainty. DB plans integrate social security into the calculation of benefits in over half of the private-sector plans in the United States (Merton et al. 1987) and in the United Kingdom (HMSO 1991a, table 7.3). Chapter 4 suggested that public pension plans are subject to frequent and abrupt changes. By integrating into and thereby offsetting these unexpected changes, pension schemes offer another insurance component. Bodie (1990) argues that such exigencies are best handled by the provision of DB plans, where the benefit formula can be adjusted, rather than DC plans, in which pension benefits are determined by fund performance.

Objectors to the view that DB plans exist primarily to provide insurance question whether such plans are necessarily superior to DC plans purchased individually or offered as a group plan by the employer. Proponents of pension plans as insurance sometimes assume that similar insurance cannot be obtained by individual employees. Such an assumption requires either the rather strong assumption that these individuals have no access to a capital market, as in Diamond and Mirrlees 1985,[9] or the perhaps more plausible argument that the employer can invest the funds at transaction costs lower than those individual employees would have to pay. However, even in the presence of adverse selection, market failure does not provide an explanation for DB plans *per se* as opposed to employer-provided plans in general.

The general assumption of capital-market imperfection would explain both the prevalence of pension schemes among large firms and firms with relatively uniform wage structures and the absence (until recently) of a well-developed individual annuity market. Company pension schemes "crowd out" independent pension provision. An obvious risk to an individual investor is investment risk in the market. Risk-averse individuals may prefer a known pension value from a DB scheme to any alternative, such as an individual DC plan, even when the latter on average outperforms the former in terms of expected return. But, as Bodie et al. (1988) point out, it is hard to find a feature of a DB plan that cannot be adequately replicated by a suitably constructed group DC plan, including a Lazear-type incentive structure.[10]

On the other side, there are potential risks attached to DB plans. The first is the risk of potential bankruptcy of pension funds. Although employers are in effect acting as financial intermediaries, this potential risk may be one reason why pension funds in the United States typically adopt more cautious investment strategies than would be predicted from the tax advantages of holding assets in the form of pension fund assets rather than taxable assets. Bodie (1990) describes private pension funds as "participating annuities" providing a guaranteed minimum benefit supplemented by increments at the discretion of the management (which may, of course, include employees' representatives among the trustees). Even so, the assigning of employees' rights in DB plans is sometimes fraught with difficulties absent from the more transparent DC valuation procedures. This issue has emerged in the context of takeovers in which control of pension funds is assumed and in the celebrated Maxwell pension fund debacle in the United Kingdom.[11]

A second source of risk arises where DB-plan benefits are not fully portable between jobs and where there is thus a discrete probability of involuntary job separation resulting in lower pension benefits. Although some penalty attached to transferability is justified in the Diamond-Mirrlees model, the consequences for final pension benefits of incomplete portability of DB-plan benefits is usually considerable.[12] In a simulation model constructed by Brugiavini and Disney (1995), the utility-maximizing individual choice between a DB plan and a generic DC plan, given identical expected values, is determined by the spread of potential rates of return relative to the (individual-specific) probability of job separation. Depending on the spread of investment risk, the risk of job separation, and the timing of the revelation of information as to those risks over the lifetime, either holding a DB plan, holding a DC plan, or holding a combination may be optimal.

A potential source of risk attached to DB plans is inflation risk, assuming that DC plans can always purchase indexed securities. In neither the United Kingdom nor the United States do DB plans provide full inflation-proofing. At first sight, this is a puzzle in the pensions-as-insurance story. Bodie (1990) speculates that this omission may stem from any or all of the following:

money illusion among employees

underestimation of anticipated inflation

the high costs of incorporating full indexation into pension schemes (implying either higher contribution rates or considerably lower pension starting values)

the proposition that individuals hold other, superior hedges against inflation, such as property.[13]

Bodie also notes that many schemes nevertheless provide *ad hoc* indexation when inflationary pressures are acute, irrespective of previously agreed limitations to indexation in the pension contract. Allen et al. (1986) point out that this strategy might represent a form of insurance acceptable to the employer and employee, so long as there is a positive covariance between fund rates of return and inflation.

Even so, the evidence of Allen et al. shows that the degree of indexation falls well below full post-retirement price indexation in the United States. The experience of the United Kingdom, where full indexation of the Guaranteed Minimum Pension in contracted-out schemes has been guaranteed by the government but where private pension providers and the public sector have bargained over who bears the remainder of the cost, would suggest that cost, rather than misperceptions of future inflation or the existence of overindexed assets, lies behind the reluctance of private providers to offer full indexation.

While "typical" final-salary DB pension plans provide insurance against longevity risk and, by suitable averaging procedures, the possibility of at least partial insurance against earnings uncertainty, the problems of incomplete portability and inadequate indexation procedures have been widely cited. Of course, DB schemes could in principle be reconstituted to provide fully lifetime-earnings-averaged price indexed annuities, at the expense of any salient incentive features. These are precisely the features that are held to be so attractive in DC plans, which are fully portable, are not intrinsically weighted toward long-tenure, high-final-salary members (Samwick and Skinner 1993; Disney and Whitehouse 1994), and can provide fully indexed annuities if required. As such, the distinction between DB and DC plans in theory is somewhat artificial; the practical differences arise from plan design rather than any intrinsic features of DB or DC plans.

The traditional argument against DC plans is that they directly expose the participant to investment risk (capital-market uncertainty), as annuitization will expose the purchaser to fluctuations in asset values. In contrast, it is asserted that in DB plans the provider insures the participant against any direct risk by pre-committing to a set benefit payment (Davies 1995). The possibility of "immunizing" DC plans, particularly against downside investment risk, is therefore an important consideration if societies are increasingly to make use of such plans. To the extent that this issue can be resolved, DC plans may provide a secure source of retirement income in the future without the inequalities in provision that arise in the typical DB formula.[14]

Aging and the insurance role of pensions

There is no clear *a priori* theorization as to how the aging of the workforce impinges on the extent and the nature of pensions as insurance. An aging workforce tends to be more risk averse on average, and to demand more insurance. However, for the reasons discussed earlier, an aging population may render backloaded DB plans harder to sustain. Borrowing by governments to finance social security deficits and a greater demand for pension insurance within an aging population,

will tend to affect the "price" at which this insurance can be bought
(i.e. capital-market values). But as DB plans mature and coverage stabilizes, the net flow of funds into existing pension schemes may ebb. If, at
the same time, continued budgetary difficulties associated with PAYG
social security systems generate an oversupply of government securities (bonds), interest rates on the latter may go up. The consequences
of a shift in the bond-equity mix for the capital market depends on the
degree of international substitutability of equities (stocks) and bonds
(Davies 1995). The issue is further complicated where the optimal
holdings of bonds and equities might differ between DC and DB portfolios, although no clear-cut predictions, either theoretical or empirical, have emerged in the literature.

High real returns are attractive to purchasers of DC-type instruments, although the combination of events outlined above may generate a shift in emphasis from high capital gains toward higher yields.
But, given the higher demand for funded pension insurance in aging
populations and the internationalization of capital markets, it is hard
to believe that aging populations will have adverse effects on particular capital markets, notwithstanding the macroeconomic considerations described in chapter 3. In general, the impact of aging
populations on capital markets, especially in the context of a general
shift from pay-as-you-go to funded pensions, and from DB to DC
plans, is an underresearched issue on which no clear conclusions
have emerged.

5.2   Can Pension Privatization Restore the Fiscal Balance?

The Pressures to Privatize Pensions
The 1980s saw increasing international interest in substituting private
pension provision for PAYG social security programs. The dynamic
behind this shift in attitude is not hard to uncover. In most countries,
the payroll taxes associated with PAYG provision rose steadily. These
rises stemmed not just from population aging but also from the Ponzi-
scheme nature of social insurance, whereby each generation would
promise itself higher real pension benefits on retirement despite an
aging population.[15] Not surprisingly, there have proved to be limits to
this process. There are adverse political and economic consequences
to raising contribution rates—politically, once these are perceived to
be another form of personal taxation, and economically, where, in an
increasingly competitive world economy with mobile international

capital, high labor costs in a particular country can deter inward investment. The alternative—allowing cumulative social security deficits—is equally unappetizing. Furthermore, the 1980s debate took place against a backdrop of governments specifically committed to tax cuts, such as the Reagan and Thatcher administrations, and "tax rebellions" in Sweden and in other countries previously noted for high spending and high taxation.

In these changed political circumstances, and given the liberalization of international capital movements, PAYG financing of social security would have been under pressure in any event. However, pension commitments made at an earlier time, when demographics were more favorable and contributors died earlier, now had to be fulfilled. Rising replacement ratios associated with growing numbers of elderly put pressure on tax rates. In turn, a vicious circle of higher contributions leading to greater evasion led many PAYG schemes toward unacceptable tax levels, and notionally funded public schemes to insolvency, in a number of countries.

Once this cycle of rising claimants, declining numbers of contributors, lax supervision, and tax evasion becomes established, the decline in viability can become spectacular. In Chile, for example, which became a path-breaking "pension privatizer," the ratio of contributors to beneficiaries fell from 8:1 in 1960 to 2:1 in 1980 (Santamaria 1992). In Turkey, a country with a relatively young age profile, the main pension scheme for employees saw this ratio fall from 3.5:1 to 1.8:1 in 10 years. And, as was suggested in the discussion of Italy in chapter 4, Turkey's experience is not atypical of the Mediterranean countries. Finally, the collapse of enterprise-based pension schemes in many of the formerly communist countries of central and eastern Europe have led to an urgent search for new modes of pension provision—a search that has also been pursued, though less dramatically, in the countries of North America and northern Europe, where the pressure on social security financing has grown more slowly.

The move toward private pension provision has varied in extent and in form between countries. One of the most dramatic transformations to a private pension system occurred in Chile after 1980; this transition, which has served as a model for several other countries, has been discussed extensively and not uncritically. Other countries have attempted to introduce funded retirement savings accounts as a complement to existing PAYG schemes, either on a voluntary basis (as with Individual Retirement Accounts in the United States) or as an additional compulsory forced saving component to the pension scheme (as in Mexico and in several other countries). In yet other cases, private pensions have been offered as an alternative to membership in a public PAYG scheme. In these countries, the provision of contracting out is used to encourage this public-private mix of provision: the United Kingdom is an illustration of this model, with Argentina as a very recent convert to this type of scheme. In addition to the Chilean case, therefore, it is useful to focus on this "mixed model" in order to see how an aging population can be accommodated.

Although these moves to privatize social security have been associated with adverse trends in dependency ratios in social security programs, it is not immediately apparent that private pension schemes *per se* offer a solution to population aging. The most naive case for such a policy envisages the government eliminating public expenditure by "privatizing" its pension obligations, so reducing the "burden of aging" on the public budget. As we shall see from case studies of Chile and the United Kingdom, however, the short-run budgetary effects of pension privatizations are generally adverse; the handling of unfunded liabilities (as in Chile) or the tax subsidies required to induce greater private provision (as in the United Kingdom) often outweigh any budgetary savings on pension expenditure in the near future.[16] In Argentina, which is adopting a similar form of contracting out in individual savings accounts, it is argued that losses in contribution revenue stemming from cuts in payroll-tax rates can be offset by increased payroll-tax revenues stemming from reduced evasion. This may be plausible in Argentina, where total payroll taxes on employees and employers come to 49 percent of gross salary (Braun et al. 1993). But the subtler *general* argument for privatization is that it transfers budgetary obligations from the future to the present; in other words, if the country in question is running a budget surplus and envisages that in future, with an aged population, the budget will be in deficit, the intertemporal transfer of tax payments may be worthwhile.

A potential for large intergenerational transfers arises through the switch from PAYG to fully funded social security, irrespective of privatization. As was mentioned in chapter 3, a switch to full funding might be attractive if real fund returns could be maintained in the face of falling population growth by simple application of the Aaron-Samuelson "rule." But a shift to full funding does not require privatization as such; it could be argued that the state can simply decide that it intends to provide social security benefits from an accumulated fund rather than by PAYG, with the buildup of the fund requiring higher contribution rates in the transition. The lesson from countries that have adopted this approach is, however, that accumulated public funds may be dissipated in public consumption or in transfers to other budgetary headings; the state cannot be relied on to discipline itself across the budget as a whole when it commits itself to full funding of the pension scheme.[17]

A further point is that privatization is generally associated with a transition to DC rather than DB pension provision—that is, to pension values dependent on fund performance rather than some formula linked to years of contribution and to earnings. Although in practice the state might offer some degree of underwriting of a substitute funded pension scheme if it replaced a PAYG scheme, the implication still remains that individual scheme members will be exposed to investment risk, and a guarantee of a fixed replacement ratio cannot be sustained. Indeed, a flexible replacement ratio is an obvious means of handling the demographic transition, as was illustrated in chapter 2.

In summary: Privatization has been seen as a transition strategy to a fully funded system, with particular advantages to countries where the population growth rate is falling. Furthermore, the associated switch to DC pension provision liberates governments from obligations to maintain unsustainable replacement ratios. An added bonus arises if the privatization increases aggregate savings rates and encourages the development of an emergent capital market in situations where capital accumulation is constrained by an imperfect capital market. These considerations have loomed as large as narrower considerations as to choice of pension provision in many countries. It is useful to appraise the experience of these policies in two very different policy environments: Chile and the United Kingdom.

Pension Privatization in Chile

Chile, in 1924, was one of the first countries to institute social insurance. It was intended that a social security fund be built up initially to finance later commitments, but in fact inflation eroded the social security fund, which had been invested in unindexed bonds and mortgages (Santamaria 1992). Consequently, the scheme operated largely on a PAYG basis. As with several other Latin American countries, population aging took place steadily after 1945: the proportion of the population aged 65 or over grew steadily from 6.9 percent in 1950 to 8.5 percent in 1985 (it is projected to rise to 9.6 percent in the year 2000 and 14.2 percent in the year 2020; see UN 1991). But from the 1960s on there was a fourfold increase in the ratio of beneficiaries to contributors, which could not be put down entirely to aging. The fragmentation of the pre-reform social insurance system, with a multiplicity of plans for different sectors of the economy, led to widespread abuse; beneficiaries obtained pensions from several different plans and targeted the plans that offered the most generous benefits or the most lax eligibility conditions (for example, public-sector workers generally required significantly fewer years of contributions than private-sector workers). Yet the majority of beneficiaries received little more than the minimum pension, which was also eroded by high inflation.

Despite low benefits for many workers and a lack of inflation indexation, contribution revenues grew slowly as earnings were underreported and contributions were evaded. Government subsidies to the social security scheme, which already accounted for 3 percent of GDP in 1980, were projected to increase tenfold by the year 2000 (Santamaria 1992; Barrientos 1993). Instead of attempting to reform the system in a PAYG context, the conservative regime decided to take the much more radical step of replacing the system with a scheme of private individual savings accounts.[18]

The 1981 pension reform

The basis of the post–1980 scheme is a system of individual retirement savings accounts instead of a state-operated PAYG scheme. Each individual employee within the new scheme has a pension savings account in one of a number of newly formed private institutions known as Administradoras de Fondos de Pensiones (AFPs), fourteen of which existed in 1990.[19] Employees' contributions, which must be a minimum of 10 percent of eligible earnings, are collected by employers and paid into the individual employee's chosen AFP. Individuals can not only choose their AFP, but can switch between them; typically 10 percent of employees have changed AFP each year (Vittas and Iglesias 1992). Voluntary contributions can be made above this amount, but employees must also pay premia for disability and life insurance (rates for which vary among the AFPs) and an additional variable commission fee (which amounts to, on average, 3 percent of eligible salary per annum).

Pension benefits can be taken in a number of ways. Retiring members can use the fund to buy a lifetime annuity from an insurance company, or can make scheduled withdrawals from the fund, or a combination of the two. The level of the scheduled withdrawal is determined by the AFP regulator on the basis of the projected life span of the contributor and his or her eligible dependents and the projected rate of return on the fund. The advantages of scheduled withdrawal are that it recovers some funds in the event of the contributor's premature death and that its transaction costs may be lower than those associated with annuitization; the drawback is that scheduled withdrawal does not provide insurance against longevity risk. In addition, the contributor can withdraw a lump sum at any time if the remaining fund is sufficiently large to provide a projected 70 percent replacement ratio thereafter.

The pension scheme is fully indexed to inflation, and the pension benefit is underwritten by the state in that the benefit is guaranteed to be a fraction of the minimum wage (the fraction determined by the inflation adjustment of the unit of account in the pension scheme). In general, employees can retire at 65 (men) or 60 (women) on the basis of the annuity provided by the savings account, or earlier if the annual pension reaches 50 percent of the individual's average indexed wage during the previous 10 years of employment.

Calculations by Vittas and Iglesias suggest that, if the retirement period is double the working period and if there are price-indexed pensions and an "excess yield" of real return over earnings growth of 3 percent, then a replacement ratio of 55–60 percent can be guaranteed for a typical age-earnings profile with 10 percent of eligible earnings invested.[20] Gillion and Bonilla (1992) calculate a somewhat lower replacement ratio of 44 percent, but with an "excess yield" of only 2 percent and with the addition of a survivor's pension. They also point to the adverse effects of periods of unemployment. These are, of course, straightforward spreadsheet calculations; the important point is that the system requires rather high real rates of return to achieve a pension of at least half of final earnings with full inflation protection. In fact, real returns averaged 12 percent per annum over the first decade of the system's existence, and adequate replacement ratios could easily be achieved if this decade's performance were to continue.[21]

The transition

A key issue in moving from PAYG social security to a scheme of individual savings accounts is how to enact the transition.

One question concerns the move from a scheme of joint contributions by employee and employer to one in which individual employees bear the whole contribution. At the time of the Chilean reform, the government required employers to grant an immediate wage increase equal to the cost of the new minimum pension contribution plus the associated survivors', disability, and health insurance, totaling 18 percent. In principle this implied a higher net wage, since participants were no longer obliged to pay their payroll contribution to the old PAYG scheme. In practice, it seems likely that employees did not receive full compensation, as subsequent wage increases were held down and new entrants to the labor market probably received lower net wages than they otherwise would have.

A second question concerns whether privatization of this kind should be optional or compulsory. Employees covered by the old system (around 75 percent of the total workforce) were given the option to remain in the old system or join the new one within 5 years (new entrants had to join the new system). But employees who chose to remain in the old system now had also to bear the employers' contribution cost as well as their own component. Almost 90 percent of employees transferred to the new scheme. However, although scheme contributors have been rising in absolute numbers, the *proportion* of affiliated members of the new schemes who are actually contributing has been falling (Vittas and Iglesias 1992; Barrientos 1993). Since evasion was widespread in the previous system, it is hard to know whether a switch to the option of individual accounts increases participation in a pension scheme.

The most thorny transition question, however, concerns the unfunded liabilities remaining from the previous scheme. Any switch from PAYG to full funding will, of course, involve higher contributions or budgetary transfers. Pressure to privatize pensions generally stems from problems of financing, but the immediate effect of such policies is to worsen the general budgetary position. In the case of Chile, since contributions were no longer being made on behalf of existing pensioners, and workers already in the workforce had acquired rights under the previous system which would mature in due course, there were immediate adverse budgetary implications. Fortunately Chile was running a budget surplus of almost 5 percent in 1980, notwithstanding the growth of the unfinanced obligations of the existing social security program. The pension reform moved the social security "budget" into further deficit, reaching a peak of 7 percent of GDP in 1984. The overall budget concurrently moved from surplus into deficit in 1983, the deficit peaking at just over 3 percent of GDP in 1985, and then gradually returned to approximate balance by 1990. Nevertheless, it is projected that the deficit in the social security budget will persist for up to 20 years.

The counterargument is that creation of savings accounts will generate private-sector savings which can in part finance the deficit—particularly if the social security reform is associated with an increase in other investment opportunities, such as a general privatization program attractive to investors. Some evidence is provided in figure 5.6, which shows that the private-sector savings rate in Chile rose from 0.2 percent in 1981 to 12.7 percent in 1989 while the public-sector savings rate halved in that period. There is no evidence of any trend in national savings as a whole, however. Investment also slumped in the middle of the 1980s, but it picked up rapidly toward the end of the decade.[22]

The means of transferring existing pension rights under the old scheme for current employees was to issue "recognition bonds" that could be redeemed on retirement. The value of each individual's bonds

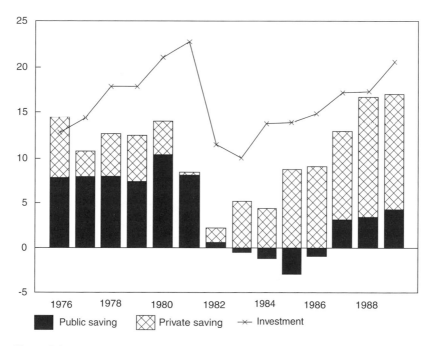

Figure 5.6
Saving and investment (percentage of GDP), Chile. Source: data from International Monetary Fund and Central Bank of Chile, cited in table 4 of Santamaria 1992.

was calculated at the time of the transfer to be equal to his or her accrued pension rights under the old scheme. These bonds accumulate real interest at 4 percent per annum, a reasonable rate of return by international standards but low by the performance of the capital market in Chile in the subsequent decade (Vittas and Iglesias 1992). This step of issuing frozen or "recognition" bonds has been followed by many of Chile's imitators in Latin America; in some cases the transitional arrangements have required that the bonds be invested in specific ventures such as new privatizations. In some cases, open-market trading of such bonds for other financial assets is permitted. The consequences of such policies for private savings rates, and ultimately for retirement incomes, are not yet clear.

The regulatory system

Compulsion is a key issue in pension policy. Membership in the new pension scheme (or the old scheme, for existing workers) is compulsory for employees and optional for the self-employed. Although there are monitoring difficulties in enforcing contribution conditions on the self-employed, it might be assumed that the attractiveness of the scheme is sufficient to encourage participation among the self-employed, who are presumed to have some financial awareness from their business activities. However, it is argued that in the case of any group for which membership is compulsory a sound regulatory structure must be in place to guarantee prudent and profitable investment.[23]

Most authorities agree that the new Chilean pension scheme is tightly regulated. Only authorized companies are allowed to participate in the system, and these are overseen by a regulatory superintendent. Each AFP is set up as a joint stock company with a minimum required capital according to size of membership. They are required to maintain "investment reserves" of 1 percent of total assets which are utilized as part of an interesting form of investor protection. The assets of an AFP are valued daily. If real returns on any given fund are twice the average among AFPs (or 2 percentage points above the average real return—whichever is the higher) over the past 12 months, the AFP has to place the whole of the difference in a profitability reserve. If the reverse is true, and the AFP is underperforming and the profitability reserve is exhausted, the AFP must draw on its investment reserve. So far, the further question of exhaustion of the investment reserve has not arisen; indeed, the "spread" of returns has tended to narrow over time. Under another provision, an AFP must also adjust its reserve position if the return halves between years, as happened between 1991 and 1992.

Of more significance has been the profitability of the AFPs, which is determined by their success in attracting members, by the profitability of their investment reserves, and by their commission charges (which have been partially regulated; for example, closure fees cannot be levied to preclude exit by members from below-average performers). Fee charges are typically flat rate and may include opening charges; initial concern that they were excessive has tended to lessen as funds have built up and commission charges have declined. As a percentage of wages, charges have evened out at around 2 percent; as a proportion of overall contributions, however, they have averaged 15 percent. Despite these high charges, at least in the first 5 years, AFPs typically made losses, although their funds earned high real returns. However, they subsequently have made very high real returns (calculated on their own assets), which, it is argued, should attract new entrants to the private pension industry and thereby force down charges. There is evidence that charges as a proportion of fund assets are falling steadily (World Bank 1994, figure 6.1) and that there are new entrants to the industry (see note 19).

Finally, the investment structure of the AFPs is tightly regulated, with limits on the proportions of the portfolio that can be invested in various types of assets. These include limits on the share of assets held in any given instrument, in any given issue of any given instrument, and in any given institution. Again the shares are monitored by the AFP Superintendent, and the limits have been altered in line with availability of opportunities for investment over time.

Is the Chilean model appropriate for an aging society?

Much of the debate concerning the Chilean reform, which has been described here in some detail, has covered aspects not connected to the aging aspect of pension reform. Concern as to the appropriate regulatory structure, for example, seems less relevant in Western industrialized countries than in developing countries. It is often assumed that the existing structure of financial regulation in the industrialized countries is more than adequate.[24] In a similar vein, the significant role of the Chilean reform in encouraging the development of a capital market may seem less relevant to industrialized countries, where sophisticated and extensive financial markets already exist. What is relevant is the context of the Chilean scheme: a collapsing PAYG pension scheme and a government bent on privatization across the economy. To the extent that more industrialized countries face similar problems of PAYG viability (associated with, if not caused by, aging populations) and of the correct mix of public and private provision, Chile's fast transition to private pensions is of more than passing interest.

The presence of developed capital markets in northern-hemisphere countries suggests that finding investment outlets for a funded privatized pension scheme is not a problem, and the existence of private pensions or other similar instruments ensures that some form of regulatory structure is in place. Furthermore, the Chilean reform appears to have raised the rate of *private* saving significantly—a relevant consideration if it is argued that an aging population needs a greater stock of assets to offset the smaller productive component of the population. As we saw in chapter 3, however, theory does not necessarily predict that the optimal capital stock *should* be higher with an aged population. More important, the transition arrangements associated with a Chilean-type reform suggest that any deficit in the public finances will be exacerbated in the short run: the ideal context for such a reform is where public borrowing is negative. But this is exactly the opposite of the position in which OECD countries found themselves in the late 1980s and the early 1990s.

In a context of public-sector deficits, the valuation and treatment of outstanding liabilities from the PAYG pension scheme are crucial to the success of the plan (for example, can the bonds covering unfunded liabilities be directly invested in privatized activities, as in some of the Latin American pension reforms?). If there are high expectations as to the future payouts of existing PAYG schemes, it is unlikely that an aging population will accept a reform that implies both lower potential future pensions and greater uncertainty attached to those returns. On the other hand, critics of the Chilean reform who argue that it places too great a burden of uncertainty on prospective scheme members (see, e.g., Gillon and Bonilla 1992) might usefully bear in mind that the promise of high replacement ratios in PAYG schemes facing aging populations will turn out to be a greater illusion.

Changing the Public-Private Mix in UK Pension Provision

Contracting out

Whereas Chile developed a private pension industry from scratch, in the United Kingdom private pensions have coexisted with social security provision for many years. Since 1978 there has been a specific system of *contracting out* by which an individual may opt for a portion of his or her pension benefit to be provided either by the state or by the private sector. From 1978 (when this scheme was introduced) until 1986, both the social security pension and the company or public-sector pension provision were required to be of the defined-benefit form in order to qualify as an approved scheme entitled to tax relief for employees.[25] Both the state component (known as the State Earnings Related Pension Scheme, or SERPS) and the component provided by a company pension scheme (the Guaranteed Minimum Pension, or GMP) related pension benefits to some formula linked to years of service and earnings. Indeed, SERPS and GMP benefits had been almost identical since 1986, both being based on average lifetime earnings.[26]

Since 1986, there has been an important development in the UK social security scheme. Individuals may now opt to contract out of SERPS, not only into an employer's DB plan, but alternatively into an individual savings account known as a Personal Pension. Furthermore, employers can now gain contracted-out status by offering a group defined-contribution plan instead of a DB plan. This relaxation of the conditions of contracted-out status explain the shift to DC plans in the private sector described in the introduction to this chapter.

As with the current Argentinian pension reform, private pension provision in the United Kingdom is "financed" by a reduction in the rate of payroll tax paid by companies or individuals that choose to opt for private provision. In the case of company provision, the employee and employer who enter into a contracted-out pension scheme pay reduced rates of National Insurance contribution. The difference between the reduced rates and the full rates (for those who remain contracted in to SERPS) is called the *contracted-out rebate*. This rebate, the reduction in the payroll-tax bill, is the offset to the cost to a company of providing a GMP. The size of the rebate was structured so as to encourage the majority of companies to contract out of the state scheme. Thus, the intra-marginal company scheme (that is, one with a high ratio of contributors to pensioners) gains an extra subsidy from the arrangement (Hemming and Kay 1981, 1982; Disney and Whitehouse 1993b); in effect the government is making a loan to the private sector on highly favorable terms to encourage it to take over future pension obligations. The gain to the government, if any, is determined by the balance between reduced current revenue from payroll taxes and the future reduction in pension payments. Clearly the key determinants of this transaction are the intertemporal "terms of trade": the rate of earnings growth and the "excess yield" of the rate of interest over the rate of real earnings growth. At the time the scheme was developed (in the mid 1970s), real returns were at low levels by historical standards.

An explicit motive for the 1986 reform was to encourage increased private provision by increasing the range of approved options available (HMSO 1985a). In the Personal Pension route, individuals opt to have their contracted-out rebate paid into an approved individual savings account by the Department of Social Security. Individuals can make additional tax-free contributions to this Personal Pension account, with an upper limit on contributions as a proportion of earnings related to age.[27] There are roughly 100 current Personal Pension providers, offering a variety of plans and a variety of charging structures, although there are usually entry costs and a flat-rate component to the charge.[28] Information on the historical returns of different companies is available, since many companies have provided similar plans for the self-employed for a number of years.

Personal Pensions can be taken in part in a tax-free lump sum; the remainder must be converted into an annuity. However, there is no requirement that the Personal Pension provide an annuity worth at least the GMP, nor is there any provision for redistribution or public subsidization of lower-yielding accounts. Investment risk is borne by the individual employee, although one may defer annuitization up to age 75 to take advantage of favorable circumstances in the capital market. However, the state provides two reinsurance aspects to Personal Pensions:

The annuity must be at least partially price indexed, and the government currently guarantees to inflation-proof above this minimum as if the GMP was being paid. Thus, in the event that the annuity is inferior to the GMP, the state indexes at a higher effective level than the actual value of the annuity.

Individuals can choose to contract back into SERPS later in their lives. The timing of this decision clearly depends in part on the yield generated by the Personal Pension. This important facet of the scheme merits further attention if the UK scheme is to be seen as a potential model for "halfway" privatization.

Incentive structure of decisions to contract out and to recontract

The decision facing an individual deciding whether to remain in SERPS or to opt to have the contracted-out rebate paid into a Personal Pension account can be illustrated diagrammatically with a case study. Here we take a professional man aged 20 who will retire at 65, with a prospective lifetime earnings profile determined by the methods described above (figure 5.2; see also Disney and Whitehouse 1992, 1993c).

It is assumed initially that real earnings grow at 2 percent per annum and that the real return on financial assets is 4 percent per annum. We calculate the increment in this worker's total pension wealth from each successive year's membership of SERPS or of a Personal Pension. In figure 5.7, therefore, the total pension wealth comprises the sum of the area under either the "PP" (Personal Pension) or "SERPS" curve, or any combination of PP and SERPS membership.

The SERPS accrual profile is determined by two factors: the age-earnings profile, purged of real earnings growth (since past earnings are revalued to retirement in line with economy-wide average earnings growth), and the ceiling on National Insurance contributions and pension entitlements, known as the Upper Earnings Limit (see the discussion in chapter 4), which in fact caps this individual's accruals once he reaches his late twenties. The SERPS accrual profile is therefore weakly hump-shaped (cf. figure 5.2).

The Personal Pension accrual profile is determined by three factors: earnings growth (which implies, *ceteris paribus*, that the individual can invest a greater *value* of earnings in the scheme if he is investing only the rebate), compound interest (which implies that earlier contributions

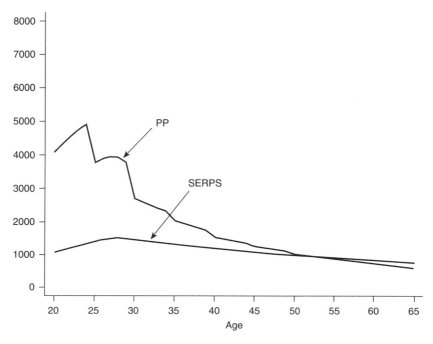

Figure 5.7
Increments in pension value from personal pensions and SERPS, United Kingdom.

accrue a higher return than later contributions), and the time path of the contracted-out rebate (which is projected to fall over time). The last effect has nothing to do with the Personal Pension reform; it stems from the earlier introduction of SERPS and the contracting-out option, when accelerated accruals of both SERPS and GMPs for early entrants meant that a higher rebate was needed to guarantee benefit levels for newly retiring cohorts. The total rebate is projected to fall from 5.8 percent (plus an extra 2 percent "bonus" for new Personal Pension optants) in 1988 to 3.4 percent in steady state in 2010. The compounding effect would by itself lead to a steady decline in the marginal accrual over time, but the distinct nonlinearity in the accrual profile stems from these other factors.

The optimal pension strategy for this particular individual is to contract out into a Personal Pension until he is aged 51, and then to re-contract back into SERPS until retirement—in other words, a mixed-portfolio strategy (even in the absence of uncertainty; see section 5.1). Note, too, that the intra-marginal subsidy, given the size of the rebate, is very large in the early years: a very much smaller rebate would have been sufficient to induce the employee to contract out of SERPS. This raises the suspicion, fully confirmed by subsequent analysis, that the intertemporal "terms of trade" to the government of this subsidy (the rebate) followed by savings on SERPS are unfavorable: the up-front cost of the rebate for the contracted-out period far outweighs the subsequent savings on SERPS. Before considering this, it is useful to note how sensitive the results are to the rate-of-return assumption. Figure 5.8 therefore plots various rates of return. At a 2 percent real return (i.e., an excess yield of zero), for example, the individual should re-contract at age 30; at a typical "excess yield" of 3 percent (an absolute real yield of 5 percent), the recontracting decision is deferred until age 56.[29]

Personal Pensions, pension costs, and the aging of the workforce
Although Personal Pensions were introduced as part of a general program of privatization measures, it is clear that, as with the principle of contracting out into DB pension schemes, the government can generate budgetary savings only where the "excess yield" of rates of return over the growth of real earnings is sufficient to induce people to contract out for a very low rebate, so that the saving in future pension costs outweighs the current loss of revenue. But it is apparent that the level of rebate needed to just induce a person to contract out[30] is dependent on age, sex, and real return. This is illustrated in figure 5.9, which

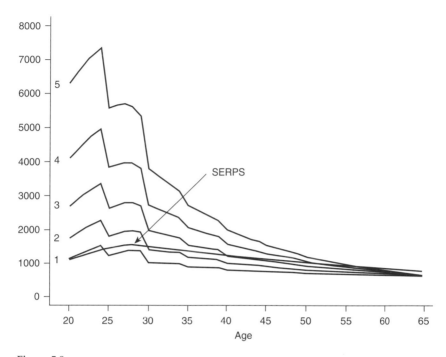

Figure 5.8
Sensitivity of increments in pension value to rate of return, United Kingdom. (Curves are indexed from 1 percent to 5 percent.).

shows what rebate would be needed, for various real rates of return, to persuade the individual at the median income specific to each age and sex to buy a Personal Pension instead of remaining in SERPS. The curves are nonlinear because, as part of the 1986 reform, the SERPS accrual rate was reduced for specific younger generations. Nevertheless, the curves are broadly upward sloping (reflecting the fact that older workers need a higher rebate to contract out), and are higher for women (who retire earlier and live longer on average, so they require a higher fund to compensate for loss of SERPS benefits).

Notwithstanding these arguments, the rebate has remained broadly uniform across Personal Pension optants.[31] The consequent intra-marginal individual subsidies imply that the government is unlikely to generate significant budgetary savings from the introduction of Personal Pensions. This point was made in a highly critical report by the National Audit Office which pointed out that the reform could lose £6.9 billion in revenue in the period 1988–1993, comparing forgone payroll-tax contributions with subsequent savings on SERPS (HMSO 1991b). Indeed, projections by the Government Actuary's Department

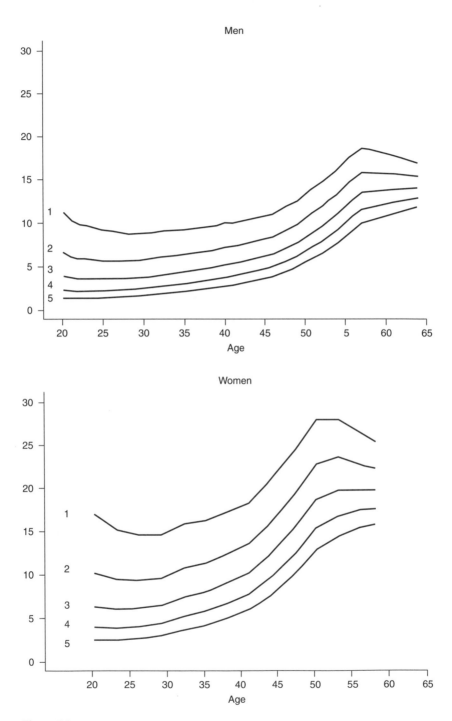

Figure 5.9
Median neutral contracted-out rebate by age and real rate of return. (Curves indexed from 1 percent to 5 percent.)

(HMSO 1990) suggest that future contribution rates will be higher, not lower, as a result of the number of optants for Personal Pensions, although it is not entirely clear how their calculations of increasing costs can be justified.

Annuitization, administrative charges, and market structure

In both Chile and the United Kingdom, the "excess" selling costs of individual retirement saving instruments, the treatment of investment risk, and the structure of the pension market have been live issues. There are lessons here for other countries that may be tempted to follow the same route: in particular the UK experience suggests that a tight regulatory structure must be in place before new pension instruments are introduced (a criticism that is less pertinent for Chile). Pension instruments are, by their nature, purchased by risk-averse individuals in the presence of asymmetric information and the scope for poor individual decision making is extensive, particularly when pension provision is traditionally the paternalist prerogative of the state and the company.

Typically, individual DC pension instruments charge higher commissions than group DC and DB plans, and these also far exceed the administrative costs of social security. If these charges reflect desirable product tailoring and risk rating, they may be justified, particularly if in compensation the purchaser can take advantage of high returns on the capital market or if the provider is prepared to undertake some degree of risk sharing (see below). But if charges reflect excess product differentiation stemming from imperfect competition in the market or from asymmetric information, they are an excess burden that should be carefully regulated. Coupled with a tendency for the insurer to paint the most optimistic picture of future returns, there may be a case for imposing strict regulation (such as capped charges for defined pension products and, as in Chile, the ability to switch products costlessly) rather than simply waiting for competition to erode sellers' margins. But it is at least arguable that pension accruals are transparent in individual DC plans, and purchasers are thereby more aware of the performance of their pension asset, adequate or otherwise. As the above discussion suggests, few people have any understanding of their likely social security outcome or of their accrued values within DB plans.

The key question of downside investment risk revolves around the choice of an appropriate investment strategy and the flexibility of annuity timing. If the insurer can construct portfolio insurance against such risk while maintaining an average market return, a higher commission is justified. In the United States, the traditional way of insuring against downside risk in DC plans is to invest DC instruments more heavily in bonds than in stocks (although so far portfolios of personal pensions have been stock-dominated, as with standard DB plans in the United Kingdom). Another strategy is to switch from equities to bonds as the investment nears the prospective date of annuitization, notwithstanding standard capital market theory concerning dynamic portfolio allocation.[32] The obvious drawback of either policy, which involves a different portfolio structure from ongoing group DB plans, is the investor's loss of the "equity premium."

An alternative, more attractive strategy is to introduce greater flexibility into the annuitization process, or, conversely, to fix the date of annuitization and use risk pooling so that the provider shares the risk. In the former case, typical strategies involve "variable annuities" (the value of which continues to fluctuate in line with the capital market) or "deferred annuities" (where withdrawals from the fund are staged over time). In the latter scenario, the insurer relies on fixing the withdrawal schedule of each individual in advance, thus forgoing any flexibility of date of annuitization. By distributing participants' withdrawals across a range of dates fixed in advance, the insurer can insure against some downside risk (for example, by pre-committing to at least non-negative changes in the real value of the fund). In addition, using market instruments such as derivatives or commodity futures to offset fluctuations in market values has been suggested. There is now evidence that such strategies are being implemented rather than remaining the province of the journals of finance theory, and the main limit on their implementation would seem to be the conservatism of insurance companies (and, perhaps, transaction costs) rather than feasibility.

A potentially more serious problem is where voluntary participation allows insurers to "cream off" the good risks (World Bank 1994, Issue Brief 11). It should be noted that "good" risks to insurance companies in the pension context are people with regular contribution histories who nevertheless die young. But it is known that, among men at least, those with regular and secure employment histories tend to live longest. These two facets therefore offset one another. In practical terms, "creaming" will tend to discriminate against women, who probably have both the risk of greater interruption to work experience and the tendency to live longer. Indeed, where the state insists on "sex neutrality" in annuity rates, the prospect of quantity rationing of annuity supply to women is enhanced. The solution would seem to be either a degree of compulsion in annuity provision or some alternative for those who cannot purchase annuities at an actuarially fair rate. Increasingly, for example, SERPS in the United Kingdom is becoming a residual benefit for those who cannot find a sensible private pension option, and it will tend increasingly to cover women rather than men.

Finally, a particular problem, specific to the UK pension reform, was the misleading advertising and inadequate regulation of Personal Pensions. Take-up of Personal Pensions was dramatic: almost 25 percent of the workforce chose to opt out of SERPS or even a DB plan into a Personal Pension in the first 5 years of operation because of "hard selling" by insurance companies, which were looking for new business after the withdrawal of tax reliefs on life insurance. Since the original contracted-out rebate could be capitalized retrospectively as a lump-sum payment into a pension account, and because transfer of the ongoing contracted-out rebate into a Personal Pension involved no explicit cost to the purchaser, many individuals who would be better off in the medium term in another pension arrangement (such as older individuals, holders of pension lump-sum payments, and existing members of DB plans) opted for the Personal Pension route. In contrast with 401(k) plans in the United States, employers in the United Kingdom rarely match contributions to Personal Pensions, especially if they operate a DB plan, and the employer's contribution to a DB plan, which is forgone if the individual opts for a Personal Pension, is usually substantial. A compensation package for "incorrect" optants (which may be around a fifth of the total) has been negotiated.

This discussion of the mechanics of Personal Pension-type instruments may seem to have shifted us some distance from the issue of private pensions in an aging society. But individual retirement savings accounts are an attractive option, taking advantage of the growing sophistication of capital markets, and are likely to be of increasing importance in other countries. The "experiments" in Chile and the United Kingdom have attracted widespread interest, and both suggest that careful regulation and provision of accurate information are required for such instruments to be alternatives to the more "traditional" routes of social security and DB plans. But, as the preceding discussion suggested, neither social security nor DB plans are risk-free in an aging society. With the World Bank also much more attracted to individual retirement savings instruments (at least in its public pronouncements; see World Bank 1994), such instruments will increase in importance over time, and their practical implementation is understood much better now than it was a decade ago.

6   Productivity, Wages, and Educational Attainment: The Impact of Workforce Aging

What is the impact of an aging workforce on productivity levels and on wage structure? Does cohort size affect educational attainment levels and participation rates? These questions are interrelated, but three distinct strands can be identified:

• If the ratio of older workers to young workers is increasing as a consequence of declining birth rates some years earlier, how will this change in relative labor supply affect the pay of older and younger workers? In particular, since earnings tend to rise with age, will the age-earnings profile be "twisted" (flattened) as a result of this demographic change? Are such effects temporary, or will members of a larger or a smaller cohort obtain relatively lower or higher pay throughout their working lives? The answer depends in large part on the substitutability of different labor-market cohorts in the production process and on the effects of cohort size on participation rates. The impact on pay structure of the entry of the baby-boom generation into the labor market in the years 1965–1975 occasioned much comment and research, especially in the United States. Findings as to the effects of a large entry cohort may, then, provide some insights into the more general relationship between age structure and earnings. The baby-boom generation is now in middle age and may continue to suffer depressed earnings relative to the previous cohort. However, subsequent fluctuations in the size of cohorts entering the labor market will have further affected age-pay relativities.

• The debate in the United States as to the impact of the baby-boom generation on pay relativities in the 1960s was closely related to a second debate concerning rates of return to education. There was concern that the size of the baby-boom cohort would generate an oversupply of educated youths from the mid 1960s on, and it was argued that the consequent low rates of return would discourage entry to tertiary education, which had been expanded in most countries since the early 1960s in order to accommodate the larger cohort. Of course, by opting for college a youngster incurs the opportunity cost of deferring labor-market entry. Thus, the consequences for educational attainment of the decline in returns to remaining in school might be overstated if the entry wage of youths in a larger-than-average cohort also decreases. In general, assessing the impact of cohort size on returns to education is not straightforward. The debate generated some mirror image-insights as the supply of young labor-market entrants has declined in the mid 1980s. Administrators, obsessed with mechanical quantitative forms of education planning, projected dwindling numbers passing through higher education; these projections often flew in the face of firm (and unsurprising) evidence that rates of return to education were once again rising in that period as the size of successive entry cohorts declined. As in the 1960s, however, the cyclical pattern of the economy rendered it difficult to separate the components of earnings change attributable to demographic factors from those attributable to other factors.

• Most difficult to unravel is the impact of a changing age composition of the workforce on overall productivity. As was mentioned in chapter 1, demographers have generally worried about the *aggregate* implications of aging on productivity: they argue that, because an aging workforce is less entrepreneurial and ambitious, it precipitates a stagnant economy. In contrast, labor economists have focused on *individual* productivity, regarding a mature population as embodying a greater stock of human capital and experience. These views are not necessarily contradictory, especially if there are productivity interdependencies or externalities, but they illustrate different "visions" of the impact of aging on economic growth and productivity. It is difficult to answer the question about aging and productivity because it is hard to find plausible measures of productivity with which to examine the hypotheses. A straightforward solution would be to look at wage rates by age, assuming that the labor market exhibited spot-market equilibrium between wages and marginal products at each age. However, the discussion of company pensions in chapter 5 gave no guarantee that lifetime remuneration would guarantee spot-market equilibrium of this kind at each age; indeed there were strong arguments that rational employers might backload pay. It would then be highly misleading to infer that the higher pay associated with experience rewarded higher productivity at the end of the working life if it was designed explicitly to encourage higher productivity earlier in the working life. Leaving aside age-earnings profiles, what "shape" might the individual life-time productivity profile exhibit? In chapter 5 it was assumed that individual productivity exhibited the "standard" life-cycle profile, with a rapid rise in the earlier years (after a period of training) fol-lowed by a decline in the rate of increase. Ultimately, perhaps, a de-crease in the absolute level of productivity would be observed, irrespective of the wage rate, as depreciation of the stock of human capital embodied in the individual outweighed the gain from addi-tional informal training at the workplace. This story is consistent with the observed quadratic relationship between years of experience in the labor force (proxying productivity) and annual wage rates in human-capital equations in what are assumed to be spot-clearing labor mar-kets. But, as was suggested above, it cannot be assumed that lifetime pay profiles fully reflect marginal productivities at each point in time. An associated problem of measurement error is that many of the com-monly used proxies for productivity, such as years of labor-market (and/or firm-specific) experience, are not very suitable, even when there is no reason to believe that the employer is distorting the age-earnings profile for incentive reasons. Moreover, early retirement may be a rational response if the "wedge" between pay and productivity becomes too large, so that the observed level of productivity of older workers is derived from a nonrandom sample. A final difficult problem in interpreting tests of human-capital models, and in treating lifetime pay profiles as productivity profiles, is aggregation. The discussion of relative supplies suggested that the extent of substitutability or com-plementarity will influence the observed age-wage relationship, irre-spective of whether we observe a "snapshot" of several cohorts at a point in time or whether we trace a particular cohort that coexists with other cohorts which enter or exit the labor market as that cohort ages. Thus, cohort effects, age effects, and other productivity effects may all interact, and uncovering the net effects of demographic changes is a complex task.

It is therefore appropriate to commence with the straightforward question of how the aging of the workforce affects the age-wage struc-ture. Did the baby-boom entrants of the 1960s face a depressed entry wage? Will this dip in wages relative to an "average" age-wage rela-tionship persist as that cohort ages? Has the entry cohort of recent

years benefited from its smaller size? These questions are examined in
section 6.1, first in the context of US research on the baby boom. The
typical production-function methodology is discussed, and the analysis is then extended to other countries.

It is apparent that, although workers of different ages make up dis-
tinctive "labor-market cohorts," workers with differing levels of educational attainment are also imperfect substitutes or even complements
in the production process. Thus, cohort size will affect earnings of various education groups differentially. Are workers aware of these cohort
effects when they invest in education? If they are, then choice of educational attainment level will also be affected by cohort size. This is examined in section 6.2.

A critical aspect of the aging of the workforce and the growing number of elderly people is the impact on participation rates of the elderly.
Discussion of this important issue is postponed until chapter 7. Nevertheless, fluctuations in the age structure of the workforce may be associated with cyclical variations in labor-force participation. Whether
such swings can be wholly attributed to demand-side phenomena
(discouraged-worker effects) or whether there is a role for changes in
the composition of the labor force by age is discussed briefly in section 6.3.

Section 6.4 discusses the question of cohort size and productivity.
The evidence as to the relationship between age, wage levels and productivity is first examined in a microeconomic context. Then models
are examined in which changes in population growth or in labor-force
growth may have macroeconomic effects on output, on real wages, on
productivity, and on unemployment. The conclusions are to be found
in section 6.5.

6.1   Cohort Size and Age-Earnings Profiles

A Natural Experiment? The Impact of the Baby-Boom Cohort on the Wage Structure in the United States in the Late 1960s

In the period from the mid 1960s to the mid 1970s, many industrialized
countries (Japan was one major exception) experienced an increase in
the numbers entering the labor market as members of the baby-boom
generation reached their late teens. In the United States, the numbers
in the labor force aged 20–24 grew from 9.7 million in 1966 to 16.7
million in 1976, and the numbers aged 25–34 grew from 16.8 million
to 23.0 million. The ratio of participants less than 35 years of age to

those 35 or greater rose from 0.46 to 0.67 over the same period (Free-man 1979).

Table 6.1 describes some key ratios for this period in the United States. By way of illustration, the first row suggests that the size of the 20–24 male age group as a proportion of the 35+ age group rose from 20 percent in 1966 to 28 percent in 1976—a rapid change in such a short period. At the same time, the ratio of the income of 45–54-year-old men to that of younger men rose from 174 percent to twice that percentage. So a 40 percent increase in the supply of younger workers was associated with a 15 percent fall in their relative wages. The second row shows a similar pattern for 20–24 female workers relative to older female workers. The ratio of numbers in the workforce rose even faster (55 percent), although the associated decline in earnings was slower (7 percent). Note that the age-earnings profile for women is flatter than that of men, a result confirmed for all the male-female row comparisons.

Table 6.1
Labor-force ratios and earnings ratios in the United States. Source: Freeman 1979, tables 4.1 and 4.2.

Ratio	1966[a]	1976[a]
Male workers 20–24 to male workers 35+	0.201	0.282
Full-time income of men 45–54 to men 20–24	(1968) 1.74	(1975) 2.00
Female workers 20–24 to female workers 35+	0.220	0.336
Mean income of women 45–54 to women 20–24	(1968) 1.38	(1975) 1.48
Male workers 25–34 to male workers 35+	0.352	0.502
Full-time income of men 45–54 to men 25–34	(1968) 1.18	(1975) 1.26
Female workers 25–34 to male workers 35+	0.276	0.487
Mean income of women 45–54 to men 25–34	(1968) 1.16	(1975) 1.05
Male college graduates 25–34 to male college graduates 35+	0.490	0.779
Full-time incomes of male college graduates 45–54 to those of graduates 25–34	(1968) 1.38	(1975) 1.63
Female college graduates 25–34 to female college graduates 35+	0.472	1.040
Mean incomes of female college graduates 45–54 to those of graduates 25–34	(1968) (1.05	(1975) 1.14

a. Except where noted otherwise.

The other comparisons in table 6.1 suggest a much weaker association of cohort size and earnings when comparing 25–34-year-olds with older workers (indeed, for women 25–34 the association of cohort size with relative earnings goes the "wrong" way). The largest change in ratios is that of younger to older college graduates, and this increase in the ratio of young to old graduates has a significant depressing impact on earnings ratios for the younger group, especially among men.

These associations between cohort size and relative earnings suggest that larger cohorts depress their own relative earnings, but it is not known *a priori* whether this persists through the lifetime. Care must also be taken in identifying the causation and the effect of omitted variables. It is noticeable, for example, that the changes in the proportions of females to males and of college-educated persons to cohort totals differ, as do the associated income changes.

The faster growth in the numbers of younger female workers may represent sorting, by which, as successive cohorts have higher participation rates, the less-productive members of successive cohorts join the labor force and depress cohort average earnings. The fact that the depressing effect of cohort size on earnings is less for women than for men may simply arise from women's flatter age-earnings profile, but it may also imply that female workers of different ages are much closer substitutes for one another than are men of different ages.

The impact of cohort size on the earnings of college graduates is another complex issue. The faster growth in the number of college places in a market where "job slots" for the more qualified are limited, may depress earnings irrespective of the size of the age cohort. Thus, the changes in income ratios are combining the effects of the size of the market for graduates and the relative size of the cohorts.

Another factor is the general state of aggregate demand for labor in the economy, which may have disproportionate effects on different age groups: for example, entry wages may be reduced significantly by adverse economic conditions, while the wages of older workers are maintained, especially where "last in, first out" seniority strategies of hiring and laying off depress the job prospects of younger workers. On the other hand, if the "wedge" between marginal productivity and wages is greatest for older workers where there is no spot-market equilibrium of wage rates for different age groups, it is the older workers whose job prospects are most at risk in a recession. Finally, it is important to note that these comparisons are affected by the significant recession that followed the oil-price shock of 1973–74.

In general, associations between cohort size and earnings derive from a combination of age effects, time effects, and cohort-specific factors, and unraveling these is a complex task. In assessing these issues, it has been common practice in the literature to utilize the production-function approach, in which workers are treated as imperfect substitutes for one another, to identify the impact of cohort size on earnings. Some studies undertaken in this framework are investigated next.

The production-function approach

Are workers of different ages substitutes? The production-function approach assumes that age groups (and sexes) are factors of production which are imperfect substitutes in an aggregate production function. Using the terminology and notation of Connelly (1986), assume that the aggregate production function contains homogeneous capital and a variety of types of "labor-market cohorts," distinguished initially solely by their age. The aggregate production function can be written as

$$Q = F[N(a), K], \tag{6.1}$$

where Q is output, $N(a)$ is a vector of workers at each age, K is capital, and $F[\cdot] > 0$. A single labor-market cohort (element of the vector $N(a)$) is denoted $n(i)$. The relation between labor-market cohort $n(i)$ and the size of its own birth cohort is

$$n(i) = \lambda(i)b(t - i)p(i), \tag{6.2}$$

where $b(t - i)$ is the number of people born $t - i$ years ago, $\lambda(i)$ is the labor-force participation rate of this cohort and $p(i)$ is the cohort's average probability of surviving to age i. Clearly λ and even p could be variables; for the moment, however, they can be taken as parametric.

To examine the effect of cohort size on earnings, we need to introduce the concept of the *elasticity of substitution* between the various age categories: a high elasticity implies that workers of different ages (and sexes) are close substitutes in production, and that the depressing effect of the size of a given cohort on its *own* total earnings is small. Then the only impact of a change in the size of the labor-market cohort is on the total labor supply and thus on average earnings. In the polar opposite case, where different age groups are not at all substitutable in production, a change in cohort size affects the earnings of that cohort only.

In investigating how changes in the quantity of inputs affect inputs' prices, the appropriate measure is the *elasticity of complementarity* (Hicks 1970), which, in this context, is the elasticity of the wage of any group with respect to a change in the size of any labor-market cohort, $\eta^{w(\cdot)b(\cdot)}$. Thus, the own and cross elasticities are

$$\eta^{w(i)bi} = \gamma_{ii}S_i \tag{6.3a}$$

and

$$\eta^{w(j)bi} = \gamma_{ji}S_{i'} \tag{6.3b}$$

where γ_{ji} is the elasticity of complementarity of the change in the relative price of the jth group due to a change in the relative quantity of the ith group, S_i is the share of group i in output, and $\eta^{w(i)bi}$ is expected to be negative but other elasticities may go either way.

The approach can be illustrated by the analysis of Freeman (1979), who uses a translog function to calculate the elasticities of complementarity, and the elasticities of factor prices to input quantities, for a range of age groups using aggregate data for the US economy for the period 1950–1974. Freeman's results are reported in table 6.2. The estimated equations exhibit potentially severe autocorrelation, and confidence intervals are not reported on the elasticities; nevertheless, most of the coefficients appear to be significant.

The results suggest that the assumption of perfect substitutability among age groups and between men and women can be easily rejected, and that the own elasticities exhibit the strongest negative effects. For example, a 10 percent rise in the proportion of the male workforce aged 35–64 depresses that group's own wage by 4.9 percent. A rise in the number of younger men has a smaller depressing effect on that group's own wage (-3.8 percent), but a rise in the number of women has a much greater effect on women's wages (-7.1 percent). Elasticities of complementarity across age groups also exhibit significant differences. Men aged 20–34 and 35–64 are weak substitutes; thus, a rise in the number of older men depresses the wages of younger men slightly, and vice versa. Young men and women as a whole appear to be marginal complements: a rise in the quantity of either is associated with a small rise in the wage of the other. It is not apparent that this last result carries over to more disaggregated research, and there is no evidence of complementarity when older men and women are compared. Capital services appear to be complementary to men. Overall,

Table 6.2
Elasticities of factor prices to changes in quantities. Source: Freeman 1979, table 4.7.

	Change in quantity of			
	Men 20–34	Men 35–64	Women 20–64	Capital
Elasticity of complementarity				
Men 20–34	−0.21			
Men 35–64	−0.25	−1.25		
Women 20–64	0.17	0.15	−5.88	
Capital	1.47	1.76	2.40	−3.95
Elasticity of factor prices w.r.t. quantities				
Men 20–34	−0.38	−0.10	0.02	0.46
Men 35–64	−0.05	−0.49	−0.02	0.55
Women 20–64	0.03	−0.06	−0.71	0.73
Capital	0.26	0.69	−0.29	−1.23

Freeman concludes that the trend in the share in total income of younger workers over the period is almost wholly explained by the changing size of their own cohort.

In Freeman's model labor-market cohorts are differentiated wholly by age, but it is apparent from table 6.1 and from Freeman's other work that age groups are not homogeneous. In principle, the workforce can be disaggregated in any dimension into heterogeneous factors of production. A natural example is disaggregation by schooling attainment. Again the implication is that individuals with different levels of schooling, and of different ages, need not be perfect substitutes.

Schooling and substitutability
Following the previous analysis, we can write the production function with heterogeneous schooling attainment as

$$Q = F[N(a,s),K] \qquad (6.4a)$$

or

$$Q = F[N(a)C(a,s),K], \qquad (6.4b)$$

where s is the schooling level and C is the proportion of each age group in each schooling group. An element of $N(a,s)$ is

$$n(i,k) = n(i)c(i,k),$$

where $c(i,k)$ is the proportion of age group i with schooling level k and $\sum_k c$ is normalized at 1 for all i. Again assume that schooling attainment is independent of cohort size. Then the proportional change in $w(i,k)$ with respect to a change in labor-market cohort size (now defined over a and s) is

$$\eta_{b(i)}^{w(i,k)} = \gamma_{(i,K)(i)}\sum_s S_{i\prime} \tag{6.5a}$$

$$\eta_{b(i)}^{w(j,k)} = \gamma_{(j,K)(i)}\sum_s S_i. \tag{6.5b}$$

These results state that the elasticity of a given wage to a change in the size of the birth cohort (given λ and p) is the *sum* of the elasticities of the wage to the changes in the sizes of all the labor-market cohorts that include members of the birth cohort (Connelly 1986). The approach is illustrated by Berger (1983), who disaggregates the "young" and "old" male participants (with $0-15$ and $15+$ years labor-market experience, respectively) into those with college education and those with high school education only.

Berger's analysis is not based purely on time-series data, although table 6.3 reports his national estimates. The standard errors are approximate (see the legend) and suggest that several of the coefficients are not significant. Furthermore, the similarity of the coefficients on capital in the various share equations and the low standard errors on the capital coefficients suggest that some aspect of the specification may be unsatisfactory: for example technical progress of a particular type may be time-trending capital's share. Nevertheless, the general spectrum of coefficients in table 6.3 are as expected, and some of the individual coefficients are of particular interest. In contrast with the findings of Freeman (1979), the elasticity of complementarity between women and young high-school-educated workers suggests a strong and significant substitutability between the two factors. Indeed, Berger suggests that the major reason for the decline in the earnings of young high-school-educated males relative to older high-school-educated males over the period 1967–1974 was the influx of women into the workforce. This accounted for half the decline in earnings, whereas the increased supply of the younger males themselves only accounted for a quarter of the decline.

Berger's disaggregation by educational status is also of interest. The calculated elasticities suggest that the most depressive effect of an

Table 6.3
Elasticities of complementarity with schooling disaggregation. Data: Current Population Survey 1967–74 using 19 regions: $n = 8 \times 19 = 152$. Approximate standard errors in parentheses (Taylor-series approximations of the variances of the share coefficients). Source: Berger 1983, table 2. Elasticities of factor prices with respect to change in number of young workers: $\eta^{(\text{young high school})}_{(\text{number of young})} = -0.0653$, $\eta^{(\text{old high school})}_{(\text{number of young})} = 0.0702$, $\eta^{(\text{young college})}_{(\text{number of young})} = -0.1469$, $\eta^{(\text{old college})}_{(\text{number of young})} = -0.0204$. Source: Connelly 1986, table 1; calculated from Berger 1983.

	Young high school	Young college	Old high school	Old college	Women	Capital
Young high school	−0.51 (0.48)					
Young college	−0.23 (0.53)	−3.45 (2.99)				
Old high school	−0.47 (0.13)	−0.43 (0.27)	−0.80 (0.08)			
Old college	−0.85 (0.36)	0.68 (0.56)	−0.20 (0.16)	−1.48 (0.96)		
Women	−1.27 (0.36)	−0.13 (0.53)	−0.40 (0.14)	−0.14 (0.32)	−0.29 (0.43)	
Capital	0.75 (0.05)	0.61 (0.09)	0.75 (0.04)	0.58 (0.07)	0.77 (0.05)	−1.12 (0.08)

enlarged youth cohort was on the college-educated young (−0.15) and the least impact was on older college-educated workers (−0.02). Conversely, the impact of cohort size on high-school-educated youth was less than that on college-educated and almost identical to that on high-school-educated older workers. The conclusion is that high-school-educated workers are close substitutes (irrespective of age) but that college workers of a particular cohort are imperfect substitutes with other types of workers and with college workers in other age groups. The increased supply of women boosted the earnings of college-educated young males relative to the high-school-educated by depressing the earnings of the latter.

Berger's results therefore suggest a more complicated story concerning the association between cohort size and relative earnings (or income shares). It appears that the increased supply of college-educated workers had a particularly adverse effect on their own earnings (and, as was suggested in the introduction to this chapter, this is not solely a demographic phenomenon: see Freeman 1989) but that the depressed earnings of less educated young workers in the early 1970s stemmed in part from other factors, such as the growth in female employment. The question then arises as to whether this observed depressing effect on cohort entry earnings persists throughout the lifetime.

Lifetime persistence of cohort effects

Welch (1979) also considered the effect of cohort size on earnings, focusing in particular on the persistence of systematic intercohort differences in earnings. Using the Current Population Survey for 1967–1975, Welch investigated whether the reported drop in returns to college education between the mid 1960s and the early 1970s was due to the business cycle or whether it signaled a change in the return on college relative to high school in the same cohort. He concluded that the key empirical issue was the drop in relative wages of the college-educated *within* schooling groups (i.e., between cohorts) rather than changes in relative wages *between* schooling groups (i.e., within cohorts).

Unlike Freeman and Berger, Welch argued that each "schooling group" (i.e., level of educational attainment) should be seen as wholly separable in the production process. Over time, each group would experience productivity change in line with initial training, subsequent on-the-job training, accrual of experience, and so on. Differences in productivity *between* schooling groups stemmed from differences in the number of workers at each productivity (experience) level *within* each group. Thus, the focus was not on substitutability between schooling groups, but on the relative earnings of different schooling groups in view of their cohort-specific average experience level (which could depend on the number in each cohort, among other things). In contrast with the model in equation 6.4, Welch is not considering age and schooling as separable forms of heterogeneous labor; rather, production is made up of disparate schooling groups composed of individuals of different ages—groups whose relative average earnings can be depressed or raised by the age structure of the group.

Since earlier years of experience in the workforce tended to be devoted wholly to learning (on-the-job training), a higher intake would tend to reduce the earnings of that schooling group by reducing its average productivity. But since the rate of earnings growth was most rapid after training, the larger-than-average entry group might subsequently see a faster rate of productivity growth than other groups.

Consequently, cohorts with depressed initial earnings could in principle "catch up" on their lost earnings.

To test the proposition that wage losses might be only temporary, Welch imputed own experience on the basis of cohort averages to form 44 "experience groups" for nine Current Population Surveys for each of four schooling groups. For each schooling group (two levels of high school and two of college), annual reported earnings were regressed on a quadratic in imputed experience, cohort size, unemployment rate, time trend, controls for missing data and, crucially, an "early career spline" (which also interacted with cohort size). This last variable, varying from 6 to 9 years for the different schooling groups, was designed to explain the steeper rise in early earnings with experience than predicted by the quadratic, interacted with cohort size to pick up any effects of cohort size on early experience.

Results showed that cohort size had strong adverse effects on both starting earnings and subsequent earnings, but that for all but the lowest education category the persistent effects of cohort size were less than the initial effects. The theoretical rationale was explained above; the econometric explanation stemmed from a negative sign on the interaction between cohort size and early career spline. Welch calculated elasticities of cohort size on weekly *entry* earnings for full-time workers, varying monotonically with schooling level from -0.082 for the lowest level to -0.665 for those with 4 or more years of college education. Interestingly, the elasticities for all full-time plus all part-time workers, and on annual earnings, were significantly higher, suggesting that larger cohort size also had adverse effects on participation and hours of work.

However, these cohort effects declined when examined over a longer period than the entry wage: the elasticities of cohort size on average measured weekly earnings (as opposed to imputed entry earnings) were far lower, varying between -0.096 and -0.218. The actual growth in cohort size from 1967 to 1975 therefore generated reductions in entry wages of 6 percent for the least-schooled category and 13 percent for college graduates. However, the faster subsequent growth of earnings of the larger cohort, relative to previous cohorts, would eradicate much of this difference, especially for the college-educated.

This last conclusion has been criticized by Berger (1985). The gist of his argument is that the "catching-up effect" stems wholly from the specification adopted by Welch, in which the "early career spline" is interacted in a particular manner. Berger's solution is to treat the Welch model as a highly restricted variant of a more general model in which all coefficients are expected to have different values during, and subsequent to, the period in which the "early career spline" is in operation. Implicitly, the "early career spline" functions as a structural break in the model of earnings, as between "young" and "old" workers.

In his more general specification, Berger finds, as does Welch, that cohort size depresses entry earnings. Interestingly, however, a cohort size × experience interaction suggests that the negative effect of cohort size on earnings appears to *increase* with experience. Larger cohorts experience both lower entry earnings *and* flatter age-earnings profiles. This result appears robust to a sensitivity analysis of where the "early career spline" is terminated, in terms of years of experience.

Unfortunately, Berger provides no numerical or simulated illustration of the magnitude of these interactive effects, and the interactive spline also appears to weaken the direct effects of experience on earnings. A simulation approach, such as that of Murphy et al. (1988), suggests, more plausibly, that cohort-size effects persist, but to a diminishing extent, as in the original Welch model. But these cohort effects are mediated by the mix of characteristics, such as skill, embodied in each age group. In all, the studies suggest that cohort effects can persist. Thus, if we combine this result with the evidence as to the impact of cohort size on entry wages from Welch, the evidence as to elasticities of complementarity from Freeman (1979) and Berger (1983), and the evidence of Freeman and Berger that earnings of college graduates are particularly affected by cohort size, the evidence for demographic impacts on age earnings profiles in the 1970s is strong.

The Experience of Other Countries

Britain
In Britain, the share of young men of working age in the male working population also rose sharply in the early 1960s, from a 10 percent average throughout the 1950s to 12.5 percent in 1965, before reverting to the previous share 10 years later. A small boom in the mid 1980s in the size of the entry cohort was followed by a projected secular decline (figure 6.1).

Rather surprisingly, time-series information as to the age structure of the working population is not readily available, although since the late 1960s repeated cross-section surveys such as the Family Expenditure Survey (FES) and the General Household Survey (GHS) have provided some information (see, e.g., Meghir and Whitehouse 1992 and Gosling et al. 1994). However, only three studies have focused explicitly on the impact of cohort size on age-pay differentials, and in particular on the earnings of younger men (for which more information can be obtained). In an aggregate time-series study for the period 1952–1979, Ermisch (1988) uses a simplified two-factor labor demand model to calculate the elasticity of young men's relative earnings to cohort size and to a number of control variables. He finds a long-run elasticity of young men's earnings to their relative supply of −0.2; this elasticity appears relatively robust to alternative specifications. The dynamic structure of the earnings models suggests that the maximum negative impact of cohort size on relative earnings occurs after 3 years, after which the effect moderates and stabilizes in about 10 years. Nevertheless, the short-run effects are not noticeably larger than the long-run

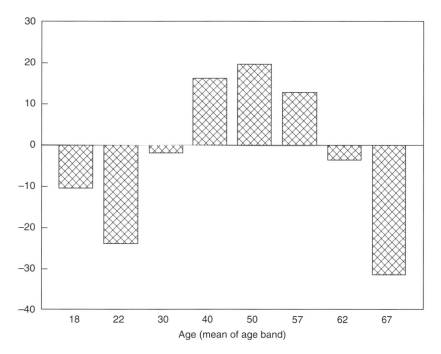

Figure 6.1
Projected percentage changes in labor force by mean of age band, Britain, 1989–2001.
Source: HMSO 1990.

effects. Like Freeman, Ermisch finds that young men's earnings are more cyclically sensitive to aggregate demand than those of older men. Nickell (1993) found a similar range of results, between −0.1 and −0.25, for an almost identical time period and data set. Wright (1989) uses pooled cross sections from the GHS to examine cohort size effects on male earnings for different age groups between ages 20 and 50. Individual earnings are regressed on quadratics in age and time, cohort size, cohort size interacted with age, and two control variables, for each of three educational attainment levels. The results suggest that cohort size variables have no effect on the earnings of those with no qualifications on leaving school, implying either that all such workers are perfect substitutes or that the "excess" supply feeds into the unemployment rate (no attempt is made to test between these hypotheses). For both groups with additional educational qualifications, cohort size is significant, as is the interaction between age and cohort size. However, the latter coefficient is positive on wages, suggesting a result, analogous to that of Welch (1979), that the depressing effect of larger cohort size is greatest in the early part of the working life. Indeed, a literal inference from Wright's result is that the earnings of larger cohorts "overtake" those of adjacent smaller cohorts by their early thirties, although it might be suggested that cohort size–pay effects of large cohorts induce "ripple" impacts on adjacent cohorts (especially those following them). Nevertheless, both British studies appear to confirm the general tenor of the US results.

Japan

A study of cohort size and pay structure in Japan by Mosk and Nakata (1985) using time-series analysis for the period 1964–1982 offers a contextual contrast to the studies of the United States and the United Kingdom. The proportion of the male population aged 15 and over which was in the 15–24 age category actually *fell* sharply in Japan from 1950 to 1980, from 31.5 percent to 18.8 percent, concealing a small "baby boom" *en route*. Over the same period, the proportion of the male population aged 55 and over rose from 16.4 percent to 20.7 percent. This aging of the workforce had an impact on the Japanese system of retirement and incentive pay scales (see chapter 5). In turn, the population *under* age 15 has grown over the period, so that a later baby boom, and then further aging, can be expected toward the end of the first quarter of the 21st century. Expectational factors may therefore be important, although these are rarely considered in the pay literature.

If the model of cohort size and age-wage profiles is correct, the Japanese experience of the 1960s and the 1970s would be of some interest in comparison to the post-baby-boom experience of the United States and the United Kingdom; predicting a fall in the ratio of wages of older Japanese workers to junior workers as the entry cohort declined in size. Indeed, there is evidence that this happened in Japan, especially in the early 1960s; however, for the decade after 1975 the earnings ratio actually tilts in favor of older workers despite a continued increase in their relative numbers. Clearly the issue is more complex.

Mosk and Nakata point to the rapid increase in the educational attainment of entry cohorts throughout the 1960s and the 1970s. This alone would be expected to induce a rise in the average relative wage of young workers through the increase in their weighted productivity. When they regress the relative hourly wages ratio of young to old workers on relative cohort size for groups separated by educational attainment, the impact of cohort size is significant, especially for workers in large firms and in comparisons among those with *less* education, but the implicit elasticity is very much lower than that found in the US and UK studies, lying in the range from -0.03 to -0.06. For college-educated workers, the results are insignificant or perverse; this may suggest that college-educated workers of different ages are very strong complements.

In common with the US and UK studies, Mosk and Nakata find that the wage ratio of younger to older workers is cyclically sensitive: entry cohorts at the peak of the cycle fare considerably better than those in the trough. But there is also evidence of a structural break in the mid 1970s, associated with the oil-price shock. Mosk and Nakata argue that this shock generated a change in the structure of Japanese industry and in its hiring procedures, especially among large companies, during which demand for new applicants fell and young workers' wages suffered. Thus, the cyclicality of the Japanese economy and the demand-side shocks are of as much importance to the structure of wages by entry cohort as the demographic factors discussed so far.

This emphasis on cyclical effects is reinforced by Martin and Ogawa (1988), who regress wage ratios of younger to middle-aged Japanese workers on cohort shares and cyclical variables for the period 1962–1981. Among men, the cohort-size effect is significant only when the cyclical variable is introduced, suggesting that a 10 percent rise in the share of workers aged 20–29 relative to those aged 40–49 reduces the former's relative pay by 1 percent. The effect is stronger for women (with an elasticity of -0.15) and in the manufacturing sector. No distinction is made between short-run and long-run effects, nor is lifetime persistence measured. Martin and Ogawa suggest that Japan's briefer "baby boom" explains the predominant effects of cyclical factors relative to cohort size. Nevertheless, the results are not dissimilar to those for the United Kingdom, and they are of the same sign as those for the United States. Cohort effects clearly play their part in the age-wage structure.

Consequences of Declining Entry Cohorts and of an Aging Workforce in the Next Decade for Pay Structure

What does this analysis tell us about the impact on pay of the changing workforce age structure in the late 1990s and beyond? So far, the investigation of the relationship between cohort size and age-pay differentials has yielded three main conclusions:

• Workers of different ages are not perfect substitutes; changes in the relative size of successive cohorts induce changes in the age-pay relationship. There is strong evidence that larger-than-average entry cohorts face depressed initial pay levels. Furthermore these pay disparities spill over into adjoining (especially subsequent) cohorts.

• Whether these pay differentials between cohorts persist as cohorts age is more controversial. Welch (1979) suggests that cohort effects on entry pay are transient, and Wright (1989) provides some evidence that cohorts with depressed entry pay may nevertheless "overtake" earlier cohorts. Berger (1985) disputes Welch's conclusion. In the British context, Ermisch (1988) finds little difference between short-run and long-run effects of age-group size on relative pay. However, it should be noted that some studies claim to be examining true "cohort" effects, whereas other studies are examining repeated cross-section comparisons of age-pay relationships. The derived econometric relationships are not identical.

• Although relative size of cohorts is an important determinant of entry earnings, and of subsequent experience, the size effect is overlain by demand factors, both cyclical and structural. All the studies agree that the ratio of young workers' wages to those of older workers is highly procyclical: depressed aggregate demand at the time of cohort entry reduces entry wages relative to present members of the labor force. Whether such demand-driven disparities persist as the cohort ages is not clear, although it seems implausible that they do. However,

severe structural breaks, such as the OPEC crisis of the mid 1970s or
the recession in the United Kingdom of the early 1980s, may have
longer-lasting effects on the employability of a particular entry cohort
and thus on its employment experience and its future wage path. In
Japan, at least, these demand-side effects may have outweighed the
importance of cohort size throughout the period. Furthermore, these
demand effects may induce *within-cohort* shifts in pay. This topic has
been analyzed in some detail in the context of widening pay inequality
in the United States in the last 25 years, and in the United Kingdom
since the early 1980s.[1] One of the clearest findings of this recent research is that cohorts entering the labor force in the 1970s and 1980s
tended to exhibit greater inequality of entry wages. This, rather than
cohort-size effects, has been the issue considered by recent research
on wage structure. Factors underlying this widening inequality may
include a reversal of the trend toward an increased share of college
graduates in the entry cohort; increased foreign competition and the
high value of the dollar (and the pound sterling in the early 1980s)
putting greater pressure on job prospects and wages of the unskilled
and the semi-skilled; greater participation of women, again typically
competing with semi-skilled and unskilled workers; and new technology, such as computers, giving greater returns to specific skills rather
than generic schooling. Although some of these arguments involve a
supply element, it is apparent that the "natural experiment" of the
effect of the baby boom at the end of the 1960s, which allowed a clear
test of the impact of cohort size on wages, could not be replicated in
the 1980s, when demographic changes were overlaid by a complex set
of events.

Projected labor-force trends and pay structure

Table 6.4 depicts the trends in labor-force and working-population
composition in ten OECD countries from 1990 to 2000, contrasted with
their experience over the period 1973–1990. Note that there is little relationship between trends in labor-force size and composition and those
of the population of working age (a point noted in the UK context in
chapter 2 above). In general the labor force is projected to grow faster
in the next decade than the population of working age in all the
countries bar Finland, and only in Austria did the labor force grow
slower than the population of working age in the period 1973–1990.

Six countries exhibit clear signs of an aging labor force in the next
decade: that is, a falling absolute number of young workers and a

Table 6.4
Past and projected labor-force and working-population changes for ten OECD countries, 1973–2000 (average annual percentage growth rates). Source: OECD 1988a; OECD countries cited by Nickell 1991.

Country and age group	Labor force		Working-age population	
	1973–1990	1990–2000	1973–1990	1990–2000
Austria				
15–24	0.4	−2.6	0.8	−2.2
25–54	1.0	0.7	0.7	0.4
55–64	−2.2	1.4	0.2	1.3
Total	0.4	0.1	0.5	0.0
Canada				
15–24	2.2	−0.2	−0.1	−0.2
25–54	3.2	1.4	2.2	1.0
55–64	1.1	1.7	1.8	1.4
Total	2.4	1.1	1.5	0.8
Finland				
15–24	−2.1	−0.7	−1.6	−0.2
25–54	1.6	0.1	1.1	0.1
55–64	−1.0	1.9	0.4	0.8
Total	0.5	0.1	0.4	0.1
France				
15–24	−1.1	−2.0	−0.1	−1.1
25–54	1.7	1.1	1.0	0.9
55–64	−0.3	−1.5	1.4	−1.0
Total	0.9	0.5	0.7	0.2
Japan				
15–24	−0.7	−1.3	0.2	−1.8
25–54	1.1	0.7	0.7	0.4
55–64	2.9	1.2	3.4	0.8
Total	0.9	0.5	0.8	0.0
Netherlands				
15–24	−0.4	−3.2	0.2	−2.6
25–54	2.6	1.4	1.6	0.7
55–64	−2.4	3.8	1.0	1.3
Total	1.4	0.8	1.2	0.2
Norway				
15–24	2.6	−1.6	0.5	−2.0
25–54	2.2	1.2	1.1	1.0
55–64	−0.4	1.7	−0.6	1.1
Total	2.0	0.7	0.6	0.4

Table 6.4
Continued

Country and age group	Labor force		Working-age population	
	1973–1990	1990–2000	1973–1990	1990–2000
Sweden				
15–24	0.2	−1.8	0.1	−1.6
25–54	1.4	0.4	0.6	0.2
55–64	−0.2	2.4	−0.9	1.7
Total	1.0	0.4	0.2	0.1
United Kingdom				
15–24	1.2	−1.8	0.5	−1.9
25–54	1.0	0.8	0.5	0.6
55–64	−1.4	0.4	−0.4	0.1
Total	0.5	0.2	0.3	0.0
United States				
15–24	0.3	0.1	−0.2	−0.1
25–54	2.9	1.4	2.0	1.0
55–64	0.1	1.0	0.6	0.9
Total	2.0	1.1	1.3	0.8

rising absolute number of older workers in the labor force. These are Austria, the Netherlands, Norway, Sweden, Canada, and the United Kingdom. Expected changes over the next decade for the UK labor force at a more disaggregated level were presented in figure 6.1.

The United States projects an almost static number of young workers and a significant rise in the number of older workers. In Japan, a similar pattern emerges in the 1990s, although the rate of growth in the number of older workers is actually slower than in the immediate past. In France there is a significant decline in the growth of all age groups in the labor force. In Finland, while the pattern of the 1990s is the same as in most of the other countries, the rate of decline of the young labor force actually slows.

What impact will these labor-force changes have on pay ratios? Assuming that the Ermisch elasticity is of approximately the right magnitude, that it applies equally to young men and women, and that the full impact is lagged 3 years, by the year 2000 average youth pay levels can be expected to range between 5 percent higher than at present (relative to real earnings generally) in the Netherlands, where the decrease in the size of the youth cohort is greatest, to about the same relative magnitude as now in the United States, where the youth cohort remains roughly its current size. These are not large effects, and they could be offset by adverse demand conditions given the procyclicality of the youth/older worker pay ratio. Furthermore, there may be considerable differences in returns among members of the cohort according to their degree of education. But it should also be noted that the effect on youth pay from Freeman's estimates (table 6.2) could be perhaps twice as high and that a higher relative wage might in turn induce participation effects relative to the option of staying in school.

Unfortunately, none of the studies cited here address the effect on relative pay of changes in the size of the 55+ age group, in part because wage levels affect retirement behavior. Freeman's results suggest an element of complementarity between young and older male workers, so that a decrease in the size of the entry cohort has a small positive effect on the pay of male workers generally. But this is not true of male and female workers, and intuition suggests that women of different ages may be substitutes in a number of occupations. Thus a combination of a smaller entry cohort and growing numbers of workers aged 50+ might depress the wages of the latter, especially those of women. However, the reduction in the size of the entry cohort mitigates the potential problem of finding employment opportunities for older workers. Again the demand conditions existing in the last decade of the century are crucial, in view of the cyclical sensitivity of participation rates of older workers.[2]

6.2   Cohort Size and Educational Attainment

The issue of educational attainment is often discussed in the framework of manpower planning or human capital, but rarely is the role of cohort size considered explicitly. A cross-country comparison of educational attainment might ideally discuss the supply of educational skills, not just in the context of demographic trends, but also in terms of the skill composition of the potential workforce as a whole. In addition, the determinants of the demand for education (that is, the willingness of young people to stay in secondary school to acquire future qualifications, or to go to college) should be considered. Yet educational planners often ignore both the overall composition of the workforce and the demand for education. Studies of educational attainment in the context of the workforce as a whole, such as OECD 1989, sometimes avoid demographic trends entirely.

In turn, studies of the *demand* for post-compulsory education that focus on individual choice rely on measurement of expected future returns to education (representative studies in the British context are Pissarides 1981, 1982) but tend to ignore the feedback effect of these choices (in the context of cohort size) on future returns. Whether individuals perceive the size of the cohort to which they belong and the implications of the choices made by that cohort in calculating these expected rates of return is a moot point; certainly the cobweb theorems of educational demand and supply discussed by Freeman (1989) suggest that rather naive partial adjustment mechanisms may characterize educational planners and participants alike, even though cobweb outcomes derive from expectations that are not "rational" (Muth 1961). So it is useful to set out a framework in which cohort size affects educational attainment and in which different types of expectational structures affect outcomes.

The impact of cohort size on choice of educational attainment level depends on several factors, which can be discussed in the context of a decline in the size of the entry cohort. First, a smaller cohort faces less immediate competition for jobs, if it is assumed that workers of different ages are not perfect substitutes. This will tend to discourage acquisition of enhanced qualifications, as immediate employment opportunities are more readily available. But this factor will be offset if the earnings of qualified workers are most susceptible to changes in cohort size (see table 6.3), so that the long-run expected earnings prospects look even stronger (depending on whether cohort effects on earnings persist). One possible outcome is a sorting procedure by which those with higher rates of time preference among the smaller cohort choose to enter the labor market immediately rather than to acquire further qualifications. Of course, a consequence of this analysis is that among *larger* cohorts, these are the individuals who choose to stay in school to acquire additional skills.

In the framework provided by Connelly (1986), endogenizing the choice to acquire extra schooling as a function of the size of the birth cohort requires an additional elasticity. Define $\varepsilon_{n(i)}^{c(i,s)}$ as the elasticity of the *share* of cohort $n(i)$ undertaking schooling attainment s given the size of cohort $n(i)$. The wage elasticity in equation 6.5 can now be rewritten as follows:

$$\eta_{b(i)}^{w(i,k)} = \gamma_{(i,k)(i)}\sum_s S_i + \gamma_{(i,k)(i)}\sum_s S_i \varepsilon_{n(i)}^{c(i,s)}, \tag{6.6a}$$

$$\eta_{b(i)}^{w(j,k)} = \gamma_{(j,k)(i)}\sum_s S_i + \gamma_{(j,k)(i)}\sum_s S_i \varepsilon_{n(i)}^{c(i,s)}. \tag{6.6b}$$

Although this looks complicated, it is simple to interpret in the case of two cohorts (young, old) and two educational levels (staying in school, leaving school). The first term on the right-hand side shows how the elasticity of the wage to cohort size of (say) the young who stay in school is affected by the sum of the wage changes of both those who stay in school and those who do not. The second term shows that these elasticities of wage changes for both those who stay in and those who leave school are affected by the responsiveness of the choice of staying to cohort size. In this simple binary choice case, the latter elasticity, ε, can be obtained by looking at how cohort size affects the probability of staying in school. The major complication in implementing such a model is obvious: the decision to stay on depends on the expected returns, which are themselves solved by equation 6.6 with the elasticity ε as one of the arguments. The model should be solved simultaneously, but it requires some assumptions as to how expectations about the future impact of cohort size enter the choice set.

Several expectation structures are discussed by Connelly (1986) and by Flinn (1993).

In the first case, young workers do not anticipate that their own actions (i.e., choice of schooling level) or the size of their cohort will affect their earnings when they are older workers. They assume that their earnings as older workers will be equal to the current earnings of older workers. By implication, the cohort has failed to note that the current earnings of older workers are affected by both the size of the young cohort and the size of the old cohort (section 6.1 above). Connelly calculates that—with these static expectations, and given the existing shares of old and young workers in the labor force, the shares in different educational levels, Berger's elasticities of complementarity (see table 6.3 above), and a 10 percent rate of time preference per year—then $\varepsilon_{n(y)}^{c(y,s)} = -1$, where y is the "young" cohort, s is college schooling as defined by Berger, and ε is the elasticity of the share undertaking schooling to the size of the cohort. This is a rather large elasticity, and its sign cannot be determined analytically. At the high rate of time preference, the cohort has discounted the future "high" return it observes among current older college-educated workers and has merely noted the low returns to a college education among the existing cohort. Accordingly the proportion seeking college entry is reduced. However, at a lower rate of time preference, and given the positive elasticity of complementarity between younger and older workers found by Berger, then the younger cohort's expected higher future earnings with schooling when older (ignoring the feedback of schooling choice on future earnings) will boost overall returns and induce greater investment in schooling as the size of the youth cohort increases, so reversing the sign of the elasticity.

In the second case, workers may anticipate that future relative earnings of older workers (themselves) will not be the same as those of current older workers. They recognize that future earnings are affected by cohort size. However, they still assume that their schooling choice has no effect on the future returns to different schooling levels. If, say, the current youth cohort is particularly large, then the *current* relative wage of older workers may be higher, especially for workers with more schooling. But these young workers now anticipate that, because they themselves are a larger cohort and they are ignoring any feedback effect of cohort size on current schooling attainment, their future earnings will be depressed by the size of their cohort. Will this lead them to invest in more schooling? Since those with less schooling are closer substitutes, the impact of cohort size on their earnings is smaller. But, from Berger's results, young and old college-educated workers are not close substitutes. Accordingly, the impact of cohort size on future earnings is greatest for college-educated workers, and the elasticity of schooling attainment with respect to cohort size is likely to be negative over all discount rates (i.e., rates of time preference).

Logically, therefore, the third alternative is that young cohorts rationally anticipate both the impact of their cohort size on future earnings and the likely decision of the cohort as a whole with regard to schooling attainment (consequent upon cohort size). This "rational" expectational hypothesis is examined by Stapleton and Young (1988) and by Flinn (1993). Stapleton and Young compute the implicit return on schooling for a baby-boom cohort (the magnitude of which approximates the US experience) and for the immediate pre-boom and post-boom cohorts. These last two cohorts, in fact, do well out of the baby boom in relative terms: the pre-boom cohort benefits from the scarcity of older workers, and the post-boom cohort benefits from the scarcity of younger workers. Since college-educated workers are again assumed to be less substitutable across ages than workers who have not gone to college, Stapleton and Young predict a cyclical pattern to college choice when cohorts fully perceive the consequences of their own size for the relative return to a college education.

Figure 6.2 illustrates their simulation results. The baby-boom cohort reaches its peak at year 0, and chooses whether to go to college at year +15. The dip in college choice is quite apparent; unsurprisingly, when the future lower returns are discounted at a higher rate, the reduction in college intake is reduced. Interestingly, too, the pre-boom and post-boom cohorts (especially the latter) increase their proportion going to college for the reasoning outlined earlier: they will benefit from the tilt in relative age-earnings profiles of the college-educated stemming from the baby boom.

If there is "full" adjustment and rational expectations are held, any variation in average rates of return to college education over time according to demographic factors is eliminated. Each cohort successfully anticipates the impact of successive cohort sizes on average rates of return, and a sorting process presumably takes place whereby those anticipating lower-than-average rates of return choose not to go to college. Where adjustment is incomplete, there will be some residual variation in average rates of return, negatively related to cohort size. However, as figure 6.2 illustrates, cohort size can set up cyclical patterns of college entry where *lifetime* effects of cohort size are fully anticipated, and this, coupled with demand fluctuations, makes it hard to unravel the impact of cohort size on average rates of return. This may be one reason why such an important topic has been relatively underresearched.

6.3   Cohort Size and Participation Rates

The long-run effects of demographic change on participation have been extensively discussed by demographic economists (see, e.g., Easterlin 1968 and Easterlin 1980). The difficulty in appraising long-run trends, such as the growing participation of married women, is that a range of both demand-side and supply-side factors underpin such shifts.[3]

So far, this chapter has focused on changes in wage structure and on the returns to education over long periods. Over shorter periods, such as decades, the major problem has been disentangling the impact of cohort size on earnings from the cyclical fluctuations stemming from the demand side of the economy. Typically, the literature on cycli-

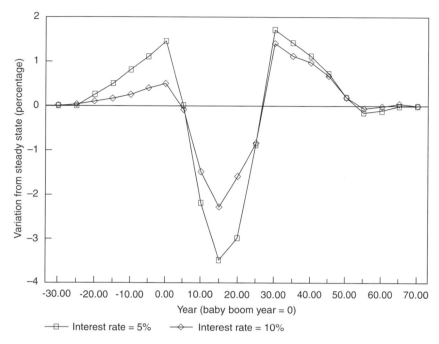

Figure 6.2
Impact of baby boom on variations in cohort percentage entering college. Source: Stapleton and Young 1988, figure 3.

cality assumes that downturns in the economy generate a "discouraged-worker effect" by which higher unemployment reduces the size of the labor force as individuals reduce the intensity of their job search when faced with a decline in the probability of obtaining work. This mitigates the impact on measured employment rates of fluctuations in economic activity around the trend.

What is the role of cohort size in all this? In view of the evidence from section 6.1 that wages do indeed adjust to cohort size, the *direct* effects of cohort size on relative unemployment rates may not be observed. But *indirect* effects are possible: for example a larger entry cohort, by depressing entry wages, may lead to changes in participation rates, especially among women. Depending on expectation structures (see the previous discussion), a reduction in wages over the shorter time horizon of the cycle may induce not only discouraged-worker effects but also "added-worker effects" (as, for example, when young women postpone childbearing and enter the labor market in order to maintain a target level of family income). To illustrate this point,

Wachter (1977) estimated equations of the following general form in a
time-series analysis of participation rates of various age groups in the
US economy for the years 1949–1976:

$$\text{LFPR}_{i,t} = f(U_t, T, p_{16-34,t}, \text{LFPR}_{i,t-1}),\tag{6.7}$$

where $\text{LFPR}_{i,t}$ is the labor-force participation rate of a particular age
group i at time t, U is the unemployment rate (designed to capture the
net discouraged-worker effect), T is a time trend (intended to net out
long-run shifts in participation propensities of particular age groups),
and $p_{16-34,t}$ is the proportion of the population between the ages of 16
and 34. The prediction is that the coefficient on the age-proportion
variable will be positively signed for members of that age group (especially young women) and negatively signed for other age groups, reflecting the added-worker effect stemming from the "twisting" of the
age-earnings profile against younger workers when there are more of
them. Secondary predictions are that inclusion of this last variable
would weaken the significance of demand-side effects through U
(which probably should be instrumented) and of the time-trend term
(which might be picking up cohort-size effects as well as capturing
any preference shifts in participation).

Broadly speaking, the results confirm the hypotheses. Labor-force
participation rates are negatively related to the annual unemployment
rate, and are time-trended negative for men and positive for women.
There is some evidence that the cohort relative size variable dampens
the trend effects for women: for example, when the relative size variable p is excluded, the time trend predicts a 2.6 percent increase per
annum (t stat = 3.6) in the participation of women aged 16–19. With
the inclusion of the relative size effect, the predicted trend is smaller
(0.1 percent) and is bordering on significance (t stat = 1.6). The relative
cohort size variable p is insignificant in the equation for men below 25,
significantly positive for all female age groups below 44, and significantly negative for all men over 25 and women over 45.

What predictions stem from this analysis? Wachter argued that the
rise in the participation rates of young women, especially in the 1960s,
stemmed not so much from a change in social attitudes as from demographic factors: the lower wages of that entry cohort precipitated enhanced participation in order to maintain target family income.[4]
Although there might be some hysteresis in participation (illustrated
by the significant lagged dependent variable), it follows that smaller
subsequent cohorts of women (facing more attractive relative wage

rates) might actually have *lower* participation rates; furthermore, with cohort effects on relative pay through the lifetime, the fastest increase in participation rates in subsequent decades would be among *older* women, who would here be the aging baby-boom generation. Finally, it should be noted in passing that age-specific participation rates correlate negatively with fertility rates; thus, the well-known modern observation that labor supply is strongly related to family composition may actually be modeling the impact of age-cohort size on fertility rates. Household composition is endogenous to the size of the cohorts containing the parents.

A recent study by Fair and Dominguez (1991) supports the proposition that cohort size affects participation rates but casts doubt on the "added-worker" implication drawn by Wachter. The problem is that Wachter's participation equation does not include each age group's own wage explicitly, relying instead on the indirect propositions that relative cohort size affects relative wages and that these wage effects generate added-worker effects (which can be interpreted as the income effect dominating the substitution effect of the wage on participation).

The approach taken by Fair and Dominguez clarifies this point. Write the basic participation equation (as consistently as possible with Wachter's notation) as

$$\text{LFPR}_{it} = \beta_0 + \beta_1 w_{it} + \prod X_{it} + \mu_\tau, \tag{6.8}$$

where i is a particular age category, w is some wage measure, X is a vector of other measured characteristics determining labor supply, and μ is the error term. But there is also a relationship between the age-specific wage and the average wage (see section 6.1 above), which can for example be written as

$$w_{it}/w_t = \gamma_0 + \gamma_1 p_{it}, \tag{6.9}$$

where $\gamma_1 > 0$ and where p is the proportion of the population in a given age category. Multiplying equation 6.9 through by w_t, and substituting into equation 6.8, we obtain

$$\text{LFPR}_{it} = \beta_0 + \beta_1 \gamma_0 w_t + \beta_1 \gamma_1 p_{it} w_t + \prod X_{it} + \mu_t. \tag{6.10}$$

Since γ_1 is predicted to be negative, the two terms commencing in β_1 should be of opposite signs. The first term, if negative, indicates a dominant income effect: a lower wage rate induces a higher participation rate. Equation 6.9 then suggests that, for any given labor-market group, the second term is of the opposite sign. The coefficients β_1 and the γ terms cannot be identified. However, Fair and Dominguez confirm that the multiplicative term is indeed negative; thus, cohort size affects relative wages. For regressions for prime-age men for the period 1954:1–1987:1, however, β_1 is negative for men and positive for women. This, Fair and Dominguez argue, suggests that the substitution effect of wage changes over time dominates for women and that the income effect dominates for men. The result for women contrasts with that of Wachter, as Fair and Dominguez interpreted it, although it should be noted that their study is at a more aggregated level and implies a very restrictive underlying utility function. Nevertheless, the studies illustrate clearly that participation rates over time are affected by cohort effects and that, crucially, these interact with the impact on relative wages described earlier.

6.4 Productivity and an Aging Population

In many ways the most fundamental question, but the most difficult to analyze, is how the relative size of cohorts affects the overall productivity of the economy. The methodological difficulties were described in the introduction to the present chapter. In particular, "aging pessimists" believe that the adverse effects of a shrinking entry cohort and an aging workforce are long-term and generate "dynamic effects" that cannot be identified by the "neoclassical" methodology (i.e., the production-function approach) that underlies much of the literature described here.

As much of this chapter has illustrated, however, there is strong evidence of feedback mechanisms by which, say, the relative supplies of factors affect their relative prices. Likewise, relative productivities should also affect relative earnings. If a country with an aged and (by assumption only at this stage) less-productive workforce has a physical capital stock of sufficient productivity and a vector of relative factor prices consistent with its relative factor supplies, then there is no reason why it should be adversely affected in its economic performance relative to competitors. Of course, comparing countries with an identical capital stock but with workforces exhibiting differential productivity growth, then real incomes will tend to rise faster in the country with the faster growth of productivity. But in any event it is not self-evident that a country with a younger age structure is the one with the faster productivity growth (as opposed to the faster *potential* for productivity growth: witness the differential rates of youth unemployment among industrialized countries).

The link between productivity and economic performance can be approached in two ways. The subsection on the microeconomic approach examines evidence on whether wage differences between individuals of different ages reflect differential productivity levels (as well as cohort size); in turn, this requires some measure of productivity levels for workers of different ages. However, the simple comparisons of task accomplishment across age groups beloved of industrial-organization specialists (leading to such statements as "younger people are more dextrous") are of little value unless the value of such tasks can be weighted in some way (and the natural method of weighting such tasks is money metric) in order to compare the value of output with the wage rate paid. Thus we pay no attention to studies that have (no doubt at length) investigated the capacity of older workers to accomplish certain physical tasks; we concentrate on the valuation of their output relative to their pay.

The next subsection investigates the macroeconomic relationship between aging and productivity by specifying under what circumstances macroeconomic performance could be affected by the age structure of the workforce in a fully specified macroeconomic model, and by then asking whether there is in fact any evidence that countries with slower population or workforce growth exhibit adverse macroeconomic performance.

Microeconomic Aspects: Are Older Workers More Productive?
Older workers typically earn higher wages, although the relationship is often nonlinear, with wage growth slowing once workers have entered their fifties (Brown 1989; Meghir and Whitehouse 1992). Do these higher wages indicate that older workers are more productive? To answer this question, it is necessary to delve a little further into the evidence, and to bring in a theoretical perspective.

Cross-section age-earnings profiles generally show a pronounced "inverted U shape" of earnings with age. The standard rationale for this is derived from human-capital theory and assumes that wages at each point in the lifetime reflect the worker's productivity. Entry wages are determined by workers' pre-labor-market investment in schooling, and this skill acquisition is supplemented in early working life by various forms of formal and informal training (the latter including both explicit on-the-job-training and experience). However, the time given over to training declines with age (Welch 1979), and the workers' embodied skills depreciate. After a time, the adverse impact of depreciation on productivity outweighs the positive effect of (reduced) increments of training. In addition, over time, there is labor augmenting technical progress in the economy, which adds to the general productivity and real-wage growth of workers. On a cohort basis, therefore, real wages tend to grow over the life cycle, but at a considerably slower rate among elderly workers. Indeed, depreciation of skills may ultimately outweigh training increments and wage growth attributable to general productivity growth, and then wages decline later in working life over time as well as on a cross-section basis.

How does a human-capital theorist test the proposition that wage rates over the life cycle measure productivity at each point in time? Human capital can typically only be proxied indirectly by measurable inputs: education by years spent in education or qualifications obtained, on-the-job training by time spent in training or by years of experience in the workforce as a whole or in the specific firm or plant. The hypothesis of diminishing time spent on training over the lifetime may be proxied by a declining weight attached to greater years of experience or by a nonlinear function such as the quadratic. In general, earnings functions incorporating quadratics in education, experience and formal training, and interactive terms perform well and are consistent with the proposition that the growth of wages over the lifetime reflects growing productivity (albeit at a slower rate in later years).

The moral of this age-productivity story for the issue of an aging workforce is that a "baby-boom" entry cohort will typically *reduce* the productivity of the workforce per capita, and indeed a workforce with a large number of middle-aged-to-older individuals is perhaps the most productive in the aggregate. Of course, this ignores any change in the embodied productivity of successive working cohorts (perhaps from improved environment and from better, or simply more, schooling); it is also consistent with younger members of the workforce having a faster *growth* of productivity. In fact this is the story told by Welch (1979), although Berger (1985) cast doubt on his empirical specifications. So the decline in the size of the youth cohort need not concern society, although the "burden of the aged" may appear later as the baby-boom cohort retires (see chapters 2 and 4 above).

An alternative view, described in part in chapter 5, is that the positive relationship of wages with age has very little to do with higher productivity with age. The shirking and incentive models of Lazear are one broad group of theories; another theoretical strand is contained in models in which wages are related to seniority through trade-union pressure or some median voting strategy among workers. In such stories, older workers are not more productive; indeed, the reverse may be the case. Though it may be necessary to pay older workers higher wages in order to attract more effort among *younger* workers (the Lazear story), the impact on aggregate productivity of an increase in the numbers of older workers is uncertain: indeed, as described in chapter 5, an aging workforce may render the incentive strategy infeasible, thus reducing productivity among younger workers (as a result of the lack of incentives, shirking., or avoidance, in addition to the adverse effects on productivity of the changing composition of the workforce).

Which of these theories of the age-wage and productivity relationship is correct? One possible approach to testing the hypothesis is obvious. Suppose we could measure the relative productivity of workers directly. If this productivity measure could be introduced into the earnings function, then in the human-capital theory it should prove a more significant explanation of earnings differences than its proxies, such as experience. Alternatively, in the Lazear story or the seniority model, where age-wage differences are not related to productivity, the additional term should make no difference to the explanatory power of the equation.

This is, in essence, the test that Medoff and Abraham (1980, 1981) proposed. They used data obtained from the personnel departments of individual companies concerning their managerial and professional staff, which included details of the standard human-capital variables: education, pre-company experience, and years within the company, plus data from supervisors' reports as to individual performance. The hypothesis was that, once included, the latter variables would supplant company experience in "explaining" age-related earnings differences. In their 1981 paper, Medoff and Abraham show that grade attained within the company was related to education level and pre-company experience. A standard human-capital regression then showed a strong quadratic relationship between years of company experience and earnings. Grade-level dummies and the human-capital variables explained 91 percent of the variance of individual earnings. Interestingly, however, introducing performance ratings (assumed to proxy productivity with error) failed to dislodge the importance of pre-company and company experience. Within-grade pay was strongly related to experience (age) irrespective of performance rating; this appeared to refute the "traditional" human-capital approach.

Further work by Medoff and Abraham suggested that additional pre-company experience and within-company experience enhanced within-grade pay but reduced within-grade performance ratings: more experienced workers tended to be less productive within grades. Although it is possible that supervisors' assessments contained a subjective component that downgraded the contributions of older workers (either through higher expectations of them or "ageist" bias), the results of several studies reported by Medoff and Abraham suggested that supervisors tend to protect older colleagues who they have known for a long period.

More important, however, is the unsurprising evidence that probability of promotion (between-grade movement) was positively related to supervisors' ratings. Thus, the Medoff-Abraham result may be interpreted as a sorting process by which workers with experience are sorted into the appropriate grades. Over time, therefore, average within-grade performance declines as more productive workers are moved into higher categories and earn higher average earnings. We might conclude that, just as the variance in earnings increases with age, so does the variance in productivity. This is perhaps less surprising than the contrasting conclusion which Medoff and Abraham obtain, and it suggests that the relationship between workforce aging and productivity is more complex than it first appears.

If performance, proxying productivity, underlies sorting within the firm, then a natural extension is to extend the sorting process to matches of individuals *between* firms, and to lengths of job tenures. This point has been taken up by Abraham and Farber (1987) and by Altonji and Shakotko (1987), who argue that seniority (experience) must be correlated with duration of job tenure. If duration of job tenure in turn indicates better "matching" of workers to the jobs in which they are most productive, then the return on seniority comprises both the standard human-capital interpretation and an indication that underlying durations of job tenure represents the installation of more productive workers in longer-tenured jobs.

This hypothesis, which draws on the "efficiency wage" literature (Salop and Salop 1976; Yellen 1984), also explains why longer job tenure is associated with higher wages: having successfully matched the appropriately productive worker to a particular job, the firm will pay higher wages to workers with long tenures to avoid the costs of turnover and training. Abraham and Farber include predicted job duration and the residuals of a regression of seniority on completed job duration, plus a quadratic in pre-job experience, in a model of hourly earnings drawn from Panel Survey of Income Dynamics data. This instrumental variable technique reduces the return on experience considerably when compared to a standard human-capital equation including a variable measuring actual experience. They infer that measured seniority is not such a significant component of earnings differences and, implicitly, that the association of age with earnings may stem from gradual matching of workers with jobs consistent with their underlying productivities. Older workers are not intrinsically more or less productive than younger workers, but they are more likely to be matched to the appropriate jobs.

Another piece of evidence concerning age-earnings profiles and productivity comes from Brown's (1989) analysis of the PSID, which yields a careful specification of the training component obtained by the individual. Brown shows that, once training both within the firm and in previous positions is entered precisely and nonlinearly, the growth of wage profiles over the lifetime is wholly "explained"; there is no residual role for seniority-based wage growth unrelated to training (here proxying productivity). Higher wages then reflect longer periods of training.[5]

How do all these studies relate to the productivity of an aging workforce? A young workforce may be more adaptable, and quicker to learn, but it will embody less training, and will not yet be sorted into jobs and into grade positions within jobs appropriate to the relative productivity differences among individuals. An older workforce will have had some depreciation of its skills, and may well be harder to retrain when the economy goes through rapid structural change, but the greater "experience" of a mature tenured workforce does embody higher productivity. The net effect of these factors is not clear; however, there is no support for the view of "aging pessimists" that an older workforce must necessarily be less productive, or that it will earn high wages inconsistent with its level of productivity.

What does this suggest for the evidence of "ageism" in hiring practices? If it is believed that there is a simple physical relationship between age and productivity, there appears to be a contradiction between the (no doubt valid) assertion that hiring practices favor younger workers and the oft-cited evidence that employers who utilize older workers are very happy with their productivity. The matching and tenure studies suggest the answer. The *variance* of actual and potential on-the-job-productivity increases with age—better matches lead to higher productivity for longer tenured workers. Shorter matches (a history of job turnover)—either through bad luck or lower productivity—are nevertheless taken as a "signal" of the latter. Older members of the workforce therefore find it harder to obtain a new job, particularly at a wage consistent with their previous hiring. Signaling a willingness to work at a lower wage is a possible strategy, but this may be taken as signaling of lower productivity instead of higher commitment to finding a job. Either way, *de facto* early retirement may be the only option for older workers in the labor market who have been less fortunate, or are less skilled. Overall, this may constitute evidence that the efficiency of the labor market in re-matching some older workers to employment may be imperfect, but the case for "productivity pessimism" with an older workforce is unfounded.

Macroeconomic Aspects: Does Age Structure Affect National Productivity, Output, and Unemployment?

What will be the effects on output, productivity, and unemployment at the macroeconomic level of a sudden change in the rate of population growth, or in the size of the cohort entering the labor market? If we ignore the effects on relative wages and on rates of educational attainment, and focus on the aggregate outcome, the impact will depend on the form of expectations held, the extent of substitutability in the aggregate production function, and the degree of flexibility in money wages and prices. In particular, in a neoclassical competitive model where there is both *ex ante* and *ex post* substitution in the production function, and where there are clearing product and labor markets, it is hard to believe that there would be any effects on aggregate output and unemployment even if the change in the size of the labor force stemming from population growth was wholly unanticipated.

Suppose, for example, that the population declines, and that this ultimately translates into a smaller labor force. The reduced supply of labor will raise the real wage (subject to aggregate productivity effects stemming from the changed composition of the labor force) and lead to the substitution of capital for labor. In the outcome, the *ex post* average level of labor productivity should depend on the elasticity of substitution between capital and labor and on the labor-augmenting or capital-augmenting bias of overall technical progress. So long as factor prices adjust, there should not be any impact on the level of unemployment.

To introduce some effects of population and labor-force size change, it is necessary to assume some form of rigidity in the product market and/or the labor market, and in the production process. In the latter case, one plausible story is that technology, once installed, operates with a fixed capital-labor ratio. This so-called putty-clay assumption suggests that changes in the composition or the size of the capital stock take time. Suppose that the labor force increases rapidly (or that its structure changes and different kinds of workers by age have different elasticities of complementarity with the capital stock). Then there may be short-run unemployment while the capital stock adjusts to the new labor force. However, this seems to be a greater problem in the face of unanticipated *increases* in the labor force (such as migration flows) rather than underlying, predictable demographic trends; in the latter case, parts of the capital stock can be left unused. Of course, if there is *ex post* substitutability in some degree, then in this case each member of the smaller workforce will operate with greater capital, and labor productivity will increase.

To examine the impact of changes in population growth in the context of wage and price rigidities, we can follow the argument of Nickell (1991). Suppose demand shocks are exogenous. If the population rises, for example, and the money supply is fixed, prices may be driven up. The real balance effect will reduce consumption. However, if the money wage is also fixed, then the real wage falls and equilibrium should be restored. If the *real* wage is inflexible, the natural rate of unemployment (NRU) is raised: the rising price level shifts the target real wage while the feasible real wage is constant (the latter is assumed to be determined by a fixed or procyclical markup). The only long-run equilibrium (i.e., without accelerating inflation) is at a higher level of unemployment. Again however in this story a *fall* in the rate of population or labor-force growth, given real-wage rigidity, will tend to *reduce* the NRU.

An alternative story is the "insider-outsider" approach. Those who are currently or were recently employed are "insiders" who are able to exert pressure on the wage bargain. A greater supply of insiders will reduce the bargained real-wage rate. However, "outsiders," such as the long-term unemployed, discouraged workers, and new entrants to the labor force, cannot exert significant pressure on the real wage. So a higher level of measured unemployment may arise when there are greater numbers of outsiders stemming from a large entry cohort. Likewise, slowing population growth reflected in a smaller entry cohort will not increase the real wage, and so unemployment will fall. But where the decrease in the size of the labor force is caused by a decrease in the number of *insiders* (say, through the introduction of early retirement) there will be an increase in the bargained real wage, and the reduction in unemployment will not be as great as when the labor-force decrease was induced by a reduced entry cohort of outsiders. Thus, early retirement of the "core" labor force is not the optimal way to reduce unemployment.

Overall, these "stories" suggest that, under certain circumstances, an unexpected increase in the labor force may increase unemployment. Conversely, a decrease in the labor force caused by a smaller entry cohort can reduce unemployment. The impact on productivity depends wholly on the nature of the production function and on technical progress. It should, however, be noted that this all relies on changes in the size of the labor force being unanticipated, despite the long information lead times provided by birth rates. It is hard to believe that this central assumption is realistic. It is not surprising, therefore, that Nickell (1991), in his comparison of growth rates of wages, prices, unemployment, employment, the labor force, and population among OECD countries in the postwar period, can find no systematic relationships between the variables of interest to us here. There appears to be no role for the growth of the labor force in aggregate wage determination, and no relationship among population, labor-force growth, and unemployment rates. The alleged deleterious effect of a declining birth rate and workforce on productivity, output, and unemployment levels must remain unproven.

6.5 Conclusions

This chapter has focused on the impact of population change on relative wages, educational attainment, participation rates among younger men and women, and productivity at both the microeconomic and macroeconomic level. It is apparent that the change in the size and age composition of the workforce has significant effects on many of these variables, but that these effects do not add up to a case for "aging pessimism."

The analysis adduced strong evidence that the "baby-boom cohort" depressed their own entry wage and possibly their lifetime earnings. A symmetrical interpretation predicts that smaller subsequent cohorts will face improved prospects in terms of relative wages. In the simplest story, fewer young workers relative to older workers should reduce pay inequality, because older workers generally earn more than younger workers. But this is far too simplistic; in the United States in particular, less educated workers tend to be highly substitutable, and the impact of cohort size would therefore be most noticeable among skilled, college-educated workers. But the impact of labor supply on inequality is mitigated by the increased supply of women and by the early retirement of less skilled workers.

Moreover, the experiences of the United States and Japan in the 1980s suggested that these supply shifts might be overlaid by significant structural changes in the demand for labor, to the detriment of less skilled workers.

Following this last point, it was also suggested that choice of educational attainment is affected by cohort size, although predicted outcomes are wholly dependent on the type of expectation structure held by successive cohorts. Nevertheless, there is evidence that a baby-boom generation may demand lower levels of post-compulsory education, and that the cohorts on each side of that generation will enhance their demand for education. Since the wages of college-educated workers are the most sensitive to demographic effects, this serves to dampen the disparity in cohort returns on education attributable to cohort size.

Fluctuations in relative wages also affect participation rates, especially among marginal groups. It has been argued that the lower relative wages of baby-boom women, in conjunction with lower prospective lifetime incomes of the household and postponed child rearing, induced greater participation through an "added-worker" effect; however, more recent evidence, while confirming the importance of cohort size in participation rates, suggests that the effect of cohort size over the cycle may go either way. In any event, cyclical demand shocks also play an important role in relative wage determination, educational level, and participation rates.

Finally, evidence in the early 1980s supported the idea that older workers received higher wages not because of enhanced productivity but because of seniority and other incentive systems, which might be undermined by population aging. Recent research has, however, cast doubt on this description of the labor market, arguing that sorting processes between jobs and within firms and correct measurement of training suggest that age-wage profiles in large part reflect differences in productivity. At the macroeconomic level, various theories by which changes in population and labor-force growth might affect aggregate productivity were examined. A decline in the growth of the population or in the size of the labor force could conceivably raise or reduce aggregate productivity growth, but if reflected in a decrease in the size of the entry cohort it would either reduce unemployment or leave it unchanged. It is hard to find theoretical models *or* empirical evidence to support the proposition that aging workforces in OECD countries will have adverse effects on productivity and employment.

Retirement: The Labor Supply of Older Workers in an Aging Society

Much of the concern about the consequences of aging for the labor market has centered on retirement behavior. "Retirement" itself is a rather imprecise concept, implying a discrete reduction in the scale of individual involvement in the labor market, either as perceived by the individual or as perceived by those monitoring the labor market. Nevertheless, whatever precise definition is adopted,[1] it is apparent that a significant labor-market phenomenon of the last 50 years has been the declining labor-force participation of older workers, especially men. For example, in the United States, the labor-force participation rate of men over 65 fell from 47.8 percent in 1947 to 20.0 percent in 1979 (Lazear 1986), although that of women stayed roughly constant at just over 8 percent. Similar declines in male participation are reported for most OECD countries.

For those over the state pensionable age, the trend is unsurprising given the income effect on participation of the rising value of, and eligibility for, social security pensions. But a decline in male participation is also evident for those below the state pensionable age. Figure 7.1 depicts the trends in labor-force participation rates among men of ages 55–64 in a range of OECD countries. This age group is typically still below the state pensionable age, but ,as the figure shows, in almost all these countries there has been a significant downward trend in participation over the period as a whole, although its character has varied considerably among them.

Figure 7.2 illustrates these trends for men and women in a different way for Britain, by tracing the (smoothed) economic activity of cohorts of workers over time through successive Family Expenditure Surveys (FESs). Four cohorts, born in 1910–1914, 1915–1919, 1920–1924, and 1925–1929, are illustrated at successive ages after age 45. Thus, the oldest member of the oldest cohort reached the age of 45 in 1955 (and

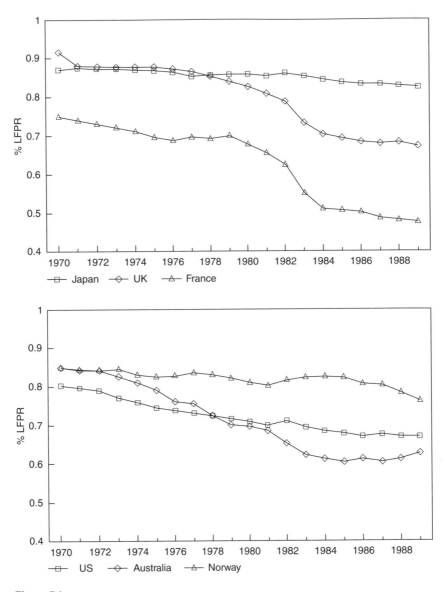

Figure 7.1
Participation rates of men aged 55–64, 1970–1989: Japan, United Kingdom, and France (top); United States, Australia, and Norway (bottom). Source: OECD 1988a.

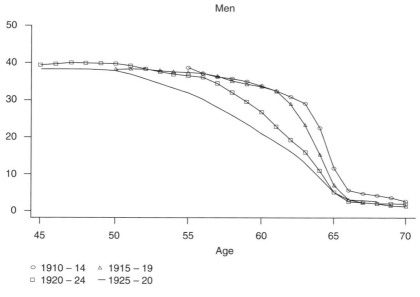

Men

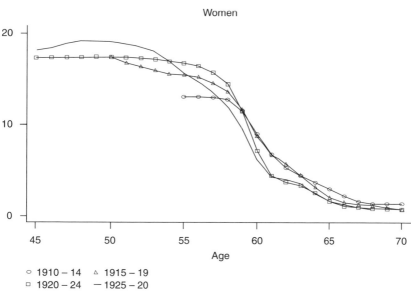

Women

Figure 7.2
Average weekly hours worked by age and cohort, Britain.

is first observed in our data in 1968), whereas the youngest individual in the youngest cohort reaches the age of 45 in 1974 and is not observed beyond age 65 in 1994. The figure depicts mean weekly hours worked across these British cohorts (including nonparticipants). Among men, the oldest cohort (1910–1914) worked on average 40 hours a week at age 45, with mean hours declining slowly to 30 hours by age 63. Between the ages of 63 and 66 mean hours fell sharply, and by age 70 average hours worked approached zero. However, the decline in hours with age occurred earlier with successive cohorts, so that the youngest cohort (1925–1929) was already averaging only 30 hours a week at age 56, and it had fallen to below 10 hours a week on average even before the state pensionable age of 65.

For women, figure 7.2 shows lower average weekly hours worked than men, owing both to women's lower labor-force participation rate and their greater propensity to work part-time. However, in contrast with men, the cohort participation profiles "cross over": each successively younger cohort tends to be working more hours in later middle age with a more rapid decline in hours as its members grow older. For example, at age 55, the oldest cohort (1910–1914) is averaging 12 hours a week, the next cohort (1915–1919) 15 hours, and the next youngest (1920–1924) 17 hours a week. At just before the state pensionable age for women, weekly hours worked begin to fall sharply. Only the youngest cohort (1925–1929) exhibits a decline in weekly hours worked at an earlier age—around age 50.

In general, hours would be expected to decline in later middle age and old age as individuals exhibit greater preference for leisure. But further investigation confirms that this reduction in average hours per worker over time stems from a greater proportion of individuals working zero hours ("retirement") rather than from a decline in average hours worked across the board, even though retirement from one job (typically a job with a pension attached) need not require complete retirement from the labor force, as in the Japanese experience described in chapter 5. Hours for those remaining in work have decreased slowly for successive cohorts, reflecting economy-wide trends, and those who continue to work after the state pensionable age typically work part-time to avoid the "Earnings Rule" (see below), but the main reason for decreasing hours before workers become eligible for social security in Britain is early retirement.

To what extent are these trends in participation in Britain attributable to the effect of changing coverage of workers by private ("occupational") pension schemes? Calculations using FES data suggest that, among pensioners, roughly 60 percent of men and 30 percent of women in the oldest cohort (1910–1914) had some income from private pensions, whereas the percentages for the youngest cohort were 70 for men and 50 for women. Furthermore, average amounts of private pension income per pensioner were highest for the youngest cohorts, presumably reflecting their longer tenure of pension schemes (Dilnot et al. 1994, figures 2.10 and 2.11).

Data from the British Retirement Survey confirm that the *pattern* of "retirement" (or, strictly, the transition to labor-market inactivity) is very different for workers covered by private pension schemes and those not covered (Disney, Meghir, and Whitehouse 1994). For the latter, the trend growth in inactivity by age after age 40 is linear (or, strictly, the hazard rate of exit into inactivity is roughly constant), reflecting increasing incidence of ill health, redundancy etc. For those in private schemes the trend is very different, with the probability of continuing to work by age "bow shaped" (that is, an increasing hazard of exit to inactivity). The likely reason is that employees covered by private pension schemes continue to work until the first date at which they become available for early-retirement provisions (see below). This will typically be at some specific date, such as "Age 55" or "Age 60," or at some fixed years of service. Since this critical point differs across pension schemes, the probability of exiting into inactivity increases as these thresholds are attained by covered workers (ibid., figure 6).

It is possible that the greater coverage of both men and women by private pensions has explained the enhanced significant drop in labor-force participation at ages such as 55 and 60 among successive cohorts. However the higher participation of women up to those ages and the general trend toward earlier "retirement" are not wholly explicable by this factor. For an explanation of these trends we would have to look at other structural changes in the labor market. One candidate would be the factors underlying the growth of women's participation in the labor force after childbearing. Another general factor could be the growth of economic inactivity among older workers on grounds of ill health and as a response to the adverse economic conditions of the mid 1970s and the early 1980s.

Reverting to the cross-country comparisons in figure 7.1, an immediate question is: Has the aging of the workforce played a part in this secular decline in participation rates among the elderly? At first sight, there is no clear relationship; the demographic trends associated with these declines in participation have differed significantly across countries. So, for example, the population aged 55–64 increased rapidly through much of this period in Japan, whereas it declined in Norway and the United Kingdom (see table 6.4). Yet in all cases the participation rate fell. OECD 1988a predicts a rise in the labor-force participation rate among this age group in the next decade in four of the six illustrated countries, and indeed OECD 1992 provides some evidence that labor-force participation rates for those over 55 stabilized in the late 1980s in Australia, the United Kingdom, Japan, and the United States. In France and Canada, however, the participation rate of people in their fifties and sixties continues to decline. The stabilization of participation rates in some countries may stem from an absence of adverse macroeconomic shocks at the end of the period, or (pursuing the analysis of cohorts illustrated in figure 7.2) may be attributable to cohort-specific factors (such as increased educational attainment) affecting life-cycle participation.

Cyclical and cohort-specific factors apart, the substantive concern then is whether, as the secular proportion of older age groups in the potential workforce grows over time, labor-force participation among older workers will continue to decline. For if the combined trends of an aging workforce and declining labor-force participation of older potential workers continue to coexist, then the extent of economic activity among the population as a whole will be curtailed. This may have both economic (see chapter 2) and social disadvantages.

It seems a paradox that, in a society where people are expecting to live longer, the age at which individuals retire from paid work is getting earlier. From a social point of view, this might be seen as a waste of human resources if older workers retain a core of skills and experience which are lost to the workforce. It is also, of course, an increasing economic burden on society if the core of "prime-age" workers is shrinking.

This waste is reinforced from the point of view of individual utility maximization by those concerned if earlier retirement is largely involuntary, stemming for example from redundancy or plant closure. Then the additional enforced leisure will have low or even negative utility, and these older displaced workers would be better off in economic activity. However, older people may find it hard to obtain paid work if job terminations are perceived as signaling low productivity and if they are thereby discouraged from searching for jobs. With re-entry after job loss hard for older workers, cohort-specific labor-force participation rates of particular cohorts may be permanently molded by adverse shocks: for example, the oil price shocks and general productivity slowdown of the 1970s and the recessions in Western Europe in the early 1980s may have induced irreversible declines in labor-force participation by older workers. Of course these shocks are cohort-specific: subsequent cohorts facing improved economic conditions may not find the same adverse "hysteresis" in their employment prospects as they grow older.

An alternative view is that the secular decline in labor-force participation rates, especially among elderly men, is an outcome of choice. For these individuals, the prospect of higher retirement income, stemming from (e.g.) the growth of private pensions and the ability to liquidate other assets such as housing equity, exceeds the utility derived from continued employment at an age when they might expect to live for another 25 years. Then the decision to retire is optimal for the individual. This view is found in Quinn et al. 1990, although the authors are careful not to equate retirement from a pensionable job with "retirement" from the labor market. However, drawing a pension may be a choice outcome and also constitute an adverse signal of a lack of commitment in the labor market, thus precluding any subsequent re-entry to the labor market if the individual regrets the apparent retirement decision.

If retirement is utility-maximizing, is there an externality or a social loss to the decision to retire? The individual could well decide to retire irrespective of whether his or her productivity is equal to or even exceeds the wage offer, as described in the next section. In a "forward-looking" (lifetime) model, the individual will evaluate the expected streams of earnings and nonwork income and the marginal utility of leisure per remaining period. This could lead still productive individuals to choose to forgo paid work. In such circumstances, it is hard to think of a social regime under which it would be desirable to force such individuals to work beyond their chosen retirement age. What is then needed, if the decline in the participation rates of the elderly is to be curtailed, is a structure of economic incentives that persuades the potential worker to continue working. Of course, even so the decision to retire may have merely illustrated that the worker's expected productivity was less than the wage for which the potential worker was prepared to supply labor (as in the Lazear model discussed in chapter 5), and so policies designed to encourage individuals to continue to work are misplaced.

Is there any credibility to the argument that retired individuals often subsequently regret the retirement decision but are unable or unwilling subsequently to obtain work at a later date? Regret might stem from a dislike of the increased leisure, or from a change in the economic environment such as increased uncertainty concerning the future generosity of social security induced by a perception of the growing burden of the elderly on government debt. In any event, this form of "regret loss" stems from a *change* in individual preferences, rather than individual loss of utility stemming from an involuntary retirement.

There is some evidence that this form of "regret loss" of utility is quite strong. A survey in Britain found that 23 percent of those under 70 but 35 percent of those over 70 interviewed thought that "the" compulsory retirement age should be raised to 70 (Casey et al. 1991), although it is not apparent what is "compulsory" about retirement. In large part this implicit regret stemmed from economic factors, as pension benefits often turned out to be less than anticipated. This has been confirmed by the 1989 Retirement Survey in Britain, which asked some 1700 retired men and women between the ages of 55 and 70 how their post-retirement income as a whole had compared with their expectation before retirement. Just 10 percent said their expectation had been exceeded, whereas over 40 percent said that their income proved to be less than they had thought it would be (Disney and Whitehouse 1996). The immediate puzzle here is why individuals in such a position could not obtain some kind of work (for example, part-time) in order to supplement their income.[2]

The aging of the workforce also has an effect on individual choice, whether subsequently regretted or not. As was suggested in chapter 6, cohort size affects wage structure, educational attainment, and consumption preferences, and we can expect differences in the labor-market behaviors of cohorts of different sizes. A larger cohort of older workers may face adverse employment prospects relative to younger workers, but these are ameliorated if the wage structure adjusts to cohort size. However, a relative decline in the wages of older workers may be more likely to induce earlier retirement (although such wage declines will also affect projected pension entitlements, which will have the opposite effect). Similarly, a larger cohort may perceive that the flow of nonlabor income (especially social security benefits) is more uncertain, and this will induce it to work longer on average as a form of insurance against a default on pension commitments by the government. Thus, there are a range of issues underpinning the relationship between retirement behavior and the aging of the population, many of which have been touched on in other chapters.

I do not intend in this chapter to survey all the literature, especially the econometric studies, concerning the retirement decision. Instead, I will focus on the aspects that relate to aging and to the previous chapters.

Section 7.1 therefore outlines a simple model of the retirement decision in a life-cycle setting and examines the consequences of changes in population age structure for the retirement decision.

Section 7.2 considers "constraints" on the pure labor-supply model of the retirement decision. These may be from the demand side—for example, where the transition to economic inactivity later in life is "involuntary," arising from a decrease in the demand for a certain type of labor. Alternatively, constraints may arise from particular disincentive effects of the tax structure in a number of OECD countries which may forestall the possibility of re-employment in the labor force after initial retirement. This issue is of some importance in considering the argument that a large retired population represents a reservoir of skills that should be exploited through paid work. However, it is suggested here that not all active policies to increase labor supply will encourage participation by the elderly.

7.1   Retirement as a Labor-Supply Decision in a Lifetime Context

Although retirement is often perceived as an institutional decision, the trends in labor-force participation before age 65 illustrated in figure 7.1 suggest that there is an element of individual choice in the retirement process. The economist's model of labor supply provides an insight into the retirement decision and into the impact of population aging on retirement behavior. The model posits that individuals gain utility from leisure and consumption, which are conveniently assumed to be separable arguments in the utility function. Consumption is obtained from income, which is derived both from accumulated assets and from earnings. The optimizing problem is general to any length of time period; it may be assumed that individuals make separable labor-supply decisions within each period or maximize their utility over the whole lifetime. In the case of variations in hours conditional on participation, within-period decision making may be optimal, but it seems likely that major participation decisions (especially the decision to retire) are made with a longer time perspective in mind.

In a general lifetime model, the individual is assumed to inherit assets A and desires to leave a fixed bequest B. With U the utility function, C standing for total consumption, L for total leisure, H for total hours of work, W for some expected average wage rate, and T for total time available (assumed here to be known with certainty), the general decision problem facing the individual or household is

$$\text{Max}U = U(C,L) \text{ subject to } C = HW + A - B = (T - L)W + A - B.$$
$$(7.1)$$

The solution of this problem, and of more complex variants, has been extensively discussed in the literature (see, for example, Killingsworth 1983 or MaCurdy 1987). The interpretation here is in the context of retirement, and it should be noted that a rationale for retirement *per se* does not exist in equation 7.1 unless some more structure is added to the problem. Thus, if the wage per unit of time and the value of leisure per unit of time are constant, there is no necessary reason for the individual to follow a continuous employment history for a part of his life $0, \ldots, R$ and then retire for the remaining period $R, \ldots, T$; a strategy of reduced but continuous employment throughout the lifetime is probably optimal.

When the model is extended to permit fluctuations in the wage over time, and when a perfect capital market exists (which also includes a supply of "fair" annuities), variations in the allocation of time between employment and leisure over time may be consistent with rational behavior (Lucas and Rapping 1969), although fixed costs of work may preclude spells of partial employment (Lazear 1986). However, a straightforward story for retirement relies on systematic change in the wage profile over the lifetime (which reflects underlying movements in the individual's marginal value product), on systematic change in the marginal utility of leisure, or on both.

Figure 7.3 provides a simple period-by-period decision model illustrating the point, with arbitrary values of the value of the marginal product of labor (MVP) and the marginal utility of leisure (MUL) plotted against age. Wages are assumed to reflect a "spot-market" equilibrium inverted-U productivity profile, and the marginal valuation of leisure is assumed to rise with age. Then individuals will work until their MVP falls below their marginal utility of leisure. Note that retire-

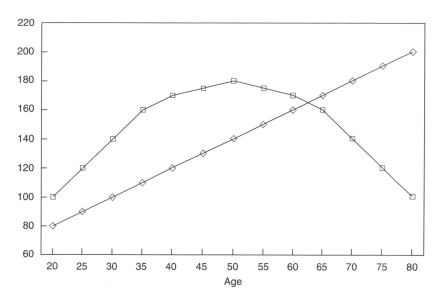

Figure 7.3
Static model of the retirement decision, with □ representing marginal value product
and ◇ marginal utility of leisure.

ment does not take place when either the MVP or the MUL is at its
maximum. Furthermore, where wages are backloaded for incentive
reasons (see chapter 5), an explicit retirement age or specific "carrots"
such as early-retirement "windows" may be required in order to implement the underlying equality of the TVP (total value product) and
total real wages paid in an implicit lifetime contract.

Pensions and Retirement
The previous model assumed that there is a perfect capital market on
which individuals can lend in order to provide an annuity on retirement (or alternatively that T is known with certainty), that there is
no earnings uncertainty (either concerning stochastic fluctuations in
earnings or in terms of earnings capacity), and that the marginal utility
of leisure varies monotonically with time. None of these assumptions
is particularly convincing, and all have been extensively discussed
in a substantial literature beginning with Yaari (1965). In particular,
the market for individual annuity purchases is generally perceived
to be rather small for standard adverse selection reasons (Friedman
and Warshawsky 1988, 1990; Brugiavini 1993), and most provision for
retirement is through institutional forms such as company pension

plans or tax-privileged retirement savings accounts such as IRAs or Personal Pensions.

Therefore, if when an individual retires his or her savings will be supplemented by institutional pension rights, any statutory provision as to how and when these pension benefits can be obtained (e.g., a fixed state pensionable age) will affect the retirement decision of the forward-looking individual consumer relative to the age at which he or she might have considered retirement had purchase of an annuity in the capital market been the only option. Although retirement "bunching" is thereby more likely, the response of individuals need not be identical, especially if returns to the pension scheme vary among individuals and where pension receipt does not always depend on the worker's having "retired" from the labor force.

Consider first social security pensions, financed by payments of taxes or contributions into a pension scheme during the working lifetime. In a typical public pay-as-you-go scheme, the analysis requires a *within-period* budget constraint by which aggregate social security taxes equal the aggregate of benefit payments in each time period. Under certain "steady-state" conditions, discussed in chapters 2 and 3, the PAYG nature of the scheme, as opposed to full funding, will have no effect on the retirement decision, because there will be no intergenerational redistribution associated with the social security program.

In practice, rates of return to pension schemes for different cohorts or generations vary significantly for two main reasons: changes in scheme provisions over time and demographic changes (see Hurd and Shoven 1985 and Boskin et al. 1987 for the United States and Disney and Whitehouse 1993c for the United Kingdom). Furthermore, nonlinear tax and pension schedules, differential indexation procedures, and differences in expected mortality also imply different returns to the pension scheme among members of the *same* cohort (Creedy et al. 1993). So the existence of public pension schemes will affect the distribution of retirement outcomes both between and within successive cohorts because of variations in scheme returns among individuals.

In the case of a funded private pension scheme, which we might initially consider to be a money purchase scheme in which lifetime contributions determine benefits; then if the market risk rates efficiently, and if no revealed information as to, for example, health affects employment status over the lifetime (see Diamond and Mirrlees 1978), the lifetime budget constraint for each individual requires that the accumulated sum of contributions to retirement equals the present value of pension rights. Retirement choice should be unaffected. But in a typical "defined-benefit" funded pension scheme benefits are not determined by contributions paid; rather, contributions are set such as to provide for future fund liabilities given the scheme's benefit formula. The aggregate accrual of pension rights typically depends on the distribution of employment tenure among participants and on variations in career and (particularly) final earnings. A consequence of within-scheme variation in returns on contributions will be variation in individual retirement behavior.

A period-by-period approach to the retirement decision building on the general labor-supply model in equation 7.1 in the context of a DB plan might assume that the individual calculates the pension increment for each additional period's work (net of pension contribution) and evaluates the marginal remuneration against the value of leisure. Denoting the wage in period t as w_t, the pension contribution as τ_t, and the per period increment in pension entitlement as $(p_t - p_{t-1})$, then the additional remuneration $\hat{w}_t$ is

$$\hat{w}_t(1 - \tau_t) + (p_t - p_{t-1}).$$

The individual will continue to work so long as $\hat{w}_t$ exceeds the marginal utility of leisure per period. Since the pension term in particular may exhibit significant discontinuities and spikes, the phenomenon of "retirement bunching" is likely, especially where some pension benefits, including social security rights, involve a fixed pensionable age (Lazear 1986) or where there is an age at which scheme retirement benefits first become available.

To put this into a life-cycle perspective, the period-by-period comparison must take account of the time path of $\hat{w}_t$ from 0 to T. The relevant criterion in a lifetime context is how an extra year's employment (and pension accrual) affects pension benefits conditional on retirement for *all* years hence. One more year's work may then shift the optimal retirement date at some future point so that, in the lifetime context, it is not simply the *current* year's pension accrual that is appropriate. In this "forward-looking" or intertemporal model, the individual is envisaged as treating consumption and leisure in a life-cycle context. He or she projects future paths of wages and pension increments through to alternative retirement dates and then solves for the optimal retirement data so as to maximize lifetime utility. If, following Burbidge and Robb (1980), leisure in working years is denoted as 0 and leisure in retirement years as 1, the maximization problem and the intertemporal budget constraint can be written as follows: Maximize

$$\int_0^R U[c(t),0]e^{-it}dt + \int_R^T U[c(t),1]e^{-it}dt \tag{7.2}$$

subject to

$$\int_0^R \hat{w}(t)e^{-it}dt + \int_R^T p(t)e^{-it}dt = \int_0^T c(t)e^{-it}dt. \tag{7.3}$$

The similarity of this more refined version of equation 7.1 with the production equilibrium in equation 5.3 is apparent. If the individual evaluates utility over leisure and consumption (equation 7.2) subject to equation 7.3, and to any fixed initial assets and bequests, maximization will in general involve consideration of the consequences for future pension streams *at all dates* of retirement of any extra period of employment, given that the value of pension rights will be linked to wage increments in a formula-based defined-benefit pension.[3] Of course, future expected wages will also affect the retirement decision; but, unlike pension entitlements, wages across time periods can be treated as separable. Again, however, new information (for example as to future employment prospects or health status) may lead to a re-evaluation of future earnings capacity, which may in turn affect the retirement decision.

Equations 7.2 and 7.3 reflect the maximization problem of the individual consumer/worker. At the same time, there is an intertemporal budget constraint facing the employer, which is similar to equation 5.3; that is, with the value of production substituting for the level of consumption in equation 7.2. For an individual valuing the consumption stream according to a "lifetime implicit contract" with a single employer, the values of production and consumption will be equated over the lifetime; but where (as is likely) job tenures are less than the employment lifetime and where pensions are not fully portable, the equality of 5.3 and 7.3 need not hold over the lifetime.

The model can be extended to incorporate the social security pension. If the state pensionable age is fixed, there may be a distinction between that age ($\hat{R}$) and the chosen pensionable age within the private pension scheme (R). The relevant budget constraint is now as follows, with the subscripts p and s denoting the private and the state pension:

$$\int_0^R \hat{w}(t)e^{-it}dt + \int_R^T p_p(t)e^{-it}dt + \int_{\hat{R}}^T p_s(t)e^{-it}dt = \int_0^T c(t)e^{-it}dt. \qquad (7.3')$$

If $\hat{R} < R$, then the state may exact some extra tax from individuals who continue to work after the state pensionable age (see section 7.2); this will be another rationale for "retirement bunching," in this case around the public pensionable age. However, the data given in figure 7.1 suggest that $\hat{R} \geq R$ is more likely for many individuals.

It is technically possible that there is no single equilibrium solution to the choice of retirement age: more than one retirement age is compatible with maximization of equation 7.2 subject to equation 7.3 or 7.3'. Where pension benefits are backloaded but the pension scheme penalizes late retirement (i.e. provides an actuarially unfair deferral formula), the path of $\hat{w}$ may be such as to generate more than one solution. In figure 7.4, $\hat{w}$ dips below the marginal utility of leisure at two points, either of which could be a possible retirement age in a static model. However, the forward-looking consumer would be able

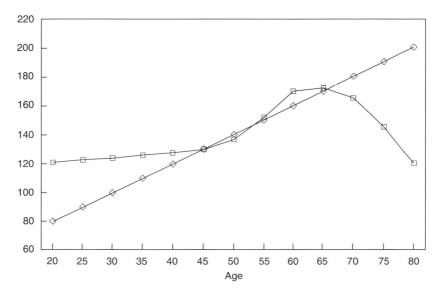

Figure 7.4
Multiple solutions in forward-looking separable model, with □ representing net wage and ◇ marginal utility of leisure.

to evaluate the utility outcome at either point and thus to derive a single optimal solution.

An Aging Population and Retirement

Now revert to the issue of an aging population and consider how the retirement decision is affected by aging in the context of the intertemporal model of choice of retirement date. The key issue is whether an aging population is likely to lead individuals to retire later or earlier than they would do in the context of a faster-growing population. By analyzing this issue, we can shed light on the pattern of retirement decisions in the future. As ever in economics, however, it turns out that an aging population pushes the retirement decision in conflicting directions. The issue can be considered in the context of a public PAYG pension scheme.

Increased longevity

If aging takes the form of increased longevity, workers can expect to live longer from any given date of retirement than in the past. This effect will tend to postpone retirement—an intuitive result of equations 7.2 and 7.3, since to achieve a given per-period level of consumption the individual needs to work for more periods in order to acquire the necessary lifetime income. Since the marginal utility of consumption in each period is thereby higher, the marginal utility of leisure is lower. The case of increased longevity is illustrated in figure 7.5. For these arbitrary values, a constant reduction in the marginal utility of leisure of, on average, 7 percent leads to retirement deferral by 5 years.

A contracting workforce

Suppose, however, that aging also implies that the size of the potential "prime-age" workforce is contracting, due to a reduction in the size of entry cohorts. In the standard framework of chapter 2, the PAYG payroll-tax rate needed to finance pensions at any given retirement age is increasing. The value of $\hat{w}$ in figure 7.3 is lower and it is apparent that this will serve to *reduce* the optimal retirement age, *ceteris paribus*. Figure 7.6 illustrates the case where aging reduces both the net wage and the MUL in every period. The net impact on retirement is uncertain, depending on the relative size of the substitution and income effects of the declines in the MVP and the MUL respectively.

A rise in the expected average replacement ratio (ratio of social security and pension benefits to earnings) without increasing longevity is

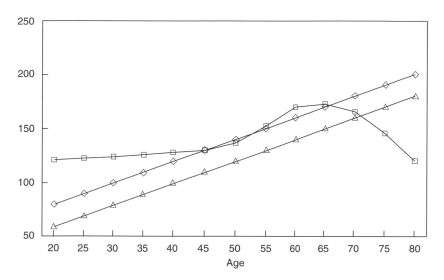

Figure 7.5
Increased longevity, with □ representing net wage, ◇ representing marginal utility of
leisure with lower longevity, and Δ representing marginal utility of leisure with greater
longevity.

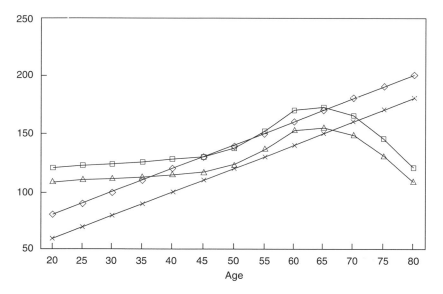

Figure 7.6
Increased longevity and higher taxes, with □ representing net wage, ◇ representing
marginal utility of leisure with lower longevity and larger workforce, and × representing net wage and Δ marginal utility of leisure with greater longevity and contracting
workforce.

straightforward to analyze where the benefit increment is strictly proportionate to income and invariant to the time at which it accrues. This operates like a decrease in the size of the workforce, raising the equilibrium payroll-tax rate and so discouraging participation. Moreover, the MUL will not be affected if the scheme is exactly actuarially neutral to the individual. These results are proved by Sheshinski (1978), who finds by simulation analysis (albeit with a particular specification of the utility function) that retirement age is extremely sensitive to changes in the replacement ratio associated with a rising payroll-tax rate. In general, it can be shown in such a framework that the effect of a change in the replacement ratio on the age of retirement will depend on the level of the replacement ratio and on the rate of growth of the labor force, which together determine the time path of the payroll-tax rate, as in the model developed in chapter 2 above. However, choice of retirement age tends to exacerbate the swings in payroll-tax rates associated with given patterns of labor-force growth and changes in the level of the replacement ratio. In a typical simulation by Sheshinski, with a 20 percent replacement ratio and a decrease in population growth from 4 percent to 2 percent, the social security tax rate rises from 7.5 percent to 10.5 percent with fixed retirement age but to 12.3 percent with variable retirement age (ibid., p. 352).

Appraisal: future trends and uncertainty
It is therefore apparent that a general aging of the population will have uncertain effects on the retirement decision: increased longevity will prolong the working life, whereas rising tax burdens stemming from pay-as-you-go financing of pensions will shorten it. As chapter 4 suggested, replacement ratios continued to rise throughout the 1960s and the 1970s, and, if anticipated, this rise may have been a major reason why the labor-force participation of those entering their fifties declined sharply in that period, especially among men for whom occupational pension coverage and uninterrupted work histories promised a high level of pension benefits. Some studies, such as that of Boskin and Hurd (1978), show that expected social security benefits have a major impact on behavior, even inducing early retirement prior to benefit receipt. This is despite the fact that social security programs will tend to offer a fixed pensionable age plus deferral terms which tend to induce "retirement bunching" around that age. However, Hurd (1990) and Quinn et al. (1990) are more cautious when evaluating subsequent studies in the United States on the impact of social security and retire-

ment which, they believe, do not show a clear-cut impact of the level of social security on participation among the elderly. They attribute the failure to find clear-cut effects to difficulties in modeling the "forward-looking" model of behavior described above, as well as to standard problems of measurement error in marginal wages and in predicting wage paths for the economically inactive.

Moreover, as pointed out above and by Burbidge and Robb (1980), the Sheshinski (1978) "substitution" model of optimal retirement by-passes all the nonlinearities in payroll-tax structures and benefit entitlements that actually exist in social security programs. In practice, the social security program is non-neutral among individuals, and taking account of these differences in rates of return there may be no clear relationship among *average* payroll-tax rates, average social security benefits, and the trend in retirement age, as Burbidge and Robb show for the Canadian public pension scheme.

Even if there has been a clear trend (driven by social security) toward earlier retirement, this trend may have ceased. First, as Sheshinski demonstrates, there are ways of structuring a public pension scheme so as to encourage deferred retirement. The most obvious is to relate the level of social security benefit positively to retirement age, arranging that the benefit deferral rate is actuarially favorable to the deferrer. A process of reform in this direction is underway in many countries and is likely to accelerate; for example, in the United Kingdom in November 1993 it was announced that the deferral rate for social security increments was to be raised from 7.5 percent to 10 percent at the same time as the first age of receipt was equalized between the sexes at the (higher) men's age of 65. Other countries have also raised the age at which the social security pension is first available and phased out early-retirement programs. Second, and perhaps fundamentally, it is questionable whether the model of retirement choice will continue to predict falling retirement age, even with rising levels of income, once uncertainty is introduced into the picture. Cutbacks in social security and adverse macroeconomic trends seem likely to reduce expectations as to future pension benefits, although payroll-tax rates in a PAYG pension scheme will be determined by *past* retirement decisions.

There is a greater weight of evidence that private pension schemes have tended to encourage earlier retirement in countries where such schemes are extensive.[4] Successive cohorts are retiring with increasing years of coverage, given the expansion of coverage in the 1950s and the 1960s in the United States and the United Kingdom, and pension benefits are playing an increasing role in determining the retirement decision. Even so, individuals have tended in the past to hold excessively optimistic expectations as to future pension benefits, and events such as the 1987 Stock Market crash and the experience of existing retirers may have forced subsequent retiring cohorts to revise their opinions. Ghilarducci (1992) describes survey data which suggest that individuals substantially overvalue their accumulated benefits in service relative to an actuarial benchmark. Disney and Whitehouse (1996) show, using UK Retirement Survey data, that only a small minority of workers retiring in the late 1980s had sufficient years of service in their company pension scheme to obtain anything close to a full pension without additional "windows" and topping up of contributions for early retirement. And further uncertainties, such as that surrounding post-retirement indexation of benefits, remain (for example, individuals may evaluate pension streams in retirement in nominal, not real terms). Thus, there are conflicting trends as to the prospective retirement behavior of individuals covered by private pension schemes. Successive cohorts will retire with greater benefits due to longer scheme durations, but may also have greater experience of prospective benefits and more realistic expectations. Insofar as this reduces subjective uncertainty it will permit risk-averse individuals to retire earlier, but insofar as this generates lower expectations of prospective benefits it will lead them to defer retirement—especially if the 1990s climate is expected to generate more "objective" risk, such as greater uncertainty as to the performance of equities (stocks) in the post-1987-crash regime. Coupled with declining prospects for social security, the balance of probabilities suggests that these conflicting trends may stabilize the retirement age, or even reverse the trend toward earlier retirement.

7.2 Constraints on Employment of Older Workers

Reported Motives for Retirement

This subsection considers whether the life-cycle labor-supply model paints an inaccurate picture of the retirement decision insofar as it assumes that retirement is based entirely on choice. To the extent that retirement is a decision forced on the individual by demand factors, or by institutional features such as a "retirement test" associated with receipt of social security or a pension, the trend toward earlier retirement could, and perhaps should, be halted in an aging population by active labor-market policies. Even so, as was noted in the introduction to this chapter, identifying "constraints" on retirement behavior is difficult: for example, when the lifetime wage trajectory is distorted by employers as an incentive device, and individuals can choose not to work for those particular employers, mandatory retirement is not a constraint on choice in a life-cycle perspective.

What evidence do we have that retirers *choose* to retire when they do? First, it is well known that there are a variety of definitions of retirement (Hurd 1990; Lazear 1986). Self-reported retirement is particularly problematic, although answers to questions concerning under what circumstances individuals would consider themselves retired are of some interest. For example, in the 1988–89 British Retirement Survey of a sample of more than 3500 people between the ages of 55 and 69, respondents variously associated the state of "retirement" with reaching the state pensionable age (even if still working), with not working and not wanting another job, with not working and not able to get another job, and with being unable or unwilling to get another job because of poor health. Given these subjective definitions, the retirement state is uncertain and should be modeled probabilistically.[5]

Table 7.1 reports individual self-assessed reasons for retirement for this UK Retirement Survey data, specifically for those who reported

Table 7.1
Main reasons for taking, or expecting to take, early retirement. (Numbers are percentages.) Adapted from Bone et al. 1992, table 5.7.

Main reason for taking, or expecting to take, early retirement	Retired from a job Men		Women		All: Retired plus not retired and working or expecting to work again Men		Women	
	<60	>60	<60	>60	<60	>60	<60	>60
Own ill health	46	29	32	14	42	26	31	11
Others' ill health	3	3	11	12	3	3	10	9
Redundancy or difficulty in finding a job	15	13	10	3	13	10	9	2
Financial inducement	22	26	7	10	22	24	7	9
Family reasons/more leisure	7	11	20	26	16	22	23	40
Other reasons	7	18	20	25	4	17	20	29
Base = 100%	196	198	293	66	210	245	311	125

having taken or intending to take early retirement relative to what they perceived as the "normal" retirement age (either in their job or in their self-assessed view of normal retirement date). Among men in their fifties, the dominant reported reason for retirement is ill health. Many company pension schemes facilitate this form of retirement. Moreover, within the social security program, disability benefits were among the fastest-growing expenditure categories in the United Kingdom in the 1980s, especially among this age group (Disney and Webb 1991). Other countries, including the Netherlands, have seen a very similar growth in disability-related retirement (Van Den Bosch and Petersen 1983; see chapter 5 of OECD 1992 for other illustrations).

Male respondents in their fifties also commonly cite "financial inducements," which are primarily temporary or permanent early-retirement provisions within company pension schemes (there are no provisions for early retirement on reduced pension benefits in the social security program in the United Kingdom). The "made redundant or difficulty in finding another job" is the next most important category in the table among this group. This factor might reflect constraints on the labor supply, so long as the individual concerned is willing to work at a wage consistent with his marginal productivity. At most, however, 15 percent of 50-year-old men are so affected. Reasons that might be rationalized in terms of the rising marginal utility of leisure account for a further 7 percent (wholly among men in their later fifties).

For older men, financial inducements and ill health are by far the strongest motives, with "rising MUL" motives now receiving the same weight as potential constraints. For women, however, the picture is rather different. Ill health, not just of the respondent, but of other family members, remains important, but it is noticeable that responses in terms of family and leisure considerations dominate other factors such as financial inducements and constraints on employment other than health. Rather strangely, the family and leisure motive becomes more dominant when the sample includes those who do not define themselves as retired (in the table). This may suggest that the MUL does not have a monotonic relationship with age, in that individuals do consider the possibility of subsequently returning to the labor force even when leisure is currently more attractive than work. However, the decay in work opportunities at given wages for workers at or above the state pensionable age may explain why many such workers do not in fact re-enter the labor market.

Thus, the main reported constraint on work in the United Kingdom for both older men and older women is ill health in later life. The evidence of table 7.1 suggests that the labor-supply decision for relatively healthy older men is dominated by shifts in the MVP and the income effects of pension receipt. For women, considerations relating to the rise in the MUL and other social obligations within the family (for example, the ill health of the husband) enter the retirement calculus. Demand constraints as such seem relatively unimportant, especially for women. This is consistent with the evidence, noted in the introduction to this chapter, that the participation of older women has been maintained (despite the decline in participation of older men).

Nevertheless, there is an important caveat to all this. Table 7.2 contains a cross-country comparison of motives for retirement among a number of OECD countries. It shows that self-assessed motives for retirement differ widely across the countries. The table confirms the importance of "ill health" as a stated motive for retirement in the United Kingdom, whereas in France "other" motives are given predominance. In the Netherlands "economic" retirement is extensive, which is not surprising given extensive coverage by defined-benefit pension plans; but this motive is given significantly less emphasis in the United Kingdom, where such plans are also pervasive. Individuals in Spain are much more likely to represent "retirement" as the outcome of a labor-market constraint; this is not inconsistent with the high level of measured unemployment in Spain compared to, say, Germany. So the results are compatible with "objective" economic differences between countries, but the disproportionate differences suggest that social as well as economic pressures, and differences in questionnaire construction, probably play a part in these differential responses.[6] To the extent that "retirement" from the labor market is a subjective state of mind, sample surveys can play only a limited part in determining its extent.[7]

Declining Job Opportunities for the Less Skilled?

One policy issue concerning trends in the United States, touched on in chapter 6, is whether declining participation of older workers, which was associated with increasing wage inequality through the 1970s and the early 1980s, arises from a change in the demand for skilled workers relative to their supply. Declining labor-force participation is noticeable for all male workers, but is particularly prevalent among workers with over 40 years of potential labor-market experience (i.e., those in their

Table 7.2
Inactive individuals aged 55–64, with work experience in the last three years, by reason for leaving last job, 1990 (percentage). Source: OECD 1992, table 5.8.

	Germany	France	Netherlands	UK	Spain
Made redundant/end of contract					
Men	1.4	9.7	—	19.4	11.6
Women	1.5	12.0	—	13.5	27.1
Total	2.8	10.6	—	14.4	15.3
Resignation					
Men	1.7	—	—	1.1	0.9
Women	3.8	—	—	4.0	3.5
Total	2.5	—	—	2.8	2.3
"Economic" retirement					
Men	35.0	18.3	59.7	8.3	18.1
Women	20.5	12.1	36.2	4.0	2.6
Total	29.5	15.9	54.1	6.0	14.2
Ill-health retirement					
Men	34.1	9.2	20.4	35.2	22.5
Women	17.8	13.5	23.8	15.9	16.3
Total	28.0	10.9	21.2	25.1	20.7
Other retirement					
Men	23.6	61.1	9.7	29.7	38.3
Women	43.1	52.2	4.9	45.1	23.7
Total	31.0	57.6	8.6	38.9	34.4
"Personal reasons"					
Men	4.1	1.7	10.2	6.3	8.8
Women	12.3	10.2	35.1	17.5	26.9
Total	7.2	5.0	16.1	12.7	13.1

late fifties and older), workers with lower schooling, workers with lower earnings, and black workers (Juhn 1992).

The *form* of this declining participation appears to be longer spells of nonemployment (whether unemployment or nonparticipation) culminating in earlier "retirement" from paid employment. It has been suggested that the growing inequality of wages in the United States, especially the significant decline in *real* wages in the lowest deciles, reflects a decline in labor-force opportunities for less skilled workers, perhaps stemming from increased competition both from other types of workers (notably women) and from foreign competition in the traded-goods sector, coupled with changing skill requirements in the economy. In other OECD countries, where the "floor" to the wage distribution seems to be more robust than in the United States, this process may take the form of rising unemployment among older workers (see OECD 1992). Incorporating the analysis of the previous chapter, a particularly adverse combination arises where a large cohort of relatively unskilled older workers face an adverse shift in the mix of demand for skills. These serve to depress their own potential real wages and job opportunities at any fixed reservation wage.

In his study of the United States, Juhn estimates wage-offer distributions for each year 1967 to 1987 together with a "participation function" which suggests that the probability of participation is positively related to the wage. So the decline in labor-force participation can stem either from a shift in the wage-offer distribution (specifically, fewer "offers" at lower wages) or from a shift in the participation function given the wage-offer distribution. Juhn suggests that the declining labor-force participation of whites for the whole period bar 1967–1969 can be wholly explained by a shift in the wage-offer distribution with a decline in labor-market opportunities for less skilled workers. For whites in 1967–1969, and for blacks throughout the period, there is some evidence of an additional downward shift in the participation function *given* the wage-offer distribution. So for white workers for most of the period, the increasing constraints on the demand for less skilled workers, leading to declining real wages for those groups, have induced a supply response. For blacks, and for white workers in 1967–1969, this has been supplemented by a shift in behavior, perhaps reflecting a change in preferences or in the availability of other sources of income. In the context of retirement, this result is of some interest. For elderly labor-market participants who are less skilled, the lack of job opportunities is reflected in a declining expected wage. Indeed, the wage effect of the depreciation of skills with aging might be enhanced, so exacerbating the "inverted U" of figure 7.3. Such a trend would generate earlier retirement, and it is hard to see how this trend could be reversed without an increased demand for less skilled workers and a stemming of the tide toward greater inequality in the wage structure. The decline in real wages at the lower end would also make the "floor" provided by the social security program more attractive, so enhancing the trend toward nonparticipation among older males. To add to this adverse set of circumstances, there is also evidence that older displaced workers generally face a much more restricted available choice set of jobs, with jobs in the same industry (often at a lower grade) or gradual withdrawal from the labor force the only feasible options (Hutchens 1993).

This trend toward greater wage inequality has been observed additionally in the United Kingdom (Freeman and Katz 1994). But even there, growing wage inequality has not been associated with declining real wages among the lower paid. It is hard to believe, however, that technological change and foreign competition have not affected labor markets in other OECD countries. Furthermore, the labor-force participation of women has also increased in all these countries. Thus, it seems likely that other policies or trends elsewhere have masked the tendency toward growing wage inequality observed in the United States. These include programs to employ hard-to-place workers, especially in the public sector (as in Sweden), generous programs of income support for the disabled (the Netherlands and to a lesser extent the United Kingdom), active policies of labor-force reduction via early retirement (as in France), labor hoarding in the public sector (as in Greece, Italy, and Turkey) and simply higher unemployment levels, reflecting the more generous "floor" of social security benefits and the downward rigidity of the lower end of the pay structure (as in almost all European countries). Thus, in Europe the decline in labor-force participation of the less skilled elderly has taken the form, not of a labor-supply reduction in the face of declining real wages, but of a discouraged worker effect in the face of fewer job offers at positive wages (a rationing of jobs for the less skilled).

Institutional Constraints: "Earnings Taxes" on Pensioners
Retirement behavior takes place within an environment defined by government policy. Eligibility for state retirement benefits is typically precluded below a certain age (although actuarial reductions are offered in some countries for early retirement, notably in Scandinavia, and in France in the early 1980s), and there may also be restrictions on pension receipt conditional on attaining pensionable age and depending on labor-force participation and other sources of income. Table 7.3 illustrates some of these institutional "constraints" on choice of date of annuitization and on subsequent employment for a variety of countries. Some examples, notably the Australian scheme, have been discussed in greater detail in chapter 4. The most obvious point from the table is that these institutional constraints vary widely. They can also have quite complex effects on labor supply and, in particular, on the retirement decision.

Table 7.3
Some salient features of social security programs. Source: Social Security Administration 1992.

	Normal pensionable age	Flexibility in pensionable age?	Restrictions on Social security receipt and participation
Australia	Men: 65 Women: 60	No	Pension is income tested and asset value tested
France	60	Retirement can be deferred after 60. Deferral accrual rate 2.5% per quarter	Must stop work with pre-retirement employer. "Solidarity" tax on other work.
(ex-W)Germany	Between 60 and 65 depending on time in labor force.	No early retirement with actuarial reduction.	Age 60–63 limited earnings to DM480 per month, 1991. Age 63–65 limited to DM1000 per month.
ex-GDR	*Men: 65 Women: 60*	Deferring age 65–67 accrues 0.6% per month. *None*	*None*
Japan	Basic Pension: 65 Additional pension: 55–60	BP: Can retire 60–64 with actuarial reduction. Pension deferral is possible.	"Retirement" a necessary condition for receipt until 70 (men), 65 (women).
Netherlands	65	No	None
Spain	Normally 65	Early retirement possible; pension reduced by 8% per annum <65	Retirement necessary
US	Normally 65 To rise to 67 in stages	Age 62–64 with actuarial reduction Deferral rate post-65 4.5% per annum	Pension reduced $1 in $2 age 62–64 for 1995 weekly earnings >$940; by $1 in $3 for 65 and over for weekly earnings >$680
UK	Men 65 Women 60 To be equalized in stages at 65	No early retirement Deferral presently possible at accrual rate of 7.5% per annum until 70 (men) and 65 (women). Unlimited 10% deferral accrual rate to be introduced.	Until Oct. 1989: If earnings above limit post-age 65/60 taxed at 100%; must not work more than 12 hours a week for state pension receipt. Both rules now abolished.

An apparently simple case is the Netherlands, where there is a fixed pensionable age and no retirement "test" for receipt of the social security pension. Even here, however, the analysis of the impact of the social security program depends on whether a "static" (single-period) or life-cycle decision framework is adopted. In the "static" model, at age 65 there is a pure income effect on participation from the state retirement pension; this will increase the likelihood of retirement. However, in a multiperiod model, if "retirement" is not a requirement of social security receipt, the present value of social security conditional on an expected earnings history can be calculated, and there is no certainty that retirement need coincide with the onset of pensionable age.

At the other extreme of complexity is the United Kingdom before October 1989, where retirement behavior was constrained by a fixed pensionable age for the state pension with the possibility of deferral for 5 years, by a retirement test, and by an "earnings rule" that effectively precluded full-time work for 5 years after attaining pensionable age. Similar taxes on earnings post-retirement and deferral rules are observed in a number of countries in table 7.3, although interestingly at widely different rates. (It is hard to believe discount rates differ so widely among populations.)

The deferral rate of 7.5 percent in the United Kingdom, given the expected longevity of 13 years at age 65, is not on average actuarially fair at any positive rate of discount for a man, although for women the option might be attractive, *ceteris paribus,* and particularly given the earlier pensionable age. Although it is to be assumed from self-selection that those men who have an expectation of greater longevity might also defer, it is nevertheless not surprising to find that participation among women in the United Kingdom in the age group eligible to defer (60–64) at 24 percent in 1990 is higher than that of men in the comparable interval (65–69) at 16 percent in 1990 (see Disney, Meghir, and Whitehouse 1994). The intention to increase the deferral rate to 10 percent should induce a substitution effect on the margin from taking the pension at 65 to deferral.

Figure 7.7 illustrates the single-period or "static" budget constraint facing an individual in the United Kingdom before October 1989 who was considering whether to take the retirement pension at age 65 and simultaneously to continue in paid work.[8] By deferring, earnings net of income tax are retained.[9] By not deferring, for earnings below £75, the pension was retained, but between £75 and £79 the pension was withdrawn at a 50 percent rate, and thereafter at a 100 percent rate

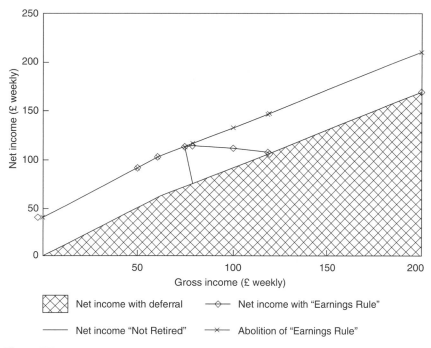

Figure 7.7
Budget constraint with earnings rule (United Kingdom, pre-October 1989).

until the pension was depleted. This was the "earnings rule" (Whitehouse 1990). An alternative constraint was that work of more than 12 hours a week was penalized by withdrawal of the whole weekly value of the pension. This is also illustrated at the diagrammatically convenient wage of £6.25 per hour, where an abrupt kink in the budget constraint is observed under both the "earnings rule" and the "12-hour rule."

Since the "earnings rule" and the limit on hours so clearly penalized employment above pensionable age associated with nondeferral, it was hoped that their abolition in 1989 might increase employment among the elderly. Not surprisingly in view of the penalty tax rate, very few people were directly affected by the earnings rule : only some 2500 at the time. However, 200,000 who deferred and 200,000 who worked fewer than 12 hours a week might be affected. But the incentive effect of this reform does not go wholly in one direction, toward higher participation. For while those who are in receipt of the pension and working less than 12 hours might increase their hours, for those who have deferred, the abolition of the "earnings rule" is a pure income effect if the deferral terms are "unfair"; such individuals can now receive their state pension while continuing to work. Since the groups are of roughly equal size and the relevant hours elasticities in relation to net wages for men are not large, the impact of eliminating these constraints on the participation of the elderly, particularly men, is probably rather small.[10]

This evidence that retirement "tests" probably have rather small effects on participation seems to be confirmed for the United States, where retirement tests appear to alter average hours worked and wages (rather than participation) and where abolition of such tests seem to accelerate the decline in labor-force participation among older workers (Leonesio 1993).

It is not necessary to describe the institutional details for the other countries in table 7.3; the broad issues are clear. Therefore to what extent might changes in the institutional constraints facing older workers alter their participation? First, it is apparent that studies of incentives in the context of single-period budget constraints may be highly misleading. The life-cycle perspective explains why retirement decisions do not in fact take place at pensionable age, where the static "income effects" of social security programs are most apparent. Second, there are both "stick" measures (raising the retirement age, or reducing the size of social security benefits) and "carrot" measures (more attractive deferral, abolition of retirement requirements for benefit receipt or of taxes on post-pension age earnings). But the analysis suggests that the consequences of stick measures may be more clear cut than those of carrot measures: the former induce simple adverse income effects over the lifetime, which may induce greater participation; the latter typically rely on combinations of income and substitution effects on participation, which may go either way. Even so, there is little clear-cut evidence that either are of great significance in explaining retirement trends in the last two decades.

"Staged" Retirement and Other Labor-Market Measures

A final issue of some interest in the context of a large cohort of older workers with diminishing employment prospects is whether some form of "staged" or partial retirement is feasible. Ideas such as a "decade of retirement" are superficially attractive; it seems likely that the marginal utility of work declines only gradually, and this may seem a route by which at least partial economic activity can be maintained in a population exhibiting greater longevity.

OECD 1992 cites two routes: "bridge" jobs and partial retirement. The former is most typically associated with the Japanese experience discussed in section 5.1, where individuals take mandatory retirement at a relatively early age from their "primary" job and then work for the company or an associated enterprise, perhaps with fewer hours and lower pay. This form of "industrial paternalism" does not now seem extensive outside Japan, and it may be declining there. Part-time work is generally lower paid and less attractive, particularly to individuals used to considerably higher remuneration. Furthermore, it is hard to see how such jobs can be developed in other economies except by "market forces." One such avenue is that an increasing share of total expenditure is undertaken by elderly consumers (see the next chapter), who may find that dealing with older workers, especially in services, is more attractive. Thus elderly consumers create jobs for older workers. This is an attractive solution but perhaps too simplistic; for example, the growth of residential-care services associated with extreme longevity has led to an expansion of employment in nursing care and ancillary activities, but these are generally staffed by younger women.

A second, more interventionist, strategy is for the government to provide an explicit "partial retirement" scheme by which individuals can obtain some social security benefits while continuing to work part-time (this should be distinguished from early-retirement schemes *per se* and from "retirement tests" which put a ceiling on tax-free earnings). Such schemes have been most popular in Scandinavia (OECD 1992, tables 5.17 and 5.18). They have typically been designed to encourage the substitution of older workers by younger workers, and they may contain a "replacement condition." As an illustration of the incentive structure: the program in Sweden, introduced in 1976, offers 65 percent of last gross earnings as compensation to workers who limit their weekly hours to between 17 and 5 less than their previous normal hours. This replacement ratio is actually more attractive than that for many workers who retire completely in other countries and the scheme has in the past reduced the compensation ratio to 50 percent. Partial retirement has proved popular but expensive in Sweden; as of early 1995 this scheme was to be phased out completely by the year 2000. Other countries that have more recently introduced similar schemes (e.g., Denmark and Finland) may also be reconsidering them in this light. Clearly there is no easy means of maintaining economic activity among older workers.

7.3 Summary

This chapter has illustrated the clear trend toward lower labor-market participation among the elderly, especially men, notwithstanding very different demographic trends across OECD countries. Greater longevity might be expected to *increase* labor-force participation rates among people in their fifties and sixties, and this observed tendency to earlier retirement might seem surprising. One cause of lower participation is the pure income effect of more generous social security and coverage by private pension plans, but the incentive effects of pensions on retirement are not always straightforward and studies of pensions and retirement behavior have not always produced clear-cut empirical results. In part, this is because pension receipt need not require "retirement" from the labor force. As the discussion of Japan in chapter 5 made clear, mandatory retirement from the "primary" job at a relatively youthful age can coexist with labor-force participation late into life.

Other factors that are clearly important in explaining the declining labor-force participation of the elderly are an increased willingness to retire on grounds of ill health, the increased participation of women, and a worsening of labor-market opportunities for less skilled elderly men. This erosion of opportunities has taken the form of declining prospective real wages in the United States and worsening job opportunities in Europe, and it is not unique to elderly men. In view of lower prospective wages, higher nonwage income (primarily pensions and disability benefits), and perhaps a higher valuation of leisure opportunities over time, the decline in participation is not surprising, even if there is some evidence that the retired subsequently regret the timing of their retirement.

The previous analysis also suggested that the rapid shift to earlier retirement in many countries may have slowed in the late 1980s, but that this deceleration may have stemmed from a slower growth of private pension benefits (and perhaps greater future perceived uncertainty as to their value). Receipt of social security, and conditions surrounding its receipt, such as retirement "tests," have probably had less effect, at least in the past two decades. Declining job opportunities for less skilled older workers, coupled with depressed wages stemming from cohort wage effects, may have had a role, and have led governments to extend programs which are effectively early-retirement programs, including wider coverage by disability schemes and the application of more lenient "work tests" for older unemployed insurance recipients. But the adverse macroeconomic shocks that led to the introduction of such programs have also led to budgetary difficulties. Increasingly, programs to encourage early retirement through disability benefits, more lenient unemployment insurance regimes, or early receipt of social security pensions are being cut back (OECD 1992).

Cutbacks in such programs and in prospective social security benefits, and later retirement ages, may be reversing the trend to earlier retirement. The interesting question is whether continued population aging by itself might also have an effect. The incentive to retire early within defined-benefit pensions may be eroded by the changing age structure of workforces (chapter 5). Greater uncertainty as to the value of social security in the future caused by higher dependency ratios may induce a "precautionary" motive for prolonged participation. But it is unlikely that the value of leisure will decrease, or that labor-market opportunities will increase (although see the discussion in chapter 6). The likelihood of policies designed to increase the participation of the elderly, such as postponement of the state pensionable age, or changes in the incentive structure of taxes for participants post-pensionable age, will be enhanced in all OECD countries. But the evidence of past impacts and policy changes (such as the abolition of the "earnings rule" in the United Kingdom) cast doubt on the strength of the participation response to such changes.

Consumption and Saving:
Life-Cycle Behavior and
Population Aging

An aging population is associated with changing lifestyles. Fewer children means falling school rolls and a declining share in household consumption for children's clothing, hamburgers, and toys. But declining family size may be associated with increased participation by women in the workforce, which increases the demand for nurseries and day care. In turn, higher household income may increase per-capita consumption of all kinds of goods and services, notwithstanding smaller numbers of children. At the other end of the age spectrum, greater longevity produces a greater demand for specialized health care for the elderly. And demographic changes also produce dramatic shifts in the behavior and geographical distribution of populations: witness the rapid growth in the seasonal migration of elderly people from north to south during the winter season in both North America and Europe.

As the working life becomes a shorter part of the total life, there is a greater demand for consumption goods complementary to leisure. Indeed, in most industrialized societies greater productivity of the workforce has been associated not so much with a substantial reduction in average weekly hours during the working life (although some reduction has typically occurred) as with a shortening of the working life due to prolonged education and earlier retirement (see chapter 7). This suggests that consumption as a whole and work may be broad substitutes whereas leisure and consumption are complements: people prefer to defer the enjoyment of leisure until after retirement. The elderly, by this token, are active consumers and net dissavers, running down the wealth accumulated during their working life.

Even without assuming any specific substitutability or complementarity between leisure and consumption, however, the standard life-cycle theory of consumption predicts a pattern of "hump saving" in the middle years of life, followed by decumulation of assets in later life. So an aging population should be associated with a reduction in aggregate saving. In similar vein, a cross plot of countries' saving rates on their aged dependency ratios should show a negative relationship. In fact, cross-section macroeconomic evidence broadly confirms this hypothesis (the evidence is presented in section 8.1), although the impact of demographic changes on saving rates over long periods of time can generally be obtained only by simulation analysis.

However, the macroeconomic evidence associating aging with lower saving appears to conflict with most microeconometric evidence concerning the validity of the life-cycle hypothesis of hump saving; this issue is investigated in section 8.2. In particular, I focus on the relationship between generations (such as a bequest motive) in the context of fewer children and a greater number of elderly people. The impact on saving of income-maintenance programs and that of reduced returns to the pay-as-you-go social security system are also considered.

If aging is associated with reduced saving, aging of a population may have macroeconomic effects, although the evidence in chapter 6 failed to confirm one potential avenue: that of lower aggregate productivity. There is evidence that slower population growth is associated with a lower rate of investment (capital accumulation) and with slower income growth. This may not be a bad thing *per se:* a reduced growth of output is still compatible with a rising standard of living if the population is actually declining, and a lower capital stock may also be desirable, so ruling out the theoretical possibility of overaccumulation of capital in such an economy (a proposition touched on in chapter 3). In addition, an aging population will affect the real rate of interest, which in the long run is determined by the supply of savings relative to the demand for investment funds. Indeed, one mechanism by which investment might be reduced is through a rise in the real rate of interest as the supply of savings declines, although the *demand* for investment will also change if technical progress is also affected by an aging population. Finally, an aging population will affect the valuation of companies in the capital market and raise their cost of capital. In particular, a prudential aging population may have invested, or may continue to invest, through institutional saving such as private pension plans (see chapter 5), and the net effect on *total* saving of changes in private saving (both individual and institutional) and in corporate and net public saving (budget surpluses and deficits) stemming from population aging may not be clear cut.

The implications of the age structure of the population for the *pattern* of consumer expenditures are considered in section 8.3, with illustrations from the UK Family Expenditure Survey. In particular, the discussion here and in chapter 9 focuses on the housing market and on health care—two areas of expenditure in which the aging of the population may have significant effects. Housing and pension rights constitute the two main assets for many elderly people. But changes in the size of the population may affect house values, and the willingness of the elderly to bequest their home. Various policies for liberating the housing equity values of the elderly are discussed.

8.1   Aging and the Macroeconomy

The Relationship between Savings and Old Age Dependency

The life-cycle hypothesis of saving posits a relationship between the age structure of the population and its national saving rate. This hypothesis of consumption and savings behavior was developed by Franco Modigliani and his collaborators in order to examine the implications of finite lives of households on consumption behavior in the context of microeconomic models of utility maximizing behavior (Modigliani 1986). With a perfect capital market assumed, a "representative" consumer from some generation with a finite expected life is assumed to choose how to allocate his or her total lifetime assets (i.e., the income stream plus any initial assets less intended bequests) over the life cycle according to preferences and the "terms of trade" between time periods: the real rate of interest. Since the later part of the life is typically spent retired from market activity, assets accumulated in the working life will be run down during this last period unless the bequest motive is particularly strong. In the basic model without a bequest motive, wealth holding follows a hump-shaped path, declining to zero at the expected date of death, if an adequately functioning annuity market is assumed.[1]

For this general argument to translate into a negative relationship between saving rates and an aging population, several assumptions are necessary. It is useful to abstract from output growth, since differential observed (and expected) output growth rates across countries might also affect saving. But in long-run equilibrium, with constant technology, the neoclassical theory of economic growth predicts that output growth *is determined by* the rate of population growth; in equilibrium the saving rate determines only the level of output per capita, not the rate of growth of output (chapter 3). These points are considered further below.

Furthermore, if the period of the working life is held constant, greater expected longevity (one facet of an aging population) may lead to an *increase* in saving in order to finance a prolonged period of retirement.[2] Even so, this positive effect on the saving of the younger age group should be swamped in equilibrium by the dissaving of the larger elderly age group. It should be noted, too, that the youngest workers are also effectively dissavers (borrowers), and that an increase in the median age of the working age group may actually lead to an *increase* in saving. Finally, different countries may have different general saving patterns, rates of technical progress, capital productivities, and so on, which make comparisons of age structure and national saving rates problematic.

Evidence for a negative relationship between the proportion of people 65 and over in the population and the saving rate in selected OECD countries is put forward in OECD 1990, with data for the period 1980–1988. The regression result

$$\text{HSR} = 0.29 \ - 0.93 \ \text{AGED} \ (n = 14, \ R^2 = 0.33) \tag{8.1}$$
$$(3.7) \ (-2.44)$$

is cited, where HSR is the net household saving ratio, AGED is the proportion of the population aged 65 and over, and t stats are given in parentheses. The coefficient on the AGED term implies a high elasticity of the household saving ratio to the composition of the population: a rise in the aged dependency ratio from 0.15 to 0.25 would imply a fall in the predicted saving ratio from 0.15 to 0.05. However, various technical problems with this study cast doubt on its central finding.[3]

Figures 8.1 and 8.2 present some comparable evidence collected by the author from published OECD data. Here the national saving ratio (NSR) and the net household saving ratio are plotted against the aged dependency ratio (i.e., the proportion of the population aged 65 and over as a proportion of the population aged 15–64). The national saving ratio for Luxembourg is implausibly high, and this country is excluded from the NSR exercise; data on the HSR are only available for 19 countries, all of which are included. The data are averaged over a longer period (1977–1992) than that used in OECD 1990.

There is evidence for a negative relationship between the two saving-ratio measures and the aged dependency ratio; however, despite the inclusion of a larger number of countries and the use of a longer time

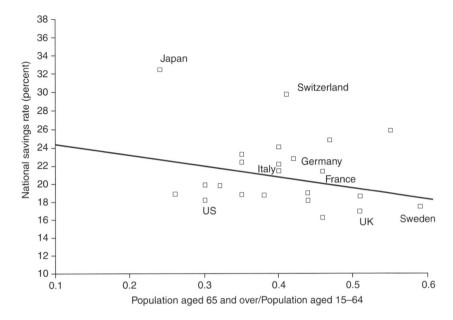

Figure 8.1
National saving rate and aged dependency ratios in 23 OECD countries (excluding Luxembourg), 1977–1992.

period (which should provide greater smoothing over macroeconomic shocks), the relationship is considerably weaker than the OECD study suggests. Indeed, the coefficient on the aged dependency ration ADR (which is a more appropriate measure than AGED) is statistically insignificant in both fitted regression lines, although this is perhaps not unexpected given the simplicity of the model specification. The regressions are

$$\text{NSR} = 0.26 \ - 0.11 \text{ ADR } (n = 24; R^2 = 0.06) \qquad (8.2)$$
$$(6.4) \ (-1.06)$$

and

$$\text{HSR} = 0.15 \ - 0.11 \text{ ADR } (n = 19; R^2 = 0.03), \qquad (8.3)$$
$$(2.7) \ (-0.80)$$

where the variables are as defined in the text averaged over the period 1977–1992.

It is clear that the implicit elasticities are considerably less than in the OECD study, as also illustrated by the regression lines plotted in

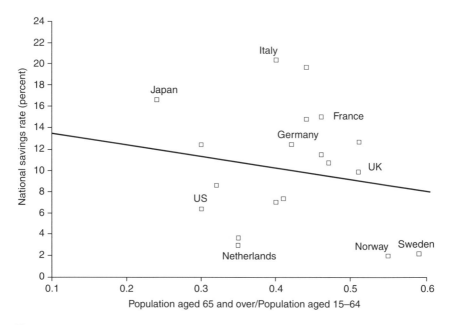

Figure 8.2
Net household saving rate and aged dependency ratios in 19 OECD countries, 1977–1992.

figures 8.1 and 8.2. Furthermore, the ADR term "explains" considerably less of the variance in the measured saving ratios, as evidenced by the lower R^2 values.

An alternative method of analyzing the issue is to look at particular countries over time, examining what happens to the saving rate as the population age structure changes. Wachtel (1984) uses this method to examine the US experience. Because demographic changes occur very slowly, long time periods have to be used, typically involving both past data and projected simulations of the future population. Wachtel's study uses data on age-specific saving rates from two cross-section data sources: the Survey of the Changes in Family Finances (SCFF) and two Consumer Expenditure Surveys (CES). The calculated saving rates by age group are superimposed on observed or projected decompositions of the population by age and income level by age for the period 1948–2050. It should be noted that superimposing cross-section proportions on time-series simulations imposes a rather strong assumption of constancy of behavior across cohorts and rules out variation in other potentially important variables.

Wachtel finds relative minor effects of age structure on aggregate saving rates. With SCFF data, the age-weighted projected saving rate falls from 14.7 percent in 1948 to 13.5 percent in 2050, as the population aged 65 and over rises from 14.9 percent to 27.2 percent. This is not a large change, and the effect is even smaller when CES data are used. Furthermore, the two data sources generate different timings of the changes in the saving rate.

A similar result for Italy is found by Cannari (1994). Using a methodology similar to that of Bosworth et al. (1991), he decomposes the aggregate saving rate at two points, 1980 and 1989, into rates by age of head of household, size of household and number of children. The object is to see whether the decline in the saving rate in the 1980s can be attributed to changes in household composition. Cannari's evidence suggests that, at most, 0.1 percent of a decline of more than 2 percent in the ratio can be "explained" by changes in the age composition of households; indeed, the other decomposition factors work in the opposite direction, predicting an increase in saving over the period.

The SCFF data used by Wachtel also decompose saving by type of assets. Expenditures on housing acquisition declines with age and therefore mirrors the decline in total saving over time as demographic aging takes place. Likewise, accumulated debt is highest among younger age groups, and as their proportion declines so too does financial debt. Investment in financial assets peaks among the middle aged; thus, following the path of the baby-boom generation through the time period, aggregate financial asset accumulation first rises, then falls, then stabilizes toward the end of the simulated period.

In a study combining time and cross-section effects, Weil (1994) examines fourteen developed countries over the period 1960–1985 using centered five-year averages (since the demographic data change only slowly). Weil regresses private savings (national, net of government) and household savings on compositional measures of the population age structure and on controls including time dummies, average and current growth rates of income, and income per capita.

Table 8.1 gives Weil's results for household saving, for a sample of nine countries over centered averages. These are compared with my own calculations, based on the nineteen sampled countries illustrated in figure 8.2, using centered four-year averages for the period 1977–1992, explicit age and youth dependency ratios, per capita current growth and average growth, a constant, $T - 1$ time dummies, and (in the fixed-effect model) $N - 1$ country dummies.

Table 8.1
Cross-country savings regressions. Sources: (column 1) Weil 1994, table 1; (column 2) author's own calculations. All regressions include time dummies.

Dependent variable:	1 (1960–1985) ln(Household saving)		2 (1977–1992) ln(Household saving)	
Country fixed effects?	No	Yes	No	Yes
YOUNG[a]	−0.002	0.018	0.178	0.753
	(0.181)	(0.117)	(0.172)	(0.408)
WORKING-AGE[b]	0.290	0.424	—	—
	(0.147)	(0.074)		
OLD[c]	−1.00	−1.36	−0.957	−2.025
	(0.32)	(0.41)	(0.417)	(0.855)
AVERAGE GROWTH[d]	3.15	—	0.145	—
	(2.29)		(0.065)	
CURRENT GROWTH[e]	−0.178	0.379	0.009	0.013
	(0.647)	(0.227)	(0.036)	(0.016)
ln(Y/N)[f]	−0.002	0.068	—	—
	(0.048)	(0.045)		
SEE	0.602	0.219	0.298	0.127
R^2	0.143	0.886	0.226	0.894
No. of countries	9	9	19	19
No. of time periods	6	6	4	4
df	43	35	68	51

a. Percent aged 0–19 in population (Weil); percent aged 0–14 / percent aged 15–64 (Disney).
b. Percent aged 20–64 in population (Weil).
c. Percent aged 65 and over in population (Weil); % aged 65 and over / % aged 15–64 (Disney).
d. Average rate of growth of per capita income over period, normalized to zero for US 1985 in column 1.
e. Rate of growth of per capita income over each period, normalized to zero for US 1985 in column 1.
f. Income per capita, normalized to zero for US 1985 in column 1.

In the Weil study, the proportion of youth has little effect on saving, and the proportion of working age is positively associated with the saving rate. There is a unitary negative elasticity of the proportion of elderly in the population on the saving ratio excluding country dummies—a result replicated in my own calculations in column 2 of the table. Including country dummies strengthens the results considerably: Weil concludes that moving 1 percent of the population from the elderly age group to the working age group will reduce household saving by between 1.3 percent and 1.8 percent (depending on whether country fixed effects are included). The column 2 result concerning the impact of the aged dependency ratio is, if anything, stronger than Weil's once fixed effects are included, although not quite as robust in terms of standard error. In column 2 the youth dependency ratio is positively but weakly associated with the saving rate, perhaps reflecting higher permanent income expectations or anticipated bequests.

The other variables merit passing attention. In theory, average growth per capita over the *whole* time period is positively related to the saving rate only if the age profile of the wealth-income ratio is assumed to be independent of the growth rate of the economy (see Modigliani 1986, and equation 8.4 below). An impact of the *current* growth rate could be compatible with the impact of transitory income on savings, but the effect is not significant. An impact of the *level* of per capita income on the saving rate is not compatible with the life-cycle hypothesis; at least in its simplest variant. Time dummies are significant, and it will be noted that the inclusion of country fixed effects improves the explanatory power of the equation fourfold.[4]

Thus, there is evidence across countries and over time of a negative relationship between the aged dependency ratio and various measures of private saving. The result is less clear cut in studies using disaggregated (micro) data, as will be shown shortly. It should also be borne in mind that *national* saving, which includes the government's net budgetary position, should certainly be adversely affected by demographic trends when the replacement ratios of social security programs are held constant, given the increasing burden of PAYG finance.[5] In turn, prospective changes in the burden of public debt may affect private saving if future repayments of debt are anticipated (Barro 1974).

Growth, Saving, Investment, and Aging

What is the relationship among growth, saving, and demographic changes? Does an aged population imply lower investment in fixed capital? In the long run, according to the neoclassical theory of economic growth (see chapter 3), the optimal growth rate of a country is determined in equilibrium by its rates of population growth and productivity growth (technical progress). This optimal growth rate is independent of the saving rate (Solow 1956; Phelps 1961). Given these parameters, the saving rate affects the per-capita amount of capital and thus the absolute levels of productivity and output per capita.

But there are diminishing returns to factors of production, and the application of the "Ramsey rules" (Ramsey 1928) places a limit on the optimal accumulation of capital. A declining population can indeed "live on its capital" and so allow low or even zero capital investment (negative, net of depreciation). But a population with a greater number of elderly dependents (due to greater longevity) may find such a strategy unattractive; a greater accumulated stock of capital allows the greater number of "passive" members of the population to enjoy a higher standard of living than would otherwise be the case.

Demographic changes can therefore affect growth directly (irrespective of any indirect effect on the rate of technical progress). The most natural avenue is the impact of the age structure of the workforce on labor productivity. However no evidence could be adduced in chapter 6 to suggest which way the relationship between age structure and productivity would go, either on theoretical or empirical grounds. Therefore, the direct effects of demographics on growth rates and capital accumulation—both the effect of changes in fertility rates inducing fluctuations in labor-market entry rates and greater longevity—can be examined directly.

In the life-cycle theory of saving, the ratio of average wealth to income, W/Y, is determined by the length of the period of retirement relative to the length of the period of labor-market activity when population and productivity growth are zero (Modigliani 1986). Suppose, however, that the population grows. Then, according to the life-cycle hypothesis, there are more households of working age (typically savers, although typically holding lower *levels* of wealth, which rise with age until dissaving starts later in life) and fewer older households (typically dissavers, although with larger W/Y ratios). In equilibrium, a growing population is associated with higher output growth and a higher saving ratio. In steady state, the growth of income is equal to the growth of wealth. Therefore,

$$\frac{\dot{Y}}{Y} = \frac{\dot{W}}{W} \text{ and } \frac{S}{Y} = \frac{\dot{W}}{W} \cdot \frac{W}{Y}. \tag{8.4}$$

This is similar to the Harrod-Domar equilibrium growth condition. Faster population growth is associated with faster growth of output (the "natural" growth rate), a *higher* saving rate, and a *lower* wealth/income ratio. Slower population growth implies the reverse. Modigliani (1986) produces cross-section evidence of a positive relationship for OECD countries between saving rates and growth rates. Our own data set for 1977–1992 gives a positive relationship, although the key coefficient is again insignificant at standard significance levels:

$$\text{NSR} = 0.18 + 1.3\,\text{GDPg}\ (n = 23; R^2 = 0.05), \qquad\qquad (8.5)$$
$$\quad\ (4.4)\quad (1.1)$$

where NSR is the national saving ratio and GDPg is the average GDP growth rate over the period. However, in subsequent research, Modigliani,[6] utilizing a panel of 21 OECD countries estimated over three time periods, obtained a well-determined coefficient of +1.8 on the GDP growth rate (t stat = 6.1).

When younger cohorts are more productive than older cohorts, the situation is more complicated. In the permanent-income approach, with infinite lives the higher permanent income associated with greater productivity will raise initial consumption and may raise the measured consumption-income ratio; however, with finite lives the total savings of younger cohorts is higher, and this should outweigh the dissaving of the older, less productive cohorts. If productivity growth generates income growth *within* the life cycle as well as "intercept" effects, then anticipation of this growth may again reverse the predicted effect on the saving ratio (Deaton 1992).

Greater longevity, associated with a longer period of retirement, should also increase the target wealth-income ratio, offsetting the negative relationship between the saving ratio and the old age dependency ratio described previously. But the situation is complicated by social security. If social security induces earlier retirement, private savings will increase. But if social security substitutes for private savings, the effect is offset. A combination of decreased fertility, increased longevity, and earlier retirement through social security should be associated with a lower rate of growth of output, but the impact on the saving rate could go either way. Figure 8.3 plots the relationship between GDP growth rates and the old aged dependency ratio across our sample of 24 OECD countries for the period 1977–1992. As predicted, there is a negative relationship, and the coefficient is closer to significance than in the cases where the saving ratio is plotted on the aged dependency ratio for the averaged cross section for the period 1977–1992:

$$\text{GDPg} = 3.76 - 3.0\,\text{ADR}\ (n = 24; R^2 = 0.11), \qquad\qquad (8.6)$$
$$\quad\ (4.8)\quad (-1.6)$$

where GDPg is the average GDP growth rate over the period.

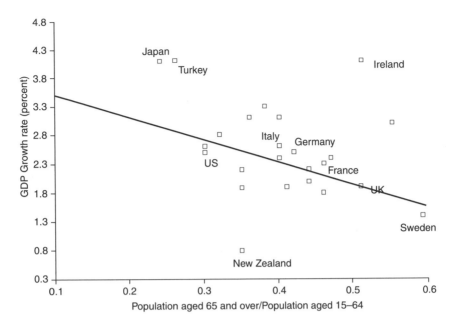

Figure 8.3
Average GDP growth rates and aged dependency ratios in 24 OECD countries, 1977–1992.

We might predict the clearest relationship to be that between fixed capital formation and an aging population. Slower population growth, involving fewer workers and longer periods of retirement, should be associated with slower growth of the capital stock, through direct output growth effects, lower saving rates, and the opportunity to dissave capital. Figure 8.4 plots the cross-section relationship between the growth rate of fixed capital formation and demographics.

The strong negative relationship for the period 1977–1992 is apparent from figure 8.4 and is reflected in the plotted regression line, which is highly significant notwithstanding the small sample size:

$$\text{gFCF} = \ 5.52 - 7.8 \text{ ADR } (n = 24; R^2 = 0.24), \qquad (8.7)$$
$$\phantom{\text{gFCF} = \ }(4.1) \quad (-2.7)$$

where gFCF is the average growth of fixed capital formation over the period.

In summary: Cross-section evidence for OECD countries suggests a clear negative relationship between the aged dependency ratio and both net household saving rates and fixed capital formation. Some studies also suggest a positive relationship between the growth of out-

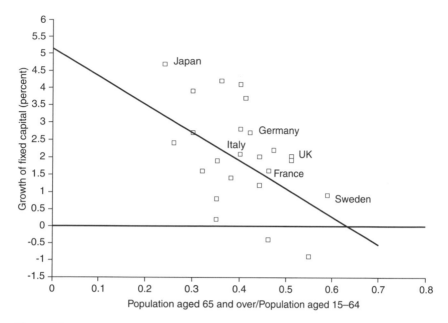

Figure 8.4
Growth rates of fixed capital formation and aged dependency ratios in 24 OECD countries, 1977–1992.

put and national saving rates, and it follows that an aging population should be associated with a slower growth of output. There is weak evidence for this last relationship here. These results in general appear to confirm that simple versions of the life-cycle hypothesis have some predictive power when examining the relationship between aging and these key macroeconomic variables. But the issue is complicated by variations over time and across countries in saving rates and growth, by the impact of government financing of social security, and by changes in retirement behavior.

8.2   Aging: The Microeconomic Analysis of Savings and Consumption Behavior

Microeconomic Evidence on the Relationship between Life-Cycle Saving and Aging

The macroeconomic evidence provides indirect support for the life-cycle hypothesis, since the observation that countries with greater numbers of elderly people have lower household saving rates is compatible with the prediction of the hypothesis that the elderly are net dissavers. However, the microeconomic evidence, drawn especially from cross-section surveys, appears to indicate that the elderly are *not* net dissavers. For example, Mirer (1979), using a 1967 US study of 8000 households aged over 65, conducted simple cross-section regressions of wealth on age and, for this age group, found no evidence of a rundown of asset holding above age 65.

In a similar exercise, Weil (1994), using the 1985 Consumer Expenditure Survey, found that elderly members of households continued to save, albeit at lower rates than middle-aged individuals, and that the only dissavers were children; thus, an age-compositional analysis of the consequences for consumption of the future aging of the US population would predict an *increase* in the saving rate, since the reduction in the number of children (so raising the saving rate) would outweigh the decline in the number of middle-aged individuals relative to the elderly (so reducing the saving rate). Other studies, such as that of King and Dicks-Mireaux (1982) for Canada and those of contributors to Ando et al. 1994 for Italy, tend to confirm the general result concerning the saving patterns of the elderly.

In general, most microeconomic tests of consumption behavior agree that an individual's consumption tracks current income much more closely than would be predicted by the "basic" life-cycle hypothesis (Carroll and Summers 1991; Deaton 1992). Among the many explanations for this finding are that individuals build up a precautionary "buffer stock" of savings, which is only gradually run down as the unknown income path is revealed (Carroll 1992); that failure in the annuity market induces individuals to save against uncertain longevity (Davies 1981); that there is a reduction in the expected net worth of social security (implicitly: see Kotlikoff 1979); that there are liquidity constraints (essentially the Keynesian model); and that there is some form of bequest motive. Attempts to differentiate these hypotheses are more than adequately summarized in Deaton 1992 and are not a central concern here.

Disaggregated cross-section studies of saving behavior among different age groups, however, contain two forms of bias, which work in opposite directions. One is a form of *attrition bias:* wealthier individuals tend to survive longest, and it is their higher wealth that is observed in the data. The cross-section wealth "transition rates," from which net (dis)saving is calculated, may therefore be biased (see, e.g., Shorrocks 1975). On the other hand, there is the possibility of *cohort bias:* if each successive cohort is (or expects to be) wealthier, the lower observed wealth of the oldest cohorts may simply stem from their lower lifetime wealth rather than from any dissaving behavior (Mirer 1979). But since the wealth expectations of successive cohorts may not be uniformly higher, whereas attrition bias is undoubtedly observed, the net effect may be to overstate the wealth position of the elderly in cross-section studies.

The obvious answer to all this to observe the saving behavior of a panel of elderly people over time. Hurd (1987), using some of the early waves of the Retirement History Survey (1969–1979), *does* find evidence that the elderly dissave: a household with a 20-year life expectancy at retirement can expect to have reduced its bequeathable wealth to about half its peak level in real terms by the time the head of the household dies.[7] However, bequeathable wealth would still remain, and the composition of wealth affects the rate of decline: households with a large proportion of wealth in the form of housing, for example, tend to reduce their wealth more slowly. Of course, the composition of wealth of a household is in principle a choice variable, although with transactions costs past decisions may not be easy to unravel. Indeed, where certain assets contain an insurance aspect, such as life insurance (Bernheim 1991), or housing (Skinner 1993), the *inability* to unravel past decisions to accumulate wealth holdings (a form of pre-commitment) may be a desirable property of the asset in question.

The effect of the bequest motive, especially in the context of an aging population, also causes controversy. Kotlikoff and Summers (1981) argued that, for reasonable cohort age-earnings and age-consumption profiles, simply not enough life-cycle saving was generated to account for the stock of capital accumulated in the United States. This conclusion was disputed by Modigliani (1986) and has been debated extensively since, although there is little doubt that richer households leave significant bequests. Of more pertinence here is the question of whether an aging population would reduce the size of bequests. If successive cohorts are wealthier, then bequests might be expected to be higher; however, greater longevity would tend to reduce bequests, with an uncertain effect on saving (Skinner 1985).

The motive for bequests is also important. If bequests are altruistically motivated, then the presence of fewer children will mean that higher *per capita* bequests (given longevity) can be made for a lower outlay of saving, thus reducing the saving of the elderly. But with more elderly savers, and greater longevity, overall saving rates might increase. If there are strategic bequests, the position is more complicated. Strategic bequests are intended to alter the behavior of potential beneficiaries, primarily children; for example, actual and potential bequests may be used as a compensation (or a bargaining counter) for services such as care and attention. Bernheim et al. (1985) support this argument with evidence from the Retirement History Survey that the "supply of attention" by children (visits, telephone calls, etc.) is affected by the potential amount of bequeathable wealth. However, the observed positive relationship between amount of wealth and attention does not hold for single children; Bernheim et al. hypothesize that the "bargaining counter" of disinheritance is much weaker in such cases than in families with several children, who might compete for the available wealth by means of attention.[8] For single-child families, therefore, the strategic bequest motive fails (as, of course it does for childless families).

Therefore, to the extent that population aging is associated with a greater number of single-child or childless families, the value of strategic bequests to the potential bequestor is weakened, and the absolute size of saving for bequests might be reduced. But there is a counterargument: a single child may require a disproportionately greater "bribe" to pay a desired level of attention to the parent; that is, the "price" of gaining attention rises as family size falls (although not in any linear fashion), and the overall effect of declining family size on bequest saving among families with at least one child is unclear.

The bequest motive raises the issue of interfamily relationships. Weil (1994) believes that it is through arguments about this that the macroeconomic and microeconomic evidence as to the effect of aging populations on saving rates can be reconciled. Consider therefore two generations: "parents" and "children." Suppose that the saving of parents is related to the number of children, and the saving of children to the number of their brothers and sisters. Denote "parents" by p, "children" by k, and the saving rate by s, with $\pi(\cdot)$ measuring the effect of one generation on the saving behavior of another. Then the saving rates of individuals of each generation are

$$s_k = \beta_k + \pi_{p,k}[1/(1 + \text{number of siblings})] \tag{8.8a}$$

and

$$s_p = \beta_p + p_{k,p}(\text{number of children}). \tag{8.8b}$$

Denote the number in each age group as n. Then the mean number of children per parent is n_k/n_p, and $[1/(1 + \text{no. of siblings})]$ is equal to n_p/n_k (see Weil 1994). Thus, the *mean* savings of the two age groups are

$$\bar{s}_k = \beta_k + \pi_{p,k}(n_p/n_k) \tag{8.9a}$$

and

$$\bar{s}_p = \beta_p + \pi_{k,p}(n_k/n_p). \tag{8.9b}$$

Total saving, S, is given by

$$S = (\beta_k + \pi_{k,p})n_k + (\beta_p + \pi_{p,k})n_p. \tag{8.10}$$

Now a regression of total saving on the fraction of the population in each age group generates the regression coefficients

$$\hat{s}_k = \beta_k + \pi_{k,p} \tag{8.11a}$$

and

$$\hat{s}_p = \beta_p + \pi_{p,k}. \tag{8.11b}$$

Weil's point is that the coefficient estimate $\hat{s}$ in equations 8.11 is neither the β in equation 8.8 nor the $\bar{s}$ in equations 8.9. The differences between equations 8.9 and equations 8.11 can be written as follows:

$$\bar{s}_k - \hat{s}_k = \pi_{p,k}(n_p/n_k) - \pi_{k,p}, \tag{8.12a}$$

$$\bar{s}_p - \hat{s}_p = \pi_{k,p}(n_p/n_p) - \pi_{p,k}. \tag{8.12b}$$

Thus, microeconomic and macroeconomic estimates of age-specific saving will differ if individuals in a given age group affect the savings of other generations. Specifically, the elderly will have higher saving in micro than in macro data if there is a positive effect of children on the saving of the elderly ($\pi_{k,p} > 0$) or if there is a negative effect of parents on the saving of children ($\pi_{p,k} < 0$) (ibid., p. 67).

In the context of an aging population, fewer children may reduce the savings of the elderly with simple altruistic bequests ($\pi_{k,p} > 0$), although, as we have seen, the prediction with strategic bequests is unclear (in effect it depends on the elasticity of the demand for attention with respect to the size of the bequest). In turn, the expectation of higher bequests *per capita* may reduce the saving rate of children ($\pi_{p,k} < 0$). So an aging population is associated with a fall in the saving rate at the macroeconomic level given these intergenerational relations, largely through the impact of expected bequests on the saving rates of both parents and children given the smaller number of children. Weil's results using the Panel Survey of Income Dynamics suggest that families which expect a bequest consume 4.8 percent more than families that do not (*ceteris paribus*). Actually receiving a bequest raises consumption by 10.4 percent.

These magnitudes are sufficient to explain the difference between the saving propensities of children and parents calculated from microeconomic and macroeconomic data. This story is plausible, and it squares with an oft-noted consequence of declining family size in industrialized countries, especially through the medium of inheritance of housing assets. However, it should be noted that other studies question the existence of strong interfamilial altruism (see the discussion in section 3.3).

Social Security, Aging, and Consumption

Chapter 3 also considered briefly the question of the optimal financing of social security programs in an aging society and the evidence as to the impact of social security on saving. As we have seen from chapter 4, pay-as-you-go social security programs imply both intergenerational and intragenerational redistribution, depending on the individual "return" on social security (if perceived correctly) and the timing of taxes and benefits. Typically, earlier generations can expect to receive a positive return on their contributions, due to receiving pensions conditional on incomplete contribution histories, as can smaller generations following more numerous generations (see chapter 10). For these generations, therefore, net social security wealth is positive and can be expected to reduce lifetime private saving below what it would otherwise have been.

However, in the context of an aging population, with the prospect of low or even negative rates of return in the future on PAYG social security, both higher *current* payroll tax rates and lower prospective benefits should combine to raise saving through a pure income effect. Moreover, as described in chapter 7, higher payroll-tax rates may also affect retirement behavior and, therefore, the allocation of labor supply and consumption over time. But the establishment of a social security "trust fund," as in the United States, should increase the consumption opportunities available to succeeding generations, thereby reducing the saving rate.

Kotlikoff (1979), using the National Longitudinal Survey, finds no clear evidence that the (net) individual value of prospective social security less payroll taxes affects saving . Households may fail accurately to predict their social security benefits, or may simply assume that the impact of social security on their *net* worth is zero. However, a measure constructed by Kotlikoff of the household's accumulated social security tax payments *is* a significant influence on saving, and it is negatively signed, with a typical coefficient of -0.67. This is far higher than a simple Keynesian elasticity of consumption with respect to marginal tax changes on disposable income, but less elastic than the -1 or less that would be expected in a full life-cycle model. It implies that households recognize that past social security contributions will lead to a pension stream in the future but are unable to project the net effect on their overall lifetime wealth position (not unreasonably, in view of the frequent changes to the social security regime in most countries). Earlier prospective retirement is also associated with higher saving, so if earlier retirement behavior is *induced* by the social security system this may enhance the net effect of tax rates on saving. However, the results do not provide overwhelming evidence that social security programs affect consumption behavior in the manner predicted by the life-cycle hypothesis.

There is one group, however, for which the operation of the social security system, or the income-maintenance program, affects consumption behavior. This is the group with very low incomes, and it has been observed that such families have disproportionately low wealth holdings, even allowing for their low income level (Hurd 1990; Hubbard et al. 1995). One plausible explanation is government-financed transfer programs that provide guaranteed minimum consumption levels on retirement. Since such programs are typically both asset-tested and income-tested, with withdrawal rates of 100 percent, individuals with the likely prospect of falling within the ambit of such programs are likely to engage in dissaving (asset disposal) before retirement so as to remain within the upper asset limit laid down by the program. Such programs exist in North America and the United Kingdom, and indeed underpin the whole social security program in Australia (see section 4.4).

Figure 8.5 illustrates the impact of such programs. There are two periods, 1 and 2, with income E received in the first period. It is assumed that preferences are homothetic and that the rate of interest and the rate of time preference are both equal to zero. If there was no income-maintenance program, then an individual with income E_1^* would choose the optimal point a^* on the budget constraint $m - E_1^*$ at the

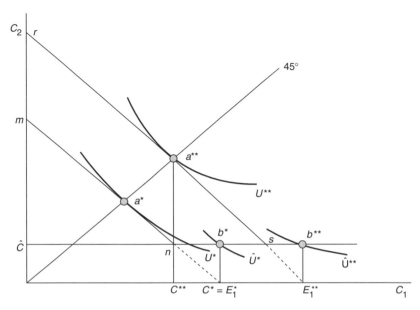

Figure 8.5
Optimal consumption with a welfare "floor." Source: Hubbard et al. 1995, figure 3.

tangent with the indifference curve U^*. However, now assume that the government offers a consumption "floor" in period 2, $\bar{C}$. Since the payment is withdrawn at a 100 percent rate per pound or dollar of wealth, the budget constraint is kinked at n. Given the preference map, the individual is now better off at b^* on higher indifference curve $\hat{U}^*$, consuming all of his own income E_1^* in the first period at C^*. Thus, the model predicts zero saving from earned income for this low earner.

Suppose, however, that the individual obtains a large increase in earned income in period 1, to E_1^{**}. The budget constraint shifts to $E_1^{**} - b^{**} - s - r$. The individual now moves to $\hat{U}^{**}$, but it will be observed that this indifference curve is dominated by indifference curve U^{**} at point a^{**}. The individual responds to an *increase* in period 1 income by *reducing* consumption in period 1 from C^* to C^{**}. In effect, the discrete jump in income allows the individual to "escape" the disincentive effect of the income-maintenance program (known as the "poverty trap" in Britain), and makes it worthwhile to save.

To the extent that an aging population is associated with an expansion of income-tested programs, this argument is potent: very low or zero saving rates can be expected among any households with low prospective lifetime earnings. This is independent of the models examined in section 3.3, which suggested that the altruism of younger generations might be exploited by such consumption strategies. However, consumption behavior of this type is a risky strategy if there is any uncertainty attached to the income-maintenance program; indeed, buffer-stock models of saving, such as that of Carroll (1992), might in general predict *greater* saving among those with persistently near-zero shocks to income, depending on the degree of risk aversion. Thus, we should distinguish between households with persistent low but positive incomes, which might engage in the strategy of consuming all income as it arises, and those with high stochastic variability of incomes (for example, a high risk of unemployment or sickness), which, if not fully covered by income-maintenance programs, would undertake buffer-stock saving. The *net* effect on saving therefore is unclear.

8.3 Expenditure Patterns and Age Structure

Budget Shares

An aging population has implications for the structure of consumer demand as well as for the overall level of consumption relative to saving. Table 8.2 illustrates differences in household consumption patterns drawn from the 1993 Family Expenditure Survey in the United Kingdom (Central Statistical Office 1994). It contrasts the average spending pattern of a household with a head under 30 to that of a household with a head 75 or older. Typically the younger household will be larger in size, with an income twice that of the older household. In fact the average weekly household spending of a household with a head aged under 30 was £258.61 in 1993; that of a household with a head 75 or older was £121.73. As the upper panel of table 8.2 suggests, there are significant differences in budget shares between the two household types: younger households typically spend more on housing, on alcohol and tobacco, and on transport. Older households spend a greater proportion of their income on food and on services. The lower panel identifies subcategories where there are disparities in the expenditure patterns; again the differences are predictable.

Can we infer something about the trends in consumer spending as the population ages from this table? The observed variations in budget shares across age groups stem from a combination of age effects, cohort effects, and differences in current and prospective income levels: the difference in the food share, for example, stems in part from the fact that younger households are better off than older households.

Table 8.2
Household expenditure shares (percentages) by age of head of household. Derived from
Central Statistical Office 1994, tables 2.2 and 2.3.

	Age of household head	
	<30	≥75
Net housing	20.3	16.0
Fuel, light, power	4.3	8.6
Food	16.5	23.5
Drink, tobacco	7.2	4.7
Clothing, footwear	6.3	4.3
Household goods	9.2	8.8
Services, misc.	9.5	12.8
Transport	14.5	8.4
Leisure	12.3	12.9
Individual items		
Children's clothing	0.9	0.0
Loan repayments	0.5	0.0
Fares	3.2	1.4
Car purchase	4.4	1.6
Meals away from home	4.3	2.5
Medical, nursing, dental fees	0.1	1.4
Domestic help	0.1	1.7
Gardening	0.3	0.8
Books, newspapers	1.2	2.3
Postage, telephone	1.8	3.2

Thus, the share of food expenditures for the lowest 20 percent of the
under-30-headed households, with an average income of £103.40, is
22.3 percent, while the share of food expenditures for the richest 20
percent of the households whose heads were 75 and older with an
average income of £212.77, is 20.6 percent.

In part, too, age differences in spending patterns may stem from
habits which are cohort-specific, related to historical events and specific technological changes. For example, the generation aged 75 and
over in table 8.2 will have entered the labor market after 1918, and both
their level and their allocation of consumption may have been scarred
by the interwar period. This might be reflected in a higher degree of
precautionary saving, in temporary saving to purchase larger items
(given an aversion to indebtedness), and in an unwillingness to spend
on "unnecessary" luxuries. In contrast individuals aged 30 and under
will typically have known relative affluence for most of their lives and

this will have affected their permanent income expectation and spending pattern: for example, an increased willingness to borrow in order to spend on consumer durables. These differences in consumption propensities may extend into retirement, so that cross-section-based inferences as to expenditure patterns may be misleading.[9]

Different age groups may respond differently to new "information" in the economy, such as new consumption opportunities or forecasts as to the state of the economy. It is commonplace to observe that an aged population is more conservative in its spending patterns and in its response to new economic information (not least because, of necessity and ignoring any bequest motive, its average time horizon is shorter), but only time will tell whether this is an age effect or whether it is specific to the cohort that lived through the interwar period and World War II.[10]

Nevertheless, there are expenditures for which the aging of the population has implications. Notable among these are expenditures on housing and on health care.

Housing
Three questions arise as to the impact of an aging population on the housing market:

• How does generation size affect the housing market and, in particular, the price of houses?

• Do capital gains or losses in the housing market (perhaps arising from cohort-size effects) affect consumption and saving? How does ownership of housing assets affect the validity of the life-cycle hypothesis of dissaving later in life?

• How do elderly households respond to fluctuations in their housing costs and values? Are "excess" housing costs a problem for the elderly?

Generation size and the dynamics of house prices
Chapter 6 described Welch's (1979) argument for a baby boom's impact on relative earnings, operating through the incomplete substitutability of different types of labor. Much the same argument has been made for a baby boom's or a baby bust's impact of cohort size on house prices, but stemming here from rigidities in the supply of housing. The argument receives its boldest statement in Mankiw and Weil 1989. Mankiw and Weil attribute the rapid rise in real house prices in the United States in the 1970s to the baby-boom generation's coming of house-buying age. Consequently, they argue, the 25 percent decline

in births from the late 1960s can be expected to generate an equally spectacular decline in real house prices in the 1990s and the first decade of the 21st century.

The "correct" methodology for modeling housing demand by age group is not immediately apparent; Mankiw and Weil utilize a simple additive function from a regression of household property values from the 1970 and 1980 US censuses on the age structure of each household's members. Age-related housing demand, by this calculation, is around zero until the late teens, peaks at age 40, and declines by about 1 percent per annum thereafter. Aggregate housing demand so calculated was some 50 percent higher in the 1980 census than in the 1970 census, stemming from a rise in real disposable income and from a change in the age composition of households in the presence of an inelastic (own price) demand for housing. Applying the calculated coefficients of age-specific housing demand to *changes* in age structure from 1940 to 2010, Mankiw and Weil predict that whereas housing demand grew by 1.66 percent per annum from 1970 to 1980 (when the baby-boom cohort reached its demand peak), the rate of growth of demand will fall steadily, to 0.68 percent from 1990 to 2000 and to 0.57 percent from 2000 to 2010 (ibid., p. 241). Given average growth of supply and real GDP, and inelastic demand for housing, this implies that house prices will decline around 3 percent per annum for most of the period 1990–2010.

It might be thought that these cohort-size-driven changes in housing demand should be predictable in advance so that supply could adjust to demand. In this case, fluctuations in real house prices would not occur (at least, not via a demographic mechanism). Why has supply not anticipated demand and eliminated this price cycle? Although Mankiw and Weil find a strong positive statistical relationship between their aggregated demand measure and the real price of housing in the postwar period, they do not observe any relationship between the size of the housing stock and demand; the stock changes are driven by an investment accelerator (relative to GDP) and by noise rather than by the size of cohorts. In a forward-looking model, investment in housing is related to the prospective price of housing and thus indirectly by demographic factors; even allowing for significant errors in demographic forecasts, however, such a forward-looking model would predict far smaller long-run fluctuations in house prices than have in fact occurred.

The Mankiw-Weil model has been extensively criticized on empirical grounds and also for its (nonexistent) model of household formation. Poterba (1991) argues that demographic changes alone cannot explain regional house-price movements, but confirms that Rational Expectations–type models of house-price movements seem to be inferior to models of extrapolative expectations. In a general model of housing demand, he argues, the stock equilibrium determines the prices of houses, with user costs (such as real borrowing costs, insurance premia, and maintenance), price expectations, and the tax treatment of housing playing roles as well as demographically induced demand shifts. In turn, the flow of *new* housing is determined by the return on housing, which in the long run should be the same as the return on other assets for the housing market to be priced efficiently.[11] Therefore, falling user costs in the 1970s stemming from low *real* rates of interest might have induced house-price rises in order to maintain asset-market equilibrium. In turn, adaptive, or extrapolative, expectations might mean that demography-driven falls in house prices might be deferred. Nevertheless, this more complex story does not rule out demography-led house-price booms and slumps[12]; furthermore, extrapolated expectations or speculative "bubbles" could not forestall underlying structural shifts indefinitely, and upward price dynamics in the housing market can easily be reversed (as was demonstrated in Canada, the United Kingdom, and the Netherlands in the late 1980s—see figures 5–7 of Poterba 1991).

Consumption of housing equity and the life cycle
Fluctuations in house prices, perhaps induced by cohort-size effects, have an impact on the net wealth positions of households. To examine some of these features in the US context, table 8.3 combines several tables from Skinner 1991. The table investigates the rising values of housing equity in the United States between 1969 and 1986 by age group. Column 2 shows that homeownership is extensive, especially among those aged between 41 and 70. Ownership of housing accounts for around 60 percent of net worth, and this is largely invariant with respect to age group (column 3). Housing debt (reflected in proportionate mortgage payments) unsurprisingly declines with age (column 4), and housing equity value rises with age until 70 (column 5). Coupled with constant equity–net worth ratios across age groups, this implies that overall asset holdings rise with age, at least until age 71+, and appears to confirm the results of studies that question the applicability of the "hump-shaped" asset profile associated with the "naive" life-cycle model of saving without bequests (see section 8.2 above). However, the attrition and cohort biases discussed in section 8.2 are also relevant here. Columns 5 and 7 together show that the average

explicitly to trade down equity. The former route exploits the asset character of housing, whereas the decision to move is interrelated with the consumption good aspect of housing; however, both "routes" involve costs, and, as the next subsection suggests, neither route may be particularly attractive for the elderly. Indeed, the typical "trigger" for releasing housing equity may be the decision to move into assisted residential care or to move in with other members of the family when the capacity for independent activity is impaired, or at widowhood. Thus, in general housing equity tends to continue to accumulate well into old age, then to be bequested on death or run down rapidly in later life if full-time care is required (Merrill 1984; Venti and Wise 1989).

The discussion so far has been in the context of the appreciation of house values in the United States over a long period; indeed, Skinner's (1991) analysis and those that utilize the Retirement History Survey (e.g., Merrill 1984; Venti and Wise 1989) cover that period of house-price appreciation. In a period of sustained rising prices, behavior may be motivated by expectational considerations, such as the extrapolative forecasts considered by Poterba (1991), which may preclude decisions that might involve the loss of prospective capital gains.[13] The experience of other countries with different house-price trajectories might afford additional insights into the life-cycle accumulation of housing equity. For example, in the United Kingdom real house prices rose by some 60 percent between 1982 and 1988, only to fall back by 15 percent by 1991 (see figure 7 of Poterba 1991) and indeed to lose almost all of the real capital gain of the period 1982–1988 by 1996.

Table 8.4 presents comparable figures for housing equity values in Great Britain in 1985 (during the house-price upswing) and 1991 (during the subsequent downswing) taken from Henley 1994. The 1985 calculations, from the General Household Survey, take account of the fact that house values are observed only for moves within the last 5 years; the appropriate selection procedure is implemented as described in Henley et al. 1994. It will be noted that there are differences between table 8.4 and table 8.3: owner occupation peaks in an earlier age group in Great Britain (35–44 in 1985, 45–54 in 1991) than in the United States. This is partly a cohort effect, although there is an overall rise in owner occupation between the sample dates stemming from the active "right to buy" policy for public housing adopted by local authorities with the active support of the Conservative administrations of the 1980s.

Table 8.4

Housing wealth by age group in Great Britain, 1985 and 1991. Source: Henley 1994, tables 6 and 7. Data constructed from General Household Survey (1985) and British Household Panel Study Wave 1 (1991).

1 Age group	2 Percentage homeowners, 1985	3 Average house value (£1991), 1985	4 Net housing equity (£1991), 1985	5 Percentage homeowners, 1991	6 Average house value (£1991), 1991	7 Net housing equity (£1991), 1991
<25	33.6	32,201	4,575	31.1	45,206	11,321
25–34	63.8	40,424	12,974	66.1	54,258	22,916
35–44	69.7	51,798	28,622	74.7	69,791	46,866
45–54	60.0	56,227	39,865	76.5	78,339	64,666
55–64	50.0	61,347	53,316	68.6	75,040	69,900
65–74	40.5	69,067	64,369	52.5	75,258	71,774
≥75	36.5	73,700	70,912	38.4	74,008	73,142

Gross housing wealth (house value) rises with age, especially in 1985. However, the positive house value-age relationship is most noticeable for net housing wealth (value less the outstanding mortgage—the equity value), which continues to rise even into the ≥75 age category. There is little evidence here of trading down to smaller *owned* housing among the elderly, although the rate of owner occupation does decline. This is probably largely a cohort effect, but it contradicts the US experience (Merrill 1984) by which more elderly people switch from renting to owning than vice versa. Merrill's result seems incompatible again with the "hump-shaped" pattern of life-cycle saving, since moving from owning to renting would be one way of liberating housing equity. But the British phenomenon of rising home equity among the elderly also contradicts the hypothesis in it simplest form. The evidence raises the possibility that individuals may have accumulated "excessive" housing (from both a consumption standpoint and an investment standpoint) in later life.

Excess housing: costs and policy

Although many elderly people own significant housing equity in Britain and North America (and, along with pension wealth, housing equity typically constitutes the main source of wealth holding in these countries), ownership of property is not without its costs: maintenance, insurance, utility costs, property taxes, ground rent, and, to a much lesser extent among the elderly than among the young, mortgage repayments. These user costs of housing may account for a significant proportion of an elderly household's income, and so the price of not downtrading or liquidating housing assets in later life may be unaffordable levels of housing costs. The obvious response to "excess" cost—moving to a smaller house or to rented accommodations—may involve transaction costs and significant psychic costs (from the move itself and from the loss of familiar surroundings), and so retention of the original property is often the norm. Thus, the apparent contradiction to the life-cycle hypothesis—that individuals retain housing assets until they die—may stem not from "non-life-cycle behavior" such as myopia or a dominant bequest motive but from constraints on behavior revealed after retirement.[14]

Feinstein and McFadden (1989) put forward evidence for the United States on what they term "inappropriate" housing among the elderly, which they define as a dwelling with the number of rooms exceeding the number of residents plus three. Using the PSID, they find that around 40 percent of households aged 65 or over are in this position. But dwelling size can always be attributable to preferences, and perhaps a more appropriate measure of financial circumstances is user cost as a fraction of disposable income, or household budget share. The distribution of budget shares reported by Feinstein and McFadden is illustrated in table 8.5; a comparable exercise drawn from the UK's 1988–89 Retirement Survey is illustrated in table 8.6.

In the US study, maintenance and insurance costs are imputed to equal 2.0 percent of house value, and measured utility costs, mortgage payments, and property taxes are included. In the UK calculation,

Table 8.5
Distribution of share of out-of-pocket housing costs in after-tax income by tenure type and age, United States, 1968–1982. Source: Feinstein and McFadden 1989, table 2.5; tabulations from PSID, average for 1968–1982.

Age	0.0–0.2	0.2–0.3	0.3–0.4	0.4–0.5	0.5+	No. of cases
Owners						
55–64	0.473	0.268	0.125	0.064	0.070	3277
65–74	0.544	0.270	0.097	0.041	0.048	3306
75+	0.559	0.246	0.103	0.043	0.049	1369
Renters						
55–64	0.450	0.313	0.133	0.060	0.044	1340
65–74	0.529	0.295	0.113	0.035	0.029	1122
75+	0.494	0.298	0.105	0.042	0.061	409

Table 8.6
Distribution of share of out-of-pocket housing costs in after-tax income by tenure type and age, Great Britain, 1988–1989. Source: Disney, Gallagher, and Henley 1994, tabulations from British Retirement Survey, 1988–1989.

Age	0.0–0.1	0.1–0.2	0.2–0.3	0.3–0.4	0.4–0.5	0.5+	No. of cases
Owners							
55–64	0.1331	0.3494	0.2213	0.1048	0.0649	0.1265	601
65–70	0.0829	0.2943	0.2886	0.1686	0.0829	0.0829	350
70+	0.0943	0.3491	0.2736	0.1981	0.0283	0.0566	106
Total	0.1126	0.3311	0.2488	0.1353	0.0672	0.1050	1057
Renters							
55–64	0.3059	0.2862	0.2336	0.1151	0.0296	0.0296	304
65–70	0.2451	0.2646	0.2918	0.1323	0.0428	0.0234	257
70+	0.3429	0.2714	0.2714	0.0857	0.0	0.0286	70
Total	0.2853	0.2758	0.2615	0.1189	0.0317	0.0269	631

maintenance and insurance are imputed to be 1.3 percent of house value but in other respects the studies are identical.[15] If we define "excess" housing costs as a housing budget share greater than 0.4, then for the United States 10.8 percent of owners and 8.8 percent of renters have a share in excess of 0.4. It is perhaps surprising that the ratios are so close for owners and renters, since renters are more mobile (Merrill 1984; Venti and Wise 1989) and might be expected to move to cheaper accommodations where housing costs are excessive. This hypothesis is borne out by the data from the United Kingdom, where the proportions with budget shares over 0.4 are respectively 17.2 percent for owners and 5.8 percent for renters (but see footnote 14). However, mean budget shares are very similar for the two studies. In both the US and UK studies, the proportions with "excess" housing costs fall with age, although in the UK data the reduction occurs only for those 70 and over.

Elderly households may in the short run reduce housing costs by economizing on maintenance and by underinsuring the property. When these costs are excluded from the UK study for owners, the mean housing budget share is halved and the proportion of owners with a ratio greater than 0.4 falls to 3.1 percent. It is also interesting to examine in greater detail the characteristics of owners in the UK who report housing budget shares in excess of 0.4. Table 8.7 presents a *probit* analysis of this probability of reporting "excess" costs, using the Retirement Survey. The table reports variable means, calculated coefficients, and, where appropriate, computed probabilities when each dummy variable is in turn evaluated at the mean of the continuous variables (log income, financial asset ownership, insurance policies, and age). The "baseline" probability for a single male owner who is fit, employed, not reported as "retired," and living in the West Midlands, is 0.1296. Being female, *ceteris paribus,* raises the probability to 0.1449.[16]

As is apparent, individuals who own outright or have higher incomes are likely to have lower housing budget shares. In the latter case, by calculating the marginal effects, we find for example that raising the weekly net household income from £100 per week to £160 per week reduces the probability of an "excess" housing cost ratio from 0.37 to 0.12. Raising the value of household financial assets from 0 to £10,000 *raises* the probability of having an "excess" cost from 0.09 to 0.13. The importance of financial assets to households with housing equity is discussed below. Demographic effects do not come through strongly, although the self-employed typically have higher housing costs rela-

Table 8.7
Excess housing budget share probit for owners: British retirement survey. Dependent variable: excess housing budget share (>0.4). Source: Disney, Gallagher, and Henley 1994; calculations from Retirement Survey.

Variable	Mean	Coefficient	S.E.	Baseline probability
Intercept	—	10.006[a]	0.975	—
Wealth and Income				
Owns outright	0.747	−1.350[a]	0.121	0.1095
Log income	4.973	−2.150[a]	0.123	—
Liquid assets	0.859	0.200[a]	0.054	—
Insurance policies	0.123	0.248[a]	0.064	—
Demographics				
Age	63.011	−0.010	0.012	—
Female	0.493	0.142	0.104	0.1449
Widowed	0.102	0.330	0.266	0.1368
Separated	0.031	0.038	0.326	0.1298
Married	0.824	0.333	0.247	0.1965
Economic status				
Invalid	0.078	−0.262	0.179	0.1253
Unemployed	0.027	0.057	0.241	0.1299
Retired	0.380	−0.373[a]	0.124	0.1020
Self-employed	0.098	0.560[a]	0.136	0.1415
Region				
Scotland	0.041	−0.798[a]	0.382	0.1227
Wales	0.063	−1.386[a]	0.402	0.1120
North	0.052	−0.746[a]	0.322	0.1216
Yorks., Humbs.	0.092	−0.444[a]	0.221	0.1211
North West	0.110	−0.262	0.208	0.1236
East Midlands	0.073	0.005	0.224	0.1296
East Anglia	0.039	0.874[a]	0.255	0.1370
London	0.084	0.810[a]	0.204	0.1444
South East	0.245	0.765[a]	0.169	0.1733
South West	0.104	0.419[a]	0.197	0.1390
N	2088			
Log likelihood	−467.286			

a. Significance at 5%.

tive to reported income and the retired (self-reported) have lower costs. As expected, there is also regional variation in the housing budget share.

If a significant minority of elderly people have "excess" housing costs, what options are open to them? The list of potential solutions includes trading down by moving to cheaper accommodations, running down other (largely financial) assets, and "equity release schemes." Although moving is the "natural" solution, it has already been noted that such a strategy involves costs; obviously, as a policy option a reduction in transactions costs might encourage homeowners to engage in more frequent "fine tuning" of their housing consumption. Methodologically, it is difficult to model moves conditional on housing costs, since tenure choice is itself an outcome of an individual's propensity to move. Feinstein and McFadden confirm earlier analyses which show that the probability of moving among the elderly is largely related to age, to changes in employment status (such as retirement), and to changes in household composition (such as children growing up or the death of a spouse). Although there are significant liquidity effects on the moving decision among renters (who are probably the more mobile individuals in any event), the evidence for financial-constraint-led moves among owners is much weaker. Thus, moving in general does not seem to be related to the financial positions of households.

The second option, running down financial assets, obtains some empirical support from analysis of the British Retirement Survey, which asks individuals aged 55–69 about the change in their financial assets since retirement. Some preliminary results are reported in table 8.8, which contains a median regression model of the absolute change in financial assets since retirement, reflated to 1988 prices. Such a regression does not provide a structural test of a life-cycle model of consumption, or indeed of any other hypothesis of consumption behavior but it can be used to illustrate the impact of housing budget shares and of housing-related behavior on financial asset holdings.

Column 2 of table 8.8 suggests that time elapsed since retirement, changes in family composition, and receipt of a bequest all have the expected effects on financial (dis)saving. Column 3 adds three significant variables: the first two show that households that have moved since retirement have, on average, financial assets some £2000 lower (reflecting transaction costs), whereas households that have moved explicitly to release housing equity (as self-reported) have gained, on

Table 8.8
Median regression model of financial dissaving by the retired. Dependent variable: change in financial assets since retirement (reflated to 1988 consumer prices). Source: British Retirement Survey, 1988–89; table from Disney, Gallagher, and Henley 1995.

1	2		3		4	
	Coeff.	S.E.	Coeff.	S.E.	Coeff.	S.E.
Time since retirement (spline segments)						
0–2 years	−698.0	326.8*	−573.3	343.9+	−687.8	452.1
2–4 years	1276.4	670.3+	−896.5	700.4	1113.0	925.2
4–6 years	−635.5	733.0	−157.2	770.2	−369.6	1019.7
6–8 years	−14.1	881.4	−340.0	948.3	−74.4	1217.0
8–10 years	−478.4	1174.7	222.6	1268.9	−348.7	1599.4
10–12 years	591.8	1559.9	−697.2	1670.6	−86.3	2132.8
12+ years	−15483.9	1842.4*	−14465.5	1997.3*	−14755.7	2577.8*
Demographics						
Widowed since retirement	320.1	482.7	652.5	528.3	417.2	681.7
Separated since retirement	−307.6	493.2	−313.6	540.6	−541.2	702.4
Other Wealth						
Insurance policies (£1000s)	5176.5	3593.4	5116.8	3927.3	151.0	490.6
Inheritance (dummy)	2168.5	403.7*	1895.6	428.6*	1457.9	565.2*
Housing						
Moved since retirement			−2199.1	590.9*	−2544.2	761.7*
Withdrawn equity			2639.9	1021.9*	2630.3	1285.1*
Housing cost "disequilibrium"			−736.0	276.7*	−588.6	359.4+
House value < £25K					−1784.7	2349.4
House value £25K–£50K					57.3	2119.0
House value £50K–£100K					−96.7	2114.2
House value £100K–£150K					−1141.2	2215.9
House value £150K–£200K					119.2	2298.2
House value £200K+					−734.8	2509.3
Intercept	−2320.2	611.7*	−1423.1	744.4+	−516.0	2268.8
Pseudo R^2	0.027		0.036		0.040	
Minimized sum of deviations	2602038		2577865		2566426	

Notes: + Denotes significance at 10%, * at 5%. Sample: Retired, owner-occupier heads of households who were not formerly self-employed, $n = 397$. Variable: Housing cost "disequilibrium" is the residuals from a regression of log housing expenditure on log income.

average, some £2600. The net impact of equity-releasing house moves on financial assets is therefore rather small. The final variable, housing-cost "disequilibrium," shows how the financial assets of households that incur housing costs greater or less than those predicted by a log-linear regression of housing costs on their income are affected. The coefficient on this variable implies that a £1 higher (lower) level of weekly housing expenditure than that predicted by income raises (lowers) the rate of dissaving of financial assets since retirement by £736. Column 4 includes banded house values in the model. Since this variable is endogenous and has little explanatory power, column 3 is the preferred specification.

Table 8.8 suggests that moving involves significant financial costs and may not release enough equity to justify the transaction. For those with financial assets, a gradual attrition of such assets is, at least for a time, the adopted solution, with house equity released later in life when a move is required by loss of physical independence or exhaustion of other resources. As Skinner (1993) points out, in any event the annuity value of a typical housing equity value is rather small until at least the age of 75. Insofar as an aging population involves greater longevity, with the most rapid increase in the numbers of those aged 75 and over, however, housing equity release may become more important.

The question therefore arises of why "equity release" schemes have not become more popular in recent years. Leather (1990) describes a number of such schemes operating in the United Kingdom. They share the characteristic that a capital sum or annuity can be obtained by using the housing equity as security, or by disposing of all or some of the housing equity in exchange for a right to continued occupancy. Examples of the former type of scheme, using the house as security, include "maturity loans" (in which repayment of the principal is deferred until sale or death) and "home income plans" (reverse annuity mortgages); of the latter, home reversion schemes are most common. Maturity loans are typically used by low income households, for example to finance repairs, because interest payments can be offset against income-tested social security payments (known in the UK as Income Support) if the household has no other financial assets. As with reverse annuity mortgages, retention of ownership means that the owner can benefit from any appreciation in house value—a facility that is lost when home-reversion-type schemes are used.

The deficiencies of such schemes are familiar. Individuals may be risk-averse as to length of life and future income flows. They may not like taking loans secured against property late in life, and may intend to leave the property as a bequest. Longevity risk is, in theory, avoided by a reverse annuity mortgage; however, given the standard adverse selection problem in the annuity market, it is unlikely that optants would obtain an actuarially fair annuity, especially since annuity values obtained from housing equity are unlikely to be large until late in life, when adverse selection as to longevity in the annuity market is most likely to be pervasive. Home reversion plans seem even less attractive, because optants thereby typically relinquish potential appreciation in the capital value of their house in practice. Evidence for the United Kingdom suggests therefore that numbers opting for these types of equity release schemes can be counted in tens of thousands rather than hundreds of thousands. Nevertheless, with an aging population, such schemes may become more attractive for the reasons outlined earlier: they avoid the costs associated with moving, and, if a bequest motive becomes less pressing with fewer children and greater affluence among the elderly, they allow homeowners to enjoy greater consumption in their final years.

8.4   Conclusion

This chapter has examined the impact of aging on saving rates and on consumption patterns. The basis of the analysis of demographic changes has been the life-cycle hypothesis (LCH) of consumption and saving. Evidence across OECD countries suggests that a higher aged dependency ratio is associated with lower private household saving and lower investment in fixed capital. There is also some evidence that population growth is a stimulus to growth and therefore to saving. Nevertheless, these trends need not be wholly alarming; a smaller capital stock may be consistent with a stationary or contracting population if factor productivity continues to increase. And chapter 6, for example, found no evidence of a negative association between the average age of the workforce and labor productivity.

The microeconomic evidence on the predictive power of the LCH is much more mixed; in particular, wealth holdings do not decline as rapidly in old age as the basic LCH would predict. However, there are biases in cross-section estimates of the age-wealth profile, and cohort analysis of individual behavior is more appropriate. Such cohort analyses do suggest stronger evidence for the LCH, but a bequest motive appears to be important for some groups (primarily the rich) and for some assets (notably housing). However, precautionary motives and preferences may retard the depletion of housing wealth as the individual ages.

The interaction between generations, and how this is affected by differential generation size, is also important. Prospective beneficiaries from bequests may spend the proceeds in advance; indeed, such behavior is one reconciliation of the microeconomic and macroeconomic evidence on the LCH. A declining number of children means fewer potential beneficiaries from bequests; how this affects the consumption behavior of both the young and the elderly depends on the model of bequests which we believe to be appropriate. Reverse altruism (that is from the young to the elderly) also depends on the willingness of the young to finance a growing burden of dependency. As PAYG social insurance schemes are cut back over time, a greater emphasis on income testing and asset testing of social security may induce changes in saving behavior among prospective elderly benefit recipients.

Consumption patterns differ between the young and the old, and change slowly. It is hard to know whether differences in consumption patterns are entirely age-related or whether they exhibit cohort-specific effects. The generation now in retirement lived through periods of war and adverse income shocks; successive retiring generations may exhibit quite different behavior: for example, a greater willingness to dissave assets and less emphasis on precautionary (buffer stock) saving motives. In general, too, the real incomes of the elderly have grown much faster than the average in recent years, although this conceals a considerable degree of inequality of income in retirement. How this will affect consumption patterns, and the size of bequests, requires further analysis.

The last section focused on housing wealth and consumption. Maintaining housing assets to death seems to be one reason why life-cycle wealth in total does not decline as predicted by the "basic" life-cycle hypothesis of saving. Demographics factors affect the story through their effects on house prices, on the distribution and allocation of housing equity, and on the strength of the bequest motive. In the late 1980s, when housing equity was increasing rapidly in the upswing of the economic cycle, there was a good deal of speculation as to the consequences of intergenerational transfers of housing wealth for future wealth distribution and saving behavior, but in countries that have subsequently seen significant real falls in housing equity values, views are now more sanguine. In the United Kingdom in the 1990s, recession in the housing market, predictions of demography-driven secular declines in housing demand, and the evidence that a significant minority of elderly people have trouble in keeping up the maintenance of their house make this prediction of extensive bequesting seem less likely. Indeed, the issue of housing equity release has been linked to the issue of the affordability of extra health and domiciliary care in old age.

Much of this book has focused on the consequences of an aging population for expenditures on social security. Another area of concern identified by "demographic pessimists" is that of health care. Greater longevity does not of itself imply improvements in health status; indeed, an increase in the population aged 75+ may be associated with a higher incidence of chronic illness and disability, which, it has been argued, will put a greater burden on society. In the countries of Western Europe this burden is typically shared by publicly financed programs of health-care provision and by private expenditures on domiciliary (at-home) and residential (nursing-home) care. A large component of care is undertaken informally, by relatives, but this still induces opportunity costs for the caregivers themselves (for example, forgone labor-market opportunities).

Public health care deserves a monograph for itself, and many have been written. In the context of aging, there is a striking parallel between public health care and pay-as-you-go social security, where the prospect of a "financing crisis" induced by aging has drawn attention to deficiencies of the program unrelated to aging *per se*. In the case of health care, these deficiencies may include underinsurance and spiraling costs in largely privately funded programs (as in the United States), an overemphasis on expensive institutional and inpatient hospital care (as in the United Kingdom), or chronic excess demand in health-care systems which are "free" at the point of delivery. In such cases, a perceived "burden of aging" has given governments the impetus to consider reforms that might have been politically infeasible in other circumstances, just as the Ponzi-scheme nature of PAYG social insurance programs has been exposed by demographic factors.

Faced with deficiencies in public-sector programs, individuals will typically wish to improve the quality of, and their access to, health care by private expenditures on insurance and treatment. A forward-looking individual with an additional demand for health care will take out insurance against ill health or disability in old age long before his or her later life, when the possibility of adverse selection may raise premium rates considerably. But myopia, inadequate insurance, and the subsequent revelation of the quality of public health-care provision (for example of residential care) may lead to greater expenditures on health care by the elderly in later life than they anticipated at an earlier stage. Thus, there may be deficiencies in private care which may induce further pressure for state intervention, even when existing publicly provided services are under pressure from costs, demography, and rising demand. The US "crisis" of health-care provision, and the attempts to reform the structure in the early 1990s, should be seen in the light.

Section 9.1 suggests that, even though much of care for the elderly is informal (unwaged), the demand for residential care will grow steadily as the population ages. Section 9.2 examines whether the US "crisis" of escalating health-care expenditures is a general phenomenon with parallels in other OECD countries, examines the forecasts of demographic effects on health-care expenditures, and describes the extent of private insurance provision in the United States and the United Kingdom.

Section 9.3 describes alternative systems of public health care, focusing on whether benefits are provided in cash or in kind (e.g., places in nursing homes) and on the degree of means testing of benefits. It also considers the development of the private market in long-term residential care and domiciliary health care, and suggests that the more sophisticated insurance products now on the market can exploit the potential negative covariances between risks associated with severe ill health and longevity.

9.1 Health Status and the Demand for Long-Term Care

Underlying the aging of society is the improvement in life expectancy. But is this enhanced longevity associated with an improvement in the physical *quality* of life? Are the medical, dietary, and public-health changes that underlie the expectation of increasing longevity also likely to improve the physical and mental capacities of the elderly? Are people aware of trends in physical and mental health among the aged, and have they made adequate arrangements in advance to deal with any eventualities that might require long-term care? All these issues have proved controversial; on some of them there has been little agreement in the literature.[1]

One obvious point is that enhanced life expectancy also increases the likelihood that an individual's last few years will be accompanied by a degenerative medical condition, such as arthritis or dementia, requiring some form of long-term care. On the other hand, it is possible that medical improvements will do much to alleviate these conditions in the future. In possible contrast, the same improvements that have forestalled early mortality from certain illnesses (cancers, heart disease) may also have improved health in these areas. Thus, as Garber (1989) points out, the debate over longevity and ill health may have clouded the more important economic issue: that a change in the *nature* of ill health may change the nature of the living arrangements required by the elderly.

Generally, living arrangements for the elderly can be divided into five types: self-sufficient living arrangements, informal (i.e. largely unpaid) care, paid community and domiciliary care, long-term residential care, and hospital care. From a narrow notion of economic cost, these options are ranked according to increasing average cost (although private costs may differ—hospital costs are often financed by the state, whereas residential care may be financed privately). In considering social costs, it should be noted that informal care often carries little explicit cost but may have significant opportunity costs, borne by the provider of the care. Informal (largely intrafamilial) care is still the dominant form. In the United Kingdom, expenditures on care of the elderly—both state funded and private—totaled £9 billion in 1992. If the hours of unpaid informal care observed in household surveys were valued at market wage rates, this would value unpaid care at £32 billion (Laing 1993). Although this is a questionable valuation procedure (observed market wages may be a poor measure of the reservation wages of unpaid caregivers), and although some informal care may actually be paid for by unmeasured cash transactions, it does show the extent of the cost that could be borne by the private and public sectors if formal care were to be substituted for informal.

In contrast, public expenditures will fall if health improvements and changes in public policy reduce reliance on hospital care, substituting greater emphasis on "care in the community" (whether residential care or greater support for informal networks of care). Institutional arrangements for public provision can also have large effects on expenditure: for example, in the United Kingdom restrictions on the number of places available in local-authority-run nursing homes in the late 1970s caused an escalation in the payment of means-tested social security benefits to individuals making their own arrangements for residential care in the 1980s. The transfer of cash limited care budgets back to local authorities under the 1990 National Health Service and Community Care Act is likely to reverse this trend (Laing 1993).

The remainder of this chapter will follow the assumption in the literature that future changes in health, in social customs, and in public policy will put greater emphasis on paid care, whether in the community or in the residential-care sector, and that services provided by this sector will not in general be free at the point of delivery. Thus, whether private savings or insurance policies are sufficient to finance individual care in old age is a key issue. As we saw in chapter 8, there may be economic constraints on choice of living arrangements associated with inability to dissave housing assets. Overannuitization of wealth may also limit the ability of older individuals to finance long-term care. Further constraints on the financing of residential care will be discussed below.

Another important issue is the nature of the "risk" associated with ill health in old age. The probability that most individuals will survive to retirement is very high now in Western industrialized countries, in Australasia, and in Japan. Abstracting from medical and health issues, the expenditure associated with a target living standard in retirement is also fairly predictable. Thus, non-health-related expenditures in retirement probably are amenable to a life-cycle saving strategy, subject to a well-functioning annuity market. In contrast, the risk of ill health in late life, and particularly the uncertainty as to the nature of that ill health, is probably less well known to the individual. In insurance terms, health status is a catastrophic risk in the sense that there is a low probability of a highly costly outcome. This would naturally invite the development of an insurance market. For even if those 75 and older face a high likelihood of requiring long-term care, the probability of surviving from retirement to this age is much less certain. Consequently, individuals may underinsure or overinsure, depending on their subjective perception of these risks, on the individual's degree of risk aversion, and on the efficiency of the insurance market. Of the two possibilities, underinsurance seems the more pervasive. Weiner et al. (1994) cite evidence from the United States that only 23 percent of those 65 and over were "disabled," whereas 69 percent of those over 85 were classified as "severely disabled." Yet only 22 percent of the "severely disabled" were in nursing homes; the vast majority were living in the community, whether by choice of the individual or of the caregiver or because of a shortage of funds.

Among the many reasons why individuals may have inadequate private insurance coverage to provide for residential care are myopia in early life, adverse selection in later life, and deductibles in "typical" health-care policies that exclude long periods of residential care or care for certain types of degenerative illness.[2] Consequently, there may be a strong case for government involvement in the regulation or even the provision of long-term health care. It has always been a puzzle, at least to this author, why the state has been happy to provide income in retirement through universal social security pensions (which seems in principle to be a market amenable to savings strategies and private provision), whereas until recently it has avoided intervention in the market for long-term health-care—a market that would seem to suffer all the potential problems of organizing insurance against catastrophic risk.

The potential costs of this government intervention, coupled with the perception that private resources are not adequate to deal with long-term health-care problems associated with aging populations, have precipitated much concern, especially in the United States, about a potential "financial crisis" in health care. Before looking at possible "solutions" to the problem and at the nature of government involvement, however, it is useful to undertake some comparative analysis of public spending on the elderly in various countries. Some interesting facts arise which suggest exercising caution before assuming that the "health-care financing crisis" often discussed in the United States is a pervasive phenomenon in other countries.

9.2   International Comparisons of Age-Related Spending on Health

The importance of international heterogeneity of health-care delivery systems is illustrated by table 9.1. The most striking aspect of this table is the disparity between population shares in the various age groups and the age-related shares of government medical expenditure. For example, in the United States the 65+ age group accounts for only 11 percent of the population but for nearly half of total public-health expenditures. In France, only the 0–14 age group obtains an "excessive" share of health-care expenditures relative to share of population. Of course, these disparities stem in part from differences in the public-

Table 9.1
Age distribution of government medical expenditure in 1980. Source: Heller et al. 1986, table 23.

	Share of medical expenditure allocated to age group			Share of population in age group		
	0–14	15–64	65+	0–14	15–64	65+
Canada	—	—	27.5	9.5	67.5	23.0
France	16.2	61.5	22.3	14.0	63.5	22.5
FRG	9.7	57.1	33.1	15.5	67.6	16.9
Italy	8.5	49.6	41.9	17.3	60.7	22.0
Japan	9.5	64.2	26.3	9.0	67.4	23.6
UK	21.4	36.5	42.1	14.8	64.0	21.2
US	9.7	40.4	49.9	31.9	56.9	11.2

private mix of health-care provision between countries. Nevertheless, there are disparities *within* public (and private) provision: for example, expenditures on public hospital care in the United Kingdom for the 75+ group were 9 times the expenditures on the 16–64 group in 1980, and in France expenditures on the 75+ group were only twice the expenditures on the 15–64 group (Heller et al. 1986, table 25).

Projections suggest that expenditures on public health care will rise by an average of 40 percent in twelve OECD countries from 1980 to 2040 (OECD 1988a). Typically, such calculations rest on assumptions as to demography, the "relative price effect" (the steeper increase of public service costs relative to private goods and services), and off-setting efficiency gains. Whether these increases are "affordable" is a moot point. Certainly the increases driven be demography alone may not be so substantial: even in one of the "worst" cases in table 9.2, the United States, Aaron (1991) projects that population aging will push up acute health-care spending by less than 2 percent of GDP over the next three decades. Laing (1993) suggests that resources spent on long-term care in the United Kingdom, both private and state financed, will more than double in the United Kingdom from 1991 to 2051, from 1.5 percent to 3.5 percent of GDP. This is similar to the increase estimated by Aaron, but it should be noted that in the United Kingdom the share of state involvement is expected to decline so that public spending may grow more slowly, as illustrated in table 9.2.

The importance of taking account of demographic trends as a whole, and not just the growth in the numbers of the elderly, is revealed by figure 9.1. Per-capita health-care expenditures peak at the two ends

Table 9.2
Real government expenditures on medical care, 1980–2025 (index: 1980 = 100). Source: Heller et al. 1986, table 8.

	2000	2010	2025
Canada	128	140	174
France	117	125	130
FRG	104	107	103
Italy	113	117	121
Japan	130	140	147
UK	105	105	115
US	130	144	180

of the age scale—at birth and among the very elderly. Consequently, countries with an increasing elderly share of a declining population, such as (ex-West) Germany, face less adverse prospects for health-care-expenditure growth than countries that face the aging of an increasing population, such as Australia and Canada. This is illustrated by tables 9.2 and 9.3. Paradoxically, measures to increase the birth rate to offset the effect of aging may obtain the "worst of both worlds" in terms of health-care-expenditure growth. A slowly growing population, with a "balanced" age profile, would minimize the increase in per-capita health-care expenditures.

The perceived prospect of a "crisis" in health-care expenditures may induce greater private provision. The Brookings-ICF Long Term Care Financing Model (Weiner et al. 1994) predicts that the number of elderly people using nursing homes in the United States will rise from 2.2 million in 1993 to 3.6 million in 2018 and the number of users of at-home care from 5.2 million to 7.4 million. Expenditures rise more rapidly, and the increase is predominantly borne by Medicare and from private patients' resources (ibid., table 1-2). But the financial status of the elderly is likely to improve, as discussed elsewhere in this book, and the extra users of private services will generally be drawn from those with larger assets or adequate insurance. For the poorer elderly, problems remain.

Furthermore, the largest proportion of health-care insurance in industrialized countries is employer-provided. Table 9.4 shows that roughly 60 percent of Americans are covered by health-care insurance provided by past or present employers. Only 12 percent have privately purchased health-care plans. In the United Kingdom the extent of health-care insurance provided by employers is even higher (Disney

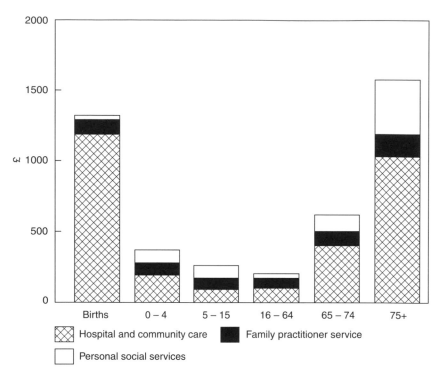

Figure 9.1
Per capita expenditures on health and personal social services (1986–87 prices), United
Kingdom, by age group. Source: Ermisch 1990.

Table 9.3
Projected percentage of government medical care expenditure on the elderly, 1980–2025.
Source: Heller et al. 1986, table 10.

	1980	2000	2010	2025
Canada	33.3	38.0	40.9	53.1
FRG	33.1	33.6	39.0	42.6
Italy	31.8	36.2	37.4	40.6
Japan	27.4	37.7	43.8	48.3
UK	42.1	44.1	44.3	49.4
US	50.0	54.4	55.6	64.6

Table 9.4
Sources of health-care insurance coverage in United States, 1992. Source: Aaron and Bosworth 1994.

	Persons (millions)	Percent
All persons	251.4	100.0
Uninsured	35.4	14.1
Insured	216.0	85.9
Sources of insurance		
Employer coverage	139.9	55.7
On own job	67.6	26.9
As dependent	72.3	28.8
Retiree coverage[a]	10.2	4.0
Non-group coverage	31.3	12.4
Medicaid	27.1	10.8
Medicare	32.9	13.1
Military	9.9	3.9
Multiple coverage	35.2	14.0

a. Insurance coverage received from a previous employer.

and Webb 1989). Of course, the problems of employer-provided health-care plans in this context are well known: benefits are typically of limited duration and may fail to cover full medical expenses. The commonest employer plan is one that provides for limited spells of leave on grounds of sickness and (typically as part of the pension plan) premature retirement on grounds of ill health (Madrian 1994). Even so, such plans typically provide the pension at an earlier date than normal retirement, without any provision for expenses associated with longevity-related illness and disability.

Furthermore, the extent and the nature of employer provision are driven by the same factors as with private pension plans (see chapter 5). For example, provision of health-care insurance by employers may be motivated by tax considerations (where such provision is taxable at a lower rate than earned income) or by the desire to provide tenure incentives. Subject to any "vesting" provisions (minimum scheme tenure) in health-care insurance, however, the incentive effects of health-care plans are much less than those associated with defined-benefit pension plans. In the latter case, benefits typically depend on duration of scheme tenure, whereas, subject to recruitment selection on grounds of potential health, provision of health benefits rests solely on health status at any point in time. Thus, the incentive effect of a pension plan in retaining labor is likely to be stronger than the offer of a health-care plan when similar plans are offered by competing firms. In competitive markets, therefore, firms may simply see health-care plans as an extra "burden" on costs with no intrinsic features. There is a tendency to erode benefits from such plans in times of recession or in particularly competitive sectors—a trend noted in recent times in the United States by Schulz (1992, pp. 193–194).

9.3 Policy Options

Public Provision of Health Care

Public, or state, support for long-term health care varies widely across countries. Two dimensions of this variation are whether cash sums are paid (and to whom) or in-kind services are provided and whether such sums or services are provided on a "social insurance" basis or on a means-tested basis.

In the case of cash benefits versus services, the nature of the service is obviously important; people are not generally given cash to buy hospital services. In contrast, whether people should be given cash to purchase residential and domiciliary care or should be offered rationed places in publicly financed care programs (typically subject to means testing and need assessment) has been the subject of debate in a number of countries, including the United Kingdom. The arguments for a cash basis are that it allows consumer choice and that, if the cash is tightly capped, it may encourage the use of cheaper care. There are also budgetary issues and questions of local autonomy—cash benefits are typically paid from social security budgets, whereas provision of services is generally financed by local agencies and administrations. This issue is important in federal structures, such as the United States, but also in more traditionally centralized administrations, such as that of the United Kingdom.

Who receives the cash benefit is also relevant. Typically, recipients of state benefits are those identified as having the need for care; examples are payments under the Canadian Health Act for nursing home care and under the Attendance Allowance in the United Kingdom. Sometimes benefits are paid to providers—for example, directly by governments to residential-care providers, but also, less commonly, to domiciliary caregivers (the Invalid Care Allowance was introduced in the United Kingdom as a benefit to be paid to individuals who spend

a large amount of time looking after a disabled person). With an estimated 6.8 million domestic caregivers in the United Kingdom, this
might seem a potentially large expenditure item, but in fact in 1991
only 159,000 caregivers qualified for ICA under tight eligibility conditions as to the time put in by the caregiver and the nature of the disability (Laing 1993).

Whether benefits should be provided universally (subject to a needs
assessment as to the nature of the care required) or means tested also
divides countries. The balance of selectivity may be weighted differently according to the nature of the service, and there are a variety of
options on offer. It is apparent that universal cash-benefit provision for
long-term care financed by insurance contributions without income
testing is an expensive option if associated with medical and hospital
treatment which is free at the point of delivery. Such a social-insurance
model is practiced for nursing-home provision in Canada, but even
there charges ("co-payments") levied toward living costs will absorb
the bulk of the income of a typical pensioner. More common are
schemes that provide medical services and some geriatric care free at
the point of delivery, but in which other residential and domiciliary
care is income tested and asset tested as well as need assessed. In
Sweden long-term-care provision is income tested but not asset tested,
whereas in Germany, the Netherlands, the United Kingdom, and the
United States varying degrees of income and asset testing are applied
(Laing 1993).

Intermediate models are also possible. In France there is a social-
insurance benefit from the health-insurance fund payable toward long-
term care, but the "hotel" element of residential care is strictly means
tested (Laing, ibid.). Yet another variant is where the social insurance
benefit is strictly related to duration. Several options are discussed and
costed for the United States in Weiner et al. 1994. Partial social-
insurance proposals costed there include the following:

(i) Home-care social insurance, as originally proposed by the Clinton
administration, would cover costs of care in the home in addition to
existing tightly means-tested arrangements for nursing care. On the
margin, this would shift the incentive toward cheaper home care because asset tests are stringent for those requiring residential care.

(ii) Home care and "front-end" nursing-home coverage, by which the
social-insurance benefit was extended, say, to finance the first 6 months
of residential care. The object of this option would be to complement

existing Medicare arrangements for the support of the majority of residential-care spells, which are typically of short duration (e.g., post-operative care). Such a strategy would provide the greatest coverage and would be an incentive for recipients not to prolong spells of relatively costly residential care excessively. It would not, however, do much for the chronically disabled.

(iii) Home care and "back-end" nursing home, the rationale for which is the exact opposite of (ii)—namely that support of nursing-home care by the public sector would be concentrated on the chronically ill and disabled. The key issue here is whether those in need of expensive care could afford to finance care privately until the end of the deductible period was attained. However such a strategy could mesh more easily with broader private insurance coverage, since the public sector would in effect underwrite the private insurance market by ultimately picking up the costly chronic cases. On the other hand, the incentive in such a structure would be to prolong spells of residential care if full costs were paid by the state without co-insurance.

(iv) Comprehensive social insurance coverage of both home and nursing care.

Estimates by Weiner et al. using the Brookings long-term finance model suggest that, with the "front end" defined as 6 months in option ii, a 2-year deductible in option iii, and a 20 percent co-insurance payment, the extra public finance costs in 1993 of these options in the United States would be (i) $21 billion, (ii) $23 billion, (iii) $33 billion, and (iv) $49 billion. These would require an increase of between 1 and 2 percent in the payroll-tax rate in 1993, rising by the year 2018 to between 2 and 4 percent as a result of the gradual aging of the population. The Brookings authors themselves propose option ii, and indeed this emphasis on subsidizing domiciliary care rather than prolonging residential care also underpins the 1990 act in the United Kingdom (which attempted to move away from social security support of long-term residential care) and a policy initiative in Germany, where a new social care benefit excluding the "hotel" cost of residential care was introduced in 1992 (Laing 1993). However, the objective of such policies seems largely to be to encourage the cheaper form of provision—home care—at the expense of more costly residential care. Such options are not considered primarily according to the criterion of what state intervention is required to supplement private insurance or a potential private market.

Private Insurance for Health Care

Insurance policies providing long-term-care insurance are relatively new; few explicit long-term-care policies were offered in the United Kingdom before 1991. The United States has more experience of a market in such policies, but even here the market has developed slowly. One constraint may be a lack of demand: Laing (1993) reports survey evidence that people regard pension insurance as more important than long-term-care insurance, and that those concerned as to their income in the event of adverse health outcomes would prefer effective home-equity-release schemes to explicit long-term-care insurance policies. But this evidence may stem from a lack of knowledge as to what is available, given that pension and housing-related financial assets have been offered for a much longer period. He reports that 94 percent of "free-standing" long-term-care policies purchased in the United States are straightforward policies offering insurance payouts subject to deductibles and, in some cases, severe exclusions (see Schulz 1992). The average age of the purchaser of such policies in the United States is 69.

As was stated above, there is evidence that individuals underinsure against events where the adverse outcome occurs with low probability but is associated with a large capital loss. As argued above, long-term health care in old age may be just such a risk, and the high average age of purchasers of "free-standing" health-care insurance may signal that only as the risk increases are individuals prepared to purchase the insurance. Conventionally, as with annuity markets, it might be argued that purchase of insurance earlier in life would avoid the adverse-selection problem inherent in such a risk and would be less costly to those demanding insurance, both through a lower premium and through fewer deductibles. Indeed, given the characteristics of the risk, it might seem feasible to require compulsory *private* insurance at an early stage against adverse health outcomes late in life. A counterargument is that, in contrast with pension provision (where the risk to the insurer is merely an unanticipated increase in longevity), the costs of future health-care provision are largely unknown—that is, there is an undiversifiable element to the risk involved, which might in fact justify greater public intervention. In the absence of compulsory insurance, the aging of the individual provides the revelation of information, to both the insurer and the purchaser, which allows an actuarially fair premium to be fixed.

The more original point is that long-term health care has characteristics which suggest that it could be sold as a joint product with other longevity-related financial assets. Assuming that catastrophic ill health and disability are associated with shorter life, then, aside from natural deterioration with age, there is a negative covariance with the annuity factors underpinning life and pension insurance. Indeed, products have now been developed in the United Kingdom through which, for a reduction in the pension annuity, a long-term health-care package can be purchased in conjunction with a Personal Pension. Likewise, life insurance can be purchased jointly with health-care insurance. Typically, in such policies, the utilization of the long-term-care element of the policy is triggered by objectively measured indicators of loss of individual physical and mental independence. There may be a tradeoff in such policies stemming from the moral-hazard problem of health insurance and the actual health care required. The development of a market in such policies requires objective, measurable indicators of need. As the market grows in sophistication, therefore, we may anticipate an increase in the demand for private health-care insurance and a broadening of the market from the upper income echelons (or those covered by company schemes) who currently purchase. Unlike the private pension market, however, the market in long-term health care may not yet be sufficiently well developed to allow it to take on responsibility for much of the provision currently undertaken by the state.

9.4   Conclusion

One of the problems in determining the impact of aging on the health-care budget is that existing difficulties in the provision of health care by the public sector have been mixed up with the question of demographic pressures on spending. Thus, aging stands in the background of attempts, for example in the United States, to broaden the social-insurance nature of health-care coverage while capping soaring expenditures in the existing health budget and keeping general public expenditures under control. The twin pressures on health-care budgets therefore stem from the aging process *per se* and the belief that greater public support of health care is required. Each may add perhaps 2 percent to the share of GDP allocated to health care for the elderly. This may be a substantial increase if publicly provided when governments are attempting to reduce the share of government activity in GDP.

One of the lessons of international comparisons, however, is that there is a good deal of heterogeneity in expenditure on the elderly, as a share of total expenditure and in the form it takes. Moves toward cheaper forms of care in several countries (for example, residential rather than hospitalized, and domiciliary rather than residential) may reduce the growth of the budget considerably. On the other hand, attempts to broaden public provision, for example by providing subsidies to caregivers in the domestic setting, may increase government expenditures substantially. And all this takes place against a backdrop of disagreement as to whether improving longevity will be associated with improving or worsening health status of the elderly and as to the nature of future improvements in medical treatment and technology.

Markets supplying individually tailored long-term health-care insurance products have been slow to develop, perhaps owing to a combination of institutional inertia and public ignorance. Insurers have been able to exploit uncertainty among individuals concerning future prospects for social security in order to sell private pension products, but the potential risks associated with disability and deterioration in old age have not had such an impact. However, it would seem that there is a potential market in packages offering long-term health care in association with pensions and life insurance, and such products are now being developed. There seems no theoretical reason why such markets should not attain much broader coverage. A long-run model of comprehensive minimum social insurance or income-tested provision coupled with privately financed supplementary provision for combinations of pensions, life insurance, and health care may be the ideal.

10   A Public-Choice Perspective

Samuelson's (1958) consumption loan model, outlined in chapter 3 above, is a model of intertemporal optimization: it examines the content and the feasibility of a hypothetical social contract that would produce a consumption pattern maximizing the utility of a representative individual over his or her lifetime for each of a series of overlapping generations. The Samuelson model has spawned an extensive literature, one facet of which has focused on the available instruments that might facilitate this hypothetical contract. Samuelson suggested manipulation of the size of the stock of money as one such instrument, but in his own subsequent work and that of other authors the existence of a pay-as-you-go social security system was seen as best able to fulfill this function of optimal intertemporal consumption allocation.

A unifying theme of the present book has been optimal behavior over the lifetime in the context of an aging population: in production and productivity, in wage setting, in retirement behavior, and in the allocation of expenditures between consumption and saving. But in a sense the most fundamental issue has been pushed to the background: the efficacy and feasibility of an intergenerational "contract" between generations over resource allocation. This chapter restores that important issue to its central position.

Whereas Samuelson and his successors focused on the form that an optimal intergenerational contract might take over time (defining optimality in a manner consistent with the modern treatment of consumption and taxation in welfare economics developed since Ramsey (1927, 1928)), other strands of thought have considered the question from the point of view of *within-period* transfers. The utilitarian framework postulated by Lerner (1959) in his riposte to Samuelson provides just such an alternative. Recall figure 2.1: the utilitarian framework argues that the social optimum is attained where *total utility is max-*

imized in each period, at $MU_{cd} = MU_{cw}$, where d indicates dependents and w workers. Altruism will generate intergenerational transfers as described in chapters 3 and 8, but utilitarian optimality typically requires further transfers by forced levy, in the form of a tax or "insurance contribution," such as to equate the marginal utilities of individuals from different generations. In the within-period framework, therefore, the possibility that this transfer is forced rather than agreed upon poses the possibility of an intergenerational conflict between dependents and workers as to whether the whole of this amount (or indeed some greater amount) is to be transferred between the generations. By contrast, the Samuelsonian "social contract," if agreed upon, implies (in theory) a Paretian improvement for all successive generations except the final one.

The starting point of the public-choice approach to intergenerational transfers is to ask whether sets of rules or institutions can be established by which distributional outcomes maximizing social welfare can be attained. The literature in the public-choice field is generally skeptical as to whether this is possible. Indeed, models presented in due course in this chapter suggest that transfers from workers to dependents between particular generations, or indeed among all generations, may be excessive when viewed either from a utilitarian perspective or from the lifetime-utility-maximizing framework of modern welfare economics. Conflict between generations as to the allocation of resources then becomes all too likely.

How does this possibility of within-period intergenerational conflict square with the Samuelson model, and how is the possibility of conflict affected by the aging of the population? The literature on intertemporal optimization shows what conditions are required for an equilibrium path to be attained and what mechanisms might be used to attain such a path. Since markets alone cannot attain the intertemporal optimum (indeed, the absence of full futures markets is a primary source of market failure), a major role for the government is implied. But there is no guarantee that the government will be able to supply the "correct" growth of the money supply, or the "correct" level of social security, or the optimal balance of overfunding or underfunding of the social security program. What levels may actually be supplied is a central concern of public-choice theory.

The reason for this failure of public provision is that in practice the government, or polity, is itself far from the benign *deus ex machina* arbiter of the social-welfare function so beloved in the field of abstract welfare economics. It is instead a set of institutions, swayed by lobbyists and interest groups, with a time horizon typically long enough only to consider the within-period allocation of resources consequent upon its economic policies, rather than the agent of long-run optimization required by economic theory. Although economists have tried to specify mechanisms (such as "policy rules') that might sustain intertemporal optimizing behavior, no government has yet been prepared to relinquish the notional freedom associated with policy discretion and with the accommodation of interest groups.[1]

This is not to suggest that the utilitarian approach to within-period transfers in some way superior to modern welfare economics and its insistence on intertemporal optimization. Indeed, far from it; modern welfare economics arose because of the self-evident fact that economic agents did not engage in interpersonal comparisons based on measures of individual accrued utility. Nor was there any evidence that the behavior of governments was consistent with the maximization of total utility, even were such a concept measurable.

In one important respect the Samuelson model provides a significant insight into decision-making processes that is not available to the utilitarian framework. In the original Samuelson model, the population is growing, with the consequence that within-period generational transfers do *not* in the optimum require the equating of marginal utilities between generations. This allows the development of a welfare-enhancing "chain" in which all generations "gain" in the form of a positive rate of return on their savings until the last generation. Pareto optimality therefore allows that such an intergenerational contract could be established and inherited by yet-unborn generations, so long as the terminal date is perceived to be indefinitely far in the future. In practical terms, because each successive generation is more numerous, it is therefore able to bear the burden of the aged of the previous generation with relative ease. As Samuelson (1958, p. 480) observes, in his inimitable style: "If we depart from the [contract], the final young will be cheated by the demise of the human race. Should such a cheating of one generation 30 million years from now perpetually condemn society to a sub-optimal configuration? Perfect competition shrugs its shoulders at such a question and (not improperly) sticks to its Pareto optimality."

Unfortunately, as described in the case studies of social security programs in chapter 4, the enthusiasm with which governments in a number of countries have embraced the concept of state pensions as "social insurance" contracts between generations rather than simply as a form of current transfer lies less in their desire for intergenerational equity than in the belief that an implicit obligation is established by which successively larger (and, it is hoped, richer) generations can afford to pay the increasingly generous pension benefits promised to themselves by previous generations.[2] A Ponzi-scheme aspect to the development of social security programs is apparent in this, but in an unsustainable form once an aging population appears.[3]

Population aging therefore throws into sharp relief the role of governmental institutions in facilitating or thwarting intergenerational transfers. Does population aging, reflected in a growing proportion of elderly people, imply a diminution or an expansion of the political and economic "power" wielded by the elderly? In the simplest format of an economic theory of democracy with majority voting, can the elderly simply vote themselves a larger share of the economic "cake"? Alternatively, does the change in the age structure heighten the perception among workers of the "burden" of the elderly, and induce them to resist more strongly the claims on resources made by the latter? Are younger workers more likely to be hostile to transfers, given their time horizon, or do they have less to lose (in the form of, say, lower earnings) than older workers? Can coalition of disparate groups be formed in order to facilitate or block such transfers? Through what mechanisms are such conflicts transmitted, and perhaps resolved? These and other questions are discussed in this chapter.

Section 10.1 investigates the determination of tax rates and social security transfers in models where these matters are settled by majority voting. It considers Browning's (1975) well-known demonstration that expenditure on social security under a scheme of democratic voting on tax rates will lead to an excessive social security budget. It also considers the possibilities of log rolling and voting cycles within this public-choice framework. The models examined differ as to whether generations vote myopically, in the assumed structure of earnings with age, and in the assumed structure of pension benefits. However, they share the common perspective that generations manipulate the voting system so as to maximize their own share of income or, in a multi-period framework, the rate of return on their tax payments. They also take explicit account of population aging and, more generally, of fluctuations in the sizes of generations (see also Boldrin and Rustichini 1994).

Section 10.2 takes a slightly different approach. The relative size of successive generations can be thought of as determining the cost, or "shadow price," of pension provision. When the shadow price of providing a good is higher, *ceteris paribus*, its supply is lower. Turner (1984) constructed a model of this type. In contrast to models in which votes are weighted by generation size, a *negative* relationship between the size of the retired generation and the level of pension provision is predicted. However, it is suggested here that an econometric model of this relationship is formally underidentified for standard reasons, given that pension provision is determined by both the shadow price and the voting model of the previous section.

Section 10.3 returns to the question of a social contract between generations and to the issue of whether successive generations can establish such a "contract" which permits an optimal level of redistribution between generations. The well-known Rawlsian approach to social contracts is discussed and extended in the present context. Barry's (1978) suggestion that transfers between generations should be seen as a public good is discussed in the context of public transfer payments between generations.

10.1   Does a Democracy Overspend on Social Security?

Majority Voting and Tax Rates

Suppose that a democracy determines levels of taxes and transfers by majority vote. There are several "generations" of equal size, each of which is represented here by an individual composite voter. Generations work for several periods and then retire (for fewer periods than they work). There is a pay-as-you-go social security program in operation, providing a pension in each generation's last period. What level of taxes and what level of transfers (in the form of public pensions) will be voted in by a majority vote of the generations alive at any one time?

Under pure myopia, and with no altruism, the answer is trivial: With the number of working "generations" outnumbering the retired "generation," a majority will vote against any tax to finance pensions. However, this relies on myopic behavior. Dropping that assumption changes the likely outcome. As a general principle, retired people have nothing to lose in a pay-as-you-go system from voting for as high a tax rate as is feasible, if they are assumed to have no taxable income.[4] The relative preference of working generations for lower tax rates, *ceteris paribus,* would stem from the length of the period over which they discount benefits back to the present. Thus, an older worker would be attracted by a higher tax rate to finance a more generous social security pension as the prospect of retirement drew closer, whereas a younger worker would tend to resist high rates of taxation for such a purpose. With a continuum of generations, the single-peak nature of preferences, and voting over one dimension (tax rates), Black (1948) and Mueller (1989) suggest that the tax rate would be determined by the preferences of the median individual, who would be a middle-aged worker in this context.[5] Although this is a general and intuitive solution, there is some mileage to be gained from an analysis of a simpler problem in which a discrete number of generations establish a tax rate by majority voting.

Following Browning (1975), and analogously to Aaron (1966), a steady-state tax-and-transfer system can be established in which the rate of return on taxes paid (in the form of future pension payments) is equal to the rate of growth of the economy. (Note again that, at present, generations are assumed to be of constant size.) This outcome can be illustrated by an amended version of the Browning model in which earnings are related to the age of the generation as well as to the time period. As in Samuelson's model, there are three "generations" (two working and one retired) alive at any one time, and it is assumed here that they are of equal size. Generations are indexed alphabetically and periods numerically.

In period 1 there is no tax-and-transfer system; it is assumed that one is introduced in period 2. Generation A receives nothing. Generation B, retiring in period 2, receives a social security pension, financed by current taxpayers (generations C and D), despite having paid no taxes itself in previous periods. (This is the key assumption of Browning's model.) Thereafter, each generation pays taxes for two periods and receives a pension in the third period. Assume that incomes double in each period and that the initial tax rate is 10 percent. The assumption concerning income growth implies a real growth of earnings for 20-year "generations" of 3.5 percent per annum, which is a not-unrealistic summation of general economy-wide earnings growth plus average (cross-section) growth of earnings with age. (In contrast, Browning assumes that earnings are invariant between generations *within* each time period.) The tax-and-transfer outcomes for six generations and five periods are illustrated in table 10.1.

Table 10.1
Rates of return to a tax-and-transfer scheme.

	Year				
	1	2	3	4	5
Tax rate	0	0.1	0.1	0.1	0.1
Incomes					
Young	C: 100	D: 200	E: 400	F: 800	G: 1600
Middle-aged	B: 200	C: 400	D: 800	E: 1600	F: 3200
Retired	A: 0	B: 0	C: 0	D: 0	E: 0
Taxes (−) and transfers (+)					
Young	C: 0	D: −20	E: −40	F: −80	G: −160
Middle-aged	B: 0	C: −40	D: −80	E: −160	F: −320
Retired	A: 0	B: +60	F: +120	D: +240	E: +480
Rate of return	A: 0				
	B: 60/0 = ∞				
	C: 120 − 40(1 + i) = 200%				
	D: 240 − [80(1 + i)+20(1 + i)²] = 100%				
	E: 480 − [160(1 + i) + 40(1 + i)²] = 100%				
	100% thereafter				

The equilibrium tax-and-transfer system in table 10.1 can be observed by ignoring for the moment periods 1 and 2 and commencing from period 3, by which time a tax-and-transfer system has been in operation for several periods. It is apparent that, by continuing the *status quo*, each generation can obtain a rate of return on its taxes (or contributions) equal to the rate of growth of the economy. This may be regarded as an equilibrium solution in the sense posited by Aaron (1966). Generation C has in fact obtained a higher rate of return because the tax-and-transfer scheme was only introduced in period 2, so this generation has paid fewer contributions in return for a full pension in period 3.

Is this tax-and-transfer configuration stable? Suppose there was a proposal that in period 3 alone the tax rate be raised to 20 percent. Such a proposal (which would, of course, appeal to generation C, which has retired) would be defeated by a coalition of generations D and E, for the obvious reasons. Note, however, that the reduction in return from agreeing to this proposal differs between the two working generations, and that in fact the older generation, D, would have the most to lose from the proposal, in view of the disparity in incomes. A rise in the tax rate to 20 percent for period 3 only would raise the return for generation C to 500 percent, reduce the return to generation D to 29 percent, and reduce that of generation E to 65 percent.

Log Rolling

Even this simple example in which income varies with age suggests the possibility of more complex solutions. The assumption that the desired tax rate would rise with age, which underpins a median-voter solution in the general case, looks shaky when earnings are assumed to vary with age. Although on the face of it a proposal to raise pensions for one period alone is defeated by majority voting, the differential reduction in rates of return for generations D and E were the proposal to have been successful allows scope for "log rolling" or other forms of negotiation between pairs of generations.

Suppose for example that generation E, the youngest generation, is the only generation with children. In exchange for generation E's voting to raise the tax rate to 20 percent to finance a higher pension, generation C could offer to introduce a child-support payment of, say, 50. This would be at the expense of the new, higher pension of 240. But with a pension reduced to 190 and the new payment of 50 to generation E, the consequences for rates of return of this one-period tax change are altered. In net terms, generation D still loses with a lower rate of return of 29 percent; however, generation C gains relative to the original position[6] (with a return of 380 percent), as does generation E (with a return of 115 percent). Consequently, generations C and E would outvote generation D in favor of the new, higher tax rate financing both higher pensions and the new child-support payment. This case, although not considered by Browning, is a familiar outcome in the public-choice literature (Tulloch 1959) and shows how majority voting can generate higher public spending overall.

Note, however, the overlapping-generations facet of the present case, which distinguishes it from much of the public-choice literature. In principle generation C could offer a competitive concession to generation D instead of to generation E in order to get the higher tax rate passed, relying on generation D's closer proximity to retirement age to appeal to it to raise pensions. Thus, higher pensions, rather than child support, might seem more attractive to generation D than to generation E, given their relative stages of life. However, generation D cannot rely on the support of generation C in period 4 to perpetuate the higher tax rate and pension, simply because generation C no longer exists, and the breakdown of the contract to provide a higher pension in period 4 to generation D is of no concern to generation E (which would have received the side payment, child support, in period 3).

It is also not certain that the outcome with log rolling is stable. Rather than negotiate with generation C, it would be rational for generation D to offer an even higher rate of child-support payment to generation E, if E thereby agrees not to vote for a higher pension in the current period. In this sense, generation E is the median voter, because a side payment to generation E is probably the optimal strategy for both generations C and D even though E is the youngest generation. (This leaves aside the questions of altruism and bequests, which further complicate the analysis.) The possibility of voting cycles' emerging is strong, with rapid formation and breakup of alternative coalitions and consequent changes in the generosity of pension provision. Critics of the application of public-choice theory in this context have suggested that this predicted instability of pension policy is a weakness of the public-choice framework, but the case studies in chapter 4 offer little evidence of stability in social security provision.

What distinguishes these models from those of chapter 3, and Aaron's in particular, is that considerations of intergenerational redistribution as well as allocative efficiency emerge. The Aaron-Samuelson model considers what configuration of returns and earnings growth would improve allocative efficiency, such as to maximize lifetime utility for successive generations. Finding "rules" that would implement these improvements is one aspect of public-choice theory. But when possibilities inherent in majority voting are considered, such as side payments or log rolling, the scope for redistribution among participants is enhanced. This is another aspect of public choice (Mueller 1989). The example here illustrates that deviations from the rule of equating rates of return to the rate of growth of the economy (so far here without either positive or negative population growth) may be voted for irrespective of the desirable long-run outcome—a conclusion that has much in common with the "time inconsistency" proposition in the context of the tradeoff between consistent and optimal macroeconomic policies.

Initial Conditions of Pay-As-You-Go Pension Schemes

As already mentioned, a key assumption of the Browning model is that full pensions can be obtained from partial or indeed no tax or contribution entitlements. Accelerated accrual of pension entitlements in the early stages of social security programs are common in practice (see chapter 4 above, Hurd and Shoven 1985, and Disney and Whitehouse 1993b), although at least some pension contributions are generally required as a condition of benefit payment in order to preserve the social-insurance character of such schemes. This accelerated accrual, rather than the possibility of log rolling, forms the basis of Browning's conclusion that democracy generates excessive social security; the demonstration is straightforward from table 10.1.

Consider the returns accrued by the three generations in period 2 from a proposal to move to a higher tax rate of, say, 20 percent. It is apparent that generation B will vote for the higher tax rate, as it is entirely costless to that generation. If we assume that generation D regarded the previous rate of 10 percent as optimal, then it will vote for the *status quo*. Thus, the crucial generation is generation C. It is apparent, Browning argues, that this generation will also vote for the higher tax rate if it believes that the higher rate can be maintained in the future. The rationale for this is that the rate of return on its contributions (taxes) exceeds the rate of growth of the economy, so greater "investment" in the program is attractive. In contrast with the previous case, generation C, by voting for the higher tax rate, does not improve its rate of return: the marginal return equals the average so long as the higher tax rate is maintained, at least until that generation is in retirement.

The key question, therefore, is this: What happens at the start of the next period with the higher tax rate of 20 percent? Generation C, having now retired, will of course vote to retain the higher tax rate. By an argument similar to the previous one, generation E will vote to revert to 10 percent. Generation D is now the key voter. Previously it voted for 10 percent, but, having paid 20 percent in period 2, this generation will be disinclined to vote for a reduction to 10 percent in period 3 if it thinks (by logical extension of generation E's behavior in the next period) that the higher pension can be retained, as is required to offset the higher taxes it paid in the previous period. So each generation changes its preferences as it moves from being the youngest generation to becoming the median generation. Any initial excess tax rate generated by the accelerated accrual of benefits is perpetuated *ad infinitum*.

In contrast with log rolling, whereby excessive social security arises, this example rests wholly on a divergence from equilibrium—in this case, from the initial conditions. If a full record of contributions or taxes was required in order to obtain a pension, generation B would not have received a pension at all, and generation C would not have obtained the higher rate of return on its tax payments that led it to vote for the higher tax rate. In general, wherever higher taxes or contributions are associated with accelerated social security entitlements, there will be an incentive for *any* subsequent generation to form a coalition with the existing elderly in order to retain the higher taxes. Logically, this would seem to preclude any public program from offering such favorable initial conditions, unless there was some degree of altruism present by which the younger working generation was prepared to accelerate the accrual of entitlements for the generation nearing retirement age without thereby perpetuating the same level of taxes in order to obtain the same rate of return for itself in future years. Thus, in the previous example, generation D would have to stick loyally to its position of a 10 percent tax rate in period 3 even though it thereby obtained a return on its taxes below 100 percent.

Since economists are skeptical as to whether altruism on a large scale underpins apparently paradoxical policies, such as accelerated accrual at the start of social security programs, the question remains as to why such policies are nevertheless implemented. One answer is that even working on a generational basis is too long a time horizon for the policy maker or, by inference, the electorate. For a mixture of altruistic and selfish reasons, a promise of higher pensions may prove politically attractive. Since the commitments build up gradually, perhaps beyond the lifetime of the current government, the problem of de-escalating rising pension commitments is left to future governments and to the votes of generations not yet in the labor market.

An *ad hoc* explanation of this kind, which in effect relies on myopia among both the electorate and the politicians, would suggest that social security commitments would continue rising until some kind of fiscal crisis brought awareness of problem to the attention of the electorate (as happened in Italy in the late 1980s). It does not explain why politicians sometimes do confront problems of pension commitments a generation or so in advance (as when the Conservative government in the United Kingdom attempted to abolish the State Earnings-Related Pensions Scheme (SERPS) in 1985 because of its rising costs 25 years hence; see section 4.2).

An alternative explanation along public-choice lines might be as follows: Low incomes among the elderly are observed. However, the extreme intergenerational redistribution associated with a one-off transfer to the current elderly, as suggested by the utilitarian, can always be defeated by a coalition of generations within the working population.[7]

At the other extreme, a proposal to introduce higher pensions some 40 years in the future, when full contribution (tax) payments have been accrued, will gain little political support from existing generations: the youngest working generation may gain and might vote in favor of this (subject to myopia), but older workers and the existing elderly have nothing to gain and would defeat it. A legislated increase in the social security program therefore requires log rolling or side payments (any compromise by which pension entitlements are accrued at a faster rate than the steady-state Aaron-Samuelson model would admit). Under such an arrangement, all generations may gain something, or may minimize their losses. However, the insight offered by the Browning model is that there is no certainty that the consequent tax rate corresponds to any long-run equilibrium. Nor is it stable in response to successive votes over tax rates, which may in practice generate ever higher public spending.[8]

The Impact of an Aging Population
In a voting framework, an aging population has two offsetting effects: The increase in the average age of the population tends to generate a higher voted pension level and therefore a higher tax rate; however, the greater burden of dependency raises the cost of financing a given level of social security benefits, and this will tend to reduce the voted level of benefits. Which of these effects dominates is ultimately an empirical question. The first of these effects is examined in more detail in this subsection; the second effect is deferred to section 10.2.

In the absence of log rolling, and with identical age-specific preferences across successive cohorts concerning tax rates, the extension of the previous analysis to the aging population case is straightforward. With pure myopia, if workers still outnumber pensioners the optimal tax rate is zero. In these circumstances, however, some autocratic rule, such as mean tax (contribution) rate by weighted generation size, would suggest a higher tax rate than the case where the population age structure was stable.

With non-myopic behavior, and with generational preferences for tax rates constrained to be non-negative up to a maximum of 100 percent, a continuum of increasing preferred tax rates with age would generate an older median voter than in the stable-population case and, thus, a higher tax rate to finance the social security pension. The exact tax rate will depend on whether a median-voter outcome is obtained by voting or whether some mean generation-size-weighted tax rate is established by the government. The mean and median preferred tax rates will differ because of the skewed age structure, and the exact rate for given age-specific preferences will depend on whether population aging is being generated by declining cohort size or by increased longevity.

The analysis so far excludes all considerations of intergenerational altruism and of differing preferences between cohorts. However, this is an unreasonable omission in view of the discussion in the previous subsection: a larger retired generation may feel enhanced altruism toward a smaller working generation and so moderate its preferred tax "bid"; in turn, the prospect of more older people may reduce the preferred tax rates of working generations. The latter factor in particular may generate a precautionary or strategic reduction in the social security demands of retired workers who do not want to run the risk of "killing off the goose that laid the golden egg," especially if workers are still in an absolute majority.

The case of a changing population structure in the context of the discrete-generation model of table 10.1 should also be considered. To abstract from the issue of accelerated accrual, only generation C (which retires in period 3) and succeeding generations are considered in the illustrative simulation in table 10.2. The baseline assumptions, given in the first three rows, are consistent with table 10.1. Thereafter, the rate of growth of the population is allowed to vary. It is assumed that generation E, which enters the workforce in period 3, is a larger generation (1.01^{20} larger) than generation D.[9] The same rate of growth is maintained by generation F, but thereafter population decline sets in at an equal rate, so that generation H is in fact the same size as generations C and D, while I and J, which only enter into the calculation of contributions (taxes), are smaller than the baseline case. A situation of a growing population followed by an aging population permits examination of both cases; however, it is assumed that average longevity remains constant throughout the simulation.

Two solutions to pension levels and tax rates can be considered. The first is close to the Aaron-Samuelson model, where the tax rate is held constant. The real value of the pension therefore rises (falls) in line with the sum of real-income growth and population growth (decline). This case is explored in the next two rows of table 10.2. Leaving aside generation C, which is still benefiting from accelerated accrual, the

Table 10.2
A tax and transfer system with population growth and decline.

Generation (number)	C	D	E	F	G	H	I	J
Year retires	3	4	5	6	7	8	(9)	(10)
Rate of return at zero pop. growth	200%	100%	100%	100%	100%	100%	(100%)	(100%)
Assumed annual rate of pop. growth	0%	0%	+1%	+1%	−1%	−1%	−1%	−1%
Social security pension per head at constant tax rate ($t = 0.1$)	129	314	551	739	1480	2957	—[a]	—
Rate of return at constant tax rate	223%	144%	121%	64%	64%	64%	—	—
Tax rate that maintains constant real pension per capita	9.3%	7.6%	10.6%	19.4%	15.8%	13.8%	—	—
Rate of return with constant real pension per capita	200%	108%	131%	107%	80%	80%	—	—

a. Not calculated.

optimum state, not surprisingly, is achieved by generation D, which is receiving a pension financed by two growing generations. Generation E, too, does better than earlier generations, since one generation involved in the finance of its pension is larger than it. Thereafter the situation reverses dramatically. The largest generation, F, experiences a rate of return below the real growth of incomes—and indeed this is the subsequent equilibrium rate of return—that is exactly the sum of the cumulated population growth rates and real-income growth predicted by the Aaron-Samuelson model.

An alternative to the Aaron-Samuelson equilibrium, akin perhaps to a purely redistributive approach, is to ask what tax rate would preserve the real value of pension in the PAYG scheme. This is calculated in the penultimate row of table 10.2. It is followed by the rates of return for the various generations consequent upon such a policy rule. The rule again varies the rates of return associated with cohort size, dampening the returns to smaller retired generations associated with larger working generations (such as D) and imposing a greater burden on working generations when the population is declining. By the time of generation H, a steady-state rate of return has been reached which is above that in the constant-tax-rate case. However, the constant-pension case requires a higher tax rate than the previous case once aging has become established.

What of the public-choice consequences of changing population size? First, a change in the rate of growth of the population, whether negative or positive, causes a perturbation in rates of return among successive generations in a PAYG scheme analogous to the impact of accelerated accrual and differential earnings in the earlier analysis in section 10.1. It was argued there that differential rates of return to successive generations encouraged log rolling, while the parallel with the impact of accelerated accrual might lead to Browning-type processes generating "excess" government spending on social security. Coalitions of generations precipitating "excess" spending on pensions is therefore again possible, although non-myopic generations, aware of adverse demographic trends, might perhaps attempt to restrict voting outcomes of this type. Second, and stemming from the first point, the steady-state equilibrium associated with a declining population, whether with constant real pension or constant tax rate, implies that successive generations will encounter rates of return below the growth rate of real earnings. Calculations by government actuaries generally work with the assumption of pensions indexed in some way to real incomes, but the consequence for implied tax rates of such a procedure, which is inconsistent with the Aaron-Samuelson model when population is declining, is clear from comparing the two cases in table 10.2.

Nevertheless, a proposal to cut the real pension in the face of falling population (say, where generations F and G combine against E) by reverting to a constant tax rate may be defeated. Although at any point in time the two working generations appear to do better by cutting pensions and reducing the tax rate, comparison of the constant-tax-rate and variable-tax-rate cases suggests that the steady-state outcome will preserve a *higher* rate of return so long as future generations continue to adopt the higher tax rate. As in Browning, the key generation is the older working generation, members of which have the incentive to switch sides in favor of the higher tax rate if the alternative implies a reversion to a lower pension in the present *and subsequent* periods. Even in the face of population decline, therefore, it is evident that, although successive generations will experience reduced rates of return on their contributions (taxes) even if the real value of the pension is maintained, cutting social security benefits may not be chosen democratically: the even lower return on the reduced pension may prove unattractive to working generations with foresight but a finite expected length of life.

10.2 Pension Provision and the "Price" of Social Security

The thrust of the public-choice theories in section 10.1 was that larger elderly generations could use the ballot box or coalitions to enforce a greater tax burden on smaller working generations. But the analysis showed that, when generations voted non-myopically, considering themselves as both workers and pensioners, steady-state outcomes depended on a range of factors, such as differential benefit accrual rates and changes in age structure associated with perturbations to the population growth rate.

Implicit in all this, however, is a model of the *cost* of social security analogous to that developed in chapter 2, which in its simplest variant was depicted by equation 2.1:

$$pD = twL,$$

where the nontaxed pension per dependent is p, the proportionate tax rate is t, the wage rate is w, and the numbers of pensioners (dependents) and contributors (workers) are denoted D and L respectively.

According to Turner (1984) and Doescher and Turner (1988), equation 2.1 may be rationalized as a behavioral equation concerning changes in the marginal cost of public provision. This rationalization of equation 2.1 implicitly requires that the marginal cost of providing an extra dollar or pound of benefit is equal to the average cost (implying that the marginal "contribution" or tax rate is equal to the average) and that this extra tax revenue yields an identical marginal pension benefit to the average (for example, transactions costs are constant at the margin). Furthermore, it has to be assumed that increments of pension tax and benefit have a neutral effect on the labor supply. This assumption might be justified by a Barro-type argument that workers perceive the increment in the social security tax as of equal value to the discounted increment in the transfer benefit accruing from it. In a fully funded scheme, or in a pay-as-you-go scheme in steady state, with the rate of growth of earnings equal to the rate of discount, such a justification might be accepted without qualms, although it fits uneasily with the analysis developed in section 10.1.

Proceeding on these assumptions, however, let us rewrite equation 2.1 as

$$\frac{t}{p} = \frac{1}{w} \cdot \frac{D}{L} \tag{10.1}$$

and, in order to consider *marginal* costs, examine discrete changes in equation 10.1. Suppose for the present that Δw is zero (in real terms). Then ρ_b, the "shadow price," of providing an increment to the pension, Δp, is

$$\rho_b = \frac{\Delta t}{\Delta p} = \frac{\Delta D}{\Delta L}. \tag{10.2}$$

This shadow price is therefore derived from the change in the old-age dependency ratio, or its components (such as the change in the proportion of the elderly receiving pensions, the labor-force participation ratio among the under-65s, etc.; see Turner 1984). It follows that we can define in principle the (shadow) price elasticity of demand (willingness to provide extra social security transfers) by workers in a single-period framework as

$$\varepsilon_b = \frac{\partial p}{\partial \rho_b} \text{ with } \varepsilon < 0. \tag{10.3}$$

It is also straightforward to define an income elasticity of demand, of the willingness to provide pensions by workers, as

$$\eta_b = \frac{\partial p}{\partial w} \text{ with } \eta > 0. \tag{10.4}$$

The supply of benefits to the provider, it was assumed, was available at constant cost. Thus ε_b shows the responsiveness of benefit provision (for example, benefit levels, eligibility, or accrual rates) to changes in the shadow price of benefits: the old-age dependency ratio and its components, while η_b, the income elasticity of benefits, shows the responsiveness of the provision of benefit increases to changes in real earnings. The signs of the two elasticities are interpretable in a straight-forward manner. One interesting aspect of this formulation, not con-sidered in section 10.1, is that a lower "price" of pension benefits will increase benefit levels, *ceteris paribus.* So a smaller elderly population relative to workers will enhance the willingness of taxpayers to provide generous pensions. This accords with special-interest-group public-choice models by which smaller groups obtain higher benefits per member on exactly the marginal cost considerations outlined here (Doescher and Turner 1988; Stigler 1971; Mueller 1989, chapter 13).

However, equations 10.1–10.4 describe only part of the process by which the level of pension benefits are determined; the missing part is of course the demand for benefits by beneficiaries (pensioners). The public-choice models outlined in section 10.1 would suggest that the demand for benefits would be *positively* related to the D/L ratio as well to any shift factors (such as lobbying, electoral preferences, and so on) that may strengthen the negotiating hand of benefit recipients. For ex-ample, the vesting of political power in the hands of political parties which have traditionally been prepared to see greater spending on so-cial welfare, such as the "old-style" Labor Party in the United Kingdom or the Democrats in the United States, may reflect both the outcome of public-choice processes and a reflection of exogenous shifts in public attitudes to a range of public issues from which pensioners, as a group, benefit.

If the underlying structural model of the demand for benefits by beneficiaries and the supply of benefits by providers[10] is likely to be underidentified, one cannot hope to recover an elasticity such as ε_b directly by econometric methods. Turner (1984) provides some econo-metric evidence for the time path of OASDI benefits from 1947 to 1977, suggesting that benefits are positively related to the wage and the labor force and negatively related to the size of the population aged over 65. This accords with the price and income elasticities of equations 10.3 and 10.4. But the wage coefficient is insignificant, and the result on the dependency ratio is also insignificant unless one includes a number of auxiliary variables which interact with the population terms to pro-duce a complex overall elasticity that is not immediately signed in a manner consistent with the story of this section.

To investigate the hypothesis for the United Kingdom, I collected a long data series (1935–1991) of average pensions, wages, prices, and numbers of contributors and dependents. Various econometric specifications provide no evidence that the "supply-price" model of section 10.2 dominates the "public-choice" model of section 10.1:

• A simple model in differences finds that changes in the real pension per capita are *positively* related to the change in the number of pensioners (t stat 3.24) and the change in the real wage (t stat 2.26). No other variables are significant. However, although there is no evidence of autocorrelation in the errors, these are distributed non-normally, and a RESET test of the squares of the regressors provides some evidence of residual misspecification.

• An error-correction model provides evidence of a positive short-run relationship between the dependency ratio and the *nominal* pension per capita with an elasticity of 0.5; the long-run elasticity, which is less well defined, is 1.1. There is again evidence of a positive effect of the real wage, with an improbably high long-run elasticity of 4. However, this provides support for the proposition that pensioners are able to share in real-wage growth, just as the variants of public-choice models (and the Aaron-Samuelson "rule") would suggest. There is some evidence that pension benefits are also affected by the political complexion of the House of Commons (higher with fewer Conservative MPs) and by the 1946 National Insurance Act. However, these events are highly correlated, since the period 1945–1950 saw the fewest Conservative MPs in the postwar period.

• Finally, an "innovations" model was constructed in which each variable was regressed on itself lagged up to three periods and the residuals of the pension series were regressed on the other series' residuals. This purged the model of any spurious time-series bias, since most of the economic series are random walks within the period. Again the only significant relationship appears to a *positive* one between "innovations" in the pension value and in the number of pensioners (t stat 1.96), although again this may be largely affected by the 1945–1951 period, in which both jumped considerably.

Overall, the results suggest some support for the public-choice framework, particularly for the majority-voting model. Less support is provided for the special-interest-group model for this period. But it can be argued that such econometric tests must be used with caution, especially for predictive purposes, and that the early postwar period was one of general optimism as to the sustainability of social security programs—an optimism that rapidly disappeared during the 1980s. The ability of pensioners to raise their incomes as a group through the ballot box or through the altruism of other generations has been weakened, with greater uncertainty in future prospects for most social security programs in the next decades.

10.3   Aging and an Intergenerational Social Contract?

Much of the theorizing so far has been based on voting models involving existing generations. A slightly different focus is required when considering the welfare of generations not yet in existence, whose compliance is implicitly required in any contractual relationship that guarantees transfers between generations. It is natural to think that the within-period redistributive framework of much of public-choice theory leads to excessive discounting of the social welfare of generations further in the future, and at the sillier extremes of political philosophy complete discounting has indeed been defended. Some of the contributors to Sikora and Barry 1978 are vexed by the issue that, if current people or resources are treated in an alternative manner, different (perhaps fewer, or less happy) people will be born in the future, and that, since every alternative policy involves a different composition of future generations, any attempt to take account of the welfare impact of present policies on any particular future generation is not permissible. This reasoning, along with several of the illustrations and "paradoxes" used to justify particular positions, would seem spurious: people do not act as if they believe this, and public opinion is fashionably environmentally conscious and concerned about the prospects for future generations. Either way, the issue of sustainable contracts between generations is again brought into focus.

What form might an intergenerational social contract take? How could the welfare of existing retired generations be protected? Clearly the answer to this last question rests in part on the extent of the belief, if any, among younger generations that they themselves will be treated equitably or comparably by future generations. Fear that if they treat their elderly dependents badly they will be treated badly by their successors may spur them to altruistic behavior. However, even this may not guarantee that they are well treated in their own retirement, particularly when some who will have to support them in their retirement are not yet "voters" in the social compact.

Samuelson (1958) argued for a Kantian categorical imperative—a rule of behavior that must bind all present and future participants in the "social contract." Such a commitment may be regarded as a "public good," and the object of such a rule is to eliminate free riding, within generations and indeed by whole generations, by which individuals take advantage of the general commitment to a policy to obtain the benefits without providing their own commitment, financial or otherwise. However, it is hard to see how free riding can be avoided in a decision-making framework in which every individual knows his own economic position and has a positive incentive to misrepresent his own preferences. Rawls (1971) provided a famous "solution" to this problem of obtaining a "just" social contract without perhaps being entirely convincing as to how his procedure would handle the potential intergenerational conflicts stemming from issues such as pension provision within PAYG social security programs.

The Rawlsian solution to the problem of social justice was to imagine that individuals could be divorced from their own personal positions, including social, economic and demographic background, when deciding on a set of just institutions that could provide resource allocations. Such decisions in this "original position" had to be made behind a "veil of ignorance" that excluded knowledge even of the probabilities of belonging to any particular state. Rawls then asserted that the principle of justice that would be established by such a decision-making procedure would maximize the welfare of the worst-off individual; this was the "maximin strategy."

In the particular context of intergenerational allocations, Rawls argued as follows:

> . . . the original position has been defined so that it is a situation in which the maximum applies [and] the veil of ignorance excludes all but the vaguest knowledge of likelihoods. The parties have no basis for determining the probable nature of the society, or their place in it. Thus they have strong reasons for being wary of probability calculations if any other course is open to them. They must also take account of the fact that their choice of principles should seem reasonable to others, *in particular their descendants,* whose rights will be deeply affected by it. (ibid., p. 155, quoted in Mueller 1989; emphasis added here)

Leaving aside the question of the maximin nature of the "just" social contract, Rawls, in common with other authors, emphasizes the intergenerational aspect of justice. However, as was pointed out by Barry

(1989), Rawls assumes that the parties to the contract know that they are contemporaries, without knowing of course to which generation they belong. However, not only are future generations not included in this "original position" in which the just contract is established; the parties do not know, when making decisions as to intergenerational justice (for example, allocations according to the maximin principle), whether they can expect to be treated (or indeed *have* been treated) by other generations exactly as they intend to treat other generations.

Barry proposes that *all* generations could in principle be represented in this "original position" in order to overcome this problem, although the artificiality of the process is perhaps thereby enhanced. Rawls himself proposes that each generation will be sufficiently altruistic toward their own immediate descendants as to permit an overlapping-generations type of social contract in perpetuity. But there is nothing concrete in the "original position" formulation to guarantee that successive generations will behave in such a manner, and it can be suggested that this is required if a contract is to be established even between existing generations.

Rawls, of course, is raising some very general issues, and we cannot perhaps expect an immediate solution to the problem at hand: that of providing some kind of social contract which generates an intergenerational allocation which maximizes social welfare. To the extent that this relies on altruistic behavior, a potential problem, raised by Veall (1986) and described above in chapter 3, is that there are two equilibria in any model of the intertemporal allocation of consumption: one based on transfers to the elderly through charity and one based on life-cycle saving. But any individual generation can switch from one strategy to another and gain a higher utility level for itself. Switching from a no-gift equilibrium (thus incurring no costs of supporting the previous generation) to a full-gift, no-saving equilibrium is the obvious strategy in such a context. Retirement consumption might be lower with such a strategy; however, with a moderate degree of altruism, positive population growth, and a high rate of discount of future consumption, such a strategy might prove attractive. But, as Veall points out, such switches would typically arise in very specific contexts: through a change in "transfer technology" (i.e. in the ability to organize a public social security scheme), a change in one of the underlying parameters of the model (for example, a *rise* in the rate of population growth), or a shock to the system (such as hyperinflation wiping out the value of private savings). Conversely, in a period with an aging population, low inflation, and greater uncertainty of future income prospects, reliance on charity or intrafamilial altruism is a high-risk strategy.

Veall's analysis of altruism is based on intergenerational gifts between members of the same family and is "one-sided" (i.e., from young to old). Implicitly, our more general analysis has posited "two-sided altruism" in which existing generations care about their descendants while the young are prepared to support the elderly (either directly or through social security transfers). The evidence for altruistic behavior described briefly in chapter 3 casts some doubt on the strength of a "pure" altruistic motive in examining intrafamily transfers. Nevertheless, even if decisions are based on self-interest, transfers may still be optimal. With a "strategic" bequest motive, as chapter 8 showed, care for parents is predicated on the possibility of subsequently receiving bequests: siblings compete to provide attention in order to gain favor with parents (Bernheim et al. 1985). Alternatively, families may provide insurance properties such as annuity markets if there is a failure of the private-sector market (Kotlikoff and Spivak 1981; Kotlikoff et al. 1987). Finally, "dynastic" models of inheritance may explain why intrafamily transfers may be maintained voluntarily, irrespective of contractual obligations established by the state.

If we extend the idea of altruism to consider generations composed of many individuals, not all related, however, the gift motive relies on extra-family altruism, which is harder to justify. Barry (1978) argues that support for future generations (but, by inference, also existing older generations) can be justified if a generation regards the welfare of other generations as a public good. In fact Barry's illustration of this idea rests on the case where, rather than the welfare of the generation being a public good, the good being provided to that generation is itself a public good or exhibits an externality. However, it is not unreasonable to envisage the case where income provision generates a consumption externality even for a private excludable good, whether within generations (if I am elderly and you give me money, I am still happier if all members of my generation are receiving money too) or between generations (a wider form of altruism than "keeping it in the family").

In a sense, the inclusion of altruism (as in Veall's model) and the argument for a public-good aspect to redistribution between generations reflect a reversion to the approach to redistribution underlying utilitarianism—without, however, requiring the strong assumptions needed to accept a utilitarian perspective. Yet it seems necessary to add considerations of this kind to the Samuelson model if an implementation of the intergenerational "social contract" is to be found. For the reasons given in this chapter, the incentives to deviate from the intertemporal allocative equilibrium seem to be substantial: variations in earnings levels, differences in pension accrual rates between generations and, of most interest in the present context, changes in the rate of population growth (especially a fall in the rate of growth, or even negative growth) all provide scope for voting strategies that lead the tax and pension scheme away from the allocative optimum. The changing pattern of social security provision in recent years suggests that the balance between allocative efficiency and a stable voted outcome has yet to be found in many countries.

There is no "crisis of aging."

Although many countries now exhibit dramatic demographic transitions, talk of a "crisis of aging" is overblown. There are in place various feedback mechanisms (notably operative parts of the price system in labor markets and capital markets as well as product markets) that generate offsetting effects.

Issues Where the Impact of Aging Is Overstated

There is no evidence of adverse effects of aging on aggregate productivity.

Microeconomic and macroeconomic studies have failed to uncover any convincing evidence that differences in demographic structure between countries and over time are a major factor in determining productivity levels (chapter 6). There *is* evidence that older skilled workers find increasing difficulties in obtaining employment (chapter 7), but this may stem from a wider disjunction between the wage structure and the supply of, and demand for, various skills (chapter 6). The wage structure, including its deferred pay component (pensions), is designed for particular incentive structures, and aging may significantly reduce the effectiveness of these incentive structures (chapter 5).

There are serious crises in pay-as-you-go social insurance programs and in health care, but these have little to do with aging.

It is common to blame "aging" for the budget deficits and payroll-tax increases associated with social security programs in the 1980s. But the sources of these (correctly perceived) crises have little to do with aging *per se.* In pay-as-you-go social insurance, financing crises have far more to do with the chain-letter or Ponzi-scheme nature of such programs as practiced by governments and voters, which pre-commit future generations to excessive forced transfers (chapters 3 and 4). Health care has its own endemic financing problems (chapter 9). In both cases, the aging of society has served a useful function in drawing attention to the unsustainability of current arrangements in many developed countries.

Issues Where the Impact of Aging Is Understated

Aging affects the pay structure and the educational (skill) attainment of the workforce.

There is evidence that cohort size affects cross-sectional age-wage dispersion and the lifetime wage profile. Educational attainment is also affected by relative cohort size, as a product of shifts in demand relative to supply (and lagged supply effects) (chapter 6). Mechanical application of educational supply planning based solely on cohort size ignores these behavioral effects and may generate highly misconceived policies.

Aging has implications for the structure of private pension plans.

Most private pension plans in North America, the United Kingdom, and other countries with sizable private provision are predicated on an incentive structure geared to a balanced, or even youthful, workforce. It is not surprising that the aging of the workforce and the growing number of retired plan members have led to a shift in the form of private provision away from traditional "defined benefit" plans. This will continue, as will an interest in privatized pension provision instead of social security (chapter 5).

Aging affects retirement behavior, but greater longevity need not be associated with a prolonged working life (chapter 7).

The ownership and the value of assets, notably the housing stock, are affected by aging.

Different age groups have different propensities to hold assets. In the standard life-cycle hypothesis, the young and the very old are dissavers and the middle aged are net savers. Consequently, cohort size will affect asset values. In particular, the demand for housing is affected by cohort size; declining fertility 20 years earlier may lead to declining house prices. But the behavior of house prices will affect the size of bequests and the market for residential care (chapters 8 and 9).

Fewer children may not lower the value of bequests.

The size of a bequest is related to the number of children. But, depending on the motive for bequests, a growing incidence of one-child families may lead to higher bequests, not lower ones. Consumption spending of donors and of recipients may be affected in anticipation of a bequest and not just after the bequest (chapter 8).

Notes

Chapter 1

1. "Each spring, President François Mitterand still awards the Médaille de la Famille Française to deserving mothers of eight or more children"—*The Independent* (London), July 30, 1991.

2. Aside from the specific approach taken by Easterlin, a standard reference is Clark and Spengler 1980. There are several specialist journals on the subject. A recent interesting collection of papers, some of which impinge on the content of the present book, is Ermisch and Ogawa 1994.

3. North America comprises Canada and the United States. Bermuda and Greenland are included in figure 1.3.

4. Comprising the Scandinavian countries, Iceland, Ireland, and the UK.

5. Including Austria, France, Germany, Belgium, the Netherlands, Luxembourg, and Switzerland.

6. Albania, Greece, Italy, Malta, Portugal, Spain, and Yugoslavia.

7. For a more general discussion see Schulz 1992.

8. See the discussion in chapter 4 below. See also Boskin and Shoven 1987.

Chapter 2

1. Although the literature on bequest motives is extensive, orthodox economics has paid insufficient attention to measurement of implicit intrafamily allocations of consumption resources. Some studies, such as Kotlikoff and Morris 1989, suggest that *financial* support of the elderly by their children is extremely limited, although social contact is often extensive and elderly members of the family may underpin market activity elsewhere in the household through unpaid support (such as care of grandchildren). See also chapter 8 below.

2. Several countries are considered in chapter 4. For evidence on the US see also Hurd 1990 and Schulz 1992; for the UK see Dilnot et al. 1994; for Australia see Foster 1988; for Japan see Takayama 1992. For recent studies of sources of household savings for a number of countries see Poterba 1994; for consideration of pension saving in particular see World Bank 1994.

3. A survey of public attitudes undertaken for the British Department of Health and Social Security in 1984 revealed that 69% of the sample were unaware that the National Insurance Contribution financed the state pension and 55% had not heard of the State Earnings Related Pension (SERPS), which was to be an important component of public pension provision and which was at that time a source of major political controversy. See HMSO 1985a, Cmnd 9519, Paper 4 for details of the study.

4. In this chapter, all total magnitudes are represented by upper-case Latin letters, all per capita or per unit magnitudes by lower-case Latin letters, and all growth rates by Greek letters.

5. Strictly $Y = (W + rK)$. Here, since $L = D$, we can normalize income as $(w + rk)$.

6. As expressed here, gifts are not tax-exempt. Where they are, the necessary tax rate is, of course, $t'(Y - G)$, where $t' > t$.

7. One strong implication is that intercountry comparisons of the "well-being of the elderly" should focus on comparable measures and should incorporate all sources of income and wealth. Unfortunately several studies in Europe, including some financed by the European Commission, concentrate on arbitrary indicators of transfers to the economically inactive, such as social security tax rates, or arbitrary projected measures of the "generosity" of parts of the social security programs.

8. The Italian projections were made before the reforms introduced from 1992 to 1995, and discussed in chapter 4 below, were introduced.

9. For the UK see Creedy and Disney 1988; for the US see chapters 2 and 3 of Aaron et al. 1989.

10. Of course, if other government expenditures are sensitive to demographic shifts, the sensitivity of the overall tax burden may be enhanced or diminished. For example, health-care costs are disproportionately incurred at birth and in the last decade of life. An aging population may have mixed effects on public health-care expenditure.

11. See Creedy and Disney 1989a and Creedy and Disney 1992. The analysis extends a model developed in Rosen 1984.

12. Equation 2.8 assumed that all members of the potential labor force L_{-1} receive a pension whether they worked or not. An alternative and simpler formulation is $D = \mu E_{-1}$, which typifies a "pure" social insurance system in which pensions are received only by those who participate. The model in this case is considerably simplified; all terms in θ drop out, including ε, and $1+\eta$ combines the effects of both population growth and any changes in the participation rate. But in practice (see chapter 4 below), "pure" social insurance schemes are unusual, with provision of some form of pension benefit or income support for retirement pensioners who have never worked or who have insufficient work histories.

13. This is not common; see section 2.2.

Chapter 3

1. This assumption is made here for analytical convenience. If expected interest rates are uncertain, the issue of the term structure of interest rates arises. Although this issue is not generally perceived to be central to the issue of aging populations and pension

provision, it has some indirect relevance. For example, a term structure is one of the few rationales that can be found for defined benefit rather than defined contribution pension plans: see chapter 5 and Bodie et al. 1988.

2. Deaton (1992) argues that the potential for "dynamic inconsistency" of intertemporal (consumption) plans has been overstated. Of course, wholly genuine myopic behavior must still be ruled out in the present framework.

3. Without further restrictions on preferences, the possibility of dissaving in periods 1 and 2 cannot be ruled out.

4. Rearrange equation 3.5' and assume that there is a positive rate of return, r, on saving (i.e. the productivity of capital outweighs storage costs). Then

$$\frac{\partial u}{\partial c_1} = R(\partial u / \partial c_2)(1 + \rho).$$

If $i(R)$ is then treated as an explicit rate of time preference, this is the so-called Euler equation of consumption that underpins Hall's (1978) analysis.

5. Aaron's proof is somewhat more general.

6. The derivation of equation 3.9, now standard in the growth literature, is summarized in the appendix to this chapter.

7. See Blanchard and Fischer 1989, especially chapters 3 and 5. Modern theories of dynamics, and especially of chaotic systems, are also relevant.

8. This can also be written with U^A replacing C, as in this model these formulations are equivalent; see Veall 1986.

9. See chapter 2 above.

10. The issue of aggregation, although examined in part by the study, seems important. Furthermore, where there is two-sided altruism (i.e., children to parents *and* parents to children) the transfer regimes may be altered by the allocation of income between parents and children, as Altonji et al. themselves point out.

11. The pure life-cycle hypothesis is also just rejected by the data: joint family incomes do have an effect on individual household consumption. See chapter 8 below.

12. In an open economy, a further constraint is that the rate of interest may be exogenous. Slowing population growth may generate a widening differential between the domestic rate of interest and the consumption loan rate of interest. This also has implications for funding policy. See Verbon 1988.

13. See the debate between Barro (1974, 1976) and Feldstein (1976).

Chapter 4

1. Where (as in the UK and the US) the tax system also provides significant tax breaks for private pension provision, the overall redistributive impact of changes to pension provision over time is more difficult to analyze. This subject is rarely analyzed in great detail, although see Disney and Whitehouse 1993b.

2. These earnings thresholds in accrual rates are termed "bend points" in the US literature. The US and Italy are among only six countries that use weighted benefit formulas

in calculating social security pensions; in Greece there are 28 "bend points" (Social Security Administration 1993). However, the two-tier schemes of the UK and Japan are an extreme form of the formula.

3. For example, a scheme where social security benefits are automatically increased for those who are particularly long-lived (e.g., 85+) may, from a lifetime perspective, disproportionately benefit those with higher lifetime incomes on average. Such payments may nevertheless be justified on some age-related need basis.

4. There was in fact a small subsidy to the National Insurance scheme from general Treasury revenues to cover the payment of pensions to individuals in earlier cohorts for whom the scheme had been in operation for insufficient time to attain the requisite contributions. This subsidy was phased out in the early 1980s.

5. By a perverse asymmetry, contracted-out pensioners were entitled to receive the difference between equation 4.2 and equation 4.1, since they were entitled to receive the difference between the SERPS payment forgone (equation 4.1) and the guaranteed minimum which it was assumed their private pension scheme would deliver (which has always been calculated by equation 4.2). The legislative change also eliminated this entitlement.

6. This confirms the model of chapter 2 and the Government Actuary's forecasts of future contribution stability.

7. Much of what follows is based on a seminar by Watsons International Consultancy in London in June 1993, and on information provided by E. Schettino of the Italian employers' federation Confindustria.

8. With the issue of "privatization" of Italian pensions now on the agenda, the issue of whether the TFR funds can form the basis of a funded private pension scheme has been raised. If the funds were structured in the past such that real returns are negative (or, at least, below market returns), with funds effectively acting as a cheap form of company finance, the question of incidence arises in guaranteeing a sufficient pension annuity from such funds in the future.

9. Currently, private pension provision is very limited: the total outstanding value of pension funds in 1991 was 6% of GDP, the lowest in any major OECD country.

10. See Rossi and Visco 1994, but also Favero et al. 1995.

11. The Australian dollar was worth £0.47 and US$0.72 in late 1994.

12. The more general issue of compulsory private pensions as an alternative to supplementary social security is discussed at much greater length in chapter 5 and in World Bank 1994.

13. Although income testing is pervasive in the Australian social security program, some benefits continue to be treated as social insurance benefits.

14. For a discussion see Creedy and Disney 1985. For a reform proposal for the UK social security system along integrated tax-and-transfer lines see Dilnot et al. 1984.

15. However, Takayama's estimated lifetime age-earnings profiles are based on cross-section data. Cross-section data alone do not really permit analysis of longitudinal (cohort) earnings profiles. Although age dummies are included, it may be that the inclusion of age dummies is too crude a control for the impact of cohort-specific effects on earnings profiles. This issue is discussed in chapter 6 below.

16. See chapters 5 and 7 below for further discussion of these issues in Japan.

17. This is discussed at much greater length in chapter 8 below.

18. See chapter 8 below.

19. It is true, of course, that the financial problems have been exacerbated by the fact that the baby-boom generation, born in the late 1940s and the 1950s, is followed by a smaller generation. But simple arithmetic predicts that difficulties would thereby arise after the turn of the century; generation size alone does not explain why these financing crises have already appeared in many countries.

20. It has been suggested that younger generations may find the intergenerational "terms of trade" less unfavorable in practice because the early beneficiaries in PAYG schemes will bequest their "excess" returns to younger generations. This would be convenient, but it would still bypass the question of whether savings were adequate, especially if younger generations anticipated the bequest. For more on life-cycle dissaving by the elderly, on bequests, and on expectations of prospective intergenerational transfers, see chapter 8 below.

Chapter 5

1. For discussions of these trends see Gustman and Steinmeier 1992, Ippolito 1995, and Kruse 1995. For a recent discussion of the range of private pension savings plans available in the US see Engen et al. 1994.

2. See chapter 7 for details.

3. See Ippolito 1985 and Kotlikoff and Wise 1985. Note, however, that there is some debate as to the appropriate method of measuring the pension liabilities of the firm (Barnow and Ehrenberg 1979; Bulow 1982; Gustman and Steinmeier 1989) and as to the elasticity of substitution between wages and pension benefits (Woodbury 1983; Turner 1987).

4. This is not to suggest that workers will be indifferent to dismissal if they have a future pension claim on the employer. Pension entitlements are usually not fully portable, and workers lose out when accruing several interrupted pension claims instead of one derived from uninterrupted tenure; for evidence from the US see, e.g., Turner 1993 and references cited therein.

5. Whether older workers are in fact more costly and less productive is discussed in the next chapter.

6. On unions and pension coverage see Freeman 1981, Freeman 1985, Allen and Clark 1986, and, for the UK, Disney and Whitehouse 1991a.

7. For further details on methodology see Disney and Whitehouse 1996. The pension-scheme characteristics are based on a matching of household data from the General Household Survey of 1987 to pension-scheme characteristics from the official survey of pension schemes. Occupation-, sex-, and age-specific earnings equations are derived from pooled Family Expenditure Survey data, and expected pension-scheme durations from Retirement Survey data.

8. Such features include nonlinear relationships between earnings and pension benefits, and transferability provisions: see Lazear 1985. It is interesting that until the passage of

ERISA in 1974 some US pension plans required workers to stay until retirement to vest benefits—this is an extreme application of Lazear's incentive device at work.

9. Merton (1985) highlights this assumption of the Diamond-Mirrlees model. It would seem more plausible to assume that individuals face capital market imperfections, such as differential borrowing and lending rates. This makes the valuation of lifetime incomes more complex (Creedy 1990), but it avoids the more restrictive limitation of no capital market.

10. In the case where the term structure of returns is such that investment in a contractual DB plan earns a superior return to a DC plan, there may be a significant advantage to the former.

11. For a discussion of pension funds' investment strategies in various OECD countries see Davies 1995.

12. See Gustman and Steinmeier 1993 and Turner 1993 for the US; see Disney and Whitehouse 1996 for the UK.

13. Indeed, some assets, such as residential property, may overindex to inflation, rising in price more rapidly in inflationary periods and falling back in times of recession. Thus, a rational individual would hold a portfolio of assets to retirement, not all of which were fully indexed. This view has been expressed by Feldstein (1983), among others.

14. This issue is considered in greater detail in section 5.2 relative to the experience of DC-plan-based "privatizations" of social security.

15. Indeed, countries with youthful populations have proved equally susceptible to overgenerous eligibility requirements and benefit levels leading to problems with PAYG financing precisely because the disciplining effect of an aging population is absent.

16. In a public-choice framework, it is perhaps not so surprising that scheme participants have to be "bribed" to give up promised PAYG benefits by tax subsidies or other transitional measures. The public-choice approach is discussed more fully in chapter 10.

17. In Mexico pension-scheme surpluses have been used to underwrite a deficit in the health-care budget. In the US the pension fund's net receipts have been used to finance general expenditures of the federal government.

18. Ironically, perhaps, in the light of its subsequent performance, the police and the armed forces exempted themselves from the new scheme.

19. New AFPs have been established as the scheme has matured—six in 1992 alone. Some of the original AFPs have merged. There is some evidence that competition between established and new AFPs has raised charges since 1992; this may be a temporary phenomenon.

20. The "excess yield" is the excess of the real interest rate (return) over real earnings growth. This has averaged 3% over each 20-year period terminating over the last 18 years in the UK; in the first years of the Chilean scheme it has been considerably higher.

21. This average concealed wide variations in annual performance. For example, the average return was 32% in 1991 and 5% in 1992. But UK data suggest that prospective yield variance tends to decline with duration of fund holding; the question is whether portfolio strategies can exploit this fact.

22. The difference between national saving (as defined) and investment is the balance of payments deficit (surplus) on current account, by national accounting definitions.

23. This section is based largely on information provided in Vittas and Iglesias's comprehensive account of the regulatory structure.

24. In view of the Savings and Loans crisis in the US and the Lloyds fiasco, the Barings collapse, and the Maxwell and BCCI frauds in the UK, such an assumption smacks of complacency.

25. The self-employed were able to invest in tax-relieved DC schemes. These s226 policies were the forerunner of Personal Pensions.

26. The minimum that a contracted-out scheme was required to offer was therefore a multiple of average earnings. But the typical DB plan would offer the more attractive final-salary basis to the pension calculation. Since 1990 deferred (preserved) benefits have been indexed to inflation but early leavers are still not compensated for real earnings growth. Under legislation introduced in 1995, the GMP requirement is abolished and DB plans are required to adopt a statutory standard approximately based on final earnings.

27. Starting at 17.5% of earnings for those aged under 35 and rising progressively with age. Contributions to approved private DB schemes are also exempt up to a ceiling. Furthermore, payments to individual pension accounts can be made in addition to other pension provision.

28. For details see Walford 1994 and the summary in Dilnot et al. 1994.

29. For further sensitivity analysis see Disney and Whitehouse 1992, 1993c.

30. This is termed the "neutral rebate" in Disney and Whitehouse 1992 and in Disney and Whitehouse 1993c.

31. In 1993 the rebate was reduced to 4.8% in line with Government Actuary projections and an extra 1% "incentive" was offered to new optants over 30. Under a key provision of the 1995 Pensions Act, the contracted-out rebate to DC plans, including Personal Pensions, is in the future to be explicitly related to age, so that (in theory, depending on the rates structure) the accrual rates track the SERPS accrual rates at each age more closely. There is to be no differentiation of rates by sex, however.

32. For the standard argument of the invariance of portfolio structure to the duration of the investment see Merton 1969 and Samuelson 1969. For an explanation of why investors may opt for a different strategy see Benhartzi and Thaler 1995.

Chapter 6

1. There is now an extensive literature on this issue, although not all of it examines labor-supply issues. For the US see Bound and Johnson 1992, Juhn et al. 1993, Katz and Murphy 1992, and Levy and Murnane 1992; for the UK see Gosling et al. 1994 (in which cohort effects receive some consideration).

2. See chapter 7 below.

3. The feedback effect of demand-side shifts on long-run demographic change is a major issue that lies outside the scope of this book, in which population change is largely treated as exogenous. The important question of trends in participation of the elderly is, however, considered in the next chapter.

4. This "added-worker effect" would be reinforced if men in the large age cohort also

had lower lifetime income expectations, leading to deferral of child rearing and pressure on the spouse to work; see Easterlin 1980.

5. The role of the "experience" variable in human-capital regressions continues to be a source of controversy, see, e.g., Brown and Light 1992 and Hou and Yang 1993.

Chapter 7

1. This issue is further considered below.

2. Some hints have been given above; this issue will receive further discussion later in this chapter.

3. See Gustman and Steinmeier 1986; Lumsdaine et al. 1990; Quinn et al. 1990; Stock and Wise 1990.

4. See the works cited in the preceding note.

5. See Disney, Meghir, and Whitehouse 1994 for such modeling of this UK data set.

6. Indeed, Quinn et al. (1990) show how, chronologically, US studies of retirement increasingly moved from a perspective and a design that perceived retirement as an involuntary decision to one in which retirement was taken on "economic" grounds connected with the time path of pension accruals and prospective wages.

7. To the extent that we are unable to assess individual motives for retirement objectively, there is some scope for analyzing retirement behavior by exploiting any discrepancies between subjective reported expectations of retirement date and actual retirement date in repeated (panel) surveys of older workers. See Bernheim 1989 and Bernheim 1990 for an illustration of this approach.

8. The "rule" was abolished in October.

9. The discounted annuity of the deferral increment is not included but is small: in April 1989 prices equal to the basic pension (for a single person, £41) times the deferral rate of 7.5% divided by (1 + the discount rate).

10. Meghir and Whitehouse (1993) suggest that the effect of the wage rate on the probability of job exit into inactivity among men in the Retirement Survey who are only eligible for social security (i.e., no private pension) is insignificantly small. This finding does not preclude the possibility, discussed in the text, that a decline in the prospective wage with age, subsequent to retirement, might preclude re-entry into the labor market.

Chapter 8

1. The annuity market is required to insure against longevity risk.

2. Although not if greater longevity reduces the conditional probability of, and therefore the demand for, bequesting; see Skinner 1985.

3. A subsample of fourteen countries is chosen, although data are available for several other countries (see below): the selection criterion is not discussed, and the time period chosen is very short. A Durbin-Watson statistic is quoted implying that there may be a panel component to the study, which suggests that time and/or country dummies

should be included. However, it seems more likely that the study simply compares country averages over the time period and that the D-W statistic is inappropriate.

4. Relative to the United States, and for the period 1977–1992, Japan, Germany, France, Italy, the UK, Austria, Belgium, Denmark, and Greece had significantly higher household savings rates, and Finland and Holland significantly lower rates, *ceteris paribus*. The other seven countries had insignificantly different savings rates from the US.

5. For illustrations in simulation models see Auerbach and Kotlikoff 1987, Auerbach et al. 1989, and Hagemann and Nicoletti 1989. Auerbach and Kotlikoff present a more sophisticated GE model which contains households, firms, and a government and in which it is assumed that agents adopt intertemporal optimizing behavior.

6. This is cited by Deaton (1992).

7. Bernheim (1987) uses the National Longitudinal Survey and, unlike Hurd, includes annuity values. His specifications suggest a slower decline in wealth after retirement. An important issue is whether transfers to survivors in the household (e.g. widows) are treated as bequests.

8. Assuming threats to give the money to charity are not credible. The single-child result is interesting, and the authors argue that "it is difficult to reconcile this conclusion [concerning single child versus multiple child families' behavior] with any known model of bequests other than [the strategic model]." However, it is possible to think of various types of self-selection where size of family is endogenous which might generate this result.

9. This issue of "habits" in consumption behavior has some aspects in common with the issue of "long-term preferences" discussed in Deaton and Muellbauer 1980 (pp. 373–378), although the latter have generally been discussed in the context of the presence of lagged values in time series estimates of consumption expenditure. Generally cohort-specific effects are subsumed under demographic and age variables in such equations.

10. The counterargument is that moderately well-off older people who have been through any part of the period 1914—1945, seeing the affluence of younger cohorts, will respond by increased consumption in retirement. Orville Metcalfe (aged 73), who summers in Spokane, Washington, and winters in Quartzsite, Arizona, put it this way: "I was raised in the Depression, on a farm in Nebraska, and we had some pretty hard times. I fought in World War II, raised four kids, and now I feel I got some time to enjoy for myself. I live comfortably, go where I want and I don't have to do anything 'cept eat." ("Snowbirds Are Go," *The Independent*, March 28, 1992).

11. This treatment of housing as an investment good understates its consumption aspect; furthermore the characteristics of housing, notably transactions costs in liquidating housing equity in the face of expected price falls, may require a "risk premium" relative to more liquid assets. However, some risk may be offset by standard portfolio diversification.

12. Stemming also from changes in the pattern of household formation, such as marriage and divorce rates.

13. This issue is considered in the housing context in Bover et al. 1989 and underpins the discussion of the consumption boom in the UK in the mid 1980s: see Attanasio and Weber 1994 and Miles 1992.

14. In answer to the natural question of "why then invest in property as an investment asset if realizing its asset value is costly?" one might point to the generally favorable tax treatment of home ownership in these countries, and to the insurance aspect of home ownership as a form of precautionary saving. If bad outcomes *do* occur in the working life or in early retirement, the property can be sold notwithstanding transactions costs; see Skinner 1993.

15. Households with low incomes and limited capital assets in the UK with mortgage payments and/or rents are entitled to social security payments (housing benefits). Housing costs are reported in the Retirement Survey net of these housing benefits.

16. By varying one characteristic at a time, we ignore the fact that, say, a woman has different mean values of the other characteristics than a man.

Chapter 9

1. Using largely self-reported data, Verbrugge (1984) details the decline in health status among older people in the 1970s in the US. However, evidence from the 1980s suggests a significant *improvement* in health status in the same age group. This may reflect underlying changes in medical treatment and technology or changes in self-reported bias and in self-awareness of health status: see Waidmann et al. 1995.

2. For examples see Garber 1989 (p. 260); for discussion see Aaron and Bosworth 1994.

Chapter 10

1. Estaban and Sákovics argue that, if it is costly to change an existing transfer institution, an equilibrium in intergenerational transfers can be achieved. But it is hard to believe that older generations cannot affect the cost of changing institutions, and other simplifying assumptions cast doubt on Estaban and Sákovics's central conclusion.

2. For a trenchant critique of the practical consequences of this behavior by the US government, see Kotlikoff 1992.

3. Had a utilitarian approach of diminishing marginal utility of income dominated, we might have expected greater emphasis on the targeting of pensions, such as means testing, and payments of pensions to the "needy" irrespective of notional contributory eligibility conditions. It is a paradox to the utilitarian approach, but not to the intergenerational contract hypothesis, that the "rediscovery of poverty" among pensioners in the UK in the 1950s and the 1960s led to legislation guaranteed to increase the generosity of benefits provided for future, richer cohorts of pensioners but did little to remedy the plight of existing pensioners (see section 4.2 above).

4. Where there are different types of taxes, generations might be expected to vote for combinations of taxes that minimize their own tax bill: for example, pensioners would prefer greater reliance on taxes on earned income rather than taxes on commodities or on wealth.

5. A simplistic application of the median-voter model in this context ignores the possibilities of investing in other assets, and thus the existence of capital markets. With capital markets, younger voters in particular might prefer negative social security. Assuming workers cannot borrow against future social security, a corner solution is possible in which the optimal social security for the median worker is zero. Models of this type do

not generally invalidate the single-peakedness condition, however; see Boadway and Wildasin 1989.

6. See table 10.1.

7. This would seem to rule out the actual illustration used by Browning (1975) in which the incomes of the working generations are equal. If, say, in period 2 both generation C and generation D had incomes of 200, it is hard to see why they would agree to pay B a pension at all. Browning never discusses *why* a pension scheme is established; he merely notes that once established it will tend to be too generous. To examine the possibility of why a pension scheme starts, it is preferable to assume that incomes of the two working generations differ and that the scope for log rolling exists.

8. An ingenious explanation offered by Thomson (1989) is that the development of the welfare state, and of pensions in particular, stems from the selfish behavior of one particular generation: the one associated with the introduction of the welfare state in the post–World War II period. Having developed redistributive policies to benefit themselves when they were young, such as family-support programs, these policies have dwindled away in favor of policies to support the elderly as this generation has aged. Thus, members of this generation have benefited at both ends of their life cycle at the expense of other generations. Disillusion with this selfish behavior has caused younger generations to turn against redistributive behavior, especially toward the elderly, and an "intergenerational conflict" is inevitable. Although this is interesting, an immediate response is that such a series of events seems inconsistent with optimal strategic voting behavior unless it is believed that successive generations have different preferences and/or asymmetric myopia.

9. The analysis is set in discrete generation sizes rather than continuous change.

10. The latter is, of course, itself a reduced-form version of the model of marginal cost and shadow price described above.

Bibliography

Aaron, H. J. 1966. The social insurance paradox. *Canadian Journal of Economics* 32, August: 371–374.

Aaron, H. J. 1984. Social Welfare in Australia. In *The Australian Economy*, ed. R. Caves and L. Krause. Allen & Unwin.

Aaron, H. J. 1985. Comment on Hurd and Shoven. In *Pensions, Labor and Individual Choice*, ed. D. A. Wise. University of Chicago Press for NBER.

Aaron, H. J. 1991. *Serious and Unstable Condition: Financing America's Health Care*. Brookings Institution.

Aaron, H. J., and Bosworth, B. P. 1994. Economic issues in reform of health care financing. *Brookings Papers on Economic Activity (Microeconomics)* 1: 249–299.

Aaron, H. J, Bosworth, B. P., and Burtless, G. 1989. *Can America Afford to Grow Old?* Brookings Institution.

Abraham, K. G., and Farber, H. S. 1987. Job duration, seniority and earnings. *American Economic Review* 77, June: 278–297.

Allen, S. G., and Clark, R. L. 1986. Unions, pension wealth, and age-compensation profiles. *Industrial and Labor Relations Review* 39, no. 4: 502–517.

Allen, S. G., Clark, R. L., and Sumner, D. A. 1986. Postretirement adjustment of pension benefits. *Journal of Human Resources* 21, winter: 118–137.

Altonji, J. G., Hayashi, F., and Kotlikoff, L. J. 1992. Is the extended family altruistically linked? Direct tests using micro data. *American Economic Review* 82, December: 1177–1198.

Altonji, J., and Shakotko, R. 1987. Do wages rise with seniority? *Review of Economic Studies* 54, July: 437–459.

Ando, A., Guiso, L., and Visco, J., eds. 1994. *Saving and the Accumulation of Wealth: Essays on Italian Household and Government Saving Behaviour*. Cambridge University Press.

Ando, A., Moro, A., Corboda, J. P., and Garlando, G. 1995. Dynamics of demographic development and its impact on personal saving: Case of Japan. Presented at Conference on the Economics of Saving and Retirement, University of Venice.

Attanasio, O., and Weber, G. 1994. The UK consumption boom of the late 1980s:

Aggregate implications of microeconomic evidence. *Economic Journal* 104, November: 1269–1302.

Auerbach, A. J., and Kotlikoff, L. J. 1987. *Dynamic Fiscal Policy.* Cambridge University Press.

Auerbach, A. J., Kotlikoff, L. J., Hagemann, R. P., and Nicoletti, G. 1989. The economic dynamics of an ageing population: The case of four OECD countries. *OECD Economic Studies* 12, spring: 97–130.

Barnow, B. S., and Ehrenberg, R. G. 1979. The costs of defined benefit pension plans and firm adjustments. *Quarterly Journal of Economics* 93, November: 523–540.

Barrientos, A. 1993. Pension reform and economic development in Chile. *Development Policy Review* 11, March: 91–107.

Barro, R. J. 1974. Are government bonds net wealth? *Journal of Political Economy* 82, November-December: 1095–1117.

Barro, R. J. 1976. Reply to Feldstein and Buchanan. *Journal of Political Economy* 84, April: 343–349.

Barry, B. 1978. Circumstances of justice and future generations. In *Obligations to Future Generations*, ed. R. Sikora and B. Barry. Temple University Press.

Barry, B. 1989. Justice between generations. In *Democracy, Power and Justice*, ed. B. Barry. Clarendon.

Bateman, H., Frisch, J., Kingston, G., and Piggott, J. 1990. Demographics, retirement saving, and superannuation policy: An Australian perspective. Discussion Paper 241, Centre for Economic Policy Research, Australian National University, Canberra.

Bateman, H., Kingston, G., and Piggott, J. 1993. Taxes, retirement transfers and annuities. *Economic Record* 69, September: 274–284.

Becker, G., and Stigler, G. 1974. Law enforcement, malfeasance and compensation of enforcers. Journal of Legal Studies 3, January: 1–18.

Benhartzi, S., and Thaler, R. H. 1995. Myopic loss aversion and the equity premium puzzle. *Quarterly Journal of Economics* 111, February: 73–92.

Berger, M. C. 1983. Changes in labour force composition and male earnings: A production approach. *Journal of Human Resources* 17, no. 2: 177–196.

Berger, M. C. 1985. The effect of cohort size on earnings: A re-examination of the evidence. *Journal of Political Economy* 93, no. 3: 561–573.

Bernheim, B. D. 1987. Dissaving after retirement: Testing the pure life cycle hypothesis. In *Issues in Pension Economics*, ed. Z. Bodie et al. University of Chicago Press for NBER.

Bernheim, B. D. 1989. The timing of retirement: A comparison of expectations and realizations. In *The Economics of Aging*, ed. D. Wise. University of Chicago Press for NBER.

Bernheim, B. D. 1990. How do the elderly form expectations? An analysis of responses to new information. In *Issues in the Economics of Aging*, ed. D Wise. University of Chicago Press for NBER.

Bernheim, B. D. 1991. How strong are bequest motives? Evidence based on estimates of the demand for life insurance and annuities. *Journal of Political Economy* 99, no. 5: 899–927.

Bernheim, B. D., Shleifer, A., and Summers, L. H. 1985. The strategic bequest motive. *Journal of Political Economy* 93, December: 1045–1076.

Black, D. 1948. On the rationale of group decision making. *Journal of Political Economy* 56, February: 23–34.

Blanchard, O. J., and Fischer, S. 1989. *Lectures on Macroeconomics.* MIT Press.

Boadway, R., and Wildasin, D. 1989. Voting models of social security determination. In *The Political Economy of Social Security,* ed. B. Gustafsson and N. Klevmarken. North-Holland.

Bodie, Z. 1990. Pensions as retirement income insurance. *Journal of Economic Literature* 28, March: 28–49.

Bodie, Z., Marcus, A. J., and Merton, R. C. 1988. Defined benefit versus defined contribution plans: What are the real trade-offs? In *Pensions in the US Economy,* ed. Z. Bodie et al. University of Chicago Press for NBER.

Boldrin, M., and Rustichini, A. 1994. Equilibria with Social Security. CORE Discussion Paper 9460, Louvain.

Bone, M., Gregory, J., Gill, B., and Lader, D. 1992. Retirement and Retirement Plans. HMSO for Office of Population Censuses and Surveys.

Boskin, M. J., and Hurd, M. D. 1978. The effect of social security on early retirement. *Journal of Public Economics* 10, 361–377.

Boskin, M. J., and Shoven, J. B. 1987. Concepts and measures of earnings replacement during retirement. In *Issues in Pension Economics,* ed. Z. Bodie et al. University of Chicago Press for NBER.

Boskin, M. J., Kotlikoff, L. J., Puffert, D. J., and Shoven, J. B. 1987. Social security: A financial appraisal across and within generations. *National Tax Journal* 40, March: 19–34.

Bosworth, B. P., Burtless, G., and Sabelhaus, J. 1991. The decline in saving: Evidence from household surveys. *Brookings Papers on Economic Activity* 1, 183–256.

Bound, J., and Johnson, G. 1992. Changes in the structure of wages in the 1980s: An evaluation of alternative explanations. *American Economic Review* 82, June: 371–392.

Bover, O., Muellbauer, J., and Murphy, A. 1989. Housing, wages and UK labour markets. *Oxford Bulletin of Economics and Statistics* 51, 97–136.

Braun, D., Cottani, J., and Lennie, S. 1993. Social Security Reform in Argentina. Presented to NBER social security privatization project pre-conference, Boston, August.

Brown, J. N. 1989. Why do wages increase with tenure? On-the-job training and life-cycle wage growth observed within firms. *American Economic Review* 79, December: 971–990.

Brown, J. N., and Light, A. 1992. Interpreting panel data on job tenure. *Journal of Labor Economics* 10: 219–257.

Browning, E. K. 1975. Why the social insurance budget is too large in a democracy. *Economic Inquiry* 13, September: 373–388.

Brugiavini, A. 1987. Empirical evidence of wealth accumulation and the effects of pension wealth: An application to Italian cross-section data. Discussion Paper 20, London School of Economics, Financial Markets Group.

Brugiavini, A. 1993. Uncertainty resolution and the timing of annuity purchases. *Journal of Public Economics* 50: 31–62.

Brugiavini, A., and Disney, R. 1995. The choice of private pension plan under uncertainty. Working Paper 95/5, Institute for Fiscal Studies.

Bulow, J. I. 1982. What are corporate pension liabilities? *Quarterly Journal of Economics* 97, August: 435–450.

Burbidge, J. B. 1983a. Social security and savings plans in overlapping-generations models. *Journal of Public Economics* 21, June: 79–92.

Burbidge, J. B. 1983b. Government debt in an overlapping-generations model with gifts and bequests. *American Economic Review* 73, March: 222–227.

Burbidge, J. B., and Robb, L. A. 1980. Pensions and retirement behaviour. *Canadian Journal of Economics* 13, August, 421–437.

Campbell, C. D., ed. 1984. *Controlling the Cost of Social Security.* Lexington Books for American Enterprise Institute.

Cannari, L. 1994. Do demographic changes explain the decline in the saving rate of Italian households? In *Saving and the Accumulation of Wealth*, ed. A. Ando et al. Cambridge University Press.

Carroll, C. D. 1992. The buffer-stock theory of saving: Some macroeconomic evidence. *Brookings Papers on Economic Activity* 2, 61–156.

Carroll, C. D., and Summers, L. H. 1991. Consumption growth parallels income growth: Some new evidence. In *National Saving and Economic Performance*, ed. B. Bernheim and J. Shoven. University of Chicago Press for NBER.

Casey, B., Lakey, J., and Fogarty, M. 1991. The Experience and Attitudes of Older People to Work and Retirement. Mimeo, Policy Studies Institute, London.

Castellino, O. 1995. Redistribution between and within generations in the Italian social security system. Presented at Conference on the Economics of Saving and Retirement, University of Venice, Italy.

Central Statistical Office 1994. Family Spending: A Report on the 1993 Family Expenditure Survey. HMSO.

Clark, R. L., and Spengler, J. J. 1980. *The Economics of Individual and Population Aging.* Cambridge University Press.

Connelly, R. 1986. A framework for analyzing the impact of cohort size on education and labor earnings. *Journal of Human Resources* 21, no. 4: 543–562.

Cozzolino, M., and Schioppa Kostoris, F. P. 1995. Contribution-based versus earnings-based retirement pension systems: Some policy proposals. Presented at Conference on the Economics of Saving and Retirement, University of Venice, Italy.

Creedy, J. 1982. *State Pensions in Britain.* Cambridge University Press for National Institute of Economic and Social Research.

Creedy, J. 1990. Measuring wealth in a simple two-period model. *Journal of Econometrics* 43: 167–177.

Creedy, J., and Disney, R. 1985. *Social Insurance in Transition*. Clarendon.

Creedy, J., and Disney, R. 1988. The new pension scheme in Britain. *Fiscal Studies* 9, May: 57–71.

Creedy, J., and Disney, R. 1989a. Can we afford to grow older? *European Economic Review* 33: 367–376.

Creedy, J., and Disney, R. 1989b. The Australian pension scheme: Some basic analytics. *Economic Record* 65, December: 357–368.

Creedy, J., and Disney, R. 1992. Financing state pensions in alternative pay-as-you-go schemes. *Bulletin of Economic Research* 44, no. 1: 39–53.

Creedy, J., Disney, R., and Whitehouse, E. 1993. The earnings-related state pension, indexation and lifetime redistribution in the UK. *Review of Income and Wealth* 40, September: 257–278.

Davies E. P. 1995. *Pension Funds: Retirement Income Security and Capital Markets, An International Perspective*. Clarendon.

Davies, J. B. 1981. Uncertain lifetime, consumption and dissaving in retirement. *Journal of Political Economy* 89, no. 3: 561–577.

Deaton, A. S. 1992. *Understanding Consumption*. Clarendon.

Deaton, A. S., and Muellbauer, J. 1980. *Economics and Consumer Behaviour*. Cambridge University Press.

DHSS 1984. *Population, Pension Costs and Pensioners Incomes*. UK Department of Health and Social Security.

Diamond, P. A. 1965. National debt in a neo-classical growth model. *American Economic Review* 55, December: 1126–1150.

Diamond, P. A. 1977. A framework for social security analysis. *Journal of Public Economics* 8: 275–298.

Diamond, P., and Mirrlees, J. 1978. A model of social insurance with variable retirement. *Journal of Public Economics* 10: 295–336.

Diamond, P., and Mirrlees, J. 1985. Insurance aspects of pensions. In *Pensions, Labor and Individual Choice*, ed. D. Wise. University of Chicago Press for NBER.

Dilnot, A. W., Kay, J. A., and Morris, C. N. 1984. *The Reform of Social Security*. Oxford University Press for Institute for Fiscal Studies.

Dilnot, A., Disney, R., Johnson, P., and Whitehouse, E. 1994. *Pensions Policy in the UK: An Economic Analysis*. Institute for Fiscal Studies, London.

Disney, R. 1995. Occupational pension schemes: Prospects and reforms in the UK. *Fiscal Studies* 16, August: 19–39.

Disney, R., Gallagher, T., and Henley, A. 1994. Excess housing costs and the behaviour of elderly households. No. 94/8, Studies in Economics, University of Kent, Canterbury.

Disney, R., Gallagher, T., and Henley, A. 1995. Housing assets and saving behavior among the elderly in Great Britain. Working Paper 95/22, Institute for Fiscal Studies, London.

Disney, R., Meghir, C., and Whitehouse, E. 1994. Retirement behaviour in Britain. *Fiscal Studies* 15, February: 24–43.

Disney, R., and Stears, G. 1996. Why is there a decline in defined benefit pension plan membership in Britain? Working Paper 96/4, Institute for Fiscal Studies, London.

Disney, R., and Webb, S. 1989. Is there a market failure in occupational sick pay? In *The Economics of Social Security*, ed. A. Dilnot and I. Walker. Oxford University Press.

Disney, R., and Webb, S. 1991. Why are there so many long term sick in Britain? *Economic Journal* 101, March: 252–262.

Disney, R., and Whitehouse, E. 1991a. How should pensions in the UK be indexed? *Fiscal Studies* 12, August: 47–61.

Disney, R., and Whitehouse, E. 1991b. Union membership and occupational pension coverage in Britain: A disaggregated analysis. Mimeo, Institute for Fiscal Studies.

Disney, R., and Whitehouse, E. 1992. *The Personal Pension Stampede.* Institute for Fiscal Studies.

Disney, R., and Whitehouse, E. 1993a. Contracting-out and lifetime redistribution in the UK pension system. *Oxford Bulletin of Economics and Statistics* 55, February: 25–41.

Disney, R., and Whitehouse, E. 1993b. Will younger cohorts obtain a worse deal from the UK state pension scheme? In *Industrial Concentration and Economic Inequality*, ed. M. Casson and J. Creedy. Edward Elgar.

Disney, R., and Whitehouse, E. 1993c. Pension Privatization in Britain: Policies and Prospects. Presented to NBER social security privatization project pre-conference, Boston.

Disney, R., and Whitehouse, E. 1994. Choice of private pension and pension benefits in Britain. Working Paper 94/2, Institute for Fiscal Studies, London.

Disney, R., and Whitehouse, E. 1996. What are occupational pension plan entitlements worth in Britain? *Economica* 63: in press.

Doescher, T. A., and Turner, J. A. 1988. Social security benefits and the baby-boom generation. *American Economic Review: Papers and Proceedings* 78, no. 2: 76–80.

Easterlin, R. A. 1968. *Population, Labor Force, and Long Swings in Economic Growth: The American Experience.* Columbia University Press for NBER.

Easterlin, R. A. 1980. *Birth and Fortune: The Impact of Numbers on Personal Welfare.* Basic Books.

Engen, E. M., Gale, W. G, and Scholz, J. K. 1994. Do saving incentives work? *Brookings Papers on Economic Activity* 1: 85–179.

Ermisch, J. 1988. Fortunes of birth: The impact of generation size on the relative earnings of young men. *Scottish Journal of Political Economy* 35, August: 266–282.

Ermisch, J. 1990. Fewer Babies, Longer Lives. Report to Joseph Rowntree Foundation, York.

Ermisch, J., and Ogawa, N., eds. 1994. *The Family, the Market, and the State in Ageing Societies.* Clarendon.

Estaban, J. M., and Sákovics, J. 1993. Intertemporal transfer institutions. *Journal of Economic Theory* 61: 189–205.

Fair, R. C., and Dominguez, K. M. 1991. Effects of the changing US age distribution on macroeconomic equations. *American Economic Review* 81, December: 1276–1294.

Falkingham, J. 1989. Dependency and ageing in Britain: A re-examination of the evidence. *Journal of Social Policy* 18, no. 2: 211–235.

Favero, C., Fella, G., and Iascone, M. L. 1995. Private saving and social security wealth: What time series evidence for Italy? Mimeo, Bocconi University, Milan. Presented at Conference on the Economics of Saving and Retirement, University of Venice.

Feinstein, J., and McFadden, D. 1989. The dynamics of housing demand by the elderly: Wealth, cash flow, and demographic effects. In *The Economics of Aging*, ed. D. Wise. University of Chicago Press for NBER.

Feldstein, M. 1974a. Social security, induced retirement, and aggregate capital accumulation. *Journal of Political Economy* 82, September-October: 905–926.

Feldstein, M. 1974b. The optimal financing of social security. Discussion Paper 388, Harvard Institute of Economic Research,.

Feldstein, M. 1976. Perceived wealth in bonds and social security: A comment. *Journal of Political Economy* 84, April: 331–336.

Feldstein, M. 1983. Should private pensions be indexed? In *Financial Aspects of the US Pension System*, ed. Z. Bodie and B. Shoven. University of Chicago Press for NBER.

Flinn, C. 1993. The implications of cohort size for human capital investment. In *Labour Markets in an Ageing Europe*, ed. P. Johnson and K. Zimmerman. Cambridge University Press for Centre for Economic Performance.

Ford, J. R. 1986. Demography and the future cost of pensioners. In *Finance of Old Age*, ed. R. Mendelsohn. Centre for Research on Federal Financial Relations, Australian National University.

Foster, C. 1988. Towards a National Retirement Incomes Policy. Social Security Review Issues Paper 6, Department of Social Security, Canberra, Australia.

Freeman, R. B. 1979. The effect of demographic factors on age-earnings profiles. *Journal of Human Resources* 14, summer: 289–318 (reprinted in Freeman 1989).

Freeman, R. B. 1981. The effect of unionism on fringe benefits. *Industrial and Labor Relations Review* 34, no. 4: 489–509.

Freeman, R. B. 1985. Unions, pensions and union pension funds. In *Pensions, Labor and Individual Choice*, ed. D. Wise. University of Chicago Press for NBER.

Freeman, R. B. 1989. *Labour Markets in Action: Essays in Empirical Economics*. Harvester Wheatsheaf.

Freeman, R. B., and Katz, L. F., eds. 1994. *Differences and Changes in Wage Structures*. University of Chicago Press for NBER.

Friedman, B. M., and Warshawsky, M. 1988. Annuity prices and savings behaviour in the United States. In *Pensions in the US Economy*, ed. Z. Bodie et al. University of Chicago Press for NBER.

Friedman, B. M., and Warshawsky, M. 1990. The cost of annuities: Implications for savings behaviour and bequests. *Quarterly Journal of Economics* 105, April: 135–154.

Fry, V. C., Hammond, E. M., and Kay, J. A. 1985. Taxing Pensions. No. 14, Report Series, Institute for Fiscal Studies, London.

Garber, G. 1989. Long-term care, wealth and health of the disabled elderly living in the community. In *The Economics of Aging*, ed. D. Wise. University of Chicago Press for NBER.

Ghilarducci, T. 1992. *Labor's Capital: The Economics and Politics of Private Pensions*. MIT Press.

Gillion, C., and Bonilla, A. 1992. Analysis of a national private pension scheme: The case of Chile. *International Labour Review* 131, no. 2: 171–195.

Gordon, A. 1985. *The Evolution of Labor Relations in Japan*. Harvard University Press.

Gosling, A., Machin, S., and Meghir, C. 1994. The changing distribution of male wages in the UK, 1966–92. Working Paper 94/13, Institute for Fiscal Studies, London.

Gustman, A. L., and Steinmeier, T. L. 1986. A structural retirement model. *Econometrica* 54, no. 3: 555–584.

Gustman, A. L., and Steinmeier, T. L. 1989. An analysis of pension benefit formulas, pension wealth, and incentives from pensions. *Research in Labor Economics* 10: 53–106.

Gustman, A. L., and Steinmeier, T. L. 1992. The stampede towards defined contribution pension plans: Fact or fiction? *Industrial Relations* 31, no. 2: 361–369.

Gustman, A. L., and Steinmeier, T. L. 1993. Pension portability and labor mobility: Evidence from the Survey of Income and Program Participation. *Journal of Public Economics* 50, 299–323.

Hagemann, R. P., and Nicoletti, G. 1989. Population ageing: Economic effects and some policy implications for financing public pensions. *OECD Economic Studies* 12, spring: 51–95.

Hall, R. E. 1978. Stochastic implications of the life cycle-permanent income hypothesis: Theory and evidence. *Journal of Political Economy* 86, no. 6: 971–987.

Hannah, L. 1986. *Inventing Retirement: The Development of Occupational Pensions in Britain*. Cambridge University Press.

Hansson, I., and Stuart, C. 1989. Social security as trade among living generations. *American Economic Review* 79, December: 1182–1195.

Heller, P. S., Hemming, R., and Kohnert, P. W. 1986. Aging and Social Expenditure in the Major Industrial Countries, 1980–2025. Occasional Paper 47, International Monetary Fund, Washington.

Hemming, R., and Kay, J. A. 1981. Real rates of return. *Fiscal Studies* 2, March: 15–25.

Hemming, R., and Kay, J. A. 1982. The costs of the state earnings related pension scheme. *Economic Journal* 92, June: 300–319.

Henderson, J., and Ioannides, Y. 1983. Dynamic aspects of consumer decisions in housing markets. *Journal of Urban Economics* 26: 212–230.

Henderson, J., and Ioannides, Y. 1986. Tenure choice and the demand for housing. *Economica* 53: 231–246.

Henley, A. 1994. The Determinants and Distribution of Household Housing Wealth in Great Britain, 1985–1991. No. 94/5, Studies in Economics, University of Kent, Canterbury.

Henley, A., Disney, R., and Carruth, A. 1994. Job tenure and asset holdings. *Economic Journal* 104, March: 338–349.

Hicks, J. R. 1970. Elasticity of substitution once again: Substitutes and complements. *Oxford Economic Papers* 22, November: 289–296.

HMSO. 1985a. *Reform of Social Security,* volumes 1–4, Cmnd 9517–9520.

HMSO. 1985b. *Reform of Social Security: Programme for Action*, Cmnd 9691.

HMSO 1990. *Social Trends*. 1990.

HMSO. 1991a. Occupational Pension Schemes 1987, Eighth Survey by the Government Actuary.

HMSO. 1991b. The Elderly: Informational Requirements for Supporting the Elderly and Implications of Personal Pensions for the National Insurance Fund, House of Commons, November 1990.

HMSO 1994. Pensions Bill 1994: Report by the Government Actuary on the Financial Provisions of the Bill on the National Insurance Fund, Cm 2714.

HMSO 1995. National Insurance Fund: Long Term Financial Estimates, Third Quinquennial Review by the Government Actuary; House of Commons Paper 160.

Hochman, H. M., and Rodgers, J. D. 1969. Pareto optimal redistribution. *American Economic Review* 59: 542–557.

Hou, J. W., and Yang, T. M. 1993. Do wages rise with job seniority? Reconsidered. Mimeo, California State University.

Hubbard, R. G, Skinner, J., and Zeldes, S. P. 1995. Precautionary saving and social insurance. *Journal of Political Economy* 103, no. 2: 360–399.

Hurd, M. D. 1987. Savings of the elderly and desired bequests. *American Economic Review* 77, June: 298–312.

Hurd, M. D. 1990. Research on the elderly: Economic status, retirement and saving and consumption. *Journal of Economic Literature* 28, June: 565–637.

Hurd, M. D., and Shoven, J. B. 1985., The Distributional Impact of Social Security. In *Pensions, Labor, and Individual Choice*, ed. D. Wise. University of Chicago Press for NBER.

Hutchens, R. M. 1993. Restricted job opportunities and older workers. In *As the Workforce Ages*, ed. O. Mitchell. ILR Press.

Inagami, T. 1980. Extension of mandatory retirement age and changes in personnel management, Japan Labour Bulletin 19, December: 12: Japan Institute of Labour.

Ippolito, R. A. 1985. The labor contract and true economic pension liabilities. *American Economic Review* 75, December: 1031–1043.

Ippolito, R. A. 1995. Toward explaining the growth of defined contribution plans. *Industrial Relations* 34, no. 1: 1–20.

Jacoby, S. 1979. The origins of internal labor markets in Japan. *Industrial Relations* 18, spring: 184–196.

Japan Institute of Labour 1988. Employment and Employment Policy, Japanese Industrial Relations Series No. 1: Tokyo.

Jappelli, T., and Pagano, M. 1993. Personal Saving in Italy. Mimeo, International Saving Comparison Conference, NBER.

Jappelli, T., and Pagano, M. 1994. Government incentives and household saving in Italy. In *International Comparison of Government Incentives and Household Saving*, ed. J. Poterba. University of Chicago Press for NBER.

Juhn, Chinhui 1992. Decline of male labour market participation: The role of declining market opportunities. *Quarterly Journal of Economics* 107, February: 79–121.

Juhn, C., Murphy, K. M., and Pierce, B. 1993. Wage inequality and the return to skill. *Journal of Political Economy* 101, no. 3: 410–442.

Katz, L. F., and Murphy, K. M. 1992. Changes in relative wages 1963–87: Supply and demand factors. *Quarterly Journal of Economics* 107, February: 35–78.

Kelley, A. 1988. The coming of age. Research Paper 194, Department of Economics, University of Melbourne.

Killingsworth, M. 1983. *Labour Supply.* Cambridge University Press.

King, M. A., and Dicks-Mireaux, L. 1982. Asset holdings and the life-cycle. *Economic Journal* 92, June: 247–267.

Koike, K. 1988. *Understanding Industrial Relations in Modern Japan.* Macmillan.

Kotlikoff, L. J. 1979. Testing the theory of social security and life cycle accumulation. *American Economic Review* 69, June: 396–410.

Kotlikoff, L. J. 1992. *Generational Accounting.* Free Press.

Kotlikoff, L. J., and Morris, J. N. 1989. How much care do the aged receive from their children? A bimodal picture of contact and assistance. In *The Economics of Aging*, ed. D. Wise. University of Chicago Press for NBER.

Kotlikoff, L. J., Shoven, J. B., and Spivak, A. 1987. Annuity markets, savings, and the capital stock. In *Issues in Pension Economics*, ed. Z. Bodie et al. University of Chicago Press for NBER.

Kotlikoff, L. J., and Smith, D. E. 1983. *Pensions in the American Economy.* University of Chicago Press for NBER.

Kotlikoff, L. J., and Spivak, A. 1981. The family as an incomplete annuities market. *Journal of Political Economy* 89, April: 372–391.

Kotlikoff, L. J., and Summers, L. H. 1981. The role of intergenerational transfers in aggregate capital accumulation. *Journal of Political Economy* 89, no. 4: 706–732.

Kotlikoff, L. J., and Wise, D. A. 1985. Labour compensation and the structure of private pension plans: Evidence for contractual versus spot labour markets. In *Pensions, Labor and Individual Choice*, ed. D. Wise. University of Chicago Press for NBER.

Kruse, D. L. 1995. Pension substitution in the 1980s: Why the shift toward defined contribution? *Industrial Relations* 34, no. 2: 218–240.

Laing, W. 1993. *Financing Long-term Care: The Crucial Debate*. Age Concern England Books.

Lazear, E. P. 1979. Why is there mandatory retirement? *Journal of Political Economy* 87, no. 6: 1261–1284.

Lazear, E. P. 1981. Agency, earnings profiles, productivity and hours restrictions. *American Economic Review* 71, September: 606–620.

Lazear, E. P. 1985. Incentive effects of pensions. In *Pensions, Labor and Individual Choice*, ed. D. Wise. University of Chicago Press for NBER.

Lazear, E. P. 1986. Retirement from the labour force. In *Handbook of Labor Economics*, volume 1, ed. O. Ashenfelter and R. Layard. Elsevier .

Leather, P. 1990. The potential and implication of home equity release in old age. *Housing Studies* 5: 3–13.

Lee, R. D., Arthur, W. B., and Rodgers, G., eds. 1988. *Economics of Changing Age Distributions in Developed Countries*. Clarendon.

Leonesio, M. V. 1993. Social security and older workers. In *As the Workforce Ages*, ed. O. Mitchell. ILR Press.

Lerner, A. P. 1959. Consumption-loan interest and money. *Journal of Political Economy* 67: 512–518.

Levy, F., and Murnane, R. J. 1992. US earnings levels and earnings inequality: A review of recent trends and proposed explanations. *Journal of Economic Literature* 30, September: 1333–1381.

Levy, M. D. 1984. Achieving financial solvency in social security. In *Controlling the Cost of Social Security*, ed. C. Campbell. Lexington Books for American Enterprise Institute.

Lucas, R. E., and Rapping, L. 1969. Real wages, employment and inflation. *Journal of Political Economy* 77, September-October: 721–754.

Lumsdaine, R. L., Stock, J. H., and Wise, D. A. 1990. Efficient windows and labor force reduction. *Journal of Public Economics* 43: 131–159.

MaCurdy, T. E. 1987. A framework for relating microeconomic and macroeconomic evidence on intertemporal substitution. In *Advances in Econometrics*, volume 2, ed. T. Bewley. Cambridge University Press for Econometric Society.

Madrian, B. C. 1994. The effects of health insurance on retirement. *Brookings Papers on Economic Activity* 1: 181–252.

Mankiw, N. G., and Weil, D. N. 1989. The baby boom, the baby bust and the housing market. *Regional Science and Urban Economics* 19: 235–258.

Martin, L. G., and Ogawa, N. 1988. The effect of cohort size on relative wages in Japan. In *Economics of Changing Age Distributions in Developed Countries*, ed. R. Lee et al. Clarendon.

Medoff, J. L., and Abraham, K. G. 1980. Experience, performance and earnings. *Quarterly Journal of Economics* 95, December: 703–736.

Medoff, J. L., and Abraham, K. G. 1981. Are those paid more really more productive? The case of experience. *Journal of Human Resources* 16, no. 2: 186–216.

Meghir, C., and Whitehouse, E. 1992. The evolution of wages in the UK: Evidence from micro data. Working Paper 92/16, Institute for Fiscal Studies, London.

Meghir, C., and Whitehouse, E. 1993. Labour market transitions and retirement of men in the UK. Working Paper 93/12, Institute for Fiscal Studies, London.

Merrill, S. R. 1984. Home equity and the elderly. In *Retirement and Economic Behaviour*, ed. H. Aaron and G. Burtless. Brookings Institution.

Merton, R. C. 1969. Lifetime portfolio selection under uncertainty: The continuous time case. *Review of Economics and Statistics* 51: 247–257.

Merton, R. C. 1985. Comment. In *Pensions, Labor and Individual Choice*, ed. D. Wise. University of Chicago Press for NBER.

Merton, R. C., Bodie, Z., and Marcus, A. J. 1987. Pension plan integration as insurance against social security risk. In *Issues in Pension Economics*, ed. Z. Bodie et al. University of Chicago Press for NBER.

Miles, D. 1992. Housing markets, consumption and financial liberalisation in the major economies. *European Economic Review* 36: 1093–1136.

Mirer, T. W. 1979. The wealth-age relation among the aged. *American Economic Review* 69, June: 435–443.

Mitchell, O. S. 1993. *As the Workforce Ages: Costs, Benefits and Policy Challenges*. ILR Press.

Modigliani, F. 1986. Life cycle, individual thrift, and the wealth of nations. *American Economic Review* 76, June: 297–313.

Mosk, C., and Nakata, Y-F. 1985. The age-wage profile and structural change in the Japanese labour market for males, 1964–82. *Journal of Human Resources* 20, no. 1: 100–116.

Mueller, D. C. 1989. *Public Choice II*. Cambridge University Press.

Murphy, K., Plant, M., and Welch, F. 1988. Cohort size and earnings. In *Economics of Changing Age Distributions in Developed Countries*, ed. R. Lee et al. Clarendon.

Muth, J. F. 1961. Rational expectations and the theory of price movements. *Econometrica* 29, July: 315–335.

Nickell, S. 1991. Wages, unemployment and population change, Applied Economics Discussion Paper 122, Institute of Economics and Statistics, University of Oxford.

Nickell, S. 1993. Cohort size effects on the wages of young men in Britain 1961–89. Discussion Paper 120, Centre for Economic Performance, London School of Economics.

OECD. 1988a. *Ageing Populations: The Social Policy Implications*. Paris.

OECD. 1988b. *Employment Outlook*. Paris.

OECD. 1989. Educational attainment of the labour force. In *Employment Outlook*.

OECD. 1990. *OECD Economic Surveys: Japan 1989/90*. Paris.

OECD. 1992. Labour force and participation of older workers. In *Employment Outlook*.

Phelps, E. S. 1961. The golden rule of accumulation: A fable for growth men. *American Economic Review* 51, September: 638–643.

Pissarides, C. A. 1981. Staying-on at school in England and Wales. *Economica* 48, November: 345–363.

Pissarides, C. A. 1982. From school to university: The demand for post-compulsory education. *Economic Journal* 92, September: 654–667.

Pitts, A. M. 1978, Social security and aging populations. In *The Economic Consequences of Slowing Population Growth*, ed. T. Espenshade and W. Serow. Academic Press.

Poterba, J. M. 1991. House price dynamics: The role of tax policy and demography. *Brookings Papers on Economic Activity* 2: 143–183.

Poterba, J. M. 1994. *Public Policies and Household Saving*. University of Chicago Press for NBER.

Quinn, J. F., Burkhauser, R. V., and Myers, D. A. 1990. *Passing the Torch: The Influence of Economic Incentives on Work and Retirement*. W. E. Upjohn Institute for Employment Research.

Ramsey, F. P. 1927. A contribution to the theory of taxation. *Economic Journal* 37, March: 47–61.

Ramsey, F. P. 1928. A mathematical theory of saving. *Economic Journal* 38, December: 543–559.

Rawls, J. 1971. *A Theory of Justice*. Belknap.

Rebick, M. 1993. The Japanese approach to finding jobs for older workers. In *As the Workforce Ages*, ed. O. Mitchell. ILR Press.

Rosen, S. 1984. Some arithmetic of social security. In *Controlling the Cost of Social Security*, ed. C. Campbell. Lexington Books for American Enterprise Institute.

Rossi, N., and Visco, I. 1994. Private saving and the government deficit in Italy. In *Saving and the Accumulation of Wealth*, ed. A. Ando et al. Cambridge University Press.

Salop, J., and Salop, S. 1976. Self selection and turnover in the labour market. *Quarterly Journal of Economics* 90, November: 619–628.

Samuelson, P. A. 1958. An exact consumption-loan model of interest with or without the social contrivance of money. *Journal of Political Economy* 66, December: 467–482.

Samuelson, P. A. 1959. Reply. *Journal of Political Economy* 67: 518–522.

Samuelson, P. A. 1969. Lifetime portfolio selection by dynamic stochastic programming, *Review of Economics and Statistics* 51: 239–246.

Samuelson, P. A. 1975a. The optimum growth rate for population. *International Economic Review* 16, October: 531–538.

Samuelson, P. A. 1975b. Optimum social security in a life-cycle growth model. *International Economic Review* 16, October: 539–544.

Samwick, A. A. 1993. Wage risk compensation through employer-provided pensions. Mimeo, MIT.

Samwick, A. A., and Skinner, J. 1993. How will defined contribution pension plans affect retirement income? Mimeo, NBER.

Santamaria, M. 1992. Privatizing social security: The Chilean case. *Columbia Journal of World Business*, spring: 39–51.

Sauvy, A. 1969. *General Theory of Population*. Weidenfeld and Nicholson.

Schieber, S. J 1984. Universal social security coverage and alternatives: The benefits and costs. In *Controlling the Cost of Social Security*, ed. C. Campbell. Lexington Books for American Enterprise Institute.

Schioppa, F. P. 1990. Undesirable redistributions in the retirement public pension schemes: The Italian case study. Discussion Paper 463, Centre for Economic Performance.

Schulz, J. H. 1992. *The Economics of Aging*, fifth edition. Auburn House.

Sen, A. 1970. Introduction. In *Growth Economics*, ed. A. Sen. Penguin Education.

Sheshinski, E. 1978. A model of social security and retirement decisions. *Journal of Public Economics* 10: 337–360.

Shimada, H. 1980. The Japanese employment system. Japanese Industrial Relations Series 6, Japan Institute of Labour, Tokyo.

Shimono, K., and Tachibanaki, T. 1985. Lifetime income and public pension. *Journal of Public Economics* 26: 75–87.

Shorrocks, A. F. 1975. The age-wealth relationship: A cross-section and cohort analysis. *Review of Economics and Statistics* 57, May: 155–163.

Sikora, R. I., and Barry, B. M., eds. 1978. *Obligations to Future Generations*. Temple University Press.

Skinner, J. 1985. The effect of increased longevity on capital accumulation. *American Economic Review* 75, December: 1143–1150.

Skinner, J. 1989. Housing wealth and aggregate saving. *Regional Science and Urban Economics* 19: 305–324.

Skinner, J. 1991. Housing and Saving in the United States. Working Paper 3874, NBER.

Skinner, J. 1993. Is Housing Wealth a Sideshow? Working Paper 4552, NBER.

Smith, A. 1982. Intergenerational transfers as social insurance. *Journal of Public Economics* 19, October: 97–106.

Social Security Administration. 1987. Economic Projections for OASDHI Cost and Income Estimates, 1986. US Social Security Administration, Baltimore.

Social Security Administration. 1992. Social Security Programs throughout the World–1991. Office of International Policy, US Social Security Administration, Washington.

Social Security Administration 1993. *Social Security Bulletin* 56, spring: 1.

Solow, R. M. 1956. A contribution to the theory of economic growth. *Quarterly Journal of Economics* 70, February: 65–94.

Stapleton, D. C., and Young, D. J. 1988. Educational attainment and cohort size. *Journal of Labor Economics* 6, no. 3: 330–361.

Stigler, G. J. 1971. The theory of economic regulation. *Bell Journal of Economics* 2, spring: 3–21.

Stock, J., and Wise, D. A. 1990. Pensions, the option value of work, and retirement. *Econometrica* 58: 1151–1180.

Takayama, N. 1992. *The Greying of Japan: An Economic Perspective on Public Pensions*. Kinokuniya and Oxford University Press.

Takayama, N. 1994. The 1994 Reform Bill for public pensions in Japan: Its main contents and related discussion. *International Social Security Review* 48, no. 1: 45–64.

Thomson, D. 1989. The welfare state and generation conflict: Winners and losers. In *Workers versus Pensioners*, ed. P. Johnson et al. Manchester University Press.

Tulloch, G. 1959. Some problems of majority voting. *Journal of Political Economy* 67, December: 571–579.

Turner, J. A. 1984. Population age structure and the size of social security. *Southern Economic Journal* 50, April: 1131–1146.

Turner, J. A. 1993. *Pension Policy for a Mobile Labor Force*. W. E. Upjohn Institute for Employment Research.

Turner, J. A., and Dailey, L., eds. 1991. *Pension Policy: An International Perspective*. US Department of Labor.

Turner, R. W. 1987. Taxes and the number of fringe benefits received. *Journal of Public Economics* 33, June: 41–57.

UN 1991. *World Population Prospects 1990*. United Nations Department of International Economic and Social Affairs.

Van Den Bosch, F., and Petersen, P. 1983. An explanation of the growth of social security disability transfers. *De Economist* 131, no. 1: 65–79.

Veall, M. R. 1986. Public pensions as optimal social contracts. *Journal of Public Economics* 31: 237–251.

Venti, S., and Wise, D. A. 1989. Aging, moving and housing wealth. In *The Economics of Aging*, ed. D. Wise. University of Chicago Press for NBER.

Verbon, H. 1988. *On the Evolution of Public Pension Schemes*. Kanters.

Verbrugge, L. M. 1984. Longer life but worsening health? Trends in health and mortality of middle aged and older persons. *Milbank Quarterly* 62, no. 3: 475–519.

Vittas, D., and Iglesias, A. 1992. The Rationale and Performance of Personal Pension Plans in Chile. Working Paper WPS 867, World Bank, Washington.

Wachtel, P. 1984. Household saving and demographic change, 1950–2050. *Research in Population Economics* 5: 217–233.

Wachter, M. L. 1977. Intermediate swings in labour force participation. *Brookings Papers on Economic Activity* 2: 545–576.

Waidmann, T., Bound, J., and Schoenbaum, M. 1995. The illusion of failure: Trends in self-reported health of the US elderly. *Milbank Quarterly* 73, no. 2: 253–288.

Walford, J. 1994. *Personal Pensions 1994*. Financial Times.

Weil, D. N. 1994. The saving of the elderly in micro and macro data. *Quarterly Journal of Economics* 109, February: 55–82.

Weiner, J. M., Ilston, L. H., and Handley, R. J. 1994. *Sharing the Burden: Strategies for Public and Private Long-Term Care Insurance*. Brookings Institution.

Welch, F. 1979. Effects of cohort size on earnings: The baby boom babies' financial bust. *Journal of Political Economy* 87, no. 5: S65–S97.

Whitehouse, E. 1990. The abolition of the pensions 'earnings rule.' *Fiscal Studies* 11, August: 55–70.

Wilson, T., and Wilson, J. 1982. *The Political Economy of the Welfare State*. Allen & Unwin.

Wise, D. A., ed. 1985. *Pensions, Labor and Individual Choice*. University of Chicago Press for NBER.

Woodbury, S. A. 1983. Substitution between wage and nonwage benefits. *American Economic Review* 73, March: 166–182.

World Bank. 1994. *Averting the Old Age Crisis*. Oxford University Press.

Wright, R. E. 1989. Cohort size and earnings in Great Britain. Discussion Paper in Economics 89/8, Birkbeck College, London.

Yaari, M. E. 1965. Uncertain lifetime, life insurance, and the theory of the consumer. *Review of Economic Studies* 32, April: 137–158.

Yamaguchi, K. 1981. Company pension plans: Present system and its problems. Japan Labour Bulletin 20, Japan Institute of Labour.

Yellen, J. 1984. Efficiency wage models of unemployment. *American Economic Review: Papers and Proceedings* 74, May: 200–208.

Index

Aaron, H. J., 40, 43–45, 50, 61, 63–64, 66, 93, 272, 288, 293–294, 296
Abraham, K. C., 185–187
Accumulation, Golden Rule of, 45
Allen, S. G., 130
Altonji, J. G., 54, 186
Altruism, 35, 50–55, 244, 247, 264, 284, 293, 302, 304–305
Annuities, 18, 108, 150–151, 203, 229, 262, 270
  failure in market for, 128–129, 240, 279
  indexation of, 130–131
Argentina, 134
Assets
  of elderly, 11, 17–18, 22, 228–229
  over life cycle, 233, 240–241
  of private pension plans, 108, 129–132, 141
Australia
  demographic trends in, 92, 273
  social security system of, 92–94, 219
  means testing in, 28, 93, 245
  private pension plans in, 108
  redistribution in, 97–98
  replacement ratios in, 94–96
  tests of assets in, 92–95
Austria, 172–173

Baby-boom generation, 4, 73, 102, 153–158, 168–169, 178–179, 181, 184, 190–191, 233, 249–251
Barry, B., 287, 302, 304–305
Bateman, H., 92, 95–97
Bequests, 4, 36, 56, 202, 229, 235, 241–244, 264, 305
  strategic, 242–243, 305
Berger, M. C., 162–164, 166, 170, 177–178, 184

Bernheim, B. D., 241–242, 305
Blanchard, O. J., 14, 45
Bodie, Z., 128–130
Boskin, M. J., 67–68, 204, 210
Brown, J. N., 183, 187
Browning, E. K., 286, 288, 290–291, 293, 297
Brugiavini, A., 91, 128, 130, 203
Bulow, J. I., 117
Burbidge, J. B., 55–56, 206, 211

Canada
  health care in, 272–274, 276
  labor-force trends in, 172, 198
  private pension plans in, 108
  Registered Retirement Savings Plans in, 109
  saving in, 240, 251
  social security expenditures in, 26, 92
Cannari, L., 233
Capital market, 37, 202–204, 229
  and aging, 132, 228
  in Australia, 96–97
  and borrowing against retirement income, 115, 129
  in Chile, 137, 139–142
  and investment risk, 131
  internationalization of, 132
  in United Kingdom, 149–151
Capital stock, 189, 237–238, 263
  and aging population, 44–50, 59, 182
  and saving, 55–56, 64, 228, 235–237, 241
Chile
  demographic trends in, 135–136
  privatization of pensions in, 132–142
  saving in, 138–139
China, 2

Complementarity
  elasticity of, 160, 189
  between leisure and consumption, 227
Connelly, R., 159, 162, 175–176
Consumption, 17, 20, 227, 240
  by age group, 247–249, 264
  and aging population, 237, 240
  and bequests, 244
  and housing assets, 253, 260–263
  intertemporal optimum, 36–40, 51–52, 110, 201–202, 205–209, 229, 304
  and leisure, 227
  and social security, 245–246
Creedy, J., 28, 54, 70–71, 79, 92–93, 101, 204

Davies, E. P., 96, 108, 131–132
Denmark, 5, 223
Dependency ratio, 12, 24, 59
  and GDP growth, 235–239
  old age, 25–26, 56, 225, 298–299
  in Australia, 92
  in Italy, 85
  in Japan, 98–99
  in United Kingdom, 73
  in United States, 62
  and saving, 229–235, 243–244
Diamond, P. A., 42, 45–46, 50, 66, 128–129, 204
Dilnot, A. W., 11, 74, 82, 107, 197
Disability benefits
  as early-retirement program, 218, 224–225
  expenditures on, 59, 268, 275, 281
  in Chile, 136
  in Italy, 87
  in Netherlands, 214
  in United Kingdom, 214
  in United States, 62, 273
Disney, R., 28, 54, 70–71, 77–79, 92–93, 109, 118, 130–131, 143–144, 197, 200, 204, 212, 214, 220, 275, 292
Divorce, 4
Doescher, T. A., 298, 300
Dominguez, K. M., 181–182

Early retirement, 29, 114, 116, 155, 196–197, 201, 213–215
  disability and, 218, 224–225
  in Japan, 123–124, 126
  labor market and, 222–225

and social security benefits, 210–212, 218–222
and unemployment, 187–188, 198–199, 214–218
Easterlin, R. A., 4, 178
Economies of scale, 2–3
Education
  demand for, 13, 161–163, 174–178
  and older workers, 215–218
Equilibrium
  in dynamic optimization models, 38, 45–46, 229, 235–236
  in labor market, 111–115, 202, 206–207
Ermisch, J. F., 167, 170, 174, 274
Euler condition, 38
Expenditure taxes, 27–28

Fair, R. C., 181–182
Falkingham, J., 24–25
Family
  aging and, 4, 227, 242, 244
  as annuity market, 305
  income sharing in, 17
  and retirement behavior, 214–215
Farber, H. S., 186–187
Feinstein, J., 256–257, 260
Feldstein, M., 44, 55
Fertility, 1, 5, 7, 10, 85, 181, 236
Finland, 172–173, 223
Fischer, S., 14, 45
Foster, C., 92–94
France
  demographic trends in, 7–8
  expenditures on pensions in, 26
  health care in, 271–272, 274, 277
  labor force in, 172, 194, 198
  lifetime wage profiles in, 121–123
  retirement in, 215–219
Freeman, R. B., 157, 160–162, 164, 166, 174–175, 218
Friedman, B. M., 128, 203
Fry, V. C., 107

Germany
  demographic trends in, 7, 25
  expenditures on pensions in, 26
  health care in, 272–274, 277–278
  lifetime wage profiles in, 131–132
  private pension plans in, 108
  replacement ratio in, 27
  retirement behavior in, 215–216, 219
Ghilarducci, T., 110, 212

Gosling, A., 167
Greece, 60, 218

Hannah, L., 110
Hansson, I., 52–53
Health care
  and aging, 267–270, 272, 274
  private insurance for, 273, 275, 279–280
  public expenditures on, 271–273, 278
  reform of, 276–280
Hemming, R., 70, 80, 143
Henley, A. G., 254–255
Hicks, J. R., 160
Hours of work, 165, 193–196, 202, 219,
    221, 223–224
Housing
  as asset of elderly, 229, 241, 251–256,
    264–265
  costs of maintaining, 256–260
  equity-release schemes, 260, 262–263,
    279
  prices of, aging and, 249–251
Hubbard, R. G., 54, 97, 245–246
Human capital, 3, 31, 154–155, 174,
    184–187
Hurd, M. D., 11, 66, 69, 204, 210, 213, 241,
    245, 292

Iglesias, D., 136–137
Indexation
  in pension plans, 128–130
  of social security benefits, 26–27, 31,
    204, 212
  in Chile, 137
  in Italy, 86, 88–89
  in United Kingdom, 72–76, 81–83
  in United States, 62, 65–66
Individual Retirement Accounts (US),
    103, 109, 203
Insider-outsider theory, 189–190
Italy, 218, 233, 240
  demographic trends, 5, 7–8
  expenditures on pensions in, 25–26
  health care in, 272, 274
  public debt in, 86, 87, 89–90, 293
  reforms since 1992, 87–90
  social security in, 84–86

Japan
  demographic trends in, 5, 9–10, 25, 92,
    98–99, 126
  expenditures on pensions in, 25–26

expenditures on health care in, 272, 274
  growth of labor force in, 172
  lifetime wage profiles in, 121–123, 127
  job tenure in, 122–123
  pension plans in, 125–126
  rates of return to social security in, 102
  retirement behavior in, 123–127, 194,
    198, 223
  savings in, 103–104
  social security system, 100–101, 219
  wages in, 168–170
Jappelli, T., 86, 91
Job tenure
  and wages, 186–187, 206
  in Italy, 86–87
  in Japan, 122–123
  and valuation of pension rights, 117–118
Juhn, C., 216–217

Kay, J. A., 70, 83, 143
Koike, K., 121–123
Kotlikoff, L. J., 54, 64, 116, 240–241, 244,
    305

Labor-force participation rate, 29, 193–
    201, 217–218, 299
  and dependency burden, 1, 29–34
  of elderly, 93, 99–100, 121–122, 126–127,
    194, 198, 218–225
Labor-force productivity, aging and,
    187–190
Labor supply. See Early retirement; Hours
    of work; Labor-force participation rate
Laing, W., 269–270, 272, 277–279
Lazear, E. P., 111–116, 122, 128, 185, 193,
    199, 202, 205, 213
Leather, P., 262
Leisure, and consumption, 227
Lerner, A. P., 20, 39, 283
Levy, M. D., 62, 66
Log rolling, 286, 290–292, 297
Longevity, 1, 5, 10, 12, 30, 32, 41, 208, 210,
    222–224, 227, 230, 236–237, 240–241,
    262, 268, 281, 295
Lumsdaine, R. L., 116

Mankiw, N. G., 249–250
Maxwell, R., 72, 130
McFadden, D., 256–257, 260
Medoff, J. L., 185–186
Meghir, C., 167, 183, 197, 220
Merrill, S. R., 254, 258

Merton, R. C., 128
Mexico, 134
Mirer, T. W., 240–241
Mirrlees, J. A., 128–129, 204
Modigliani, F., 229, 235–237, 241
Money
 and intergenerational social contract, 40, 284
 utilitarian perspective on, 13
Morris, J. N., 54
Mosk, C., 168–169
Myopia, 37, 41–43, 256, 271, 287

Nakata, Y.-F., 168–169
Negative income tax, 74, 97, 245
Netherlands, 251
 growth of labor force in, 172–174
 private pension plans in, 108
 retirement in, 214–215, 218–220
Nickell, S., 168, 189–190
Norway, 172–173, 194, 198

Old Age, Survivors, and Disability Insurance (US), 61–63
 financing of, 63–65
Overlapping-generations models, 12–14
 and capital stock, 4–49
 and pension provision, 36–40
 and strategic behavior in, 51–55

Pagano, M., 86, 91
Pension plans
 aging and, 116–120
 in Chile, 117–119, 132–142
 defined-benefit, 108–120, 154, 253
 defined-contribution, 108–110, 135–151
 fall in employee coverage by, 109
 rationale for, 110–117, 127–131, 275
 regulation of, 140–141, 151
 and retirement behavior, 203–207, 211–212
 in United Kingdom, 70, 142–151
Personal Pensions (UK), 72, 103, 109, 144–151, 204, 280
Phelps, E. S., 45, 235
Ponzi scheme, 41, 60, 91, 267, 286
Poterba, J. M., 250–251, 254
Production function
 and growth theory, 44–45, 57–58
 and cohort size, 156–164

Productivity
 age composition of workforce and, 182–188
 aging and, 2, 188–190, 198–199, 236–137
 growth of, and dependency burden, 28–34, 43–44
 pension provision and, 111–116
Public-choice theory, 284, 286, 290–294, 301
 and aging population, 294–298
Public debt, 50, 55–56, 63–64, 86, 89–90
Public goods, and intergenerational transfers, 303, 305

Quinn, J. F., 116, 199, 210

Ramsey, F. P., 236, 283
Rates of return, 39, 56, 289–290, 295–297
 on education, 153–154, 175, 178
 in private pension schemes, 129–130, 204, 211
 to social security in Japan, 102
 to social security in UK, 77–80
 to social security in US, 66–68
Rawls, J., 287, 303–304
Redistribution
 between generations, 17–19, 204, 291, 304–306
 in Italy, 90–91
 in Japan, 102
 in United Kingdom, 76–78
 in United States, 66–67
 utilitarian models of, 19–23, 283–284
 within defined-benefit pension plans, 117, 120
 in Japan, 101–102
 in United Kingdom, 79–80
 in United States, 67–68
Registered Retirement Savings Plans (Canada), 109
Replacement ratios, 22–23, 26, 28–34
 in private pension plans, 118
 and retirement, 210
 in social security systems,
 in Australia, 94–96
 in Germany, 27
 in Italy, 86, 90–91
 in Japan, 101
 in United Kingdom, 75–77
 in United States, 62, 65–69

Robb, L. A., 206, 211
Rosen, S., 31, 66

Samuelson, P. A., 13, 18, 20, 35–36, 39–40,
  45–47, 49–50, 283–285, 293–294, 296,
  303, 305
Samwick, A. A., 128, 131
Sauvy, A., 2–3
Saving, 11
  in Australia, 92–95
  in Chile, 139
  in Italy, 91
  in Japan, 100, 103–104
  over life cycle, 13, 36–50, 227–235, 239–
  247, 263–264
  life-cycle hypothesis of, 12–14, 45, 222–
  230, 236–237, 240, 256, 263–264, 270
  Permanent Income Hypothesis of, 36,
  235, 237, 249
  and social security, 53–56
Schulz, J. H., 276, 279
Sen, A. K., 49
Shakotko, R., 186
Sheshinski, E., 210–211
Shimono, K., 101
Shoven, J. B., 66–68, 204, 292
Signaling, 187–188, 198–199
Skinner, J., 131, 241, 251–253, 262
Smith, A., 53
Smith, D. E., 116
Social insurance paradox, 40, 43–44, 50
Social security
  in Australia, 91–98
  credibility of, 42, 291
  in Italy, 84–91
  in Japan, 98–104
  in overlapping-generations models,
  46–50
  pay-as-you-go vs. fully funded, 18, 26,
  53–56
  rationale for, 22, 41–42, 275, 287–293, 305
  and retirement behavior, 193, 204, 210–
  211, 218–224
  and saving, 244–247
  strategic behavior toward, 52–53,
  291–295
  in United Kingdom, 69–84
  in United States, 61–69
Solow, R. M., 44, 235
Spain, 215–216, 219
Stapleton, D.C., 177–178

Stears, G., 109
Stuart, C., 52–53
Substitution, elasticity of
  between capital and labor, 159–161, 188
  between income and leisure, 208–209,
  211, 220, 227
  between social security and private
  saving, 44
  between younger and older workers,
  159–164, 170
Support ratio, 102
Sweden, 25, 173, 223, 277

Tachibanaki, T., 101
Takayama, N., 102–103
Tax allowance, 28
Taxation, 18, 27–28, 295–297. *See also*
  Negative income tax
Time preference, 37, 39, 45, 245
Turkey, 60, 218
Turner, J. A., 287, 298–300

Unemployment
  and aging workforce, 4, 125, 188–190
  and participation, 24, 180–182, 191,
  215–218
  and saving, 246
United Kingdom
  consumption expenditures in, 247–248
  contracting out in, 69–71, 142–149
  demographic trends in, 15, 25
  expenditures on pensions in, 26,
  300–301
  growth of labor force in, 167, 173
  health care in, 267, 269, 272–274, 276,
  278, 280
  housing market in, 251, 254–256,
  259–262
  Personal Pensions in, 72, 103, 109, 144–
  151, 204, 280
  private pension plans in, 117–120, 128
  rates of return in, 77–80
  replacement ratios in, 75–77
  retirement behavior in, 194–197, 214,
  218–221
  social security system of, 69–73
  State Earnings Related Pension Scheme
  in, 69–73, 81–82, 143, 293
  wages in, 166–168
United States
  demographic trends in, 7, 9–10, 25

United States (*cont.*)
 expenditures on pensions in, 26, 48, 300
 401(k) plans in, 109, 151
 growth of labor force in, 173
 health care in, 267–268, 271–275, 277–279
 housing market in, 249–253
 Individual Retirement Accounts in, 103, 109, 203
 integration of pension plans in social security in, 128
 Old Age, Survivors, and Disability Insurance in, 61–65
 public debt in, 63–64
 replacement ratios in, 62, 65–69
 retirement behavior in, 193–194, 210, 215–219, 222
 saving in, 244–246
 wages in, 156–166
Utilitarianism, 13, 19–23, 39, 283, 285

Veall, M. R., 52–53, 304–305
Venti, S. F., 254, 258
Vittas, A., 136–137
Voting cycles, 286, 291, 305

Wachtel, P., 232–233
Wachter, M. L., 180–182
Wages
 age-wage profiles and pensions, 111–116
 in Japan, 121–122
 cohort size and, 156–171, 200
 and participation, 178–182, 202–203, 205–206, 220–221
 and productivity levels, 183–188
 real, 30–31, 43–44, 253, 301
Warshawsky, M., 128, 203
Webb, S., 214, 275
Weil, D. N., 233–235, 239, 242–244, 249–250, 253
Weiner, J. M., 270, 273, 277–278
Welch, F., 164–166, 168, 170, 184, 249
Whitehouse, E., 77–79, 130–131, 143–144, 167, 183, 197, 200, 204, 212, 220–221, 292
Wise, D. A., 116, 254, 258
Wright, R. E., 168, 170

Yaari, M. E., 203
Young, D. J., 177–178